Booktalk! 4

Selections from *The Booktalker* for All Ages and Audiences

Edited by Joni Richards Bodart

THE H. W. WILSON COMPANY
NEW YORK
1992

JR
0285
Bodart

Front Cover: Students in Mr. J.B. Doze's Advanced Placement Sophomore English class, International Baccalaureate Program, Smoky Hill High School, Cherry Creek School District, Aurora, CO, May 1992. Cover photos by Jerry Walters of Monty Nuss Photography, Littleton, CO.

Library of Congress Cataloging-in-Publication Data

Bodart, Joni Richards
  Booktalk! 4: selections from The Booktalker for all ages and audiences / edited by Joni Richards Bodart.
      p. cm.

  Includes bibliographical references and index.
  ISBN 0-8242-0835-8
  1. Book talks.   2. Public relations—Libraries.
  3. Libraries and readers.   4. Books and reading.
  I. Booktalker.   II. Title.
  III. Title: Booktalk! four.
  Z716.3.B637   1992
      021.7—dc20

                                                                    92-13556
                                                                    CIP

472179   *Printed in the United States of America*

CONTENTS

DEDICATION

To my nieces and nephews,
Whose addiction to reading anything and everything
They can get their hands on
Never ceases to make me enormously proud of every one of them,

And to their parents,
Who made sure that their homes were full of books
And many chances to curl up and read them.

Sarah, Kelsey, and Abbie Boos
Drew, Doug, and Julie Wallen

Christy and Curtis Boos
Ceci and Mike Wallen

INTRODUCTION

It all started a long time ago, in 1979, when I was not even close to the person I am now and had no idea of what the future might bring. I was a young-adult librarian, and I wrote a how-to manual for booktalkers called *Booktalk!* On publication day I had all the jitters of a first-time author, but to my relief the book did well, and eventually I was able to expand it in a second edition (*Booktalk! 2*) and a supplementary volume (*Booktalk! 3*). Then, in the fall of 1988, when I was teaching in library school, it started all over again. I was sitting in a colleague's office talking about research—the exhaustive (boring!) scholarly research required of professors—and suddenly found myself thinking instead about what I *really* wanted to do. Why? Because my colleague said, "Joni, did you know that your face lights up when you talk about booktalking, and you look like a different person? Why don't you think about how you could publish booktalks more frequently. . . . What about a booktalk subscription service?"

That was the spark of inspiration that led to *The Booktalker* newsletter, and ultimately to the book you now hold in your hand—a collection of about half the talks and articles that appeared in the newsletter over a three-year period (the other half will be collected in *Booktalk! 5*). *The Booktalker* was published by the Wilson Company five times a year from September 1989 to May 1992, as a pull-out section of their journal, *Wilson Library Bulletin*. Since then it has been published as a semi-annual volume by Libraries Unlimited.

Editing *The Booktalker* has been one of the most exciting and challenging opportunities of my life. It propelled me out of the 9-to-5 world where I had assumed I would always live and into the frightening, uncertain, intoxicating and addictive world of the freelancer and entrepreneur. Volumes have been written about the joys of "doing your own thing" versus the prospects of going down in flames; maybe I'll write one of those books myself someday, but at the moment I'm still living the story—loving the freedom and sense of commitment, biting my nails over the frustrations and finances—and don't yet know how it will end.

So *The Booktalker* definitely comes under the heading of adventure, with all the ups and downs that implies. In going over the material that went into the newsletter for the past three years, I am amazed at the variety of titles, presentation styles, and ideas we made room for—truly something for everybody. The talks and articles you will find here were mostly published during the first year and a half of the newsletter; the books have copyright dates of 1988 to 1990, with the majority published in 1989. I'm delighted to have the opportunity to collect this material, because I know (from your letters and phone calls) how irritating it was to miss out on an issue (or lose it to a more aggressive colleague) and how difficult lost issues were to replace.

The titles included here cover almost every subject one could do a booktalk about, whether addressing adults, teenagers, or children. The contributors take many different approaches, some that may fit in easily with your own style and others that may present a challenge. If you're under the gun, preparing for a school visit that's coming up next week, you can find "quick fixes" here: talks you can adapt easily, about titles your class will like. But if you have more time, here's your chance to experiment: to rediscover an old favorite from fresh point of view or try out a new kind of presentation. Or you may find yourself intrigued by a talk on a book you've never read, and add one more title to that list of things you're going to read just as soon as you have time (and maybe sooner!). Browsing through booktalks can be an excellent way to expand both your professional and your personal reading horizons.

The five articles reprinted at the start of this volume show booktalkers in the field—braving stagefright and inexperience to spread the word about reading, trying different approaches with different audiences, developing techniques to make talks more effective, and dealing with the myriad of situations that novices and experts alike encounter in a day's work. I hope that you'll find both inspiration and practical tips for your own presentations in these accounts—and even some ideas for extending the range of your library's programs.

The one thing this book doesn't do, and isn't meant to do, is provide detailed "Square One" instructions on how to write and deliver booktalks and how to set up a booktalking program. That information appears the text of *Booktalk! 2*, available from The Wilson Company. There and in the companion volume, *Booktalk! 3*, you'll also find more examples of talks that work. And if you and your colleagues are interested in a workshop or a presentation on booktalking and young adult librarianship, please get in touch with me at the address below—there are few things I enjoy more than convincing people, whether they are librarians, teachers, or students, that booktalking is the most effective way to create legions of enthusiastic readers.

If, when you read the talks in this volume, you think to yourself that you could do as well, please consider trying out for the *New Booktalker* (the version now being published by Libraries Unlimited). Take a moment to send me two of your best booktalks and a short description of your experience. And *don't* say, "Oh, I'm just a beginner; I could never do that"—look over the information on what a booktalk is and how to write one in *Booktalk! 2* and give it a try. You may surprise yourself!

But now it's time for me to sign off and give you a chance to explore some of the fascinating books and ideas that are waiting for you just a few pages on. I hope you'll find these articles and talks as helpful and enjoyable as I have, and that you'll let me know how you've used them, and what else you may need in your work.

Have fun, and Happy Booktalking!

—Joni Richards Bodart
8236-A West Morraine Avenue
Littleton, CO 80123
July 1992

ACKNOWLEDGMENTS

First of all, there's no way I could have put this book together without the contributions of more than eighty booktalkers from all over North America. Their names are listed in the Contributors section, and you'll see them again throughout the book as you read their talks and articles. Some of these people have worked with me since 1979, when the original *Booktalk!* was published; others have come on board only recently. They are librarians, teachers, students, free-lancers, retirees (and even a bed-and-breakfast owner!)—men and women of all ages, from every part of the country and even from Canada. What they have in common is a dedication to bringing books and readers together, and they demonstrated that a thousand times over in the work they did for *The Booktalker*. These people volunteered to write talks and articles, frequently on tight deadlines; they delivered wonderful material by mail and fax, rewrote when necessary, and then volunteered for more— generously giving me (and you) the benefit of their experience, ideas, energy, and talent. Thank you, one and all. *The Booktalker* would never have existed without your enthusiastic support.

I'd also like to thank *The Booktalker*'s subscribers, and especially those who expressed their enthusiasm by writing, calling, or just coming over to talk to me at workshops and conferences. Editing *The Booktalker* has been an adventure, but adventures have their ups and downs. I cannot count the number of times when a letter, a phone call, or a conversation has helped me remember just why I'm doing this— for each of you and for the children, teens, and adults who profit from your work. Thank you for keeping my head small enough to get my hat on, for keeping my vision clear, and head and heart aimed in the right direction. Please don't stop letting me know what you think, what you like, what you don't like, and what you need for your work. The relevancy of *The Booktalker* (and now *The New Booktalker*) depends not on me but on you.

Patty Campbell has been my friend, colleague, mentor, sometimes fiercest critic and always most loyal supporter for more years than either of us really want to admit. She encouraged me when *The Booktalker* was just a dream, gave me ideas and suggestions to help it improve, held my hand when necessary (even long-distance), and did everything a friend could do, including invite me when I needed it most to visit the avocado ranch she and her husband David own, in partnership with Rufus, their avocado-eating dog.

Cathi MacRae has also gone far beyond the call of either duty or friendship, administering comfort and criticism, listening to my joys and frustrations, and even contributing booktalks. She too has been there for me since the beginning of *The Booktalker*, and has brought valuable ideas to it all along the way. Her husband Robin Dunn is a newer friend, but one who has taken an interest in the project from the moment he heard about it, generously offering his insights as a publisher and reader.

Martha Franklin cheerfully functioned as local editorial consultant, house- and cat-sitter, and taker of phone messages whenever she could. And she once spent most of a long weekend helping me send out a shipment of books to contributors and then did about half of another shipment on her own, when I was called out of town in the middle of the job—thanks to her, we stayed on schedule.

There are also people at Wilson who helped make this venture possible—and no doubt more than I am aware of, since it's a long way from Denver to the Bronx. First Norris Smith, who did the in-house editing and generally kept the fires of one kind or another under control—not always an easy task. Bruce Carrick and Frank Miller were willing to take a chance on a new and different publication, and Mary Jo Godwin graciously shared not only the pages of *Wilson Library Bulletin* but also her own ideas and reader responses.

I would be remiss if I forgot to thank my family, especially those in Colorado—my aunt and uncle Joan and Chuck Lamb and their daughter, Patty Comer. They know first-hand how difficult those early issues were. Over the 1989 Christmas vacation, they pitched in every way they could, from hauling books to hauling me around, and Patty has even tried out booktalks on her own kids. Finally, Mother has always encouraged me to try for what I wanted, even when it meant a big reach.

So to all of you who contributed in your own unique and special ways to making the past three years of *The Booktalker* a success, thank you, thank you, thank you. *Booktalk! 4* did not emerge from a vacuum, but from a matrix of dedicated professionals and supportive friends and relatives. I could *never* have done it without you.

—J. R. B.

CONTRIBUTORS OF BOOKTALKS

Bette DeBruyne Ammon
Missoula Public Library
Missoula, MT

Mark Anderson
Fairfax County Public Library
Fairfax, VA

Barbara Bahm
Tonganoxie High School
Tonganoxie, KS

Kathleen Beck
Koelbel Public Library
Littleton, CO

Jeff Blair
Olathe South High School
Olathe, KS

Marvia Boettcher
Bismarck Public Library
Bismarck, ND

Julie Bray
Jasper County Public Library
Rensselaer, IN

Maggie Carey
The Barstow School
Kansas City, MO

Sandra Carpenter
Hamilton Elementary School
Hamilton, KS

Nancy L. Chu
Western Illinois University
Macomb, IL

Mary Cosper
Terrebonne Parish Library
Houma, LA

Bernice D. Crouse
Fulton County Library
McConnellsburg, PA

Cathy Crowell
Oswego High School
Oswego, KS

Dorothy Davidson
Jackson Elementary School
Abilene, TX

Diane L. Deuel
Central Rappanhannock Regional
Library
Fredericksburg, VA

Barbara Diment
Santa Fe Elementary School
Kansas City, MO

Judy Druse
Washburn University
Topeka, KS

Susan Dunn
Salem Public Library
Salem, OR

Paula Eads
Booklegger Project
Fremont Main Library
Fremont, CA

Marilyn Eanes
Grisham Middle School
Austin, TX

Kathleen B. Ellis
Berkeley Carroll School
Brooklyn, NY

Steven Engelfried
Alameda County Library
Pleasanton, CA

Sister M. Anna Falbo, CSSF
St. Aloysius Gonzaga Convent
Cheektowaga, NY

Susan R. Farber
Ossining Public Library
Ossining, NY

Lesley S. J. Farmer
San Domenico School
San Anselmo, CA

Eileen Gieswein
Lincoln Elementary School
Concordia, KS

Anna Biagioni Hart
    Sherwood Regional Library
    Fairfax County Public Library
    Alexandria, VA

Barbara Hawkins
    West Potomac High School
    Alexandria, VA

Mary Hedge
    La Porte County Public Library
    La Porte, IN

Di Herald
    Mesa County Public Library
    Mesa County, AZ

Mary K. Hobson
    Vermillion Primary School
    Maize, KS

Betty A. Holtzen
    Abilene Public Library
    Abilene, TX

Donna Houser
    School District 257
    Iola, KS

Doninique Hutches
    Booklegger Project
    Freemont Main Library
    Fremont, CA

Olivia D. Jacobs
    Wichita High School Heights
    Wichita, KS

Rebecca E. Jenkins
    Tempe Public Library
    Tempe, AZ

Kelly Jewett
    Georgetown Public Library
    Georgetown, DE

Patrick Jones
    Tecumseh Branch
    Fort Wayne Public Library
    Fort Wayne, IN

Susan A. Jones
    Pleasanton Branch
    Alameda County Library
    Pleasanton, CA

Carol Kappelmann
    Dover Grade School
    Dover, KS

Eldean Kechely
    Mickle Junior High School
    Lincoln, NE

Patsy Launspach
    Indian Ridge Middle School
    El Paso, TX

Frances W. Levin
    Bentonville, AR

Anne MacLeod
    Booklegger Project
    Fremont Main Library
    Fremont, CA

Mary Macneil
    Shimek Elementary School
    Iowa City, IA

Cathi MacRae
    Boulder Public Library
    Boulder, CO

Rene Mandel
    Framington, MA

Cecelia May
    Lawrence Public Library
    Lawrence, KS

Wanda McAdams
    Booklegger Project
    Fremont Main Library
    Fremont, CA

Diantha McCauley
    Augusta County Library
    Fisherville, VA

Jan McConnell
    Kansas City Public Library
    Kansas City, MO

Kaite Mediatore
    Emporia Public Library
    Emporia, KS

Kathy Ann Miller
    Student, School of Library
        and Information Science
    Emporia State University
    Emporia, KS

Rosemary Moran
    Martin East Regional Library
    Tulsa City-County Library System
    Tulsa, OK

Paulette Nelson
    Minot Public Library
    Minot, ND

Linda Olson
    Superior Public Library
    Superior, WI

Amy L. Oxley
    Indianapolis-Marion County
    Public Library
    Indianapolis, IN

Sue Padilla
    Ida Long Goodman
    Memorial Library
    St. Johns, KS

Paula Paolucci
    Hamilton Public Library
    Hamilton, Ontario, Canada

Kimi Patton
    Booklegger Project
    Alameda County Library
    Fremont, CA

Susan Perdaris
    Fairview Elementary School
    Olathe, KS

Kristina Peters
    North Carroll Branch
    Carroll County Public Library
    Greenmount, MD

Robbi Povenmire
    Mesa, AZ

Faye A. Powell
    Spauldings Branch
    Prince George's County Memorial
    Library System
    District Heights, MD

Marianne Tait Pridemore
    San Jose Public Library
    San Jose, CA

Ann Provost
    Shawnee Mission Schools
    Shawnee Mission, KS

Tracy Pruitt
    Jayhawk-Linn High School
    Mound City, KS

Terrie Ratcliffe
    Irving Public Library
    Irving, TX

Douglas Rees
    San Jose Public Library
    San Jose, CA

Blair Reid
    Carroll County Public Library
    Westminster, MD

Margie Reitsma
    St. Mary's-St. Catherine's School
    Remsen, IA

Tracy Chesonis Revel
    Sussex Central Junior High School
    Millsboro, DE

JoEllen Rice
    Booklegger Project
    Alameda County Library
    Pleasanton, CA

Susan Rosenkoetter
    Rochester Public Library
    Rochester, NY

Kim Carter Sands
    Rindge Memorial School
    Rindge, NH

Suzi Smith
    Maxwell Park Library
    Tulsa City-County Library System
    Tulsa, OK

Pam Swafford
    Teachers College Resource Center
    Emporia State University
    Emporia, KS

Sharon Thomas
    Goddard Junior High School
    Goddard, KS

Sarah M. Thrash
    Seaford District Library
    Seaford, DE

Pamela A. Todd
    John A. Logan College
    Carterville, IL

Rosanne Tricoles
    San Jose Public Library
    San Jose, CA

Diane P. Tuccillo
    Mesa Public Library
    Mesa, AZ

Cara A. Waits
    Tempe Public Library
    Tempe, AZ

Melinda D. Waugh
    Topeka Public Library
    Topeka, KS

Paula J. Wertz
Bradford County Library
Troy, PA

Lenna Lea Wiebe
Clearwater Middle School
Clearwater, KS

Patricia Willingham
Kent Library
Southeast Missouri State University
Cape Girardeau, MO

James Witham
Lexington Public Library
Lexington, KY

Melanie L. Witulski
Holland Branch
Toledo-Lucas County Public
Library
Toledo, OH

Susan Wolfe
Central Dauphin School District
Harrisburg, PA

Sue Young
Ysleta Independent School District
El Paso, TX

ARTICLES

"I Did It!"
Reflections of a First-Year Booktalker
By Jeff Blair
Librarian, Olathe South High School, Olathe, KS

[The events described in this article took place at the junior high school in Junction City, KS, when Jeff Blair was librarian there.—*Ed.*]

I thought that I had them hooked with the first book. But it was a class of seventh graders, so who could be sure? The book was *The Boy Who Reversed Himself*, by William Sleator, about a junior-high girl who is having inter-dimensional occurrences in her locker—a topic I was sure would catch somebody's interest. I even threw in a reference to chocolate-chip cookies, to appeal to their basic appetites.

When I finished the talk, I noticed that I wasn't shaking or sweating heavily. I moved on through the stack of books, picking up a little more confidence with every one of them. I had stacked the deck (stacked the stack?) so that I got to end with a booktalk in which I bellow like an irate king. That, I figured, would be an effective grabber for the finish. But I really hadn't expected the crunch around the reserve cards afterwards. Most of the class was up there, throwing elbows.

I had never had any serious doubts of my ability to booktalk, but seeing that sort of response made me feel as if I'd finally made the majors. I could booktalk to junior high kids, and they'd want to read the books!

The only previous booktalking experiences I'd had were in the YA and Children's Lit classes I took getting my MLS. Joni Bodart was my instructor for both courses, so we did have booktalking assignments. But I had only done three short talks in front of a live audience, and that had been a jury of my classmates, not a roomful of seventh graders.

I had decided to plan my first program around the William Allen White Award nominations. This was a logical choice, since the nominees were all books that the kids were being encouraged to read anyway and would later be asked to vote on. And it was a practical choice for

1

me: by sticking to the list I avoided a lot of nervous decision-making my first time out.

Later on in the year, I did a series on mystery stories and spooky books for Halloween, and then a program featuring ten or twelve books that I personally enjoyed (and had ordered for the library). I wish I had had the time to do more during the spring, but by then research projects were taking up most of the hours I had used for preparing talks. The more I looked around at the collection, the more I realized, too, that it was going to take me some time to build up enough talks to be able just to grab books off the shelf and go into a classroom. (Still have so much to read!)

Throughout the year, I was almost overwhelmed by the reserve list response from the students. I experienced that classic situation in which ninety-three people, about one-eighth of the student body, want the same book and the librarian has only one copy. (I had to promise some of the seventh graders that I would see that they got their turn by the time they came of age.) A more common problem was that the same lump of kids would slowly work its way through the reserve list on each title, so that some students would be next in line for three or four books at a time.

I can't say that I've had any major disasters while booktalking (yet). Had a few books that wouldn't stand up, used a wrong name all the way through once, and had a few flubbed lines, but over about four hundred talks, that's an acceptable margin of error.

My only real regret about this first year of librarianship is not having been able to do more booktalking. A school librarian's life is a busy one, so I didn't get a chance to work up talks on Hi-Lo books, historical fiction, or humor, as I had intended. But I've already started getting ready for next year. "So many books, so little time," as the famous librarianesque lament goes, but I'm determined to make Year Two even better.

Booktalking to Tough Kids
An Interview with Joanne Rosario
By Joni Bodart

Last summer at the Dallas ALA, the Young Adult Services Division of the American Library Association sponsored a preconference on booktalking, presenting a wide variety of ways to promote books and encourage reading. One of the speakers was Joanne Rosario, the Vocational Schools Specialist for the New York Public Library. Her work takes her into some of the toughest schools in the city, and she has found it not only challenging but rewarding. Joanne talks to about 3,500 kids annually, visiting about 150 classes a year in twelve of New York's vocational high schools. The vocational schools offer a basic high school curriculum plus occupational training (in auto mechanics, secretarial skills, carpentry, and other trades) to a large, multi-ethnic population of city teenagers. These kids may be street-smart, but they're not academically inclined. Many read below grade level, and some are more fluent in a foreign language than in English. Some are frankly bored with education and eager to be out earning a living; almost none are automatically respectful of adult authority.

To Joanne, these students are exactly the people the library needs to reach, for their future and for its own. She visits classes in English, remedial English, and English as a second language, as well as Special Education classes. The "blackboard jungle" image, she says, is greatly exaggerated—she has found the students responsive and has never felt herself in any danger, even in the two schools that have been forced to install metal detectors. She just uses common sense to decide what is and isn't appropriate. She talks to the faculty before her visit and takes their advice about where and where not to go, and she walks from class to class during the regular breaks, when the halls are busiest. In case she is stopped by a hall monitor, she always carries identification, giving not only her name and position but also the names of the teachers whose classes she'll be visiting.

Since the class period is only about 40 minutes long, Joanne uses all of it. She starts her presentation with a booktalk, something that's a guaranteed winner—a "boys' book" with lots of action, a low reading level, and a plot that the kids can identify with. (Her current favorite for this slot is Jay Bennett's *Long Black Coat*.) Then she explains how to get a library card, where the nearest branch is, and what services NYPL offers to teenagers. She does some more booktalks and then gives the kids a chance to look at the titles she's mentioned, and to talk with her about whatever problems they may have had with the library in the past. She usually presents from six to eight books during each class period.

At some point during the presentation, she makes sure to explain what to do if you have an overdue book—like, overdue for years. Some kids may have checked out a book when they were younger and incurred a fine that they couldn't pay. So they never brought the book back and now can't get another card. They may never visit a library again because of a problem with one book. Joanne talks individually with these kids after class, evaluates their situation, and then (if it's appropriate) gives them a note to take in to their local library—a note that allows their fines to be remitted and gives them a chance to get another card. She talks with local branch librarians ahead of time, so that they know the kids may be coming in, or sends the kids to the Nathan Straus Young Adult Library at the Donnell branch, which is specially designed for teenagers.

Here are some of her tips for talking to tough kids in tough schools:

1. Don't be afraid to visit these classes. Leave your good jewelry at home if you want to (she doesn't), but with or without it you are not likely to be in any physical danger. Just remember to use your head, and don't panic when you see or hear things you probably wouldn't in the average school.

2. Find out about the class before you go. What is the average reading level? What titles have been or will be assigned in class? Select titles on the basis of the class composition and reading history.

3. Don't automatically accept a teacher's evaluation of a class. Just because the students give the teacher a hard time doesn't mean they will treat you the same way. Let them know right away that you aren't a teacher and they don't have to take notes. This isn't school—this is for fun.

4. Make sure the teacher stays in the room with you—this isn't a chance for a quick cup of coffee in the teachers' lounge. You are an entertainer, not a disciplinarian. The teacher needs to stay in the classroom and perform that function.

5. Begin with an exciting booktalk, not a boring lecture on the Dewey Decimal system—which may be more or less what the kids expect! Catch their attention right away. And if they don't want to listen to the information on the library services, you can point out that if they are quiet so you can get through with this part, you'll do some more booktalks. (It works!)

6. Don't be too concerned about the kids who don't seem to be listening, or assume that if they have their heads down on their desks they aren't paying attention. Often they *are* listening, and ask the best questions after you're finished and want to look at all the books.

7. Do be concerned about a teacher who isn't listening. If the teacher isn't paying attention, the students will feel that they don't have to either. Be sure to explain to teachers that their attention is important—this isn't a time to grade papers.

8. Bring a variety of books with you—several reading levels, different subjects—something to interest as many class members as possible.

9. Do feel free to cancel a visit if you arrive to find a substitute—the kids usually feel this means a free-for-all day, and may be uncontrollable. This is especially true if you have several classes scheduled with that same person. Of course, if you decide to give it a try and find that the substitute is able to maintain order, by all means continue.

10. Do feel free to pack up and leave before you are finished if the class is uncooperative and the teacher cannot maintain order. You and your presentation deserve their attention and respect and if you don't get it, don't spoil your day and endanger your self-confidence by continuing to fight a losing battle. Pack up your things, make sure that the teacher knows exactly why you are leaving, and go. It may also be appropriate to stop at the school library or office and explain to the librarian or principal why you are leaving. (Joanne hasn't done this very often, but has found it to be very effective when she has had to.)

Talking to tough kids can be very satisfying. Even teachers may be amazed at the rapt attention you are able to command from students who are usually noisy and uncooperative. But your highest compliments will be from the kids themselves. No matter how tough they are, they still enjoy a good story!

Don't Tell, Sell:
Putting Hooks in Your Booktalks
By Patrick Jones
Manager, Tecumseh Branch, Allen County Public Library, Fort Wayne, IN

As we've all discovered, many members of the teenage audience are non-readers, either never turned on to books or already turned off. And without a push, they're likely to stay that way—few can expect to earn "peer points" for reading (the dread geek factor); fewer still will be receptive to someone from the library coming to talk to them about it. All day kids are assailed by voices telling them things: early in the day at school, it is "talking heads" at the front of the room putting them back to sleep; late in the evening it is MTV, HBO, CD, and the WWF. Somehow librarians have got to break through the surrounding noise and make books interesting.

That's where "hooks" come in. What is a hook? It's whatever immediately catches your attention and holds your interest—the thing you can't ignore and can't forget. Every YA book has a hook: it can be a character, a plot device, or even the author's style. The hook is the answer to that eternal teenage question: "Why should I want to spend my time reading this book?" A hook in a book makes it different from any other book; a hook in a booktalk makes that difference known.

So, how can hooks be taken from books and used in booktalks? First you have to find them. In *Buck*, by Tamela Larimer, the hook is that Buck has a deep secret. The booktalk can begin with questions to teenagers about keeping secrets ("How many of you have kept a secret?"). It can then move on to giving hints about the secret ("Promise me you won't tell anyone") and finally to a punchline ("Hey, want to know a secret?"). Upon hearing a talk like this, one girl went straight to the library to check out the book, read it that night, then went around school the next day offering to tell her classmates the secret—for a dollar!

Using hooks not only requires changing the focus of the talks themselves but also reevaluating your assumptions about booktalking—you're not there to praise books but to persuade people to read them. When you think about it, booktalking is a performance art. The elements are all there: a captive audience, a presenter onstage (or in front of the room), and certain expectations. The audience may expect to be entertained, informed, or enlightened. The booktalker is hoping to get the audience interested in reading. Performance techniques can be used to meet the audience's expectations and "sell" the book, and models for these are all around in various media.

Movie previews are an excellent example of what booktalks should do. These trailers present the key elements of a film in an interesting, fast-paced fashion. In much the same way, music videos are built around vivid images paired with catchy music. Popular songs have hooks—listen to "Like a Rolling Stone," by Bob Dylan. From the bang of the opening drumbeat to the wail of the final chord, this song bristles with hooks, the most powerful being the question that explodes in each chorus: "How does it feel?" From "Rock Around the Clock" to "Like a Prayer," all popular singles are built around catchy hooks.

Stand-up comics provide another model. Not that booktalkers should imitate Jay Leno, but there's something to be learned from a comedian's timing and from joke construction. Jokes have a grabber for an opening and end with a punchline. A booktalk can be constructed in the same way. Though the last line doesn't have to be funny, it does need to register with the audience. Composing the talk so that the title of the book can be used as the punchline can be a very effective technique.

A model closer to home is storytelling. Not only does storytelling, as practiced by many librarians, use basic hooks—linking sound and movement, developing characterization and suspense—it also demonstrates the necessary shift in attitude. Many librarians who tell stories "switch" from being librarians to being storytellers, a change in role that reflects a change in objectives. Librarians may tell kids about books and stories, but storytellers excite them through performance.

Do librarians doing booktalks make a similar switch? Do they shift from being librarians to being performers? Do they realize, like many children's librarians, that after the teacher introduces them to the class, it's show-time? Making the switch from librarian to performer is the first step to using hooks effectively.

Hooks are more than a matter of style. They are the tools of the trade, the means used to get and hold the audience's attention, so that you can sell them something (something like reading). After accepting that a booktalk is a performance and admitting that you do want to influence your audience, you'll find yourself handling your material differently. Learning to perform your talks instead of just reciting them will help you develop you own unique performance style, best suited for getting your message across. It might be nice to stand up and gush about this wonderful YA novel, but will that sell the book? No, but arousing the audience's curiosity about the plot, playing on their sympathy for the central character, entertaining them with a lively, teasing presentation—that may do it.

What follows is an alphabet of hooks. Each one represents a different spin or angle that can make a booktalk unique, intriguing, and therefore memorable.

Audience participation: Get the audience to repeat the title or a key phrase from the book like a refrain. The repetition alone will help sell the book; giving the audience a part to play is even better.

Boring, but . . . : Start with dry facts, then jump to a shocking event.

Cliffhanger: The classic hook. Bring the audience to the edge, then stop.

Dialogue: Copy dialogue from the book and read it with the audience. Talking with, not at, the audience will increase the energy level in the room.

Empathy: Ask questions to put the audience in the shoes of the character. If the theme of the book is loneliness, then build a booktalk using a series of rhetorical "How does it feel?" questions. For most teens, reading is as much an emotional experience as an intellectual one, and an invitation to share feelings can be a powerful hook.

First sentence: Read only the first line (of Kafka's *Metamorphosis*, for instance) for a short but effective book-hook.

Gross-out: Read or describe the goriest, grossest scene in the book.

Headlines: Refer to an article in the news, then link it to a book (good for contemporary biographies; also for crime or survival stories).

If/then: Present the booktalk in the conditional mode ("If . . . , then. . . . "); let the audience think of other possibilities.

Jump-cut: Jump quickly from one scene to another; let the audience deduce the connection.

Know a secret: Talk about it and around it, but don't tell it.

Linking: Link the book to a popular movie with a similar theme or setting.

Mystery: Turn the book into a game of Clue, and invite the audience to play.

Next line: Read a dramatic scene from the book; stop just before the punchline.

O. Henry: Create one set of expectations, then pull the rug out with a trick ending; save a vital piece of information till the very end.

Props: Use an object to lead in to a scene, or to help act it out.

Questions: Ask a series of these to set a mood or to pique curiosity.

Reaction: If you want a reaction, do something to create it—plan not only what you want to say but also the kind of reaction you want to inspire.

Sounds: Use sound effects (snap your fingers, clap your hands, stamp your foot, etc.).

Themes: Talk about several books that share the same theme (one of the titles should be well-known).

Understatement: Present strange happenings in a deadpan manner.

Violence: Describe a fight or a murder.

What if?: Present the moral dilemma facing the central character.

X-rated: Best example—read the warning from *A Very Touchy Subject* (Strasser).

You: Relate events in the book to events in the listeners' lives.

Zonk: Save one "can't fail" talk in case all the others do. But if you've got your hooks into the audience, they won't!

With thanks to Nancy Currie and Ellen Kimmel for their excellent comments and suggestions.

Senior Booktalking
By Cecelia May
Head of Reference, Lawrence Public Library, Lawrence, KS

It must be stage fright again. Why else would all these evil thoughts be lurking about? I can't go through with this tomorrow, I feel sick.

Maybe one of the kids will be sick in the morning. Maybe the car won't start. Maybe everyone else in the department will be sick and I'll have to stay at the library. Maybe. . . .

You'd think I'd be past this point by now, or at least would have learned to recognize the symptoms before running through my litany of excuses. I *am* prepared. I have done this before. They will love me again, as they always do, and I will feel great afterwards. But rationalization never works, and I really don't want it to. I have done booktalking without this energizing panic driving me on, and it was less than the best for all of us.

Booktalking and stage fright go hand in hand for me. So, twelve times a year, on the second Wednesday of each month, I tie myself in knots, load my arms with books, and hit the road. Before the end of that day, I will have visited groups at two nursing homes and two retirement centers; the next day I will share what I have with a group at the county senior services adult day program and a group at a local mental health center. For about twenty to thirty minutes, I will talk with each group about the books I have selected for that month, sharing, telling the story, reading excerpts aloud, booktalking.

This challenge was inherited as part of my position in the Reference Department. Booktalking was new to me at that time, and I was less than elated. I followed directly in the footsteps of the individual who had set up the program with vision, enthusiasm, and hard work, and I wasn't sure I could keep the ball rolling. Now, nine years later, even with recurrent butterflies, I feel the sense of success that comes from doing something that is tremendously satisfying, immensely appreciated, and fun. The confidence I feel has come gradually, however, and it has come through a learning process of trial and error.

That process extends to logistical details, as well as considerations of selection, preparation, and presentation. For instance, calling the day before my visit to remind the activity director or program contact that I plan to be there that month just as scheduled helps both of us. (Librarians aren't the only people with crazy schedules.) The day and time of my visit are the same each month for each group; alterations in the set schedule can be negotiated as necessary, but keeping those to a minimum seems to work best.

Selecting books to talk about each month has become an intriguing hunt, a good part of the fun. "Selection" actually means a constant, ongoing search, as I juggle ideas and title suggestions with the books I can get my hands on, and then prune the stack down to a manageable size, putting aside the books I've pulled out for another time. The best-seller list, the new-book shelf, and magazines such as *Ladies Home Journal* and *Reader's Digest* that feature books in each issue are good current-awareness tools. Periodicals such as *Publishers Weekly* and *Kirkus Reviews* contain advertising and reviews for new titles, usually in advance of publication. Articles in the local newspaper about authors, regional or otherwise, will suggest titles to follow up on with a booktalk. If people have been hearing about the book, or can expect to hear about it soon, they'll be interested in a booktalk.

Oldies are goodies too, and recommendations from other staff members and patrons, as well as suggestions from group members themselves, can also provide ideas. "What was a book you really enjoyed reading?" is more than a conversation-starter for me—I'm still working my way through a fascinating shelf of fiction by George Barr McCutcheon, a best-selling author of the early 1900s, introduced to me by one who enjoyed him then! Browse your library shelves in certain areas—movie stars, folklore, railroads, comic strips; or compare one of the newly published etiquette books with an old standard. Look through the books returned by patrons: a well-worn, tattered cover can be as attractive as a shiny new book jacket.

As is the case with any booktalking venture, this hunt for titles to talk about also requires keeping in mind the age and lifestyle of the audience. Patrons in this age group grew up in more straitlaced times, and some of them may be put off by rough language or explicit descriptions of sex or violence. You need to be sensitive to their sensitivities, though you don't have to confine yourself to bland content—old people have seen a lot of life. Subjects of general interest seem to work best as openers, so I pattern my programs accordingly. Books that jog memories are very effective for generating interest, involvement, and even discussion, especially with individuals who may no longer be actively reading. And anyone at any point in life can benefit from a broadening of horizons; a book about a foreign country can be an occasion for reminiscence if you've been there, excellent enticement or preparation if you're planning to go, or a fantastic exercise in armchair traveling.

Booktalking to senior citizens requires some additional considerations, then, in selection, but preparation is equally important for success. As in preparing for any program, read the book and think about it from the point of view of your prospective audience. Booktalks for the senior audience are not so much intended to entice people into reading as to make contact, stimulate thinking, and even entertain. For that reason, details about the author are often included, researched if need be, to add human interest to the talk. (One February, Danielle Steel's latest book was included in my program—"Love" was a theme that month—along with copies of the children's books she has written and information from several magazine articles about her and her family.)

Booktalking to senior citizens also requires flexibility in presentation. The groups on my circuit are diverse. At the two retirement centers, audiences will include many who are still reading and enjoying books on their own, though often only in large print. At the adult day program I talk to a lively group of nonreaders—people who for one reason or another never got the habit but welcome the chance to hear and discuss stories and plan activities. The people at the two nursing homes are usually no longer able to read on their own, but they enjoy listening and being read to, looking at pictures, and simply being visited. "Coffee-table" books are good to include occasionally for this audience, and an entertaining book from the children's collection can be fun to read aloud. The visit with the group at the mental health center—not necessarily senior citizens—was arranged by request, fits easily into my schedule, and is valuable for the nonthreatening personal contact it provides the audience, as well as for the exposure to literature and reading.

Booktalking to adults and senior citizens continues to be a challenge. It can stimulate new connections between patrons and books, and it serves a real need that exists in the community. It is good public relations for the library, a great outreach program. And for me it is one of the most rewarding areas of library work—the stage fright is worth it!

Booktalking the Bluebonnets
By Dorothy Davidson
Librarian, Jackson Elementary School, Abilene, TX

[The titles mentioned here are from the 1991-92 TBA list, which follows this article.—*Ed.*]

The Texas Bluebonnet Reading Program is designed for students in grades three through six. The Bluebonnet year opens when a new list of titles arrives in January. These are the nominees for the Texas Children's Choice Awards, and students who have read five or more of these books can vote for their favorites at the end of the year. Children take their choices seriously, and as an elementary school librarian, I focus my booktalks on this program. As soon as the list arrives, I check the shelves for titles already in the collection and order those I don't have.

The serious work begins in the summer, when I read the twenty books that have been nominated. I try to read each book in one sitting, but one or two are always too long to read in that amount of time, and of course interruptions do occur, even during the summer. As I read, I take notes on such things as the names and ages of the main characters and the setting and approximate date of the story. I also note brief background information and clever phrases. Jotting down page numbers from the book itself helps me retrieve exact information and any additional details I may need when I come to write the booktalk. I consult the blurb on the jacket and the summary on the reverse of the title page, but I do not use those exact words in the booktalk, and only rarely do I use any of those details. Working from my notes and my memories of the book, I then write a formal booktalk, editing it as many times as necessary to be sure the wording is accurate, varied, and suitable for third- through fifth-grade students. If I can't seem to get it right, I put the talk aside for a few days and then make a fresh start. The final step is to type each booktalk on a 4 x 6 index card.

For the actual presentation of the booktalks, I have a fresh, new copy of each of the twenty titles. All the books on the current list have Bluebonnet stickers on their spines, so that students can pick them out easily from the shelf, and I draw attention to this feature. I try to state the title and the author of the book early in the presentation, but the first line of each talk is a "grabber," a quote or a question relating to the book, such as "What if you awakened in the middle of the night looking like a wolf, with hair sprouting out all over your body?" (*Weird Wolf*), or "The strange man standing silently at the cabin door looked like a wild creature in his ragged clothing, *but* he had Mama's *locket* in his hand!" (*Weasel*). In the course of the talk, I may briefly mention special features like the postcard illustrations in *Stringbean's Trip to the Shining Sea*, the color photographs of actual storms in *Storms*, or the borders framing the illustrations in *The Diane Goode Book of American Folk Tales & Songs*. With fifth- and sixth-graders, I may mention things like the pronunciation guide and bibliography in *Shaka: King of the Zulus*, and the "B" in the call number; or the illustrated glossary and "Geological Timetable for Giraffes" in *Giraffes, the Sentinels of the Savannas*. Available time dictates the amount of this information I use. In closing each booktalk, I mention the title and author again and encourage readers with endings such as "Why did the kittens suddenly stop what they were doing and race to the kitchen as fast as they could go, and what is 'snot stew'? For the answers to these questions, and for a fun book to read, try *Snot Stew*, by Bill Wallace," or "To discover what Emma and Bertie built in the sand, and what happened to it, read *The Village by the Sea*, by Paula Fox."

In scheduling classes into the library, the teachers allow one hour of library time for booktalks, part of which I set aside for the students' own discussions. Third-grade students also need a thorough explanation of the Bluebonnet program because they are participating for the first time, so booktalks for that grade have to be very concise. I close the class session by reading aloud one of the "picture book" titles on the list: *The Wall* or *Sky Dogs*. Then I say, "You have now heard one Bluebonnet book read aloud, and you may place a dot on the chart when it is convenient with your teacher." Charts are distributed to the teachers at this time, and students receive bookmarks bearing the list of titles. They are encouraged to write their names on their bookmarks and to check off books as they are read. And they're reminded that they will be able to vote for their favorite titles next January.

Writing my booktalks out beforehand helps me make a better presentation—one with variety instead of repetition, and one that focuses on the important elements of each book. And the actual job of writing fixes the book in my mind, so that I will be able to recommend it to readers in future years. The Bluebonnet lists constitute a valuable reservoir of recommended reading. While a list is current, some of the children may have trouble getting hold of the most popular titles, which are likely to be checked out; and the younger children may need time to "grow into" the more difficult books.

By the time students reach the fifth grade, they often think they have "read everything in the library." So, near the end of the school year I present booktalks to fifth-graders using this introduction: "These books are a few of my favorites; some of them are selections from the Bluebonnet lists prior to this year. Others are books that you might like to re-read, or books that were always checked out when they were on the Bluebonnet list."

Time spent carefully preparing booktalks will pay off. These talks may be used at a later date to further emphasize and encourage the reading of quality literature.

Texas Bluebonnet Award Master Reading List
1991–1992 TBA Program

Anderson, Joan. *The American Family Farm*. Harcourt 1989.
Bunting Eve. *The Wall*. Clarion 1990.
Byars, Betsy. *Bingo Brown and the Language of Love*. Viking 1989.
   [See page 35.—Ed.]
Conrad, Pam. *Stonewords: A Ghost Story*. Harper 1990.

Cuyler, Margery. *Weird Wolf.* Holt 1989.

DeFelice, Cynthia. *Weasel.* Macmillan 1990.

Durrell, Ann, col. *The Diane Goode Book of American Folk Tales & Songs.* Dutton 1989.

Fox, Paula. *The Village by the Sea.* Orchard 1988. [Page 237.—Ed.]

Houston, Gloria. *The Year of the Perfect Christmas Tree.* Dial 1988.

Janeczko, Paul B., sel. *The Place My Words Are Looking For.* Bradbury 1990.

Reeder, Carolyn. *Shades of Gray.* Macmillan 1989.

San Souci, Robert D., retel. *The Talking Eggs.* Dial 1989.

Sattler, Helen Roney. *Giraffes, the Sentinels of the Savannas.* Lothrop 1990.

Scieszka, Jon. *The True Story of the Three Little Pigs.* Viking 1989.

Simon, Seymour. *Storms.* Morrow 1989.

Stanley, Diane and Peter Vennema. *Shaka: King of the Zulus.* Morrow 1988.

Turner, Ann. *Grasshopper Summer.* Macmillan 1989.

Wallace, Bill. *Snot Stew.* Holiday 1989.

Williams, Vera B. *Stringbean's Trip to the Shining Sea.* Greenwillow 1988.

Yolen, Jane. *Sky Dogs.* Harcourt 1990.

BOOKTALKS

An Acceptable Time
By Madeleine L'Engle

Grades 7-12

An Acceptable Time   **Grades 7-12**
By Madeleine L'Engle

Polly stood on the star-watching rock in her grandparents' back yard. It was one of her family's favorite spots. It was here, many years ago, that her mother and father, Meg and Calvin, had gazed at the stars and talked about the wrinkle in time. It was on this rock that Polly's uncle Charles Wallace had met Progo, the cherub with many eyes, and years after that, Gaudior, the time-traveling unicorn.

But now, as Polly stared, there was a sudden strange shimmering in the air. Then there was a flash as if from lightning, but no thunder. The ground quivered slightly under her feet, then settled. Where the fertile valley had been, there was now a large lake. A girl was approaching, dressed in soft leather leggings and a tunic, with her hair in a long black braid. Her name was Anaral, she said; she was a druid. At that moment Polly knew she was not in the year 1989. Like her mother and father and uncles before her, Polly had moved through time. She had stepped through the time gate at the star-watching rock into another world, three thousand years in the past.

—Kaite Mediatore

Across the Creek   **Grades 5-9**
By Marya Smith

When twelve-year-old Ryerson's mother died and his father's job kept him traveling, Rye had to go stay with his maternal grandmother in a small sleepy town. He missed his mother terribly, but looking at old black-and-white photos of her when she was a little girl made him feel better. He couldn't look at the color pictures of his grown-up mother with her baby—him—it hurt too much. It also made him angry, because she had promised to stay with him and now she was gone.

But when Rye went to the old creek, where his mother had played as a child, he knew she had kept her promise.

Kneeling on the other side of the water was his mother, his mother from her old childhood photos. A girl of seven, she was quietly and contentedly building something with pretty stones and weeds. Breathlessly, Rye crossed the creek and without a word began to help her.

The rest of August they met there. Rye whittled carvings for her design and she kept building. There was no need for conversation. His mother hadn't changed. She always sat and listened to him, showing love and care in her eyes and face. And there was no need for names or introductions—he knew they knew each other. He accepted that she couldn't bring him anything from her time. All he cared about was that she had returned just to be with him.

Then school began. Rye missed the bus, but not what was waiting for him at his new school. Standing in the only neat line in the busy hall was a group of special students. Rye thought he would go insane, that his life was shattered, when he spotted in that line the girl from *Across the Creek*.

—*Faye A. Powell*

The Adventures of   Grades 5–9
High John the Conqueror
By Steve Sanfield

A hundred and twenty-five years ago, during the days of slavery, about four million men, women, and children had to live in inhuman conditions. But even though the slaveholders tried to take away everything, the slaves held fast to their human spirit. Out of this spirit rose a folk hero known as High John the Conqueror, a bold and witty slave who loved living. He tried to do as little slaving as he could, but Old Master could never figure out if John was working for or against him.

Whenever Old Master was feeling mean or angry he would take it out on the slaves. One time Old Master told the slaves that all the catfish in the big pond were off-limits—the slaves could only take the other fish. Of course these other fish were tiny perch, no bigger than a baby's hand.

All the slaves except John gave up fishing in the pond. High John continued to try his luck every Sunday. He was so bold he would keep any catfish he caught, and he was so crafty that no one ever caught him—until late one Sunday afternoon.

John was asleep, dreaming happily of freedom. Who should come along but Old Master! Old Master saw that eight-pound catfish hanging from the willow branch and he was sure he had finally caught John. He woke John and said, "Nice day! How's the fishing?" with a smile that wasn't so nice. John was scared, but his mind was a-scrambling and a-thinking. Why, you could almost hear those brain cells moving around in his head. Again Old Master said, "I asked you, John. How's the fishing today?"

John spoke very sadly. "You know, Massa, I've been having a terrible time today, a terrible time." And John told Old Master that the old bull catfish had been stealing his bait and just wouldn't stop. John told Old Master that there was nothing he could do but to catch that catfish. Then John said, "But I'm done fishing now, so I guess I might as well turn him loose."

John untied the catfish and flung him back in the pond, picked up his pole and bucket and started home, leaving Old Master staring at the ripples in the pond and scratching his head. He knew something was wrong, but he couldn't catch John out.

And that's only one of High John's escapades—you'll find the others in *The Adventures of High John the Conqueror.*

—*Susan Wolfe*

Afternoon of the Elves   Grades 4-6
By Janet Lisle

Every school has someone like Sara-Kate. She's the odd person who dresses in strange clothes and who says and does the most peculiar things. Hillary had no intention of being weird old Sara-Kate's friend. Hillary was a part of the special group that wore the trendy clothes and gossiped and giggled together. Hillary was sure she didn't need anyone else in her life—until Sara-Kate told her that there were elves in the back yard.

It was extraordinary. The elves had built their village in Sara-Kate's junky, overgrown yard, right behind her broken-down house. There among the weeds, broken glass, car tires, and rusty machines were little elf houses, a tiny well, and even a Ferris wheel. Hillary's own neatly tended yard didn't seem nearly as nice compared to that. Hillary's cool friends didn't seem nearly as interesting as the blunt and mysterious Sara-Kate. Catching a glimpse of an elf became more important than almost anything.

The elves had worked their magic on Hillary, it seemed, but was it them or was it Sara-Kate? What was going on at Sara-Kate's house, anyway? Why had no one seen her mother, and why were there never any visitors?

The Afternoon of the Elves became a bigger mystery than even Hillary could have imagined. Was it elfin magic or not? You will have to decide for yourself when you too discover Sara-Kate's secrets.

—*Sue Young*

Alessandra In Love   Grades 7-9
By Robert Kaplow

When Alessandra fell in love with Bayard Lees she did what any fifteen-year-old would do in that kind of situation—she stole his English folder and read every essay, quiz, paragraph, and book report he'd ever written. But that was last year. Now Alessandra is sixteen, more mature . . . and in love again, this time with Wyn Reed—tall, dark, and handsome (and self-centered). Alessandra is thrilled when she finds out Wyn likes her, but the trouble is, Wyn likes his ex-girlfriend Debbie just as much.

—*Kaite Mediatore*

An Almost Perfect Summer   Grades 7-12
By Rona S. Zable

A summer job on Cape Cod. It really is too good to be believed! After all, how hard can it be, working a mother's helper next door to one of the world's greatest beaches? Ellen's an ambitious young writer, and she's already imagining the story: she sees herself in a glorious natural setting, taking care of two adoring children and falling in love with the mysterious, dark-haired stranger next door.

But the two adoring children turn out to be Monster Marcie and her brother Derek. (Ellen hasn't figured out what's wrong with Derek yet.) The dark-haired stranger next door is real, though—but is he all that he seems? Ellen's summer may not be so perfect after all.

—*Nancy Chu*

Alyssa Milano: She's the Boss   Grades 5-9
By Grace Catalano

Do you know where you can see Alyssa Milano every week? On *Who's the Boss*—she's Samantha! It sounds glamorous, doesn't it, being a teenage TV star. No school, no chores, no worries, and lots of money. Well, it's not like that at all. Alyssa's life's not really so different from yours. She lives with her mom and dad and her younger brother Cory, whom she sometimes babysits.

How many of you have seen the musical *Annie*? When Alyssa was a little girl, she saw it on stage and thought, "I can do that!" So when she was eight years old, she auditioned and got a part—she became one of the "orphans," singing and dancing in the roadshow as it toured the country. Then, after appearing in a few other plays, Alyssa won a role in the 1983 movie *Old Enough*. Her big break, though, came when she auditioned for a star part in a new television series.

When you read *Alyssa Milano: She's the Boss*, you'll discover a star who's a lot like you, and you may want to follow in her footsteps!

—*Wanda McAdams*

Angela, Private Citizen   Grades 3-9
By Nancy K. Robinson

Angela Steele, six years old, was the first one awake on this most important day. She was very excited. All week long her parents had been preparing for just this day, and now it had finally come.

Angela had spent the week trying to help. She knew there was so much to do that sometimes her parents were tired and cross, so she helped by answering the phone; also by trying to keep her older brother and sister from arguing, running to their rooms, and slamming the doors. But April 15th had finally arrived, and her family was ready to pay their income tax. Angela was so proud.

Angela knew that the money her parents paid to the government was important because of a thing called the national debt. She had been shocked to learn that the government was spending more money than it had in the bank. The government needed help! Then Angela had a really brilliant idea. *She* would help by paying her income tax too. After all, she did have $4.53 saved since Christmas. All she would need was a 1040 tax form.

The form was just like a workbook page in school. There was a space for her name and all kinds of fill-in-the-blanks. Angela filled them all in. The spaces she could not write in, she colored. Then she got out her best stickers to decorate the pages. Now all she had to do was mail the form and her $4.53 to the President.

To find out what happened to Angela and her $4.53, read *Angela, Private Citizen*, by Nancy K. Robinson.

—*Linda Olson*

Any Woman's Blues   Adult
By Erica Jong

Leila remembered qualifying at the AA meeting. It was like childbirth, or falling in love.

"I was born in a trunk in a silversmith's shop on Eighth Street to an alcoholic mother and father. The strain of living by my wits seemed so desperate that I tried in every way I knew to eradicate my wits—pot, coke, drugs—until I could feel nothing. . . . nothing but the love leaching through my fingertips onto a canvas. In my clearest moments, I invoked my muse. But always there were days when I could not pray, could not paint; and then I would try to stoke the fires with pot, with wine, with coke—or with my real drug, my main drug: men.

"I would cling to a love as if the force came through him, and after a while I would come to believe that it was he, not I, who made the work come true. Then, inevitably, I would start to abuse myself by giving myself over to him. And he, knowing I had given away all my power, would leave me and find another woman." Always in Leila's life, men appear as if by magic. Bad magic. It's seductive sorcery, to be experienced only by the unafraid: the unafraid of obsessions, power sex, filthy sex, skinless sex. And it's a hard blues sleight of hand as Erica Jong unpeels the masks of love and womanhood. Are you woman enough?

—*Lesley S. J. Farmer*

Anything to Win   Grades 7–12
By Gloria Miklowitz

I'm Cam Potter. I play football, and every girl in school hangs on me—except the one I want. Laurel Greene makes my hands sweat, but she couldn't care less about jocks. And that makes me mad! Half the guys in my school wish they were in my shoes. If you're real good at sports, no one pushes you for grades. You get respect from everyone, even the teachers. You're having fun doing what you like doing best, and girls go crazy just to wear your varsity jacket. The crowds yell your name as if you were a rock star. You get invited to all the parties that count. Who wouldn't like that? Laurel, that's who.

So I decided she's just a stuck-up air-head. She doesn't know the first thing about life. Doesn't she realize that the only thing that matters is winning?

Well, I'll show *her*. Coach called me into his office a while ago. A recruiter's been around to see him, and he says State is going to offer me a scholarship! I hadn't realized until that moment just how much I wanted it. I felt a grin start in my chest and spread right through me.

The only thing I gotta do is gain thirty pounds by January. He says I need the bulk and the power if I'm gonna be worth it to State. When I tell him I already pig out on milk shakes and ice cream sundaes and don't put on an ounce, he says, "There are other ways."

He's talking steroids. I know it and he knows it. I've got a card with an address and a phone number, and Coach says they'll have me looking like Charles Atlas in two months. So just wait till Laurel Greene hears about State. And don't give me any static. Any player who's any good takes steroids. For a girl and a four-year scholarship, wouldn't you?

Read *Anything to Win*, by Gloria Miklowitz, and see if Cam gets the girl and the scholarship, or something else—something he didn't bargain for.

—*Tracie Pruitt*

Away Is a Strange Place To Be   Grades 6–8
By H. M. Hoover

The year is 2349. Abigail Tabor lives with her Uncle Moochi on Earth. He owns the Inn at St. Anne's, a lodge where people who live on artificial habitats come for a luxurious vacation. Uncle Moochi wants Abby to take over the Inn when he decides to retire, but Abby doesn't like that idea. At least, she doesn't think she does. She wants to choose her own future when she grows up, as Uncle Moochi chose his.

One of the guests at the inn is a twelve-year-old boy—just Abby's age—whom she can't stand. Bryan Bishop is the son of very rich parents who live on Triark, an artificial habitat orbiting in outer space, and he is a pain in the neck. He thinks Abbey should do everything that he wants to do, and he's *always* right. He hates this vacation on Earth, this dumb planet with its stupid people and their backward ways.

One evening, Abby's uncle tells her he's arranged for her to take dear Bryan to the amusement pier. A driver will carry them there, and they are to be back at the Inn by eleven. All goes well at the pier until Abby notices that someone is following them. She grabs Bryan's arm and urges him to run back to the car with her. When they pause to catch their breaths, a woman approaches. She reaches out for Abby's arm; Abby feels a sharp pain in her wrist and then blacks out.

The first time she wakes up, she thinks she's having a nightmare. She is enclosed in a tube, there's a voice coming from her pillow telling her to be quiet, and there is some sort of feeding tube in her arm. The voice goes on to announce that she is a lucky winner, and that she is now a Young Pioneer going to live on a new habitat, VitaCon. She and the other Young Pioneers will help build VitaCon into a super-habitat. But Abby is still groggy; she slides back into sleep.

When she wakes at last, the feeding tube is gone and she is in a dormitory. The room is a long, curving structure with rows of beds along the two walls. There is an overhead camera that runs on a track, passing over Abby's bed ever two minutes or so. And all the other girls are wearing the same pink outfit she's got on.

Meals for the Young Pioneers are served in a huge dining room, boys and girls eating together. During her first visit there Abby spots Bryan, but posted around the dining room are guards, called instructors, armed with guns that fire jolts of electricity, so she can't go over to him. Soon their group leader, Mr. White, is introduced. The Young Pioneers are then told what their future will be. They are here to build VitaCon, and they will spend the rest of their lives on this habitat.

Abby knows then that she cannot live like this. Somehow she will have to escape. She and Bryan are assigned to the same work unit, and much as she dislikes him, she realizes that if she is to escape, she will have to have his help. Because Bryan was born and raised on a habitat, he will know how the city is laid out, where the loading docks are, and how to get to the top of those loading docks. Once there, Abby can sneak aboard a cargo ship and find her way back to Earth.

But Bryan gets suspicious when Abby starts asking lots of questions about habitats, and when Abby tells him what she plans to do, he insists on going with her. When Abby refuses, Bryan threatens to tell Mr. White of her plans. Abby's back is against the wall. She can't live like this much longer—all she thinks about is getting back to Earth. Now Bryan is going to Mr. White. There's only one thing to do: *run!*

—Paula Eads

Backstreets: Grade 7–Adult
Springsteen—The Man and His Music
By Charles Cross and the editors of *Backstreets* magazine.

Who do you think of when you hear someone called "The Boss"? Do you know who made simultaneous covers of *Time* and *Newsweek* in 1975? Do you know who Asbury Park, New Jersey's most famous citizen is? Who's been called "the future of rock 'n' roll"?

If you answered "Bruce Springsteen" to those questions, then this book is right up your alley, or rather, up your backstreet. This in-depth look at Springsteen and his music contains rare interviews with Bruce and band members, a list of every concert appearance, candid photos, a session-ography listing all released and unreleased recordings, and more.

From Asbury Park to Thunder Road, from "Rosalita" to Patty Scialfa, from obscurity to "Bossdom"—if you're interested in the life and works of Bruce Springsteen, this is the book for you.

—Jeff Blair

Baily's Bones   Grades 3–9
By Victor Kelleher

At seventeen Kenny's the oldest of the three of us. He's also the simplest, if you know what I mean. In fact, Alex and I look after Kenny. Mr. Clever Alex gets exasperated because Kenny is too big to have the mind of a little kid, but I've just always figured Kenny needs us so he can keep singing his doop-a-doo song, his safe song. It's always been that way. Except for this past vacation, when Mom went researching her old gold mines up on the Northern Tablelands for six weeks. She brought the three of us along to stay in an ancient, run-down cottage that was the original house on the Arnolds' homestead.

Looking back, I can see things were off right away—starting with Kenny finding the bleached human bones in the gully, and old Mrs. Arnold and her son Geoffrey warning us away from there, and the image I kept having, almost like a memory, of his broken bleeding body on the rocks below, with the sound of a woman wailing. By the time Rose, the Aboriginal woman who works for the Arnolds, told us that the gully had been the site of a horrible massacre of her people a hundred years before, we were already in over our heads. Kenny—our brother—was possessed by the ghost of Frank Baily, whose journal suggested we were all on a collision course with a vengeful reenactment of a brutal murder.

You understand, we *had* to try to prevent history from repeating itself. We had to save our brother.

—*Kim Carter Sands*

Balyet
By Patricia Wrightson

In Australia there is a legend about Balyet, an Aborigine girl doomed to live forever, always alone, because of a stupid mistake she made in her youth. Jo's heard the story, but doesn' think it has anything to do with her. So while her mother is away, Jo decides to go visit some friends who are camping in the wilderness. She'll stow away in the trunk of a neighbor's car—Mrs. Willet is going out there to tend the ancient, sacred sites of her people, near the campsite where Jo's friends are. Jo has no idea of the danger her being there will create, especially when Balyet senses her presence, longs for her company, her youth, and her understanding. Will Mrs. Willet be able to keep Jo safe when Jo keeps breaking her promises to her?

—*Sarah M. Thrash*

The Band Never Dances   Grades 7-12
By James David Landis

Half of the power of rock 'n' roll comes from the silent rests between the notes. And half of Judy Valentine's music—and life—comes from the memory of her dead brother.

Jeffrey always wanted to be a star, to stand out. He'd dress outlandishly, only to be copied next season by the rest of the kids. When he decked himself out in a full tux, he said that he had nowhere else to go. Little did Judy know that her brother had decided to go out—permanently. He left a suicide note on her drums: "Why do I feel there's no me inside me? I won't even miss myself. But I'll miss you. You're the only thing I've ever been good at. Don't change. Just grow. Remember, the band never dances. P.P.S. Now the only thing left of me is you."

After that, Judy didn't want to share her life with anyone else. She shut them all out, even her parents, who couldn't face the loss of Jeffrey either. So Judy danced with herself. Getting good grades. Trying to laugh. Practicing her drums. Writing songs. And waiting to become sixteen years old, when she would be Jeffrey's age, so she'd have his permission from beyond the grave to go find her band.

And find her band she did. "Band seeks drummer," said the notice.

"I'm calling about your ad for a drummer."

"What about it?" He sounded very far away.

"I'm a drummer."

"You sound like a girl."

"I am."

"I don't work with girls."

"I don't work with idiots. Good-bye." But Judy didn't hang up.

They called the band Wedding Night. It had a lead singer who looked like a ghost, an electric bass player who stood like a tall black tree, a piano player who walked off a concert stage to join them, Mark the Music, and Judy Valentine, the tiny girl drummer who hid behind her drum kit and wrote personal, mysterious lyrics.

A lot of folks came to their concerts and listened to her music. And what those folks wanted most was to get Judy up front, to love her. But all Judy wanted to do was be invisible—and to keep Jeffrey close to her, closer than anyone else.

—Lesley S. J. Farmer

Been Clever Forever   **Grades 7–12**
By Bruce Stone

I have been clever forever. In fact, I was born smart, but the commotion didn't start until I was in the first grade. That was when I listed ten questions that should be answered in an appropriate course of study. Some of the questions were:

1) Why are all magazine subscriptions sent to Boulder, Colorado?

2) Where has Donald Duck left his pants?

3) What becomes of the roaches you flush down the toilet? and

4) Why is aluminum foil shiny on one side and dull on the other?

I didn't think my questions were all that weird, but they were the start of yearly meetings between my parents and teachers They also got me put into special classes for the gifted. Being smart means you are expected to do great things, which doesn't necessarily follow. All I wanted was to be left alone—fat chance! However, I have finally made it to high school, and after a clash with my biology teacher, I realize that the world is as confusing and chaotic to adults as it is to me. I'll need all my cleverness just to survive!

If you want to find out whether I survive high school and if I ever manage to succeed, just read my story in *Been Clever Forever.*

—Barbara Bahm

Before the Wildflowers Bloom   Grades 3-6
By Tatyana Bylinsky

It's 1916. Carm and her brothers and sisters live in a coal-mining camp in Colorado. The girls dream of pretty dresses and parties. The reality is yellow dust and the taste of coal in the air. The whole family dreams of a homestead near Aguilar. The reality is saving enough money to leave the mine and buy the cattle for a ranch.

Carm's story is one of hope, of tragedy, and of one year, 1916, that changed her life forever.

—Carol Kappelmann

A Begonia for Miss Applebaum   Grades 7-12
By Paul Zindel

"To any kid who reads this: Something terrible has happened. There are no lies in this book and nothing phony. We are writing it on an Apple IIE during our computer class at high school while most of the other kids are playing Donkey Kong and Demon Attack. We have to tell the whole story because we thought what we were doing was right. Well, maybe it wasn't. Maybe we were very wrong. We still don't know. Maybe you will understand and be able to help us. Please don't think we meant to hurt Miss Applebaum. Please don't think that at all. Sincerely, Henry and Zelda."

It all started last September 9th around 8:30, when we burst into the third-floor science lab to sign up as lab assistants with Miss Applebaum and discovered that she wasn't there. The man who *was* there—her replacement, Mr. Greenfield—told us she had retired. Something in the tone of this voice wasn't quite right, and we got suspicious and decided to investigate. After all, Miss Applebaum was not an ordinary teacher—in fact, she was an extraordinary and special teacher in every way. Like the time she brought over seventy cocoons from Central Park and hung them from threads in the windows. A month later we came to class and there were seven million baby grasshoppers leaping all over the desks and causing a riot. Then another time she explained in complete scientific detail how doctors force a tapeworm out of a patient by giving massive doses of laxatives and then search through buckets until they find the worm's head. Every year Miss Applebaum baked bohemian ceramic earrings in the lab incubator and sold them to other teachers as Christmas or Chanukah gifts, and whenever she wanted to feel especially special, she wore a black homburg hat.

So you can see why she was our very favorite teacher, and why we just couldn't let her disappear without a word. But we never thought that taking a begonia to her as a retirement present would change both our lives, and how after that day, nothing would ever, ever, be the same.

—*J. R. B.*

The Believers
By Rebecca C. Jones

Grades 3–6

Do you believe in miracles? Tibby Taylor does. She's already had one miracle in her life and now she's praying for another. The first miracle happened when Tibby was interviewed on the network news by gorgeous newswoman Veronica Taylor. Veronica thought Tibby was so cute that she decided to adopt her. Tibby's natural mother had died when Tibby was four and she had been placed in one foster home after another until Veronica came along.

Veronica was always adopting sad cases. The one before Tibby had been a three-legged dog named Lou Grant. But Veronica doesn't stay in one place for very long; she's always moving on to the next big story, the next chance to make it to the big time, to Washington and the nightly news. So both Lou Grant and Tibby end up spending most of their time with Veronica's Aunt Evelyn. Lou Grant doesn't mind—that dog just loves Aunt Evelyn. But Tibby minds—a lot. She wants a chance to spend some time with her new mother. She wants Veronica to come home for more than just a brief visit.

So Tibby's in the market for another miracle. The first one got her a new mother and she hopes the second will make that mother come home to stay.

And now she's met a group of people called the Believers who think their prayers can help Tibby get her miracle. Aunt Evelyn says the Believers are very dangerous because "their leader has brainwashed them into thinking they don't need schools or doctors or anything. They think God will take care of everything." But Tibby sees the Believers as a group of loving people who really care for her. They're helping her pray for her miracle. But the miracle that Tibby gets won't be what she expects at all.

—*Marianne Tait Pridemore*

Best Friends Tell the Best Lies   Grades 7–12
By Carol Dines

Being fourteen isn't easy for Leah—especially after her best friend Tamara announces that her own mother is a murderer! Tamara is a terrific friend—unconventional, smart, and funny— but she does tell wild stories, and sometimes Leah doesn't know if she ought to believe them. But Leah's very loyal to her friend.

Then Leah's mother starts dating this dumpy-looking Mexican named Jose, who's nothing at all like her wonderful, dashing father. Leah can't understand what her mother sees in him.

When Tamara confesses that all her stories are lies, Leah realizes that she can't depend on anyone—not her mother, not even her best friend. What's truth anyway, and where can she find it? "Integrity" used to be one of those words that you always hear and never think about. Now it's got to be more than that.

—Barbara Bahm and J. R. B.

The Best Place to Live Is the Ceiling   Grades 7–12
By Barbara Wersba

Would you be willing to assume soneone else's identity to take an exciting trip to a foreign country? Even if it meant that you might get caught and arrested? Even if you found out that the identity you'd borrowed was going to plunge you into a situation like a James Bond movie? Sixteen-year-old Archie Smith is a lonely kid from Queens, New York, who, because of a strange coincidence, finds himself facing these very decisions.

Archie feels that his life is going nowhere, and his kind but busy father barely has time for him. There are only two things that make Archie happy. One is watching old movies, dreaming of being like the dashing, handsome heroes on the screen. The other is staring out the window of the restaurant at Kennedy Airport, watching the planes take off and imagining all the exotic places they are going.

It is in that restaurant, one afternoon when Archie is feeling particularly depressed, that something happens to change his life. A young man, about Archie's size and coloring, gets sick and passes out. After the ambulance has come and taken the man away, Archie realizes that the man's black bag is still sitting there, left behind. Nobody else seems to have noticed. Archie takes the bag and quietly opens it. Inside he finds a passport, some money, a hotel reservation—and a plane ticket to Switzerland. Archie sees the man's name—Brian Chesterfield—and suddenly, on a whim, he makes a decision: Archie Smith will become Brian Chesterfield, and leave on that flight to Switzerland. Archie can't imagine anything more exciting than a trip to a foreign country—a chance to ski the Alps. He figures his new identity will provide the change of perspective he needs to turn his life around. But Archie's life gets turned practically inside out when, instead of the fun-filled ski trip he was expecting, he finds himself tossed into a dangerous adventure, a world of intrigue, and an unexpected and very unusual romance.

—*Diane P. Tuccillo*

Best Witches: Poems for Halloween   **Grades 3-4**
By Jane Yolen

Halloween Poems
Compiled by Myra Cohn Livingston

Halloween: Stories and Poems
Compiled by Caroline Feller Bauer

[A booktalk for mid to late October]

You guys getting ready for Halloween? [This should draw the answer, "Yes!" If you are doing the talk in early October, or if the answer is "No," ask, "Are you *thinking* about getting ready?"]

What are you going to need? [Should get replies. If not, ask, "Will you need a hat?" and so forth. Let the children respond, but don't let them go on too long or wander too far afield.]

But, you know, you're going to need one more thing . . . a poem! [This will probably be met with a certain scepticism.]

No, really. Picture this: it's getting dark on Halloween, but it's still too early to go out. The doorbell rings. You open the door. There are three witches there. They are not early trick-or-treaters—they've come for dinner. What can you feed them? "Witch Pizza"! [Hold up the Yolen book. Open to page 9, and read or recite; make sure the kids see the illustrations.]

No anchovies,
Lots of cheese,
Amanita
Mushrooms, please.

Top with herbs
Both hot and chivey,
And some extra
Poison ivy.

You really need to know this. You have to be careful dealing with witchy things. Otherwise . . . [Read or recite Yolen's "Fossilot"—and do show the illustration on page 16!]

You cannot find a Fossilot
Except in ancient stones,
Where imprints of its teeth and claws
Lie jumbled with its bones.

Some scientists cleaned up the bones,
Arranged, then tried to date them.
But when they had the jaw complete—
It turned around and ate them.

So . . . let's say your witches do eat dinner (and don't eat you!). Now what? Well, before you leave the house, you'll want to make sure your pumpkin is set up [read or recite "Pumpkin" by Valerie Worth on page 38 of the Bauer book]:

After its lid
Is cut, the slick
Seeds and stuck
Wet strings
Scooped out,
Walls scraped
Dry and white,
Face carved, candle
Fixed and lit,

Light creeps
Into the thick
Rind: giving
That dead orange
Vegetable skull
Warm skin, making
A live head
To hold its
Sharp gold grin.

Are you in the right mood to go out into the night? Good! Just take your friends and go. [Read or recite "We Three" by Lilian Moore on page 23 of the Livingston book—and show the illustration!]

> We three
> went out on Halloween,
> A Pirate
> An Ape
> A Witch between.
>
> We went from door to door.
>
> By the light
> of the moon
> these shadows were seen
> A Pirate
> An Ape
> A Witch between
> and—
>
> Say, how did we get to be *four?*

You may feel you'd better pray. Try this [read or recite from Livingston, page 16]:

> From Ghoulies and Ghosties,
> And long-leggity Beasties,
> And all Things that go bump in the Night,
> Good Lord deliver us.

Have a safe Halloween—if you can. And don't forget to bring a poem, just in case.

To deal with witches: Jane Yolen's *Best Witches.*

For stories and recipes as well as poems: *Halloween: Stories and Poems.*

And for very scary poems and drawings: *Halloween Poems.*

—Rene Mandel

Bethie   Grades 7–12
By Ann Rabinowitz

Beth thought she had gotten over her parents' divorce six years ago.
It hadn't been easy—learning to accept her new stepmother, dealing
with her mother's depressions, and then meeting her mother's new
boyfriend.

Somehow Beth had survived and grown. But now it was happening
all over again—to her best friend Grace. All those scary feelings of loss
and rejection came rushing back.

She and Grace had been friends for years, and though they lived
miles apart they always spent their summers together on Cape Cod.
Beth had always been especially fond of Grace's father. He was such
a kind and gentle man. She just didn't understand how he could aban-
don his daughter Grace. And Grace didn't even know the worst part
yet. What would Grace do when she found out? How would she feel
when she learned that her father was already in love with someone else?
He was getting married and moving all the way across the country to
start a new life with another woman and her two children. How could
he do that to Grace?

And then Grace found out about her father in the worst possible way.
She didn't cry or rage, she was quiet—too quiet. She was like a mine
waiting to explode on contact. It seemed to Beth that she was the only
one to notice, but even she didn't realize what was about to happen.

—*Marianne Tait Pridemore*

Better Mousetraps: Grades 5–12
Product Improvements That Led to Success
By Nathan Aaseng

Many inventors are famous, yet there are people just as famous who
never invented the products they're famous for. Instead, they took
things that were already in existence and made them better.

Take George Eastman, of the Eastman Kodak Company. Cameras
had been in existence for years when Mr. Eastman came along, but taking a picture wasn't that easy. A good half-hour might pass while the
photographer got all the heavy equipment set up. Because of Mr. Eastman's improvements, we can now take pictures with a camera as small
as this [show a Kodak Instamatic] at the touch of a button.

Shaving used to be a much longer process too, because razors had
to sharpened. In the late 1890s a man named King Camp Gillette be-

came obsessed with creating a detachable, disposable blade. Finally, in the early 1900s, he succeeded, and a Gillette razor [show one] is still a common household item.

Another common item by the early 1900s was factory-made bread. But its quality declined as manufacturers tried to produce it more and more cheaply, and soon it was about as substantial as cotton fluff. Finally, in 1937, Margaret Rudkin decided to make mass-produced bread with natural, fresh ingredients. People liked the taste of it so much that her bakery became a family business and then a large corporation. The name of the bread [show a Pepperidge Farm bread wrapper] came from the pepperidge trees at Mrs. Rudkin's country home.

So being the inventor of a product doesn't guarantee success. But if you can improve on someone else's invention, the customers will come calling.

—*Mary Hedge*

[This booktalk may follow the talk on page 89 about other books written by Nathan Aaseng.—*Ed.*]

Beyond Safe Boundaries   Grades 5-9
By Margaret Sacks

I grew up in South Africa, and until I was eleven nothing happened to disturb my peaceful world. We were white and my father was a dentist, so we lived in a comfortable house in an all-white neighborhood, with a garden and three black servants.

I knew that you weren't allowed to eat off servants' plates and that my nanny Lena, even though she was an adult, had to have my mother's permission to travel after dark. My father had to have his dental offices remodeled because his white patients complained about blacks using the same facilities. He had to set up two offices in the same building—one for whites and one for blacks. But my life was untouched by injustice or violence. It was there all along, but I never saw it. *My* world was one of privilege and abundance. It was only after my sister Evie went away to the University of Johannesburg that my world began to change.

Evie went away angry—angry at my father for marrying again. It was Lena, our black maid, who seemed to look into the future, although at the time I could not see any value in her warning. I thought that Evie would be much happier when she got away to the University, but Lena said, "Bad thing for unhappy gel to leave her house. She can get into big trouble outside." Lena was right. Evie's journey was to involve our

entire family in the racial unrest in South Africa and change my view
of my homeland forever.

—*Marianne Tait Pridemore*

Beyond the Reef   Grades 7–12
By Todd Strasser

Last year while we were on vacation in Florida, my parents fell in
love with Key West, just like all the other tourists. But what do *they*
do? They quit their jobs, sell the house, and move down here for keeps!
Dad's started diving for sunken treasure, something he's wanted to do
all his life; I've never seen him so happy. And Mom's started writing
a novel.

But lately things haven't been going so well. When we first started
treasure-hunting, Dad and I found some gold coins, but now all we're
getting are beer cans and rusted shopping carts. Mom's hit a snag in her
novel and can't write anymore. To top it off, our boat's been vandal-
ized—the natives here, the conchs [conks], don't like Dad and me diving for their treasure. We've been hanging in, but now the money's
about run out, and Mom wants to give up and go back to New York.
I know Dad won't quit diving, but I don't know how she'll react.
Doesn't she realize how hard we're trying? We could strike it rich any
day now!

—*Kaite Mediatore*

The Big Bang   Grades 7–12
By James D. Forman

There's a theory that says a few billion years ago there was just one
incredible fireball of matter that exploded and made all the galaxies,
including the Milky Way. They call this the Big Bang Theory. *My* Big
Bang was puny in comparison—but it was bigger than anything I'd ever
want to go through again, and it changed my life forever.

The night of the Big Bang was the first Saturday night of spring
break. My dad and stepmom were in Palm Beach, and my older brother
Jeff and I were headed to a party. Jeff and his buddies sometimes let
me hang around—mainly because of my camera. I was always taking
pictures, and they kind of liked that. Jeff had my dad's van, so he was
in charge of picking everybody up. We were all headed to Greg Lawrence's basement for pizza, music, and a good time. So far, so good—

and as soon as everyone was there, the beer started flowing. But when the pizza was gone and the beer was nearly gone, Jeff decided to go cruising. Everyone piled into the van, and we took off.

The first hint of trouble I can remember is Jeff and Marty, his girl, arguing about something. Then she got out of the van—she wouldn't ride with him because he was drunk. I think if I'd had the guts, I would have gotten out too, but I didn't. I don't remember much after that. About all I remember is a bright light, a fire, and I think an explosion. I found out later that I was the sole survivor. My brother Jeff and seven of his friends were dead. I'm sure there's something else I should remember, but I can't, not right now at least.

Will Chris ever remember all the details of the accident? And if he does, will those memories destroy him?

—*Linda Olson*

Bingo Brown and the Language of Love   Grades 4-6
By Betsy Byars

Bingo Brown knows the language of love—that is, he knows how to have a conversation with a girl—but little does he know that it is going to cost him fifty-four dollars and twenty-nine cents. The love of his life, Melissa, has moved to the end of the world (that's Bixby, Oklahoma) and now his mom says no more phone calls. What's poor Bingo to do?

To make matters worse, before he can even defend himself his parents drop the real bombshell—his mom runs away to Grammy's claiming she needs more space, and his dad refuses to answer any questions.

Just when Bingo thinks nothing worse can happen, Billy Wentworth, the GI Joe nerd from next door, asks Bingo to dogsit his poodle Misty. There is nothing Bingo hates more than being stared at by Misty. His mom says that it is just known as eye contact, but who wants eye contact with a dog?

Then there's Cici, the big blonde, who's trying to make her way into Bingo's life. Cici wants Bingo, Bingo wishes Melissa were back, and Billy wants Cici. How complicated can life get? To find out, read Betsy Byars' *Bingo Brown and the Language of Love.*

—*Paulette Nelson*

Birthday Poems   Grades 3–4
By Myra Cohn Livingston

What if I ask you which one day of the year is special just to you? It's a day you anticipate and make secret plans for, months ahead of time. Your birthday? Right! And what if somebody wrote a whole book of poetry about this special celebration—well, that's just what you'll find in *Birthday Poems*, by Myra Cohn Livingston.

How do you like to spend your special day? Some people have summer birthdays and choose to savor a day out-of-doors, as in "Beach Birthdays." The birthday person becomes royalty on this special day—king or queen of the sand castle. Or what about a visit to a museum where there are dinosaurs galore—that sounds like fun too. And that's just how Jan spent her "Dinosaur Birthday." But wait! "Michael's Birthday" party was at the nature trail, where everyone hiked and saw deer tracks and "Dick and I picked lots of twigs / To make the fire start/ So we could roast our hot dogs / And the food was the best part!"

Do you like party games? *Birthday Poems* tells us about everyone's reaction to the memory game Tray—"Laura giggles, and I try, / Chris gets mad enough to cry." And watch out for "Pinning the Tale on the Donkey" (especially if you invite someone named Charlotte to your party).

No matter what part of the celebration is your favorite—invitations, fancy table settings, presents, a cake with lots of icing, or wishes that might come true—you'll find a poem in this book to make you wish the magic day would come tomorrow. Or maybe next week would be better—we'll need time to plan.

—*Mary MacNeil*

Blitzcat   Grades 10–Adult
By Robert Westall

She felt his presence, yet every instinct told her that he was moving farther and farther away . . . and so her journey began. Nothing mattered except finding him. Through the war-torn rubble of England and France, and even on the bombing runs, she looked and lived for nothing else.

Through it all, she made many acquaintances, from a tough, battle-hardened sergeant to a rookie rear-gunner who adored her. And each gained something and grew a little stronger from having known her.

Gunners were a superstitious, nervous lot, and rear-gunner Tommy was no exception. Therefore, when she chose him, he took it as a sign. Everyone knew that black cats were supposed to be lucky, and she was just a small, plain, deaf black cat—or was she? No ordinary cat would have a name like Lord Gort—and that *was* her real name.

Then one night she proved what an unusual cat she really was. Suddenly she sensed its presence! Tommy, on guard duty, strained his eyes from the turret window and saw nothing. She tensed, and with lightning speed pawed at the window. Tommy looked again, closer this time, and something *was* there, moving among the clouds—a Jerry night-fighter, hoping to pick off more planes! Slowly Tommy brought the gun around and aimed at the German plane, and he and Lord Gort waited for just the right moment.

To discover if Lord Gort and Tommy survive and if she is ever to be reunited with her beloved Geoffrey, read *Blitzcat*, by Robert Westall.

—*Suzi Smith*

The Blood-and-Thunder Adventure   Grades 3–9
on Hurricane Peak
By Margaret Mahy

The Unexpected School is built on the side of Hurricane Peak. The mountain got its name from the hurricane that circles the top every three hours. The hurricane is about the only thing that's regular at the Unexpected School.

For one thing, they don't teach math or science there; instead, they teach various forms of magic. That stands to reason, since the Deputy Principal is a sorcerer who regularly has to saw children in half so that there will be enough students in the classes. For another thing, the Head Prefect is a talking cat.

Huxley and Zaza Hammond are sent to this strange and wonderful school and are soon involved in a blood-and-thunder adventure that includes villainous villains, heroic heroes, mystical forests, and more excitement that you can shake a magic wand at.

Is there anything that *can't* happen at the Unexpected School? Read this book and find out!

—*Jeff Blair*

Bo Knows Bo   Grades 7–Adult
By Bo Jackson and Dick Schaap

So you think you know Bo, do you? You know all about the baseballs he blasts off his bat like Patriot missiles, his ninety-yard blitzkriegs through the best D's in the National Football League. OK, but how about the five guys in a Mustang who tried to run him down, just for being black? Or the time he showed the fat end of a baseball bat to some crackers in a Memphis parking lot? Bo don't take no diddley, you understand. But there's more to the man than the baddest ballplayer in all the land. If you don't know Bo's biggest thrill (happened in the hospital), you don't know Bo. If you don't know what he's going to do when he hangs up his spikes and cleats (Bo's nuts about kids, especially kids who need help), you don't know Bo. And if you think he's just stomp and strut and swagger, you've been watching too much Bo-gus TV. This book'll set you straight. (And there are even great pictures, too—check out Bo in his Superman suit.)

—Jim Witham

Borgel   Grade 7–Adult
By Daniel Pinkwater

One night, Uncle Borgel tiptoed into my room in the middle of the night and pressed a note into my hand, inviting me to his room in one hour. For once, I didn't have to wear a tie. I was used to strange invitations like this from Borgel. No one was sure if he was really our uncle or not. He had shown up on our doorstep one day with thirty-two rather large and lumpy valises and moved in, announcing that God in his wisdom would reward us for taking in a homeless 111-year-old relative. He basically stayed in his room, brewing strange pots of tea and retorting with a loud "Phooey" if anyone anywhere in the house (he had excellent hearing) suggested that he might be better off in a rest home.

As I mentioned, I would occasionally get invitations to Borgel's room (with the admonition to wear a tie) for tea and conversation. We'd sit amidst the thirty-two valises and discuss buttons, deodorants, records, Chef Chow's Hot and Spicy Oil, and other wonders of the universe.

At the time, I didn't realize how out of the ordinary this particular visit was going to be. This time, Borgel, Fafner (the family dog), and I went out into the night, hot-wired a 1937 Dorbzeldge sedan, and set off to explore the time-space continuum. I discovered then that Borgel routinely traveled through time and space, and was used to adventures of this sort. I certainly wasn't!

But this wasn't going to be a typical time-space adventure, even for Borgel. We found ourselves involved with a strange creature named Freddie who caught us up in his quest for the cosmic Great Popsicle. The only trouble was, if Freddie did find the popsicle, it could mean the end of time and space as we know it (or don't know it. It all depends).

Come travel with Borgel and me as we explore (and hopefully save) the time-space continuum.

—Jeff Blair

The Boy Who Lost His Face Grades 5-9
By Louis Sachar

Scott had been David's best friend since second grade, but recently Scott had made some new friends—Roger and Randy, two of the coolest guys at school. Scott told David that he'd have to act cool too if he was going to hang out with them, so when the three boys decided to steal Old Lady Bayfield's snake-head cane, David went along with the plan. Randy tipped Mrs. Bayfield over in her rocker while Scott grabbed the cane. Then Roger poured a pitcher of lemonade over her face and tossed the pitcher through her front window. All David did was flip her off. But he was the one who got the full force of her anger. As he looked down on her, she shouted, "Your Doppelganger will regurgitate on your soul!"

Well, Randy had told David that Old Lady Bayfield was a witch, and that she had stolen her husband's face while he was sleeping and mounted it on her living-room wall. That was supposed to scare David, but it didn't—he didn't believe in witches or curses. That is, not until strange things began happening to *him*. Then he started to wonder. How would his own face look, hanging on Felicia Bayfield's wall?

—Kathy A. Miller

The Boy Who Owned the School Grades 5-8
By Gary Paulsen

Self-esteem . . . I guess you could say that that's been my problem all along. A lack of it, that is! And I don't think you'd blame me either.

I probably have one of the ugliest faces in the world, I'm almost blind without my glasses, and my body resembles a string bean. To make matters worse, my older sister is a beauty queen. No kidding! She's already won all sorts of titles, and my parents are too busy launching her career to pay any attention to me. Don't get me wrong, it's not that I want attention. On the contrary, I know for a fact that when people notice me, *bad things happen.* So I've sort of perfected the art of being invisible, and I could have stayed that way forever if it hadn't been for my English teacher. It's all her fault! In spite of my best efforts she noticed me, and now she's got me working with the stage crew for the school play. I *know* something's going to go wrong, very wrong! To find out what it is, join me in *The Boy Who Owned the School.* Who is he? Me, of course, but you'll never believe how it happened!

—*Sister Mary Anna Falbo, CSSF*

Brushy Mountain   Grades 5-9
By Patricia Pendergraft

Tice Hooker was the meanest man who ever walked on Brushy Mountain. That's what everybody said, and Arney agreed. Old Man Hooker was the "nastiest, most no-goodest old hoot-owl ever." He'd threatened to kill Arney's dogs. He'd thrown Granny Stallcup out of the shack she'd rented from him for ten years just because she'd gotten a little behind in her payments. Arney's ma had to take Granny in to live with them because there was no place else for her to go. Old Man Hooker had even scared Arney's little sister Sal when she was taking a short cut through the cemetery.

Arney vowed to do something about that man. He got his chance one Sunday after church, when Hooker fell into the creek and didn't come up. Should Arney be a good person like his pa and save Old Man Hooker's life? Or let that ungrateful skunk drown?

—*Lenna Lea Wiebe*

Buffalo Brenda   Grades 5-9
By Jill Pinkwater

My first day of junior high had a grim beginning. I missed the bus! When I finally got to school, I had to wander around the halls until I found Room 212. There I met a sour-looking, thoroughly disagreeable teacher named Mr. Osgood.

It was there, before Mr. Osgood and my peers, that I first laid eyes on one Brenda Tuna, who is now my best friend and co-conspirator. I, India Ink Teidlebaum, should have known that my life would never be the same!

Brenda decided that we should go out for an extracurricular activity in order to make our mark in school. Little did I know that the *Florence Weekly Crier* (sometimes referred to as the *Florence Weekly Flounder*) was to be our target! Little did I know that our extracurricular activities would involve a riot, horseburgers, Mr. Osgood, and finally our forced resignation!

However, that was long before Brenda's *really* big idea! If you'd like to know what to do when facing an enraged adult buffalo or how to survive really wild and unbelievable adventures, read *Buffalo Brenda*, by Jill Pinkwater.

—Suzi Smith

Burnt: Grade 10–Adult
A Teenage Adict's Road to Recovery
By Craig Fraser and Deirdre Sullivan

Craig was all-American boy from a loving, middleclass family—an honor student at a prestigious private school, a member of the student government, and a peer advisor, popular with students and teachers alike. But Craig was also one of the school's biggest drug users and dealers. Beginning with alcohol in the sixth grade, he soon graduated to pot, coke, LSD, and speed, buying and selling huge quantities of cocaine and other drugs to support his expensive habit.

In *Burnt*, you can follow Craig on his journey from drug addciton to recovery, and discover not only what it's like to be trapped within the darkest depths of drug addiction but also what kind of courage and strength it takes to make the journey back.

—Barbara Bahm

Buster Midnight's Cafe   Grade 10–Adult
By Sandra Dallas

You want to know about Butte, you go over to the twenty-four-hour Jim Hill Cafe & Cigar Store on Silver Street and ask for me and Whippy Bird. The front is covered in stainless steel just like an old North Coast Limited streamliner, and in the window is a blue neon champagne glass with pink bubbles coming out of it, as flashy as May Anna's diamond earrings, which she left me in her will. Your better class of tourists, they ask about the history. Whippy Bird likes to go into detail about the copper kings who got rich here, and also, it's the place where Buster got his start. If she's feeling sassy and has the time, she draws it out so those people are sorry they asked. If she's busy, she lets them get to the big question right away. But mostly, she makes the tourists get around to it on their own, with a lot of hemming and hawing.

This particular tourist (a real windbag, I thought) had to talk about everything on the menu first. Your fatties surely like to talk about their food. Then after he ordered a short stack of pancakes, he cleared his throat. "You from around here?" he asked in a kind of casual way.

"I been a native all my life," Whippy Bird said.

"You know, I read Marion Street was from Butte."

"Marion Street?" Whippy Bird asked. "Is that a person or an address?" (She pronounces it "ay-dress.") I've heard Whippy Bird ask that about a thousand times, but I always have to put down my coffee and laugh. You see, me and Whippy Bird know that Marion Street took her name from an ay-dress. When May Anna Kovaks wanted a fancy name, me and Whippy Bird looked up at the street sign and got the same idea at the same time. May Anna thought it was the funniest thing she ever heard. She was lucky she wasn't standing on Porphyry Street when we got the idea.

With his Expand-O waist riding halfway to his armpit, that tourist said in a low voice, "I heard Marion Street used to be a hooker here."

His wife punched him in the arm and said, "Now, Harold."

Whippy Bird was flipping a pancake just then. She turned around and let the pancake land on the floor. "Marion Street was a hooker? You mean a whore?" She said it so loud you could hear her outside, only nobody from Butte who was walking by ever paid her any mind because she's said it so many times before.

The tourist turned as red as Heinz-57 ketchup. Then Whippy Bird slammed down his short stack, which was even shorter since one of the pancakes was on the floor, turned back to the grill, and pretended to cook, but I know she was laughing.

The pancake on the floor was a good touch. The timing doesn't always work out like that. "I guess when you get to be as beautiful and as famous as Marion Street, people just naturally say nasty things about you." Whippy Bird clucked her tongue. "And her being dead like she is! She was just as famous as Marilyn Monroe. And just as sad. You know she was older 'n me?"

The rest of us, we got old, but not Marion Street. She's frozen as a Hollywood Sex Goddess now, and people remember her the way she looked when she died in 1951. You don't think, Why, she'd be in her seventies now.

"Did you know her?" Harold was back in the saddle.

"Did I know her? I guess me and Effa Commander knew her better than anybody." Whippy Bird is always willing to share the credit.

"Do you know about the Love Triangle Murder?" Nothing could stop that boy now.

"That was a long time ago," Whippy Bird said.

Me and Whippy Bird don't like it when the tourists ask about the murder. With May Anna and Buster gone, me and Whippy Bird are the only ones still around who know what really happened, and we never talked.

After the tourists left, Whippy Bird put down her pancake flipper and said "Effa Commander, it's time somebody told the truth about the May Anna Kovaks-Buster McKnight murder. And you are that person—you owe it to Buster and May Anna and the world!"

Back in the old days, when we were five years old in Butte, Montana, Whippy Bird, May Anna, and me, Effa Commander, called ourselves the Unholy Three. And now that I'm the only one left, it's surely right that I tell the true story of *Buster Midnight's Cafe.*

—*Cathi MacRae*

[Except for the last paragraph, the text of this booktalk is composed of selected quotations from pages 3–10 of the book.]

The Butterfly Jar
By Jeff Morse

Grades 3–9

We had a jar with a butterfly.
We opened the lid and it flew to the sky.
And there are things inside my head
Waiting to be thought or said,
Dreams and jokes and wonderings are
Locked inside, like a butterfly jar.
But then, when you are here with me,
I can open the lid and set them free.

And the poems in this book are set free for you and me—to enjoy, to share, to laugh over, and to wonder at. Here is one about how to trick a head-biting monster:

There was a time when I was small
That every night in bed
A monster used to come
And want to bite me in the head.
But I could trick him every time
As easy as could be,
I'd just crawl in and put my head
Down where my feet should be.
That so confused the monster
As he lifted up the sheet,
He would go home sad and hungry
'Cause he hated eating feet.
Yes, every night he found my toes
And that was such a bore,
He left for good,
    and now he doesn't
Bug me anymore.
(I think he's after my sister, though)

Ever wonder what it would be like "if purple was the only color in
the world"?

You would read about "Snow Purple and The Seven
    Dwarfs."
You would sing about "The Purple Grass Growing All
    Around, All Around,"
And you would drink purple juice for breakfast.
You'd write with chalk on the purpleboard,
And cross the street when the light turned purple,
And visit the President of the United States in the Purple
    House.
You could even write a poem that begins:
    "Roses are purple, violets are purple . . . "
It's a good thing there are other colors.

Now I'll leave you with a poem about things that come in twos.

Lots of things come in twos—
Ears and earmuffs, feet and shoes,
Ankles, shoulders, elbows, eyes,
Heels and shins and knees and thighs,

Galoshes, ice skates, mittens, socks,
Humps on camels, hands on clocks.
And heads on monsters also do—
Like that one . . .
  right in back of you!

—Diane L. Deuel

C, My Name Is Cal   Grades 7-8
By Norma Fox Mazer

The other day when I was in the mall, a spooky thing happened. I saw my father—at least I saw a tall man, slightly balding, in a worn blue sport jacket, who looked exactly like the photo I have of my father.

I didn't tell anyone about seeing him. I definitely didn't tell my mom. She and my father got divorced when I was five. He took off, and my mom won't talk about him—she doesn't even like to hear his name. I also didn't tell my friend Garo, either. Garo thinks I'm tough, can handle anything, and have all the right answers. I didn't want to lose his respect. But I guess the real reason I didn't tell anyone is that it might have been a mirage, seeing what I wanted to see.

After all, why would my father suddenly show up? In eight years, he's never come to see me, he's never called. All he's ever done is send me three picture postcards, each one from a different place.

A week later, when Garo and I were standing in line for the movies, I saw the man again, but this time I managed to tell myself all the good sensible reasons why that person going out of sight could *not* be my father. Later, though, when I was telling Mom about the coincidence of seeing this man who looked like the photo of my dad, first in the mall and then again across the street from the movies, I sensed something weird in her reaction. What was it she was keeping from me—and why?

—Olivia D. Jacobs

The Call of the Wolves   Grade 3-Adult
By Jim Murphy

What would you do if you suddenly found yourself all alone, far from friends and family, and unable to find your way home? In Jim Murphy's *The Call of the Wolves*, a young wolf finds himself in just this situation—separated from his pack and alone in the icy Arctic.

He and his pack have been following a herd of caribou for eight days over steep and dangerous terrain. They have traveled far; they are hungry. Finally, one of the caribou can go no further. In a snowy Arctic clearing, the wolves close in on the sick, weak animal that is no longer able to outrun them. Just as they are about to attack, a plane of illegal hunters zooms over the area. Wolves and caribou frantically scatter as gunshots break the silence of the snowy wilderness.

One young wolf, eager to escape, runs in the opposite direction from the others. He soon realizes he is being followed by the plane of hunters. As he runs, he comes face to face with his only route of escape—a plunge over a steep cliff. His instinct to survive is strong. He launches himself over the cliff, dropping into a mound of branches and snow. His rear leg crumples beneath him as he struggles to escape the plane that continues to pursue him. He scrambles on three legs into the protective trees that hinder the hunters' view. Alone, hurt and hungry, the young wolf curls up in the snow for a night of rest, knowing that the next day he must find his pack, even though he doesn't know where he is and has no trail to follow. Will he be able to do it? He will have to contend not only with cold and snowy weather, but also with other animals who may attack him boldly now that he is alone.

What can one young wolf do, alone in the Arctic with no pack to help him? Will his instinct to survive be strong enough to overcome his confusion, his injury, and his weakened condition?

—Susan Wolfe

Can't Hear You Listening   Grades 7–12
By Hadley Irwin

I was *so* embarrassed!! Mom was on that TV program last night with the reporter asking her about her newest "Help Yourself" book. She was wearing *my* new jacket and *my* favorite pair of stone-washed jeans. At least she couldn't wear my new Reeboks—they're too big for her. She's been going through the alphabet: *Help Yourself with Anger, Help Yourself with Beauty,* and the latest—*Help Yourself with Companionship.* When the reporter asked her, "What's next?" and Mom said, *"Help Yourself with Daughters,"* I could have just *died*! My speech teacher was going to tape this for class. The worst part of all was the reporter asking Mom my name. When she said, "Tracy Spencer," he cracked up—obviously he was an old-movie buff too, but *I* hate Spencer Tracy!

Mom has been so busy working on her books and her trial separation from Dad that she hardly seems to listen to me any more. The morning after the program, she asked me what I thought about it. I asked for jelly on my sandwich. I was thinking about going to a movie at the mall with Amy and Mary Agnes, and Mom said, "Well, what did you think?" "About what?" "About North Dakota seceding from the Union!" "Oh, you mean the interview last night?" *I* think we have a problem communicating. At least my part-time father talks to me as if I'm a human being!

I didn't really let it bother me so much until Stanley, who has been my friend forever, began acting weird. It started at a party one night last spring. Stanley had one glass of beer and acted as if he were stoned out of his mind. Over the summer he borrowed money from me, forgot to pay it back, and then asked for more. That is *not* the way Mr. Potential CPA usually operates! Then he called late one night, begging me to come and get him—he had blacked out and didn't know where he was or how he got there. He *said* he had only one drink of beer, but it didn't sound like just one beer to me!

Is Stanley taking *more* than beer? I can't talk with Mom or Dad or even my best friends . . . no one will listen. I don't know what to do, but I *have* to do something soon or something terrible will happen to Stanley. . . . *Help!*

—*Marvia Boettcher*

Caribbean Canvas   Grade 10-Adult
Compiled by Frané Lessac

Let's take a journey to the Caribbean Islands. Tropical breezes, rustling palms, blue water lapping the white sand, sweet fruits, rhythmical drums—all can be ours in *Caribbean Canvas.*

But today I recapture the islands'
bright beaches, blue mist from the ocean
rolling into fishermen's houses.
By these shores I was born: sound of the sea
came in at my window, life heaved and breathed
in me then with the strength of that
turbulent soil.
(Edward Brathwaite)

You'll see the people of the Caribbean in the paintings and hear them in the poetry—poems about living, dying, dancing, gambling, loving. Listen to the "Market Women":

> Down from the hills they come
> With swinging hips and steady stride
> To feed the hungry town.
> They stirred the steep dark land
> To place within the growing seed.
> And in the rain and sunshine
> Tended the young green plants,
> They bred, and dug and reaped.
> And now, as Heaven has blessed their toil,
> They come, bearing the fruits,
> These hand-maids of the soil.
> Who bring baskets down,
> To feed the hungry town.
>   (Daisy Myrie)

Consider what "An Old Jamaican Woman Thinks about the Hereafter":

> What would I do forever in a big place, who have
> lived all my life in a small island? The same
> parish holds the cottage I was born in, all my
> family, and the cool churchyard.
>   (A. L. Hendricks)

And imagine what it would be like to swim with a school of tropical fish:

> So for an hour, an age, I swam with them,
> One with a peace that might go on forever . . .
> Till, of a sudden, quick as a falling net,
> Some thought embraced them, I watched them go
> Tidily over the reef, where I could not follow.
>   (Barbara Howes)

If you cannot get away to the Caribbean Islands just now, a journey through the sights and sounds of *Caribbean Canvas* is the next best thing.

—Diane L. Deuel

Celine   Grades 10-12
By Brock Cole

That day I walked home from school carrying "Test Patterns," the
great painting of my junior year, which had hung for a week outside the
principal's office and might have stayed there until the end of the term,
except that someone had written "sucks" after my name in the lower
right-hand corner. I was upset. I had had to walk home because the
driver wouldn't let me take "Test Patterns" on the bus. There was a
strong wind from off the lake, and at every intersection it tried to tear
the painting out of my hands . . . When I reached the building where
Catherine and I are living, it was a total mess.

Catherine is my twenty-one-year-old stepmother. We don't get along
too well. My father, a French professor on a lecture tour in Europe,
thinks that Catherine and I will grow to love one another. Just before
he left on this impromptu tour, he noted that Catherine and I must
have much in common since we are "so nearly the same age."

I am doing my best to get along. After all, my father and I have
worked out a deal so that I can spend the summer with my friend in
Italy. All I have to do—as my father puts it—is show a little maturity,
which I've doped out to mean: Pass all your courses, avoid detection
in all crimes and misdemeanors, don't get pregnant. There are only
three more weeks of school, and I've been doing great at showing a little
maturity. What could possibly go wrong?

—*Olivia D. Jacobs*

The Cellar   Grades 5-12
By Ken Radford

While rummaging through the dusty old cast-offs in the dark corners
of the attic, Sian finds a jewelry box that plays a haunting Welsh lullaby.
She also finds a diary written in old-fashioned, faded script. She shivers
as she reads the eerie words set down long ago by a girl named Sarah
Jane. The writing mourned for a mother who went away, never to
return, and cursed a Devil-man who locked Sarah Jane in the cellar
where no one could hear her cries.

Sian is relieved to realize that the diary cannot be true—the house
has no cellar. Then she and her friend David discover a door, a door

that has been sealed for years behind a brick wall in the little room below the stairs. Now opened, it leads to a long-forgotten cellar.

Faced with the possible truth of the diary, Sian feels somehow compelled to discover what happened to Sarah Jane. Her thoughts echo with Sarah Jane's words: "If I should . . . go away forever, then search for me under the full moon. That's where I shall be waiting."

Waiting for whom? Waiting for what? Sian wonders, as she begins her descent into the shrouded past, her descent into *The Cellar*.

—Tracy Chesonis Revel

Changes in Latitudes   Grades 7-12
By Will Hobbs

Change comes so quickly sometimes, when you least expect it, and afterwards nothing is ever the same again. Travis's life changed when he saw his mother with another man, and realized why his dad hadn't come to Mexico with them for a week at a fancy seaside resort. It changed again when he and his little brother Teddy swam with the sea turtles, as beautiful and graceful in the water as they were awkward and ungainly on the land. These were Teddy's favorite reptiles, and they were an endangered species. Life was never the same for Teddy, or Travis either, after they saw the mountain of slaughtered sea-turtle carcasses, dead because their eggs were believed to be aphrodisiacs that would make a man more of a man.

Change happens, life changes, and you have to figure out how to cope. That week Travis discovered just how very difficult coping can be. It's not hard to betray a brother. It's as easy as saying a few words or swallowing an egg. Just think of yourself first, and the rest is easy.

—J. R. B.

Charlotte Shakespeare and   Grades 5-6
Annie the Great
By Barbara Ware Holmes

What do you do when your best friend is the smartest, most talented person in the school, but no one knows it? Charlotte Cheetam has that problem, but she knows what to do and she does it! She sets out to make her best friend, shy Annie Block, the star of the sixth-grade class play. Charlotte, known as Charlotte Shakespeare, has written a humorous, scary, Halloween play about a little witch named Carlotta who likes to lie. Charlotte convinces Annie that she has to try out for the lead part and beat Miss Know-it-all Tina. So Annie practices faithfully and builds up confidence, but all her confidence, and all Charlotte's too, is shattered when she has a practice audition in front of her classmates. "Dot me here, dot me there, dot me, dot me everywhere. Through my skin and underwear, dot me magic if you dare," Annie barely whispers. As Charlotte sits at her desk and hears her beautiful words suddenly turned into some boring, stupid rhyme, she begins to doubt Annie's acting ability. But determined not to let Miss Know-it-all win, Charlotte asks her dad to give Annie a crash course in acting. To everyone's amazement, on the day of the tryouts Annie does a great job and gets the star part. But getting the lead role may be a bit more than Annie *or* Charlotte has bargained for. That's only the beginning of the adventures of *Charlotte Shakespeare and Annie the Great.*

—*Amy L. Oxley*

The Chessmen of Doom   Grades 5-9
By John Bellairs

Why a dead eye in a room with no view?
Why pallid dwarves on a board that's not true?
To pull the hairy stars from their nest
And give sinful humans a well-deserved test.
(If you solve this riddle you may wish you hadn't.)

Armed with this cryptic message, the elderly, eccentric professor and his teenage friends, John and Fergie, embark on a strange mission. In order for the professor to inherit a huge estate from his deceased brother Peregrine, he must spend the summer at the desolate, deserted mansion.

As they arrive at the mansion, they discover a giant tomb, with a massive statue of an old man who, the professor says, is Peregrine. On the base of the statue they see the word *Resurgam.* The professor says that is Latin for "I shall rise again."

That night they find the bronze doors of the tomb forced open. The next morning they discover an attic room with the windows boarded up—the "room with no view," perhaps.

Day by day, more terrifying events occur, and the boys begin to wonder whether they'll even survive the summer.

—*Carol Kappelmann*

A Child's Treasury of Animal Verse　　Grades 3-9
Compiled by Mark Daniel

My dog's so furry I've not seen
His face for years and years:
His eyes are buried out of sight,
I only guess his ears.

When people ask me for his breed,
I do not know or care:
He has the beauty of them all
Hidden beneath his hair.
　　(Herbert Asquith)

Almost everyone loves animals, whether pets at home or beasts of
the farmyard and the forest. And many poets have written of creatures
great and small. There are poems about cuddly kittens and fearsome
crocodiles, about faithful dogs and three little mice, a silly goat and a
ferocious tiger, even the birds and the bees. Snakes aren't the kind of
animal you expect to find in a poem, but they're in this one . . .

The birds go fluttering in the air,
The rabbits run and skip,
Brown squirrels race along the bough,
The may-flies rise and dip;
But, whilst these creatures play and leap,
The silent snake goes creepy-creep!

The birdies sing and whistle loud,
The busy insects hum,
The squirrels chat, the frogs say "croak!"
But the snake is always dumb.
With not a sound through grasses deep
The silent snake goes creepy-creep!
　　(Anon.)

And here is a poem about a bird that doesn't live in a tree:

I am the pirate's parrot,
I sail the seven seas
And sleep inside the crow's nest—

Don't look for me in trees!

I am the pirate's parrot,
A bird both brave and bold.
I guard the captain's treasure
And count his hoard of gold.
(Anon.)

Artists also use animals, as subjects for their paintings. They have found them at home [p. 6-7], on the farm [p. 30-31], in the forest [p. 115], and at the zoo [p. 75]. Between the poems and the pictures, you are sure to find your favorite animal here.

—*Diane L. Deuel*

Children of the River   Grades 7-12
By Linda Crew

The rules of the Khmer culture don't work in America, half a world away from Cambodia. Sundara tried to obey the old rules, but it was hard, since they didn't fit the way she lived now. And when Sundara broke the rules, her Aunt Soka, who was her guardian in America, told her she was shaming her entire family, and even threatened to kick her out in the street.

But, Sundara wondered, was she really shaming her family in Cambodia and her aunt and uncle in America by making friends with Jonathan and having lunch with him? Did her parents really expect her to go ahead with the marriage they'd arranged for her years before? And worst of all, why hadn't she heard from them? Would she ever see her own family or Cambodia again?

Torn between two cultures, Sundara didn't know which way to turn. No matter what she did, she would disappoint someone: Jonathan, her aunt, her family—or herself.

—*Donna Houser, with J. R. B.*

Chinese Handcuffs   Grades 10-12
By Chris Crutcher

My name is Dillon Hemingway, and I'm seventeen years old. But I was only nine years old when Stacy caught me with Chinese handcuffs. We were at the carnival, and she came up to me and shoved a woven straw cylinder stuck on the end of her index finger at me. "Stick your finger in!" I did, and discovered that I couldn't get away. No matter how hard I pulled, the cylinder just got tighter and tighter. "Chinese handcuffs," Stacy said "Neat, huh? You have to know the secret to get out. The gypsy lady said it was the secret of life."

Well, that gypsy knew what she was talking about. The way to escape *was* one of the secrets of life—at least, of my life. In order to get my finger out of that straw tube, I had to push my finger into it, not try to pull it out. The harder I tried to get away, the more I pulled against the tube, the tighter I was trapped. The only way to get my finger out of that tube was to quit trying to escape and release the pressure.

Now I'm caught in another version of Chinese handcuffs—only the finger in the other end of the cylinder belongs to my brother Pres, who's dead. He shot himself in front of me one Saturday morning at dawn two years ago. He said he wanted to get some target practice—I didn't realize the target would be his head.

But I'm not the only one struggling to get out of an impossible situation. Jennifer is, too. She's become the main lady in my life, but even though we're best friends, she's never let anything romantic get started. I couldn't figure out why, till she told me about her Chinese handcuffs: about how first her father and now her stepfather sneak into her room late at night and molest her. She can't remember the first time it happened—she was too young, maybe only three or four. She told twice— once on her father, when she was in second grade. Her mother kicked him out, but then, just a few years later, she married T.B. and it started all over again. When Jennifer tried to tell on T.B., no one believed her. He was too smart. He got out of it, made Jennifer look like a liar, and then he killed her dog, just as he had promised he would if she ever told. Jennifer never told again—that is, until she told me. And she made me promise never to tell anyone else, no matter what. She was scared T.B. would do more than just beat up on her mother. He might also start doing the same things to her little sister that he was doing to her. She was caught, and she couldn't get out.

Chinese handcuffs—you can't pull away, you have to give in. Can Jennifer discover how to escape? Can I?

—J. R. B.

Chocolate-Covered Ants   Grades 3–6
By Stephen Manes

Have you ever read *How to Eat Fried Worms*? Think you might ever want to try it? No? Well, what about chocolate-covered ants? It's simple—all you need is a chocolate bar, some ants, and a microwave! Or maybe it's not so simple, when your mom discovers what a mess you've made and *really* lays down the law!

That's what happens to the kids in this book. If you've ever wondered what ants taste like, this is the book for you. But I warn you, after you read it you may never want to look at chocolate-chip ice cream again!

—*J. R. B.*

Choices   Grades 7–12
By Elaine Scott

Beth, Carl, and Jed, along with other students from Millington High, started the night's adventures with revenge in mind and perhaps a little fun besides. But what seemed to be the beginning of an evening of pranks between rival schools turned into a nightmare of crime.

Over the years the rivalry between Woodrow and Millington High had created traditions. Woodrow typically painted yellow claw tracks, symbols of their mascot, the Eagle, down the center of the streets and up the light poles, and then bombed Millington's signs with rotten tomatoes. Millington typically sprayed green cougar paws on the driveways and retaliated with green peppers.

This year, however, things had gone too far. Someone had taken the Crouching Cougar, the plaster statue of Millington's official mascot. That night, groups of Millington students, intent on liberating the cougar, armed themselves with green spray paint and descended on Woodrow. In the rampage that followed, some students went way beyond covering the yellow claw tracks with green cougar paws. Windows were smashed, tennis nets cut down, and gym mats sliced.

Then suddenly came the shout, "Cops!" and kids scattered in every direction. Even though Carl and Jed were with her, Beth might as well have been alone. Green paint running down her arm and streaking her jeans, she was caught by the glaring spotlight and the officer's questions.

Charges were pressed, and Beth O'Conner—a senior elected by her peers to be Clara Cougar, the symbol of school spirit—now stood alone—searched, photographed, fingerprinted, and jailed.

Can this once-popular member of the Millington Misses endure silence and ostracism by her classmates? Will the truth about the "theft" of the statue finally be revealed? What choices will Beth, her family, her classmates, and her school officials have to make?

—Olivia D. Jacobs

Choosing Sides   Grades 5-6
By Ilene Cooper

Sixth-grader Jonathan Rossi plays center for the Wildcats, the basketball team at Kennedy Middle School. His afternoons are filled with endless practice sessions with Coach Davidson, who thinks a tough regimen of drills and push-ups will whip the team into shape and make them win for a change. More than pleasing Coach Davidson, though, Jonathan tries to please his father, the sports fanatic, by doing his very best on the court. Except that Jonathan's best isn't turning out to be very good, no matter how hard he practices. Besides that, basketball takes up a lot of time, effort, and thought. Jonathan begins to realize that he'd rather spend that time hanging around with his friends Ham and Bobby. He'd rather spend that effort on a special contest, The Battle of the Books. And he'd rather think about Robin, the girl he likes, instead of basketball plays. But Jonathan hates to shatter his father's dream of having an all-star son. Sometimes, though, a son needs to think of his own feelings first, and Jonathan must decide if he is strong enough to stand up for those feelings and choose the side that's right for him.

—Diane Tuccillo

The Christmas Cup   Grades 3-4
By Nancy Ruth Patterson

Ann Megan McCallie will never forget the summer before third grade. That summer her teeth refused to grow back in, Doc Butler told her she had to wear an eyepatch, and she attended her first auction. Megan handled the teeth and the eyepatch rather well, but the auction started something she would never forget.

The auction was scheduled on a day that turned out to be hot. Megan and Nannie, her grandmother, made lemonade to sell to the people who came to bid. As the day wore on, the lemonade ran out, but Megan stayed on to listen to the auctioneer announce the last few items for sale. As the auctioneer held up a rusty tin milkshake cup, Megan listened to the comments from the audience. When the opening bid was lowered to five cents, Megan surprised herself and everybody else by calling out "Five dollars!"—all the money she had made that day selling lemonade. Amid the laughter and jeering, Megan proudly carried her treasure straight home to the kitchen, where her Nannie suggested a plan to change the rusty old milkshake cup into something beautiful. It would become a Christmas Cup, and only Nannie and Megan knew what beautiful surprises would come from it.

—Paula J. Wertz

Circle of Light   Grades 5-9
By Elaine Corbeil Roe

Lucy is known as the brain of her eighth-grade class at St. Margaret's, so it shouldn't have come as a complete surprise when her teacher, Sister Andrew, asked her to represent the school in a scholarship competition. Lucy is against the whole idea. Not only will it mean a lot of extra work, but it will take away from the time she can spend with her friends. Besides, she doesn't think she has a chance of winning, and the prize is something she doesn't even want: a four-year scholarship to a convent high school. Lucy is happily anticipating entering Rockford High, the public school, next year.

She has already said no to the competition, but Sister Andrew begs her to reconsider one more time and ask her mother for advice. Lucy knows the decision must be hers alone. Even her brother's comment, that this would be an honor for the family and the school, does not change her mind. She is determined to say no for the last time that afternoon after school. But before Sister Andrew can even ask the question, Lucy hears herself saying, "I'll do it." The challenge has been accepted, and because of that her life will never be the same.

—Anne MacLeod

Cleaver of the Good Luck Diner   Grades 3-6
By James Duffy

Dad gave us Cleaver as a good-bye present. He said Cleaver could take his place at the Good Luck Diner, and ever since Cleaver joined our family we *have* had good luck. Cleaver is the watchdog at the diner. Last year a robber came in and wanted all the money from the cash register. Fortunately, when Mom went to get the money she stepped on Cleaver's tail and he let out a yelp and scared the robber away. Later, he also scared a skunk, which you probably won't think is very good luck, but I wrote a composition about it that my English teacher really liked. She said that I was a born writer, even though my grades in English weren't great. But the best luck that Cleaver brought was the time he got lost in a snowstorm and Mom couldn't find him. And to see why that was so lucky, you'll just have to read *Cleaver of the Good Luck Diner.*

—Paula J. Wertz

Come the Morning   Grades 7–12
By Mark Jonathan Harris

Do you ever wonder when you pass the homeless on the street where they came from, how they ended up there?

Constance and the three children had come from Texas to Los Angeles to find her husband Clyde. It had been five months since Clyde had left them in El Paso in the middle of the night. Five months and not a single word, until the hundred-dollar money order arrived. The message had been short, not sweet: "I don't want to drag you down any more. You'll be better off without me." But there had been a return address printed in delicate grey type on the back of the fancy envelope. Talking it over, Ben and his mother Constance had finally agreed that Clyde wouldn't have sent a return address unless he wanted to see them. So Constance, thirteen-year-old Ben, nine-year-old Felice, and three-year-old Jube set out to find Clyde and a better life.

They arrived in LA at the Greyhound bus station and discovered that the cab fare from the station to the address on the envelope would be $25. That would leave them with very little money, but they had to find Clyde. So all four piled into the cab with their two worn suitcases, containing all they still owned in the world, and set off in search of Clyde and a new and better life. Constance had faith that "Weeping may endure for a night, but joy cometh in the morning," but it was not to be.

—Marianne Tait Pridemore

Connections: Grades 7-12
Short Stories by Outstanding Writers for Young Adults
Edited by Donald R. Gallo

We all make connections with other people, some deliberately, some by accident. Sometimes that connection becomes a lasting bond, and sometimes it's only a casual tie, that breaks with just the slightest tug. It can be a face-to-face connection or one by mail or by computer, but no matter how the connection is made or how long it lasts, it changes things for the two people involved, either a little or a lot.

Let me introduce you to one of the people in this book that I connected with. Angus Bethune is the first person I met, and, I think, the most memorable. He's just been selected Senior Winter Ball King, something that obviously has to be a joke, since Angus is as far from the kind of Adonis that usually reigns over the ball as any one person can be. To begin with, he has four parents, two biological and two step. Not so unusual, you say? But his parents are paired up a little differently from the average ones. His two dads are married—to each other! So are his two moms. And since neither of his parents is exactly small, Angus is a big kid—always has been. Not exactly someone you could overlook. He says he's really fat—I have my doubts. You can't play the kind of football that he does and still be as fat as he says he is; there's just no way. But tonight he doesn't want to hear the fat jokes or the faggot jokes he's had to listen to all his life, he doesn't want to be the laughingstock of the Winter Ball, he wants *normal*. He wants *socially acceptable*. You see, the Queen of the Senior Winter Ball is Melissa LeFevre, the girl of his dreams (and *only* his dreams), and after she and Angus are crowned, they'll have to dance together. Angus figures that this will be his moment, his only chance to hold Melissa in his arms, and he wants it to be perfect. He's been in love with her ever since kindergarten, when she dared a kid named Alex to stick his tongue on a car bumper in minus thirty-five degree weather because he called her a "big fat snotnosed deadbeat." Angus was always looking for creative ways to retaliate against his own name-callers, and when he saw the patch of Alex's tongue stuck to that frozen bumper he knew he was in the company of genius. And beautiful genius, too—a tan, long-legged blonde with brown eyes who just made Angus ache every time he saw or thought of her. And now he was going to have to hold her in his arms and dance with her while the whole school watched. Maybe if he was lucky, he wouldn't crush her feet by accident, wouldn't be laughed at, wouldn't embarrass her too much, maybe. . . . Well, I'll let you find out what happens to Angus after he walks into the high school gym that night.

All I have to say is that it was nothing like what he'd expected, or even what he'd dreamed.

—*J. R. B.*

The Covenant: Grade 10–Adult
Love and Death in Beruit
By Barbara Newman and Barbara Rogan

Lebanon, once known as the Switzerland of the Middle East, is now a shambles. Terrorist forces operate there, political infighting is rampant, and peace and truth lie buried in the rubble. Yet for a brief moment there was hope, when a young president named Bashir Gemayel tried to unite the Lebanese Christian forces and create a better future for his country.

At the same time, Barbara Newman, a Jewish investigative reporter for television, was conducting her own search for truth in Lebanon. Bashir loved his country and his family. Barbara loved her work and her daughter. And Bashir and Barbara loved each other. Their story is a covenant. First, Barbara promised to tell the world about Bashir and his cause, to show how Bashir provided a beacon of enlightened leadership to his people. But second, Barbara promised to find Bashir's killers. For soon after Bashir became president, at age thirty-four, he was assassinated, and his country plunged again into darkness and war.

Barbara was in the United States at that time, but she had to return to Lebanon somehow. At his grave she knew: "He was my friend. And for that I owe him something that may be within my power to give: perhaps not justice, but truth."

Lebanon becomes more real in this personal account. Politics and journalism take on human form and human frailty. And, although Bashir believed strongly in destiny, that destiny assumed a flukish individuality, tangled in love. *The Covenant* will change your mind about Lebanon, just as a covenant changed Barbara's life forever.

—*Lesley S. J. Farmer*

Cruel Tricks for Dear Friends Grade 10–Adult
By Penn [Penn Jillette] and Teller

Come on, admit it. You've got a secret desire to humiliate the people you claim to respect. You'd like to make them all look like dopes, and you'd love to take money from them at the same time. What greater fun is there in the world?

But beware! You've got to get them before they get you, and that's where *Cruel Tricks* comes in handy. With the guidance and inspiration of Penn & Teller, you can cash in on the months and years that you've used in nurturing intimacy with the saps around you and twist it for your own personal gain and satisfaction.

Learn the secret of dumping hundreds of roaches on David Letterman (or anybody else, if Letterman isn't available), see how to chop a snake in half, and master the art of tying knots without letting go of the ends of the rope.

Yes, *Cruel Tricks for Dear Friends* will start you on the road to fame and stardom as a cut-rate magician, and strip those lameheads who have the nerve to consider themselves your associates of their dignity and self-esteem. There's not a better bargain around.

—Jeff Blair

Dagmar Schultz and the Angel Edna   Grades 3-9
By Lynn Hall

It's the Big 1-3. Thirteen years old, and Dagmar isn't a kid anymore. She's now an official teenager, with all the rights and privileges of teendom.

To Dagmar, the most important of these is The Right to Date, even if she can't go out alone with a boy, or go anywhere in a boy's car, or go very far, or stay very late, or go out with someone her family doesn't know. She can still date! All she has to do is find a boy.

Well, that, and find a way to get around her Guardian Angel, Aunt Edna, who showed up on the night of Dagmar's birthday. Edna's been dead almost a hundred years, but she has some ideas of her own as to what sort of love-life Dagmar should have before she's twenty or thirty years old—none! And some of Edna's ways of keeping boys and Dagmar apart are anything but angelic.

Who will win this battle of wills and wits? Will Dagmar ever get that all-important First Kiss? Will Aunt Edna ever come around to twentieth-century thinking? The answers are in *Dagmar Schultz and the Angel Edna.*

—Jeff Blair

Dagmar Schultz   Grades 3-9
and the Powers of Darkness
By Lynn Hall

Now if you were going to meet a witch, where do you think it would be? Dagmar meets a witch (well, actually a warlock) in the little town of New Berlin, Iowa, in—of all places—the bowling alley. And he promises to grant her heart's desire if she will do him just one little favor. That little favor turns out to be not so little, and not so simple either, but Dagmar is sure it will all be worth it. Afterwards she'll get her heart's desire: James Mann will fall madly in love with her!

—*Frances W. Levin*

Dangerous Ground   Grades 5-6
By Gloria Skurzynski

For five years, eleven-year-old Angel has lived in Wyoming with her tough-talking Great-Aunt Hilda (or Ant Hil, in their own private joke). Angel's parents are "wildcatters," oil-field workers who travel all over the country. Angel spends the school year with Ant Hil and summers traveling with her folks. The long separations from her parents are painful to Angel, but she and Ant Hil have come to love each other, even if they don't talk much about their other feelings, especially not the painful ones.

Just before sixth-grade graduation, Angel's parents tell her that her mom is about to have another baby and they've bought a house in Texas. Angel will no longer have to live with Ant Hil.

The news could not have come at a worse time. Lately, Ant Hil has been "forgetting" things and making serious mistakes. Once she put a whole load of dirty dishes in the oven and turned on all four burners! Angel's best friend Sara has a grandmother in a nursing home who is suffering from Alzheimer's disease, and Angel worries if her dear aunt has the disease too. Or is she losing her mind? Who can Angel talk to?

Ant Hil brings everything to a head when, after a last picnic together, she takes off with Angel for a very dangerous last adventure in Yellowstone National Park, which nearly costs them their lives.

—*Susan A. Jones*

Dead Poets Society   Grade 7-Adult
By N. H. Kleinbaum, from the filmscript by Tom Schulman

The time is 1959, the hundredth anniversary of the founding of Welton Academy. Welton is a sort of Ivy League training school. Most of the boys who attend school here have already had their lives planned out for them by their parents. They'll go on to become doctors, lawyers, or heads of major corporations. The school's reputation is based on Tradition, Honor, Discipline, and Excellence, and these tenets are drummed into the boys every day. There's not a lot of room left in the students' minds for thoughts of their own.

The teachers all seem to have come out of the same mold as the school's crusty old buildings. And most of them look as though there ought to be ivy growing on them as well.

That's part of the reason that John Keating stands out. Of course, anyone who likes to stand on his desk to get a fresh perspective is going to be noticed. But Keating's different in other ways too. The young English teacher tries to awaken a sense of individuality in his students. He urges them to "seize the day," to live each moment to its fullest.

The students do try to seize their days, both as individuals (bucking the pre-programmed lives that have been laid out for them) and as members of the newly revived Dead Poets Society, a collective that Keating helped to found back during his own days at Welton.

But the boys learn that there's a big difference between seizing a day and being able to hold on to it. Traditions don't die easily at a place like Welton, and they can exact a tragic price.

—*Jeff Blair*

Dear Mom, You're Ruining My Life   Grades 5-6
By Jean Van Leeuwen

I've always known my dad was a little weird, walking around with his head full of mathematical calculations. And my brother, Bradley . . . well, the only way to describe him is "total slob." His knees are always coming out of his jeans, and he's usually wearing an old ripped sweatshirt. But now I've started to notice my *mom's* peculiarities. She's not like other moms. She stays at home all day and writes poetry, and she doesn't wear stylish clothes or make-up like my friends' moms do. She says she prefers her old clothes because they're more comfortable. Well, comfortable is *not* how she makes me feel in public. I've tried to tell her that life for an eleven-year-old girl is difficult enough without having to worry about what your mom will do next. Being the tallest kid in your shcool with feet the size of pontoons doesn't exactly win you any popularity contests, you know. Anyway, what happened yesterday really made me angry, so I wrote my mom this letter:

Dear Mom,

You're ruining my life. How *could* you break your promise to me? I can't take you anywhere! You always embarrass me. Why can't you act like a *regular* mother? You said that if I let you play in the parent-child volleyball game, you wouldn't show off and you'd only hit the ball when it came right to you. So why did you break your promise to me and make a *spectacle* of yourself by chasing after a ball that was almost out of bounds? If that wasn't bad enough, you spiked the ball over the net so hard that it hit Brian Finnegan, of all people, right in the nose, Brian had to go to the nurse's office and put an ice-pack on his nose, and now he's going around school telling everyone that my mother ruined his career as a movie star. I think I'll start shopping for a new mom!

Your perfect daughter, Sam

—*Kathy Ann Miller*

The Delphic Choice
By Norma Johnston

Grades 7-10

Seventeen-year-old Meredith has been looking forward to spending the summer in Istanbul, Turkey, where she'll be a companion to her two young cousins and her aunt, who's facing a high-risk pregnancy. Her uncle, Mark Greystone, also faces high risks, in his work there as a hostage negotiator. It all sounds exotic and exciting, and things promise to get even more exciting after Meredith meets handsome Brandon Hurd on a stopover in Greece. However, excitement turns to danger when an American journalist and an Anglican priest are kidnapped by Arab terrorists—and Uncle Mark disappears trying to save them.

As her aunt's condition deteriorates, Meredith has to handie mysterious phone calls, a masked intruder, anti-American demonstrators, and a fatal bombing. She's not sure whom she can trust. The servants seem to disappear just when they're needed. Amina and her family, who live next door, are friendly and helpful when crises occur, but Amina is hiding something. Could it involve her Arab boyfriend? Meredith can't even confide in Brandon completely—his interference has already ruined one arranged meeting with the kidnappers. She definitely doesn't want to follow the orders of the American government officials, who seem more concerned about power politics than her uncle's safety.

Finally Meredith decides she must take charge and save her uncle, even if it means putting her own life in danger.

—*Susan Rosenkoetter*

The Devil's Arithmetic   Grades 7-12
By Jane Yolen

[Before starting this talk, write J197241 on the board.]

J197241. That's who my captors think I am. The Nazi Devils put that number on me forever. I'll answer when they call this number, but that's not who I really am.

Chaya. That's who everyone from the Polish village thinks I am. A man and woman claim to be my aunt and uncle. They love me. They take care of me. They call me Chaya, but that's not who I really am.

Hannah. That's who I think I am. At least I used to think that. I remember a life so different. Another place. Another time. Another world. Clock radios. Pizza. (What's pizza?) I have Hannah's memories, but that's not who I really am.

J197241 . . . Chaya . . . Hannah . . . who am I? I don't know who I really am. It's so confusing. Only one thing is clear. If I am to survive, I must learn the Devil's Arithmetic:

J—Jew. I am a Jew.

1—Me. I am all alone.

9—German for "no." No, I will not die here.

7—Each and every day of the week I stay alive.

2—My aunt and uncle, who are also in this camp.

4—My family, I think. I can't seem to remember.

1—I am here alone. Here. Alone in this place. Alone in this time. One more day alive plus one more day alive equals one more day to remember.

That's *The Devil's Arithmetic*, by Jane Yolen.

—*Tracy Chesonis Revel*

Dinosaur Mountain: Grades 5–12
Graveyard of the Past
By Caroline Arnold

Curious about dinosaurs? What do the names Tyrannosaurus, Stegosaurus, and Apatosaurus bring to mind? Here is a book about the different species that once roamed North America, and the best place to see their fossil remains just as they are being uncovered—at Dinosaur National Monument in Utah.

Author Caroline Arnold takes you on a trip through time as she describes the important discoveries made at this site, beginning with the excavation in 1909 of the most complete Apatosaurus skeleton ever found. How did these creatures live? Why did they suddenly die out? What other, smaller animals lived at the same time? What plants? At Dinosaur National Monument, scientists continue to uncover answers—and also more questions.

You can observe these scientists at work. Imagine yourself in a visitors' center, where an entire side of the building is nothing but dinosaur fossils, still embedded in rock, still being carefully excavated as you watch. If you are curious about dinosaurs and how their skeletons are discovered and uncovered, *Dinosaur Mountain* can show you all about it.

—Susan Perdaris

Dissidents   Grades 7–9
By Neal Shusterman

Three o'clock. Time to play basketball. Derek was ready with his Spalding leather basketball, CD player, and Chicago Bulls jacket. But the only guy around to catch the ball was a bronze statue named Vladimir Ilyich Lenin.

Oh, yeah. There was also a big black sedan following him, creeping along like a slow black bull. But Derek was determined to shake them off his tail. Down an alley, onto Olimpiyski Prospekt, dribbling beside the Kremlin Wall.

But then his high-top shoes betrayed him. Derek was used to wearing his shoes with the laces untied, trailing behind him. Today he tripped, flying head over heels, the basketball sailing ahead. The black car screeched to a halt in front of him, and the basketball rebounded off the hood. Derek was in for it.

Two men in sunglasses peered at him. "Derek, you're a real pain." The hunk's bad breath hit Derek. "Your mother won't be happy."

"I don't need a bodyguard!" yelled Derek. "Just because I'm the ambassador's son!" He spun the ball on his finger. "Be useful, and find me a basketball court."

"It's almost dinnertime," growled Bad Breath. "Climb in the car." Derek grumbled, "It's impossible to get a straight answer from anyone who works in the government."

Derek's world was full of "nyets." His so-called friends at the Anglo-American school were first-class jerks. His twelve-year-old sister Dayna was Mom's perfect little darling. His Dad had died two months ago. And the girl of his dreams was a Russian with a dissident father in exile. And she didn't like Americans. Derek's headache began to get worse as he thought about it, so he turned up the volume on the TV. "I hope those James Bond videos get here soon!" he muttered.

Another possibility would be to escape: join the dissidents himself. Would Derek dare?

—Lesley S. J. Farmer

The Dolphins and Me **Grades 3-6**
By Don C. Reed

Have any of you ever seen trained dolphins perform, either at Sea World or on television? Have you ever wondered how they were taught to jump through hoops and do back flips and other exciting tricks?

In this book, the author, who was a diver at Marine World in California for many years, takes us into the world of captive dolphins. Dolphins are highly intelligent mammals, each with its own distinct personality, and Don introduces us to several of these beautiful, playful, and sometimes aggravating creatures. There is Arne, an aggressive male who makes sure everyone knows who is Top Dolphin as he rams and butts the divers. And Lucky, who charges a killer whale and barely escapes with his life. Lucky also calls a performers' strike and won't let any of the other dolphins perform! One of the trainers has to perform instead in the dolphins' place, including gulping down a fish reward!

What do dolphins think of humans? How smart are they? We can read of the strange and dramatic events the author observed in his many years of working closely with them, but until humans and dolphins can communicate in a common language, we'll never know how intelligent these friendly creatures really are, or what kind of strange fish they think *we* are!

—Diane L. Deuel

Don't Look Behind You Grades 7–12
By Lois Duncan

The world as April Corrigan knew it ended on a Tuesday afternoon in May. Someone tried to shoot her father while he was giving testimony during a drug-smuggling trial. The Federal Witness Relocation Program can protect the Corrigans, but only if they cooperate. Now April and her family must give up everything—their home, friends, jobs, hobbies, names, even their grandmother and their dog. For April it's just too hard. She can't stand leaving her boyfriend without even telling him why, missing the prom, never playing tennis again, cutting off her long blonde hair. In a desperate attempt to hold on to her old life and old identity, April makes a phone call. And that one call puts all their lives in danger once again.

Could you change everything that's unique about yourself to save your life? Not just the things you want to change, but the things that really add up to you? Could you become a completely different person—look, act, and live the way someone else says you must? Maybe you wouldn't react the way April did—but then again, maybe you would! Find out, in *Don't Look Behind You.*

—Kaite Mediatore and J. R. B.

The Dream Collector Grades 7–12
By Joyce Sweeney

Have you ever wished for a magic wand or a genie in a bottle so you could have whatever it is that you want more than anything else in the world? Magic wands and genies don't exist, but how 'bout a wish book, one that's guaranteed to work?

When Becky finds the wish book in the mall bookstore, she can't believe her luck. Now she can get everyone in her family exactly what they want for Christmas—all they have to do is write down a wish in the front of the book and then follow the instructions inside. Scott wants a $500 bike, Julia wants to be a published poet, Tim wants a kitten, and Becky wants to go with the gorgeous guy who just moved in across the street. Even her parents have wishes—her father keeps his to himself, but her mother says she wants to be very, very rich.

As they begin to follow the instructions in the book, Becky sees all their wishes coming true, even hers. But other things are happening too, and the wishers don't seem as happy as they used to be, or as they expected to be when they got just what they'd always wanted. Even Becky begins to wonder if John is really the one she wants to date, when his friend Tom seems so much more interesting.

If you had a wish book, what would you write in it, and what would you do to make that wish come true? Think hard about it, because you may be like Becky, and discover that wishing and having are not the same thing. If your wish is guaranteed to come true, you'd better be careful what you wish for—you just might get it!

—J. R. B.

The Dying Sun   **Grades 7–12**
By Gary Blackwood

There's a poem by Robert Frost that goes, "Some say the world will end in fire / Some say in ice." In the year 2050, you can have it both ways.

A new Ice Age has begun, pushing glaciers and ever colder air down over most of the North American continent. As the glaciers slowly advance, most of the population of the United States retreats south, into northern Mexico. The land is choked with people. There are no private homes, and whole families live in tiny one-room apartments. And it's hot, blazing hot all the time.

A lot of the Mexicans resent these newcomers, and some have organized themselves into the so-called Mexican Liberation Army. They vent their rage and frustration in bombing attacks and armed assaults on the gringo immigrants.

Of course if you want to get away from the heat and the gunfire, you can always move back north and make the trade for cold and isolation. There are hundreds of abandoned farms to be had in Kansas and Missouri. The land there is far enough ahead of the glaciers' advance that there are still a few months during the year when you can try to raise cold-weather crops and eke out a living.

That's the choice that James' parents make, and they leave for Missouri. James chooses not to leave the only life he's ever known and stays behind in Mexico. It's the right choice for him, he thinks, until he's drafted into the militia and watches his best friend lose a leg to a MLA pipe-bomb. He decides that life up north on the freezing edge of the glaciers can't be any crazier than this, and he sets off to try and make it in the land of the dying sun. Will James' world end in fire or in ice?

—Jeff Blair

Earth to Andrew G. Blechman   Grades 3-4
By Jane Breskin Zalben

It's hard to be the fourth-grade Henny Youngman when nobody knows who Henny Youngman is. It's not that Andrew doesn't try. He's got his own bag of joke material and he's signed up for a comedy correspondence course, but it's just not doing the trick. That's where Mr. Pearlstein, Andrew's upstairs neighbor, comes in. He's a former vaudevillian and performed with Youngman himself. He and Andrew work up a deal. He will teach Andrew his 101 best jokes if Andrew will tutor him in Hebrew so he can finally be Bar Mitzvahed.

It's an arrangement that works out well for both of them, but especially, it seems, for Mr. Pearlstein. Andrew notices that something is happening between Mr. Pearlstein and Andrew's grandmother. They even go out on a date!

Is Andrew ready for a new grandfather, even if he does tell good jokes?

—Jeff Blair

Education of   Adult
a Wandering Man
By Louis L'Amour

To Louis L'Amour, books were as important as food or water, or even air. When he found a bookstore on the island of Sumatra—not exactly around the corner—he thought he was one of the luckiest men alive. And when he discovered a shelf of books in an abandoned miner's shack in the California desert, he devoured those books as though they were food and water—and perhaps they were. Food for the mind, in any case. This was all part of L'Amour's program for self-education, set down in an easy-going, rocking-chair style in his memoir, *Education of a Wandering Man*.

L'Amour was never happier than when he could go to a new place, seek out the old-timers, and coax them into telling stories about local history. And as this book unfolds we find that L'Amour was one of his own most fascinating characters. If in one of his novels you have read about a lone rider picking his way along the mesa rim, here you will find out how the real-life loner felt as he walked away from a hobo campfire in the chill of a New Mexico desert morning. (And because it's Louis L'Amour, you'll also find out what books he had in his satchel at the time!)

L'Amour's fame and his fortune came mainly from writing Westerns, but his interests were much wider than that. He had a firm belief that the history of mankind held clues to our own age—and maybe to our future. And as he traveled around the world, he began to suspect that he wasn't the only one with an urge to wander. He discovered that there were German communities in Texas and Arab colonies in Southeast Asia—irrefutable evidence of our incurably itchy feet. Gradually, L'Amour began to wonder if one day wandering human beings would colonize outer space.

This book is much more than the story of a struggling young writer in the thirties, or the story of a writer who went to war. It is the account of a man who had a wonderful capacity to be continually fascinated by life. And as he shares that fascination, Louis L'Amour will help you see possibilities that you never saw before. He was quite a fellow, and it's a real nice story.

—*Mark Anderson*

Effie's House   Grades 7–12
By Morse Hamilton

In her mind's eye she pictures him. He is driving into the city. It is dusk, and he is the only one on his side of the road. Everyone else is headed out of the city towards home. He is coming for her, driving slowly, timimg his pace to allow darkness to fall completely. In her mind she sees him parking two doors down from her house. He gets out of the car and starts walking toward the house, always staying in the shadows. Now he is at the house, staring (well, more like peeping) into the living-room windows. He is probably hoping for a glimpse of her mother. But this is not in the plan; she is worried that neighbors might see him. With a little cough she moves forward, from her hiding place in the garage, and asks, "What took you so long?"

This is how Effie has always pictured her father coming for her, to take her away. Away from her too-busy mother, away from three former stepfathers and one looming stepfather-to-be.

In reality, Effie's father was killed in Vietnam when she was a baby. But when you're fifteen and running away, you need to believe someone is there to guide you and keep you safe. Even if that someone is dead. In fact, there are only three things Effie trusts on the road: the first is her father, the second is the priest whom she met at the hospital, and the third is this notebook, where she writes her story—*Effie's House*.

—*Linda Olson*

Eighty-Eight Steps to September   Grades 3-6
By Jan Marino

Amy's home is high above town—eighty-eight steps high. It's always easy going down, but the trip back up is slower. She and her best friend Celie often stop and sit on the steps and talk . . . and dream. But she and her brother Robbie race up the steps on their way home. Robbie always wins. It's really neat to sit at the top and look out over the town and the harbor, with the lights of Boston in the distance.

And it's great looking forward to summer vacation. Already, Robbie and Amy are building a doghouse for the new puppy they're going to get. But then Robbie isn't able to beat Amy up the eighty-eight steps any more. In fact, he has to stop and rest—twice. There are trips to the doctor, specialists, and finally Robbie has to stay at the hospital. Amy begins to wonder whether life will ever be the same again.

—*Carol Kappelmann*

El Güero: A True Adventure Story   Grades 3-6
By Elizabeth Borton de Treviño

Have you ever gone to school thinking you were in for another normal day, when suddenly—bam!—your whole world was turned upside down? Well, that's what happened 'way back in 1876 to Porfirio Trevino (better known as El Güero—"the blond one") when his father was exiled from Mexico City by the new president of Mexico. His entire family had only a few hours in which to pack their belongings, settle their business, and start out by wagon on the long journey to a Mexican outpost in Baja California. El Güero thought of the trip as his first Big Adventure, but it turned out to be an adventure filled with hardship and danger. Along the way the family had to deal with bandits, sickness, and pirates who marooned them on a desert peninsula, far from their destination. They were finally rescued and taken to their new home— only to discover even greater danger awaiting them there! Join El Güero as he journeys into the wild country and struggles to save his father from prison and possible execution!

—*Sister M. Anna Falbo, CSSF*

Empire's Horizon   Grade 10-Adult
By John Brizzolara

Something was waiting for him here. Something he'd been hunting for a long time. Although he couldn't have put the feeling into words, that was exactly what reporter Martin Cain sensed as he stepped off the transport ship into the sweltering heat of the desert planet Darkath.

It wasn't a spot many people would choose to visit. But as a frontier correspondent Cain had already traveled to most of the other planets within the Terran Empire. Officially, he reported on alien customs and cultures for the curious Terran citizens on the home planet. Unofficially, he pursued his own desperate search for a culture or a civilization that could provide a better reason for living than his own. Among fellow reporters, Cain was known as a sort of reverse missionary.

And now his search had brought him to Darkath, the most remote planet in the galaxy. Cain knew that Darkath was occupied by two fierce and feuding native tribes, the Dhirn and the Khaj. The Empire had maintained its control over the planet all these years by fueling the hatred between the two tribes—the old tactic of divide and conquer. It was a good tactic while it lasted, but rumors were circulating that renegade warriors from both Darkhani tribes were banding together, joining forces to drive the hated Imperial troops from their planet.

Although Cain didn't know yet if the rumors about the tribes were true, he did sense that the Empire's rule here wasn't going to last much longer. It would end because a power much larger than two native tribes was behind this revolt. Cain could sense the presence of this power as he stood in the crowded spaceport. It was almost as if the power—whatever or whoever it was—had come to greet him. It felt mysterious and yet vaguely familiar. And then he understood. This was the power he had pursued across all the planets of the galaxy. Or had it been pursuing him?

—*Margie Reitsma*

The Empty Sleeve   Grades 5-12
By Leon Garfield

When Peter was born at the chime of noon on a Saturday, the strange old man made a dire prophecy: "The chime-child will see ghosts and commune with the devil," he intoned. Moments later Peter's twin was born, a pale and sickly copy of the lusty Peter.

The old man appears again on the twins' fourteenth birthday, the very day when hot-tempered Peter, who dreams only of a sailor's life, is bound out as apprentice to a locksmith instead. The old man seems to know how Peter longs to go to sea, for he brings a gift for each boy—a beautifully crafted ship in a bottle. The only difference between the two ships is the name engraved in tiny letters across the stem—one is the *Peter*, the other the *Paul*. The letters are so tiny that Peter never notices when his despised, saintly twin Paul secretly exchanges the bottles.

Peter finds the locksmith trade to be just as confining as he had feared. If only he can get his hands on twenty pounds, he can buy passage on a ship as a cabin boy. Soon a means of making extra money presents itself: all he must do is steal the key to the gate to Cucumber Alley, so that other apprentices can escape for nights of revelry. Peter does it, but then he's terrified. His every move is being stalked by a ghost—a ghost with an empty sleeve. *The chime-child shall see ghosts. . . .* Now Peter is even more desperate to get away, so when Lord Marriner offers to buy the ship in the bottle for twenty pounds if Peter will also bring him certain keys, he agrees immediately, and is sucked into a devilish scheme.

In the meantime, back home, Paul watches with mounting horror as the ship that rightly belongs to Peter begins to fall apart before his very eyes.

—Diane L. Deuel

The Engineer of Beasts   **Grades 7–Adult**
By Scott Russell Sanders

"Call me Mooch," a fiery-haired girl growled as an old man tried to pull her out of the jaws of the lion.

"Save her!" cried some of the schoolies. "She's dead meat," said other schoolies. When the thirteen-year-old girl reappeared, apparently unharmed, the crowd left, bored. "Go recycle your brains!" she yelled after them.

"Who do you think you are?" glared the aging engineer. "*I* build and repair the animals around here."

"Well, then, you're just the guy I want to see." The girl was gripping a screwdriver in one fist and a circuit probe in the other. "Why are you making a stink? I just fixed your pussycat so he won't make any more wacko speeches. Just natural sounds." Mooch patted the lion's ropy mane.

Orlando, the engineer, stopped short. "How did you do that?"

"Easy. I learned about machines by tinkering with the security devices at the orphanage. Anything to escape from there."

Orlando was a sucker for a story, and hers would be a humdinger.

Several months later, Mooch was still around—as Orlando's apprentice in his mechanical zoo. The animals not only worked better, they seemed more natural. Mooch's programs had given them back their wild souls. And when the official Overseers reprimanded Orlando for the animals' aggressive behavior, Mooch led an animal brigade to freedom and revenge. Could she succeed, or was she doomed to failure?

—Lesley S. J. Farmer

Enter Three Witches   Grades 7–12
By Kate Gilmore

Double, double, toil and trouble,
Fire burn, and cauldron bubble!

Everyone has heard this familiar witch's chant. You get a picture of an ugly old hag with a wart on her nose tossing a toad into a big black kettle and waving her broomstick over it. Well, not all witches look like that, or act like that either. Just ask Bren. He's surrounded by witches.

Witch 1: Miranda, his mother, tall, blonde, beautiful, and jealous of Bren's father's new girlfriend. No telling what she'll do. Witch 2: Rose, Bren's grandmother, a professional fortune-teller with the original bad attitude. And Witch 3: Louise, Miranda's friend, a voodoo priestess who insults Bren's father, curses at chickens, and refuses to clean the house properly. Not to mention the odd assortment of minor characters in Bren's life, such as his mother's "all-knowing" cat Luna and his grandmother's "spirits from beyond"!

Difficult as it may be for Bren to live here in the House of Usher, he just can't bring himself to go live with his father instead. Bren's dad moved out the day he found a baby bat in his Gucci shoes and a python in his underwear drawer.

While Bren tangles with year-round Halloween at home, school presents problems of a similar nature. This year's play is *Macbeth*, and his mother thinks she'll make a fine consultant. Then there's Erika, the new girl with the part of First Witch. Bren wouldn't mind watching her for the rest of his life, but does she have to play a witch? Doesn't he have enough witch trouble? He's got about all the witches he can handle—can he take on one more?

—Kaite Mediatore

Erin McEwan, Your Days Are Numbered Grades 5-8
By Alan Ritchie

Erin hates math more than anything else in the world. She doesn't understand it, she never has and she never will. To make matters worse, her sixth-grade teacher is thinking about holding her back a year just because she's having so much trouble with numbers. Except for math, the worst thing Erin can think of is to be held back while all her friends go on to seventh grade. "It's not fair," she tells her parents, "I can't help it—some people just aren't made for math!"

Erin's mother doesn't like math either, so she's totally sympathetic to her daughter's plight. As a matter of fact, math is the cause of Mrs. McEwan's troubles too. She's just been fired from her job in a gourmet grocery store, not because she isn't a good cook but because she has such trouble with figures. Erin goes to the store one day to see the owner and somehow gets talked into working a few hours a day after school and on weekends. Erin doesn't really want the job, and she knows that her mother will have a fit if she finds out, but she also knows that her family needs the money. Then the unthinkable happens: the owner, Mrs. Sbrocchi, nominates herself as Erin's math coach and decides that doing the store's books is the best practice Erin can get with numbers!

Mrs. Sbrocchi is one of those unmentionable people who think that math is a piece of cake. "It's easy," she keeps telling Erin. Well, it may be easy for her, but for Erin it's pure torture. So now she's stuck: stuck with a job she isn't supposed to have, an unemployed mother, an unsympathetic teacher, and a boss who seems bound and determined to make her suffer, all in the name of education! Whether you like math or not doesn't really matter—either way you'll enjoy discovering how Erin solves the problem!

—Susan Dunn

Eva   Grades 7-Adult
By Peter Dickinson

Eva woke up on her back in a hospital bed. She couldn't move anything but her eyelids. Her mother was hovering over her and murmuring reassuring things. There'd been a car wreck, she'd been in a coma, but now she was fine, and soon the doctors would let her begin to move. Later, when she could control her left hand, they gave her a small black keyboard that made sounds when she pressed the keys and talked for her. It also controlled things in her hospital room, like the mirror. She could make it show her everything in the room—except the bed with her in it. It was a long time before they let her see herself, and when the mirror finally focused on the bed she knew why. It wasn't that she didn't recognize the small figure on the bed—she did, and moved her left hand to make her keyboard speak. She said, "Hi, Kelly." Kelly was the name of a small black female chimpanzee that Eva had known from the research pool of chimps at the Institute.

Eva had been in an irreversible coma after the wreck, but the doctors had saved her—they had transplanted her brain into Kelly's body. For the rest of her life, Eva would have the mind of a human female and the body of a female chimpanzee. She was alive—or *was* she?

—*J. R. B.*

Everyone Else's Parents Said Yes   Grades 3-6
By Paula Danziger

Countdown. Only five more days, fifteen hours, and thirty-two minutes until Matthew Martin's eleventh birthday party. But Matthew's got big problems. His mom's a health-food nut who won't serve potato chips or ice cream. His sister Amanda has arranged the first date of her life for the exact same day as his party. His best friend Joshua is mad at him. And all the girls in the sixth grade are ganging up on him at once. What's a guy to do?

Fight back! Get even! Matthew's got his computer, his Whoopee cushion, and his Gummy Worms. Nothing's going to ruin Matthew's birthday party!

—*Kaite Mediatore*

F is for Fugitive   Adult
By Sue Grafton

For seventeen years, Bailey Fowler has been on the run. Somebody murdered the town tramp on the night she discovered she was pregnant, and Bailey was convicted of the crime. But he escaped from prison and went underground. Only a fluke has brought him back to the arms of the law.

His father, now at the verge of death, wants only one thing: to clear his son and redeem the family name. To do so he hires Kinsey Millhone, a female private investigator.

Kinsey soon learns that digging information out of a tiny beachfront community is no easy task. She uncovers old wounds that have been festering below the surface of the town, and they erupt in even more killing. Before she knows it, Kinsey has become a fugitive herself.

—Jeff Blair

The Face on the Milk Carton   Grades 7–12
By Caroline B. Cooney

How would you feel if you were having lunch with your friends in the school cafeteria and suddenly saw a picture of yourself on the back of a milk carton? Yourself as a kid—the caption says you were stolen from a shopping center in New Jersey twelve years ago, when you were only three years old. Everyone at the table thinks that you're joking, but you're not—you can remember that dress, and then later you realize you can remember the shopping center, and walking with someone who was going to buy you an ice cream soda.

That's what happens to Janie. She's fifteen, with parents who love her and a totally normal life—until she sees that picture. She doesn't know what to do—does this mean that the parents she loves so much stole her from somebody else? Will she have to go live with people she doesn't love, doesn't even remember? Her friends laugh, they don't believe her—maybe she should just keep quiet and pretend it never happened. But what can she do about all those memories that keep coming back, stronger and stronger, memories of another life and of another family? She *has* to do something—but what?

—J. R. B.

The Facts and Fictions of Minna Pratt   Grades 3–6
By Patricia MacLachlan

It wasn't that Minna was ashamed of her parents. She just wished they were more like other people's. Lucas had folks who talked about regular, real-world things, and he lived in a beautiful home where the maid served delicious meals. There weren't any strange little notes stuck up all over the place, or baskets of mismatched laundry, or haphazard, thrown-together suppers. Minna's mother was different—

she was a writer. Cooking and housekeeping were *not* her priorities. Minna's dad was a psychologist, and he loved his wife just the way she was.

Why couldn't her mom ask normal questions, like "How did your day go, dear?" or "Did you practice your cello? You'd better, if you want to win that competition!" Instead, she might suddenly say, "Minna, do you ever think about love?" or "What is the quality of truth?"

Embarrassing! Weird, even. But what about Minna? Would she really be happier in a nice, normal family?

—*Carol Kappelmann*

The Faery Flag: Grades 7-12
Stories and Poems of Fantasy and the Supernatural
By Jane Yolen

Do you like to have the creepy-crawlies make a trip down your spine when you read a short story? Has a poem ever made you smile and then, on second thought, made you shiver? How about a familiar story that has been turned inside out in such a funny way that you want to read it aloud to anyone who'll listen? If these things sound good to you, you are going to like *The Faery Flag*. All these things and more happen in this lovely concoction of short stories and poems about the eerie, fantastic, frightening, and funny.

Try the tale of the manush-bagha, the man-ghost that eats flesh. The British colonel in "Wolf/Child" couldn't believe such a thing existed, even in India. When the natives warned him about the power of the ghost, he knew they were just silly and superstitious. It was easy for him to smile at their fears. What the colonel didn't know about wolves, the children raised by them, and the carnivorous spirit might turn out to make him *dead* sure.

Did you ever wonder what happened after the story was over, when "they all lived happily ever after"? A verse about Beauty might make you think twice about settling down with a Beast.

Delightful is the word for these tales and poems from a master of the written word, and nobody will want to miss them.

—*Sue Young*

Faithful Elephants: Grade 3–Adult
A True Story of Animals, People and War
By Yukio Tsuchiya, translated by Tomoko Tsuchiya Dykes

In Tokyo there is a wonderful zoo, with many marvelous animals, and in the midst of this zoo, not far from where the elephants perform their tricks for the crowds, there is a tombstone. It is a memorial for three other elephants, faithful elephants who died terrible and courageous deaths during World War II. Their names were John, Tonky, and Wanly, and they were victims just as surely as the soldiers who died on the battlefields.

You see, toward the end of the war, Tokyo was bombed over and over, day and night. The zoo administrators and the Army became concerned about what would happen if one of those bombs fell on the zoo, and the dangerous animals escaped. So the Army ordered that all the dangerous animals be killed in order to protect the people of Tokyo. One by one the animals died—the lions, the tigers, the bears, the big snakes—all were poisoned. All but the elephants. They refused to to eat the poisoned food, and when the keepers tried to administer the poison in a hypodermic, the needles broke because their skin was so tough and thick.

So it was decided to just not feed them, so that they would starve to death. Their keepers, the men who had cared for them and taught them many tricks, were forbidden to give them either food or water, no matter how much the elephants wanted and needed it. John and Tonky and Wanly had no way of knowing why no one brought them food, and why there was no water. They responded by doing the only thing they knew how to do—they performed their tricks over and over again, even after they had grown so weak they could not stand, because those tricks had always brought them rewards in the past.

They were not at war. They weren't on *either* side. They didn't even know what war was, or that it was going on around them. Yet they were among its victims.

Perhaps the memory of their sacrifice can help us see the value of peace, of settling differences without guns or bombs.

—J. R. B.

[This is a disturbing story, and although it is presented in a picture-book format, it should be used with discretion with young children.]

Fallen Angels   Grades 10–Adult
By Walter Dean Myers

Richie Perry was seventeen and in the army—and in Vietnam. That wasn't how it was supposed to be: the army doctors had said his knee was too bad for 'Nam. The rest of his unit went to Germany while he was waiting for the medical paperwork to come through. But the papers were delayed, and before they could arrive, he'd been shipped out—to 'Nam.

At first it didn't seem so bad. He met a lot of great guys—like Pee-Wee, who talked a lot about killing Cong, until he found out what that really meant, and Jenkins, who could imitate anyone perfectly, without half trying. He made them laugh—until he stepped on a land mine. No one told Ritchie what it would be like to watch a friend die, or how it would feel to look at a stack of empty body bags and know that he could be in one of them the next day, that someone could be writing a letter to his mother just like the ones he'd written to his friends' mothers.

Richie had enlisted because he couldn't afford college and didn't think he could get a job that would pay enough to support his mother and kid brother. The army was a salary and three meals a day—it didn't sound that bad. Nothin' better to do.

But no one told him the real story, about how war eats you up from the inside and makes you angry and afraid, wanting to hurt back, even if your enemy is another teenager who's just as angry and frightened as you are. Richie didn't know what 'Nam was like, but he learned fast, and in *Fallen Angels* he shares his story with you.

—*J. R. B.*

Falling for a Dolphin   Grades 10–Adult
By Heathcote Williams

The man who rented him the wetsuit had told him, "Just call its name. We call it 'Dolphin.' You just call out 'Dolphin' and it comes."

The man drifts on the sea a half mile from shore, suspended between one world and another like a hang-glider lost in unmapped continents of clouds. He tries not to think of jellyfish or sharks. He wants to see the dolphin that was orphaned long ago by fishermen's nets.

He taps with a clutched pebble. He waggles his fingers in the water. He calls. But no dolphin. He drifts. Suddenly, adrenalin makes his body shudder like a rocket on takeoff. A lone creature lies beside him in the water. Twelve, fifteen feet long. Half a ton in weight. Sleek and silvery as the moon. Eye to eye.

Heathcote Williams in his slim, magical volume *Falling for a Dolphin* invites you to play along with an astonishing new friend. Experience this story and you may wonder how humans have the audacity to claim they are the only creatures with self-awareness.

—Tracie Pruitt

Families: Grades 3-6; Adult
A Celebration of Diversity, Commitment and Love
By Aylette Jenness

What is a family? It's the people who love you and take care of you, and whom you love and care for in return. Not all families look alike—some are made up of a mother, a father, and their children, but there are lots of other people who can join in a family.

There are lots of people in Tam's family—two parents and five kids. Three of the kids, including Tam, are adopted. Hakem lives with her mother and her brother Amos. It's OK with Hakem that her father doesn't live with them, because, she says, there might be a lot of fighting if he were there. Laney's family is really big—62 of them get together for special occasions! That means that there are lots of people to do different things with, and Laney likes it that way. Tina moved in with her adoptive family just about a year ago. Helen, her new mother, had always wanted to have a daughter, and after her divorce, when her sons were grown, she decided to adopt a teenager—Tina. So now Tina has a mother, grandparents, and big brothers—and a home she won't ever have to leave. Jaime's family is from Mexico, and they speak both Spanish and English. He has four brothers, and his father has to work two jobs to take care of them all. Jaime wants to be a lawyer when he grows up.

Ananda lives with her family in an ashram, Eliot and Jody live in families with gay parents, Eve has two homes and two families—one home with her mother and one with her father and stepmother. Mattie lives with her own son, her parents, and her younger brothers and sisters. Jennifer and her mother live in a commune with a group of other people who have decided to stay together and be a family.

Families don't always look alike. Some have one or two or three or four parents; some have a lot of kids, others just one; and some include more than two generations. But no matter who is in your family, the important thing to remember is that no family is just like any other—and that's okay.

—J. R. B.

Family Pictures   **Adult**
By Sue Miller

What kind of pictures flash through your mind when you think about your family? Have you ever compared them to a sister's or brother's or even your spouse's memories of the same event? You might be surprised; I was.

I can still remember that evening. It was the summer of 1983, and I had come home to Chicago for a visit. While I was there I went to a party with my father and his fiancee Tony. I was just leaving when I got involved in a conversation with an older woman who used to move in the same social set as my parents, years before. At first she couldn't seem to remember my family. And then she placed us. "Oh yes," she said. "Now I remember. You were the family with that tragic retarded boy." Later that same evening when I recounted the incident to my mother, I emphasized how preposterous the woman's reaction was. Out of all the stories, achievements, and heartbreaks that accumulate around a family of six children and two adults in approximately twenty-five years, the only thing this woman could remember about the Eberhardts was that one of the children had been retarded. My response to the incident was clear: how could this woman dare interpret my family through that one fact? My mother's was quite different. Her voice was very matter-of-fact when she answered me. "No," she said. "No, to me that doesn't seem preposterous at all."

At first my mother's response startled me. Later it puzzled me, and still later, drove me to reflect on my family's past. And the more I reflected, the more pictures emerged from my memories: pictures of my family over the years. What I was looking for, I suppose, was the crucial picture: the one that would explain why my parents' once-good marriage had ended in divorce, why my talented brother Mick had spent his entire life chasing failure, and why I, the other family rebel, had chosen to begin a marriage that I knew would never work.

I didn't find it. But I did discover that my mother's and my reactions that summer evening were more similar than I had thought. Because when I examined all the pictures about my family that were in my head, I discovered that Randall, my autistic brother, was present in every one. Whether he was actually visible or not. Randall, who had never spoken to me in words, now screamed at me through memory.

So, like a good photographer, I've decided to arrange all of these family snapshots and show them to you. Perhaps you will see something different than I do. Or maybe when you finish looking through the

Eberhardt pictures, you'll feel the urge to re-open your own family album and examine the pictures you find there. Because we all know the old saying: One picture is worth a thousand words.

—*Margie Reitsma*

Family Portraits: Remembrances Adult
Edited by Carolyn Anthony

Fragments. Touchstones. Burning memories brought back by the turn of a phrase or the turn of a cheek. Twenty writers celebrate the influence of family in *Family Portraits*.

Joyce Carol Oates hears her father playing the *presto agitato* of Schubert's "Erl-king" on the piano and reflects, "Most of us 'know' family members . . . in the way we 'know' familiar pieces of music without having the slightest comprehension of their thematic or structural composition. We recognize them after a few notes, that's all."

Susan Kenney keeps her own collection of fragments pertaining to family life. A two-by-three-inch photograph shows a fat-cheeked baby standing in a hoopskirt-type wooden walker, reaching out to pat a dog's nose. It is her father, a lifelong friend to all dogs.

Gloria Steinem keeps snapshots in her mind: "Lying in the bed my mother and I shared for warmth, listening on the early morning radio to the royal wedding of Princess Elizabeth and Prince Philip being broadcast live, while we tried to ignore and thus protect each other from the unmistakable sounds of the factory worker downstairs beating up and locking out his pregnant wife."

Gail Godwin keeps an old magazine from 1945 containing two love stories, one by Kathleen Godwin and the other by Charlotte Ashe. Her mother wrote both, revealing two sides of her personality.

Wallace Stegner sums up the spirit of *Family Portraits* in a letter to his dead mother: "Your kind of love, once given, is never lost. You are alive and luminous in my head." And Susan Allen Toth remarks:"He [my father] left me his burden of unfulfilled promise. Without having to be asked, I picked it up."

Discover these and other memories in *Family Portraits*.

—*Lesley S. J. Farmer*

Family Pose   Grades 5-6
By Dean Hughes

David had been running for three days. He was tired, he was hungry, and he had found out how cold and wet Seattle could be in November. He had had enough of street doors and park benches, so he thought he had found heaven when he was able to sneak into the Hotel Jefferson and curl up in a hall doorway. That is, until he was suddenly shaken awake by a man in a bellboy's uniform.

Paul, the night bellhop at the Hotel Jefferson, had found the kid curled up in the hallway. He tried to talk him into going home or getting help from Social Services, but the boy threatened to run again. Finally Paul risked his job and allowed the boy to sleep in an unused room, hoping to convince him to get help, and hoping that maybe tomorrow the boy would at least tell him his name. One night stretched into two, then three, until David had become an unofficial resident of the hotel. And as he got to know Paul and the other people who worked there and heard their stories, he found himself part of something very much like a family.

—Sue Padilla

Family Reunion   Grades 5-9
By Caroline B. Cooney

Shelley would like to be part of a normal family, one that's a little less colorful than the one she has now. She lives with her father, who has just married for the third time; her impulsive brother, who is always starting trouble; and a new stepmother. Her real mother walked out on the family to go live with a charming Frenchman. This is not your average family—Shelley has three times as many parents as most kids, all doing their own thing. To make matters worse, she also has an aunt, uncle, and two cousins whose noses seem frozen in the air. They consider themselves The Perfect People, so you can imagine what they act like.

Just when Shelley is ready to enjoy a quiet summer, her perfect aunt decides to hold a family reunion. And when Shelley gets there, she realizes that there are family secrets, and she's bound and determined to uncover them. Will that make it easier for Shelley to understand her family? Or will the reunion *and* the family fall apart?

—Barbara Bahm

Fifth Grade:
Here Comes Trouble
By Colleen O'Shaughnessy McKenna

Grades 5-9

I knew this party was a mistake from the beginning but, you see, it was Marsha's signpost party. In Marsha's family, a girl's eleventh birthday was supposed to be celebrated as a Signpost to Maturity. A signpost party meant that childhood was almost over and adulthood just around the corner. Marsha decided, for her signpost, on a boy/girl party. The first boy/girl event ever in our group! Everyone was excited, even the boys, but I couldn't help feeling this was a bad idea.

Then Marsha's cousin Carole got in on the act, helping Marsha prepare for the party. She was thirteen and knew everything about being a teenager. Carole decided that Marsha's room was too childish, so everything had to go, from stuffed animals to the mouse family Marsha's dad had given her. Carole also decided that, to make this an extra-special signpost, Marsha needed to pierce her ears. I didn't like the way Carole was changing everything and Marsha just going along with her, but what could I do except go along too? Then Carole said that Marsha needed a pair of expensive gold hoops for her newly-pierced ears. I soon realized that Carole's way of getting these earrings was to lift them. I left; I wanted no part of Carole and this new Marsha.

I knew this party was a bad idea from the beginning, and now with less than twenty-four hours to go, I wonder if there will even *be* a party. Read *Fifth Grade: Here Comes Trouble* by Colleen McKenna to find out.

—Linda Olson

Fighting Back:
What Some People Are Doing About AIDS
By Susan Kuklin

Grades 7-Adult

AIDS: Acquired Immune Deficiency Syndrome—an acronym that was completely unknown a few years ago. This innocent-sounding syllable now has the power to strike panic in our hearts, to set off waves of anxiety and even loathing. In the news we hear constantly of the numbers of new cases that have been reported, and the predictions of thousands more to come. We hear how doctors and scientists are working, struggling to come up with a vaccine, a reliable test for the virus, maybe someday even a cure.

What we do not hear and may not even know about is what is being done now, on an individual basis, by ordinary people (not scientists or government officials) to help those who are suffering from the disease.

Fighting Back is the story of Group 7, one of several groups in an organization of volunteer "buddies" dedicated to helping AIDS patients cope with day-to-day life. For the eighteen men and women who make up Group 7, "help" may mean household chores, financial advice, or simple nursing care. But a lot of the time, "help" means just being a friend and going with your buddy to the movies, or listening quietly to the fears and regrets of a young person whose life is being cut short.

It is not easy watching a friend cope with an illness, especially a terminal illness. The members of Group 7 are not heroes or headline-seekers. They are people who value life, and who want to make life and death a little more bearable for their friends, any way they can.

—*Linda Olson*

Fire in the Heart   Grades 5-9
By Liza Ketchum Murrow

"I'm writing about your deceased wife, Ashley O'Connor," the letter began. Molly hadn't meant to read her father's mail, but she couldn't imagine why anyone would write about her mother, who'd been dead for ten years. And she couldn't understand why her father seemed so upset about the letter, either. He tore it up, but later she saw him tape it back together and stuff it in his shirt pocket.

Fourteen-year-old Molly's curiosity is aroused, and she realizes that she's never known much about this woman who died in an accident when Molly was only four. Against her father's wishes, Molly begins to piece together the story of her mother's life and death. On visits to her grandmother and aunt, she gathers a few photographs and some family letters and papers. But these bits of information only deepen the mystery. Why was her mother in a mountainous area of northern California, and not in Vermont with her family? Who was Paul Leone, the man who died with her when the truck she was driving skidded off the treacherous mountain road and crashed in the river below? And why doesn't Molly's father want her to learn about her mother?

As Molly gathers clues about her mother's death, she knows that only by going to California can she answer the questions to her satisfaction. Is she going on a wild goose chase, as her family believes, or on a treasure hunt?

—*Rosemary Moran*

Five Against the Sea   Grade 10–Adult
By Ron Arias

What bothered Gerardo most at first was meat. Or rather, the lack of it. For all of his thirty-three years, he'd been a picky eater. Even though he fished for a living, he hated to eat what he caught. He'd much rather bite into a thick piece of beef, chicken, or pork. He proudly referred to himself as a carnivore, a word whose sound and meaning he thought suited him perfectly.

But when you're adrift on the ocean, you can't be quite so finicky. You have to eat to survive. The secret to eating anything, even the rotten, stinking food that they had on board, is hunger. You stop smelling and tasting and just swallow. Anything to fill your belly.

For five months Gerardo and the other four crewmen of the *Cairo II* did whatever they had to do to survive. Caught off the coast of Coast Rica in a storm, they drifted in their crippled craft for 4,500 miles, setting a record for the longest period that anyone has ever been adrift on the open sea. But setting records wasn't foremost in any of their minds: survival was. Survival against the sea that was steadily trickling into their boat, against the sharks that circled outside, against the lack of fresh water and the ever-mounting despair and the differences between crew members that bordered on violence.

This is the story of the men of the *Cairo II* and their families. A true story of courage and survival.

—Jeff Blair

Five Finger Discount   Grades 5–9
By Barthe DeClements

It wasn't that Jerry didn't love his dad—he did A lot! In fact, getting a letter from his dad always made him feel better. But Jerry didn't want anyone to know where his dad was living right now, or why he'd been sent there.

Jerry and his mom had moved to a new town where she worked as a waitress while Jerry tried to adjust to his new school. His mom didn't earn a lot of money, even though she worked long hours. And so far, the only friend Jerry had been able to find was the girl next door, who was in his fifth-grade class. Jerry couldn't believe his ears when he found out that Grace's father was a preacher. All this time when she called herself a PK he had thought she meant "Prisoner's Kid," like him—not "Preacher's Kid"!

Jerry was pretty sure Grace and her family wouldn't want anything to do with him once they heard that his dad was in jail for stealing. So when a tough little fourth-grader figured out Jerry's secret, Jerry had to figure out a way to keep him quiet—or it would ruin everything.

—Wanda McAdams

Forgotten Girl   **Grade 5–8**
By Hila Colman

Have you ever felt like the forgotten member of your family? Then you can identify with Kelly, the Forgotten Girl. After Kelly's father died, her mom went back to school and became a successful lawyer. And now she's decided to run for mayor. Eliot, Kelly's older brother, thinks that's terrific; he's playing a major role down at campaign headquarters. But their mom doesn't appreciate Kelly's efforts to help, because she always seems to wear the wrong clothes and say and do the wrong things. It's an old story—Eliot is always perfect and always does things that please their mother. But once Kelly was in a store when Eliot was accused of shoplifting. Was it really just an accident? What about the money that came up missing at campaign headquarters? Maybe Kelly isn't the only imperfect person in her family!

—Marilyn Eanes

The Fortunate Fortunes   **Grades 5–12**
The Problem Solvers
The Rejects
The Unsung Heroes
By Nathan Aaseng

Amazing stories are lurking behind many common household items. For instance, there's probably no one here who doesn't know what this is [hold up a can of Classic Coca-Cola]. Coca-Cola is the most familiar trademark in the world. But do you know who invented this drink? It was concocted by John Styth Pemberton over a hundred years ago, as a medicine for relaxation, and for relief from headaches and hangovers. His bookkeeper wrote "Coca-Cola" in the calligraphy that is still used on the label today. However, Mr. Pemberton died before his medicine became a popular soft drink. He had no idea that his recipe would make other people millionaires.

Of course, not all inventors die before their products take off. One man who did become a millionaire from his invention was Charles Darrow. He invented Monopoly. He got the idea from a similar board game called The Landlord's Game. But when Mr. Darrow submitted Monopoly to Parker Brothers, the company found fifty-two reasons why it wouldn't sell. Luckily, Mr. Darrow didn't give up. Parker Brothers eventually bought the patent, and Monopoly became the largest-selling board game of all time.

Something else that many households have is this [hold up a facial tissue]. What do you call it? Most people call this a Kleenex, even though Kleenex is just one brand of facial tissue. But Kleenex was the first brand on the market, and the name is often used for any sort of facial tissue. At first, facial tissue was advertised and sold to clean off makeup. Then, after many people admitted that they really used it for blowing their noses, it was marketed as a throw-away hankie—and sales sky-rocketed.

A rather new addition to some households is a Jacuzzi. The man who invented it, Candido Jacuzzi, had a son who needed water therapy, and he got tired of taking him to the hospital so frequently. Then people who examined his invention discovered that they *enjoyed* these relaxing whirlpool baths, even though they didn't need the treatment. Now we often call any kind of hot tub or whirlpool a Jacuzzi.

All these stories and others are told in four books by Nathan Aaseng: *The Unsung Heroes*, *The Rejects*, *The Fortunate Fortunes*, and *The Problem Solvers*. Take a look at these and discover the stories behind Hires Root Beer, Gerber Baby Foods, Orville Redenbacher Popcorn, and Band-Aids. After you read these stories, you may never take another product for granted again!

—*Mary Hedge*

Forward Pass   **Grades 7–12**
By Thomas J. Dygard

When football coach Frank Gardner made his surprise announcement to the team about a new player, no one said a word. The players were more than surprised—they were stunned speechless. It was bad enough adding a new player at the second game of the season, but *this* player. . . .

At the game, some people noticed the new player right away; others did not. Up in the press box, the sports reporter for the *Morning Herald* and the game announcer gawked at the starting lineup: there was the high school basketball star listed as wide receiver.

In the stands the principal's face registered shock, and the basketball coach was enraged. How dare Frank Gardner rob the basketball team of its best player?

Across the field the opposing team didn't seem aware of a a new number on the field, number 89. But then something happened that *everyone* noticed. The basketball player, number 89, caught a twelve-yard pass, even though the Aldridge High Panthers had never used a passing strategy before. Well, they'd had no one to catch passes—until now! Then Nelson Nutting, the coach of the Randville High Tigers, took a good look at this new player and got mad.

He charged across the field, shouting and waving his arms at the referee. The referee hadn't noticed the new player either, but now he walked over to Coach Gardner to ask a question. "Coach Nutting says your 89 is a girl. Is that true?" Coach Gardner looked at the referee, smiled, and answered, "Yes"!

If you want to know what happened when a girl joined the Aldridge Panthers football team, read *Forward Pass*—and find out.

—*Kaite Mediatore*

Four Past Midnight   Grade 9–Adult
By Stephen King

It's making you think and then think again, wondering just what "reality" means, that Stephen King is good at. In a dark basement, bending over the washing machine lit only by a single bulb, you hear a noise and freeze, holding your breath, waiting for whatever you will see next, and where it will take you. Walking up the stairs late at night, you notice a flicker of shadow just as your head clears the top step, a flicker of shadow in the pool of light spilling from your open bedroom door, as if something inside had moved—yet you are alone in the house, and all the doors and windows are locked. Reading all afternoon, you don't notice how dark it's grown, until something moves just at the edge of your vision, and you feel the hair on your arms and at the back of your neck rise in response to some threat you can only guess about. Is it real or is it just your imagination? Things that go bump in the night, that follow you down the hall, waiting till you turn off the light, lurking behind half-open closet doors, those things don't really exist in our explainable concrete world—*do* they???

King can tear gaping holes in the thin fabric that protects the known from the unexplainable—the horrid, the evil that exists in that other world he creates, where the worst is waiting to happen, over and over

again. And through the holes in that barrier between us and them, between reality and insanity, *they* come—staggering, stalking, creeping,
crawling, any way they can, but always sinister, always horrible, and always, always deadly.

And then, through the rips in that fragile barrier, from what we hope
and pray is unreality, into our everyday world the creatures come. . . .
This time they are led by the langoliers, who can make even the safest
reality disappear, can leave you hanging in midair with no safety net—
unless, of course, you're lucky enough to be asleep when they arrive.
They are followed by the Library Policeman and the deadly-sweet gray-
haired spinster librarian he works with—surely the best possible reason
to get your books back on time, *no matter what!* John Shooter is just
a simple country man from rural Mississippi, but he has a mission, a
deadly mission of revenge. Don't get in his way. The Sun Dog and his
hideous snarl is the only picture a new camera will take—and that may
be enough to convince you to think twice about the convenience of Po-
laroids.

So now King invites you to let these creatures pull you back with
them, into their own terrifying nightmare worlds. But remember, once
you have visited there, you can never completely escape, for you carry
the tatters of their hideous almost-and if-it-is-God-help-us-reality with
you back into your daily world. And the next time a door swings shut
when no one's touched it, and the shadows settle over a strange
hunched shape, or you hear the soft pad of footsteps just after you turn
out the light, it won't be the wind or the dresser heaped with folded
laundry or the cat coming to curl up at your feet. You'll know that the
gauzy barrier has been torn once again, and this time it's *you* they're
coming after—and this time they're *not* in a book!

—*J. R. B.*

The Fourth-Grade Dinosaur Club   Grades 3–6
By Larry Bograd

Have you ever wanted to be famous? I guess everyone does. Well,
Billy knows what he'd like to be famous for. He wants to dig up the
biggest dinosaur bone ever! Billy is founder and president of the
Fourth-Grade Dinosaur Club. It's not a big club really, just two
members: Billy, who is president, and his friend Juan, who is vice
president. But they share their interest in dinosaurs, although Billy does
go a bit overboard at times—he eats, breathes, and lives for dinosaurs.

For once, though, Billy has other things on his mind. Mainly, how not to lose his friend Juan. Juan has some pretty big troubles. He's being picked on and bullied because of his Chicano background. He was given a dunking at the neighborhood pool. He got a black eye there, too. In the school lunchroom some kids squirted him with mustard and stole part of his lunch. And both times Billy was there, and he just stood and watched, even when Juan called to him for help. Some friend, right? It's not that Billy doesn't care, he does! It's just that the kid who has been picking on Juan is Reg North, and Reg and his friends are *big*. They've not only terrorized Juan, they've also damaged and destroyed parts of Juan's family's grocery market—Reg is in the big leagues when it comes to being a bully. But Billy *has* to do something, or he will lose his best friend. Juan is already upset with Billy and has told him that he's not much of a friend. What can Billy do?

Well, he sees a chance to save his friendship. He fixes it so that he and Juan are made partners for the three-legged race on their school's field day. Now they will have to practice together if they want to win. This is Billy's first step to getting his friend back. They'll be racing against Reg North, and if they lose they will lose a lot. But if they win they'll win a lot more than just a race and a ribbon. They could win friendship and respect. So call to order *The Fourth-Grade Dinosaur Club*.

—*Paula Paolucci*

Fowl Play, Desdemona! **Grades 3–9**
By Beverly Keller

It all started the week before Thanksgiving, when Sherman Grove, our landlord's son, came by to walk to school with Antony and me. "So what are you doing for Thanksgiving dinner?" I asked Sherman. He just about bit off my head with his answer. What's making him so touchy, I wondered.

That day at school, I, Desdemona, got the dubious honor of making posters for the school play, *The King and I* (in other words, the job was dumped on me). Time was short, so I asked Sherman to help out. He spent a lot of time working in the storeroom by himself, and when I finally got a look at what he'd done, I couldn't believe it. Instead of advertising the play, he'd made posters of turkeys, which said:

Thanksgiving's No Treat
For the Bird You Eat
and

Don't Make Thanksgiving a Fowl Holiday!
Spare a Turkey's Life
and
Give a Turkey Reason To Be Thankful
Have a Vegetarian Holiday Dinner

Sherman was an animal rights activist! No wonder he'd been so touchy when I asked him about Thanksgiving dinner!

Now time was really short, and Sherman had used up all the poster board that we needed to publicize our play. But we solved that problem—we turned Sherman's posters over and advertised *The King and I* on the back. Then we put up our signs in store windows all over town, two messages in one. Sherman was very pleased.

Next his enthusiasm for animal rights got me and my friend Laurelle involved in printing Save-a-turkey flyers to insert in the play programs. I was supposed to pick up the leaflets at the printers', but I must have taken the wrong package. I didn't notice what the flyers really said until some of the programs had already been given out. Instead of our vegetarian flyers, they were advertisements for male exotic dancers!

Well, anyway, this whole mess got my dad and Laurelle's mother introduced, and who knows what may develop now—they're both single parents, and it could get very interesting. But in the meantime, what *are* we going to have for Thanksgiving?

—*Betty A. Holtzen*

Francie and the Boys   Grades 7-12
By Meredith Daneman

Quiet, dreamy, thirteen-year-old Francie has never imagined performing on stage, so when she is singled out as one of the six girls who will act in a play at Dubb's School for Boys, she's astonished. Her family and friends are amazed. Despite her parents' objections, she becomes involved in the production, even though she doesn't know a thing about acting. Or about boys.

—*Barbara Bahm*

Frank and Ernest   Grades 3-9; Adult
By Alexandra Day

Have you ever stopped to eat at a diner and listened to what the waitress said to the cook as she turned in your order? Did it make sense, or did it sound like this: "Burn one, pin a rose on it and take it through the garden with frogsticks, and shake one in the hay." Wonder what you'd get if that was your order? What about a hamburger with lettuce, tomato and onion, an order of fries, and a strawberry milkshake?

Now you obviously wouldn't hear anything like this outside a diner or a luncheonette, but what if you knew just a few words of Diner-ese yourself? Imagine how surprised people would be if you ordered your meal in their language! For breakfast you might ask for a stack of Vermont with moo juice, or some Mike and Ike to go with your wrecked hen fruit. Then you might decide to have hounds on an island for lunch, along with your Atlanta special and a houseboat. But to really make someone who doesn't know what you're talking about sit up and take notice, just say, "I'll take a twist it, choke it, and make it cackle!"

—J. R. B.

Franky Furbo
By William Wharton

My dad writes children's stories for a living. You've probably heard of him—William Wiley. His stories are pretty famous; in fact, people all over the world read them. Especially his series of stories about Franky Furbo, the super-fox. I *know* you've heard about him: the fox who's smarter than any human being. Franky Furbo can fly, speak all the languages in the world, turn himself into a man when he wants to, and do all kinds of other neat stuff.

When I was a little kid I loved to hear my dad's Franky Furbo stories. My favorite has always been the first of the series, the one that explains how it all started. You remember—an American and a German soldier are pinned down under an artillery barrage, in Italy during World War II. They're both going to be killed, but Franky Furbo saves them. He shrinks them so they're small enough for him to carry back to his house, and then he nurses them back to life. While they're recovering from their wounds, Franky teaches both men to bury their hatred and to live in peace. Then, when they're fully recovered, he sends them back into the human world to teach other people what they've learned. The theme continues through all the other stories. Franky Furbo is always trying to save the human race from its own hatred and destruction.

I used to think my dad always pretended that Franky Furbo was real because he didn't want to spoil the stories for me. But now that I'm older, I've begun to wonder. Surely Dad knows that I'm old enough to tell the difference between reality and fantasy. So why does he go on pretending, insisting that Franky Furbo really exists, and that all the stories about him are true?

Maybe Dad never really recovered from that shock he had during the war, when he almost died during an artillery bombardment. After all, the army doctors gave him a Section Eight medical discharge—he was suffering from delusions, they said, as a result of his injuries. You see, Dad told the doctors that he and the German trapped with him in the attack had been saved by a *fox*. A fox named Franky Furbo. That was over twenty-three years ago, but Dad says the same thing today.

—*Margie Reitsma*

The Fringes of Reason: Grade 7–Adult
A Whole Earth Catalog
Edited by Ted Schultz

Does your Cabbage Patch doll send you psychic messages? Is there really a five-mile-wide Happy Face on the surface of Mars? Are there pictures of demons engraved on the Canadian dollar bill? Ever been kidnapped by extraterrestrials or had a saucer crash-land in your back yard? Is it possible to boost your brain power electrically? Is the earth really hollow?

These and other questions about unusual phenomena, eccentric beliefs, and new-age science are all explored in this Whole Earth Catalog. If there's something strange in your neighborhood, the answer to what it is and what to do about it will no doubt be found here.

—*Jeff Blair*

G is for Gumshoe   Grade 9–Adult
By Sue Grafton

Have you ever heard of a place called The Slabs? If not, you haven't missed much. When my new client asked me the same question, I drew a blank. Irene wasn't really surprised. The Slabs is just a collection of concrete slabs out in the Mojave Desert. It was a Marine base during

World War II. All that's left now are the foundations of the old barracks. Every winter thousands of people move their trailers in to escape the cold to the north. It's all very primitive, not a single modern convenience for miles around, but living on The Slabs is dirt-cheap.

Irene's mother, Agnes, was a resident of The Slabs. Unlike the seasonal nomads, she enjoyed living there all year round. But now Agnes was missing. She hadn't contacted Irene in six months. At age eighty-three, Agnes was independent and very vocal about it, so Irene hesitated to send out a search party. But perhaps it was time to brave her mother's wrath. Something could be wrong. In desperation, Irene called me.

I'm Kinsey Millhone, private investigator. Some of you may have heard of some of my other cases. This missing-person job seemed pretty routine, almost like a vacation. Just run down to the Mojave and check it out, right? But things began to get a little complicated even before I headed for the desert.

An old friend in the public defender's office at Carson City, Nevada, called to drop a bombshell. There's a contract out on me. Some guy I helped to put behind bars is out to get even. It's hard to believe he thinks I'm that important. Lee recommends I get a bodyguard, maybe another PI named Dietz. What can he do to protect me that I can't do myself? Forget it! I can handle it alone.

But The Slabs is a pretty scary place to be when someone takes a shot at you. I realize that now. At first I thought the flat tire came from an ordinary piece of scrap metal. Oh, it was metal all right, but it was a .38 slug, and it came from the red pickup that tried to run me off the road.

Now I'm on the road again, with the same red Dodge bearing down on me. My attempts to outrun it have been futile. He continues to hit me, plowing into my VW, ramming it into an irrigation ditch. I feel bruised and broken all over. Is he coming to finish me off? Only one thing puzzles me: Why would a contract killer bring a child along for the ride?

—*Bernice D. Crouse*

A Gallery of Dinosaurs and Other Early Reptiles **Grade 3–Adult**
By David Peters

Hey, everybody, don't take a nap—
It's time to listen to my dinosaur rap!

Dinosaurs lived a long time ago—
What happened to them, nobody knows.
Science explains it with a whole lot of words;
Some people think they turned into birds;
Maybe a meteor swooped down and got 'em,
Or they stuck in the tar and sank to the bottom.
Whatever happened, one thing is true:
You'll never see a dinosaur living in the zoo!
The only place to see them, the only place to look,
Is to go to the library and search in a book.
A book like this will bring lots of smiles
From its pictures of dinosaurs and other reptiles.
Just about a hundred, just for you,
Some you'll have heard of and some are new.
Dinosaurs and reptiles pictured everywhere,
So get yourself ready and pull up a chair!
It's the book for you, reptilian readers—
A Gallery of Dinosaurs, by David Peters.

—Jeff Blair

The Game of Life
By Norma Howe

Grades 7–9

Rocky thought that life had no meaning. And for the moment, Cairo Hayes had no answer. Which was unusual for Cairo. Particularly since she felt that Rocky was *the* great example of the meaning of life.

To show you: Cairo's mom wanted to play bingo. And for some strange reason, she had to have Cairo with her when she did. "You can do you homework at the mall while I'm playing." Cairo didn't like this idea at all, and her mom got desperate. "I'll probably live to regret this, but here's what I'll do." She took a deep breath. "I'll let you get a puppy." Cairo had been begging for a dog since she could talk. "A live one?" she asked incredulously. "Oh, funny," Mom said. And it was at the first bingo night that Cairo met Rocky, who worked at a fast-food joint in the mall. Now if that wasn't meant to be, what was?

And there were the Rogers, who collected cats like coupons and disposed of them just as easily. Which could be awful, but Cairo had to feed the cats some weekends, and while she was in the grocery line to buy catfood, she saw a diet plan that would just suit her obese relative Lucille.

Of course, the meaning of life might also be a strangely stacked deck. There was Heather, Cairo's older sister. She'd been enough of a flake as was without falling for Allen, a thirty-year-old environmentalist and self-styled songwriter. Heather said it was all in the stars. Cairo's down-to-earth little sister had done a whole science project on the fallacy of astrology, but that didn't deter good old Heather. Even when Allen started hitting her for up for a few bucks every couple of days—and then hitting her for real.

And there was Rene with the honesty test, and Grandpa B. and the dog park, and Uncle Larry and the Egyptian slides.

Well, it all works out. But how? That's *The Game of Life*, and you'll have to read it and play it to believe it.

—Lesley S. J. Farmer

Gameplay
By Kevin J. Anderson

Grade 10–Adult

Gamearth was a hexagonal fantasy game created by Melanie, David, Scott, and Tyrone. For two years they had played it every Sunday evening, and David wanted to quit. He wanted to quit so much that he created a vile and terrible monster, capable of overcoming all the other characters in the game. End of game, he hoped. But his friends wanted Gamearth to go on. They would fight to avoid an end, even if it meant bending a few rules. What they didn't realize, though, was that the game's characters might take drastic measures of their own to keep on living. . . .

It was Thallis' death that changed the picture for Delreal the warrior. He avenged his friend's death by slaying the ant-queen Ryx, but the conquest held no pleasure. The adventure wasn't *fun* (which was the primary rule of Gamearth). Delreal had always assumed that he would play and fight and fight and play forever, that he and the other characters would never die. But now Thallis was gone. The game had changed, with the suddenness of a slap in the face. In his heart Delreal vowed to continue the quest despite the Outsiders, no matter what the roll of the dice. . . .

Melanie too had been saddened by Thallis' death. He had been one of her favorite characters. But she felt a certain thrill, because something unique was happening with Gamearth. The characters were starting to live their own lives in between the Sunday gaming sessions.

Which is reality? The world of the players or the world of the game?

—Lesley S. J. Farmer

Genie with the Light Blue Hair   Grades 5-9
By Ellen Conford

Genies today are just not what they used to be. I mean, when you read the stories of long ago, about magic lamps and three wishes, you know that the person making the wish got everything he or she wished for, no trouble, no hassles. My genie doesn't work that way. Yes, you heard right! I have a genie, and you are welcome to him: I think he's defective!

Let me tell you how I acquired this dubious genie. It happened on my fifteenth birthday. Now, one thing you have to know is that I have always been a very practical person, so I expected the usual practical birthday presents from my family. And I got them: From my parents, a dictionary, a pen, and book called *The Complete Guide to Movies on TV*. From my brother, a wallet. All very practical so far. But in the evening my aunt and uncle came over for a gala birthday dinner, and that's when things started to go wrong. Their gift to me was a candleholder in the shape of a teapot. Not exactly what I had always wanted, but what can you do? I might never have known I had a genie if it hadn't been for the storm that night. The storm was pretty bad, and because of it the lights went out. That's when I lit my new candle. To say I was shocked is the understatement of the year. For coming out of the teapot candleholder was a blue, cigar-smoking genie by the name of Arthur, who happened to look a lot like Groucho Marx.

Well, once I had recovered from shock, I started thinking about what my first wish would be. Since my room was beastly hot, I wished that it should be cooler—but I was expecting an air conditioner, not six inches of snow!

Now you know what I mean when I say my genie is defective. He has never produced exactly what I've wished for, not even once! If you want to know about the other crazy things Arthur's done to me, read *Genie with the Light Blue Hair*, by Ellen Conford.

—*Linda Olson*

Get Help: Grades 5-9
Solving the Problems in Your Life
By Sara Gilbert

Have you ever had questions about drinking or drugs, problems with parents, problems with eating (or not eating), thoughts about suicide or running away from home? Or maybe you have worried about your body or your appearance, or about work and money and paying for college.

Get Help: Solving the Problems in Your Life will let you see that you are not alone with your question or problem. Sara Gilbert discusses people who can and want to help you. "But," you may be thinking, "it'll be hard to tell someone, 'I need help.'"

Get Help not only explains why it's hard to say those three words, "I need help," but also explains why saying them is important and can take away that "alone" feeling. *Get Help* says it's okay to have a problem . . . the mistake is not dealing with it—ignoring it and hoping it will go away by itself.

This book won't solve your problems, but it will show you how to get help so you can solve them yourself.

—*Dorothy Davidson*

Ghastlies, Goops & Pincushions: Grades 3-4
Nonsense Verse
By X. J. Kennedy

Meet Agatha Goop with a whale of a whoop and Aunt Gilda who wears twelve hat-pins. Find the Gnomes from Nome and Flossie Fly, as well as My Uncle Demented.

This poet, X. J. Kennedy, spins words into some of the silliest and funniest situations imaginable. My favorite goes like this:

> The horn on our pickup truck
> Stayed stuck—
> All night it went on beeping.
> The neighbors all
> Began to bawl,
> "Hey, knock it off! We're sleeping!"

> The firemen sprayed
> Some foam and made
> Our poor truck cease to bellow,
> But now we ride
> To school inside
> A gooey white marshmallow.

It goes without saying that if you enjoy silly situations, you will laugh and bellow with this collection of hilarious and outrageous poems.

—Susan Wolfe

Ghost Abbey   Grades 5-9
By Robert Westall

Maggi's only twelve years old, but ever since her mom died she's had to attend school *and* keep house for her father and her twin brothers. Life doesn't seem very promising—until the invitation arrives. It's a letter from an old friend of the family, offering Maggi's father a job restoring a rundown abbey out in the country. This could be a chance for the whole family to make a new start.

The old abbey just feels right to Maggi, from the very beginning. There's a lot of cleaning and repair work to be done before the place can be opened as a hotel, but the country air is fresh, the gardens are beautiful, and Maggi makes some new friends. So she isn't too scared at first, when she hears strange voices chanting, or when the service bells to ninety-nine rooms all ring at once—before they're even hooked up. But when she walks into a room and sees a man dying from wounds received three hundred years ago, the abbey becomes a place of terror.

Maggi is the only one who understands that the abbey is really alive. It is a beautiful place to live if you are "nice" to it—but hurt the abbey in any way and it will strike back. . . .

—Susan A. Jones

Give It Up, Mom   Grades 5-9
By Mary Robinson

Even though she had quit smoking, I could tell that smoke would be coming out of my mom's ears soon. She was really mad, but it wasn't *my* fault—I'd just been doing my class project.

See, for my Social Living class we're supposed to pick a cause, for an "Impact on the World" project. I couldn't think of a better cause than getting my mom to stop smoking. And after I nagged at her, she agreed, and said she'd go along with my project. At last, I thought.

But it's a harder assignment than I ever expected. Sure would help if Mom would take it seriously! *I* do—I arranged a solemn Last Cigarette Ceremony for her, I worked out a schedule of things she could do whenever she had a nicotine fit, and I left notes all over the place to remind her of how proud I am that she's quitting.

Then I had the brainstorm that got her so steamed up. I put flyers up all over town asking people not to sell her cigarettes and even offering a reward to anyone who caught her smoking. She made me go and take them all down, but at least she didn't get to buy any cigarettes. That time.

I haven't given up yet, though.

I have a lot more ideas—ones that could make her even madder. To find out what they are, you'll have to read *Give It Up, Mom*, by Mary Robinson.

—*Jeff Blair*

Glass Slippers Give You Blisters   Grades 5–9
By Mary Jane Auch

Kelly and her two best friends are entering Riverton Junior High. Being sixth graders, they're at the bottom of the totem pole socially. They decide to try out for the annual school play. Maybe that will increase their visibility. Her friends both get parts, but Kelly gets stuck painting scenery and helping with the lights.

Kelly knows her mother won't want her to be involved with the play in any capacity, so she lies, and tells her mom she's joined the Home Ec Club, which meets every day after school. But her grandmother knows the truth—she even helped Kelly get her backstage jobs. Kelly is caught in the middle—there's no way she can please both these women. And what about doing what is right for *herself*? Is there a way out, or will Kelly have to sneak around backstage forever?

—*Paula Eads and J. R. B.*

Going Green: Grades 3–12
A Kid's Handbook to Saving the Planet
By John Elkington and others

If you think "going green" means leaping about with Kermit the Frog, you're wrong! In this case, "going green" refers to the earth and how one person can make an incredible difference in saving our planet. That one person can be *you*. . . . really! In this book, you'll discover how to become a green consumer and choose products that don't harm the earth; you'll find out about acid rain and the greenhouse effect; you'll learn about energy saving, composting, and recycling. Most of all you'll realize that even one person can start a movement toward a cleaner world and a healthier environment. Are you that one person? Get ready to go green after you read *Going Green: A Kid's Handbook to Saving the Planet*.

—*Bette DeBruyne Ammon*

The Golden Bird
By Hans Stolp

Grade 5–Adult

Hello! My name is Daniel. I'm eleven years old. I have cancer. I've been in the hospital for five months now. Since I've been here I've learned to read people's faces—there's not much else to do. My doctor comes in to see me every afternoon. He doesn't say much, but I can tell from his expression whether he's pleased or not. Today he's not pleased. He frowned when he looked at my chart, and two deep wrinkles shot straight up from his eyebrows. My mom cries a lot. I can always tell when she's been crying because her eyes get so red. I asked her once why she cries. She said that she feels sad because I'm so sick and there is nothing that she can do about it.

My stomach hurts. It's the cancer. I wish the pain would stop. I know I'm going to die. I'm scared! Mom and the nurses try to comfort me, but only Victor's visits seem to help me not be so afraid. Victor is a beautiful blue bird who comes to talk to me. I remember the first time he came. It was as if his feathers glowed like a beautiful blue light. And he flew right through the window glass without breaking it! That's the way he always comes. He comes to see me every day now, and always when I'm alone. Victor is sent by the golden bird who is building a nest near the sun. Victor says that the golden bird will lay eggs in the nest. When all the eggs have hatched, the golden bird will come for me. He said that I should watch the cherry tree outside my window. When it is full of bloom, the golden bird will come soon. He also told me that the golden bird said not to be afraid; it won't be long.

I told Mom and the nurse about Victor visiting me once. They told me that I have wonderful dreams. Why do grown-ups always think you've been dreaming when there's something they can't understand? Do *you* understand? Will you wait for the golden bird with me?

—*Sandra Carpenter*

Goodbye Doesn't Mean Forever   Grades 7-12
By Lurlene McDaniel

Sequel to *Too Young To Die*

In some ways Melissa Austin, even if she's fighting cancer, has so much more than Jory Delaney does. Everyone has this image of Jory as frivolous and shallow. For years she's dated and partied and lived exactly as she pleased, but there is a void inside her. Her parents, when not shuttling off to exotic locations on business, try to manage her life like another one of their real estate deals. That's why Jory spends so much time at Melissa's, where she feels like a member of the family.

Except toward Michael. Jory is in love with Michael, Melissa's dark-haired, blue-eyed brother. He's twenty-two, but he seems older. For as long as Jory has known the Austins, Michael has been the real father of the family. After Mr. Austin walked out, Michael took over his role. Now, between his jobs and his classes at the university and an occasional ride in his hot-air balloon, Michael seems to have no life of his own. Jory longs to change that. She could be so much to him, if only he'd let her.

Jory wishes there were something she could do for Melissa too. Something that would make the pain go away, and turn their senior year together into the very best year any two seniors ever had.

—*Judy Druse*

Grass   Grade 10-Adult
By Sheri S. Tepper

Grass was its name, for that was what covered it, the whole planet— seas of rippling, multicolored grass. Some of it was striped, some colored in waves or blotches. Great sweeps of grass taller than ten men, soft mounds of grass like moss underfoot. But everywhere there was grass. And scattered in the grass were small villages, walled to keep the grass at bay, and the estancias of the aristocrats, where today Diamante bon Damfels waits to go out on her first hunt, to climb onto one of the mounts for the first time, locking herself in place, to see the hounds chasing down the fox—the mighty fox, the implacable fox, the fox who knows that they are coming.

But the planet Grass is unique in other ways as well, and one of them is now of vital importance. A plague is sweeping the galaxy—a fatal, incurable virus has been found on all the known worlds. All except

Grass. The plague does not exist on Grass, and victims of the plague, when they come to Grass, are cured. Not many can come—the Grassians are not hospitable to foreigners, who are allowed only in the port city, Commoner Town. They are even reluctant to accept the ambassador and his family who have been sent from Terra with an undercover mission—to find out the secret of the planet's mysterious immunity. The ambassador and his family are an odd lot: Rigo—estranged from his wife, full of anger and rage, not the perfect choice for a diplomat; Marjorie, his wife—sensitive, understanding, stubborn, valuing all forms of life, no matter how bizarre; Stella—a smaller version of her father, like him reaching out for what she wants with no thought of others; and Tony—like his mother gentle and sensitive, a charismatic person who draws others to him.

They have brought six Terran horses with them, for they have been told about the fox hunts that the aristocracy of Grass enjoy. But they are forbidden to ride their horses in the hunt, or even to participate in it. However, they have been invited to watch a hunt, and when they see the creatures the Grassians call hounds, mounts, and foxen, they understand why they can't take part. The hounds are as big as Terran horses, muscled like lions, with broad triangular heads and lips curled back to show jagged teeth and fangs. They are silent, and their long tongues drip onto the path as they trot through the courtyard looking at each of the hunters gathered there. The mounts are terrifying, and the Terrans stand looking at them from the safety of a high balcony, unable to believe what they are seeing. These monsters are huge, twice as tall as the hounds, with long curved necks spined with arm-long scimitars of pointed, knife-edged bone, longest on the head and midway down the neck, shorter at the lower neck and shoulders. Their eyes burn red, and their backs are armored with hard and glistening hide. They make no sound at all. As each of these Hippae (for that is what they are called) approaches a hunter, it bends one of its forelegs so the hunter can climb on. The riders each slip a metal ring attached to reins over one of the lower spines and jam the toes of their boots into the pockmarks in the sides of the Hippae, locking themselves in place. They ride leaning back at a sharp angle, the lower spines of the mounts just a few inches away from their bodies. The hunters ride in silence, just as the animals run—an eerie, almost evil silence, and as Marjorie looks at the faces of the mounted hunters, she sees that they are wiped clean of any emotion, empty, staring. The riders make no effort to control the mounts, simply going where the Hippae choose to go. The hunt goes on for hours, as the hunters hold themselves on their mounts, muscles cramping, not daring to make even a whimper of pain that might attract the attention of their mount or, worse, of the hounds that run beside them. The hunt ends when a fox is treed—a fox as unlike Terran foxes as the hounds and the mounts—and screams defiance at the sky before it is killed. The Terrans have an impression of fur or scales or fangs, and then it's all over. Or is it? What is it that makes the Grassians keep riding to the hunt, even after many have been maimed, some killed, and young girls have disappeared? Their losses are not even acknowledged, and the hunts go on.

The Hippae are not what they seem, but creatures more vicious that the Terrans can possibly imagine. Marjorie discovers a secret cave and begins to try to unravel its mysteries. Perhaps it is *not* the aristocracy that rules the planet of Grass—after all, the commoners look down on them, and Hippae seem to control them. Can Marjorie, the few commoners she has made friends with, and an old priest with a passion for archaeology figure out what the Hippae are planning in time to stop them, and prevent the Plague from destroying all human life?

—J. R. B.

Great Disasters: Grades 3–Adult
Dramatic True Stories of Nature's Awesome Powers
Edited by Kaari Ward

It was probably the loudest noise ever heard by human ears, an explosion that burst with the force of one million Hiroshima bombs and was heard across seven percent of the earth's surface. Nearly 3,000 miles away and four hours later, it was mistaken for the distant roar of heavy guns.

The event was the explosion of the volcano Krakatoa in 1883. As many as 90,000 people died as a result of that blast. Tides and weather patterns halfway around the world were affected for months.

This is just one of nearly eighty natural catastrophes documented in this book, including plagues, earthquakes, tornadoes, blizzards, and tidal waves. Be a witness to them all, as the fury of nature changes the course of history, the lives of human beings, and the face of the earth itself.

—Jeff Blair

The Great Man's Secret
Grades 7-12
By Pieter Van Raven

Paul Bernard lost his legs in a secret "accident." For years all he has done is sit, eat, sleep, brood, and write in his isolated hilltop house on the California coast. Paul Bernard is a great writer—so great he won the Nobel Prize for literature. But he refused it. Just as he now refuses all public appearances and interviews. His daughter Lorna and his housekeeper Mrs. Bailey are the only people he sees—until Jerry Huffacker bikes up the hill to the great man's house for an interview for his high school paper. Surprisingly, Jerry is allowed to talk with the great man and is asked back the next Saturday and the next . . . until finally he and Lorna are allowed to share *The Great Man's Secret*.

—*Sue Padilla*

Growing Up Adopted   Grades 5-12
By Maxine B. Rosenberg

Have you ever wondered what it would feel like to be adopted? The kids in this book can tell you—they've *all* been adopted.

Jamie feels great about her family. She loves having seven brothers and sisters, all of different nationalities. Jamie's parents don't see any of the differences and love all their kids equally. Being adopted is super for Jamie!

Many kids are told that they were adopted, but not Joe—he had to hear it on the playground when the other kids were teasing him. The truth about his birth-parents had always been hidden from Joe, so naturally he felt it was something bad—something to hide "under rocks with snakes and tarantulas." Joe's always looked so different from his brothers and sister. Now he wishes he had blood relatives, so he "could look like someone else and have roots."

Many adopted kids get teased about looking different. Mark, a Korean boy, has always felt like an American, but when he asks the girls in his high school out on a date, they won't go.

Amy, like many others, doesn't want to get together with her birth-parents—she just wants to see what they look like. Will she grow up to be like them? Melissa, going on twelve, is afraid that when she has children she will abuse them, just as her biological mother did. And Chris wonders if his birth-mother has the artistic ability he does, and if he looks like her.

Marsha actually did get in touch with her biological mother. What a disappointment—she was very cold and didn't want to have anything to do with Marsha. So Marsha's just glad that her adoptive Mom and Dad truly love her, even if her birth-mother doesn't.

All the stories are different, all written by people who've been there. Read *Growing Up Adopted* and see how it really feels to grow up as an adopted child.

—*Maggie Carey*

Growing Up Western   **Grade 5-Adult**
Edited by Clarus Backes and Dee Brown

Fishing with your half-Indian friends, herding your dad's cattle into pens, and carrying a loaded rifle were all part of life if you were growing up in the West in the early 1900s. A boy's day was filled with chores—feeding chickens, filling coal buckets, and branding cattle. However, there was also the fun of swimming naked in the creek, learning the new game of baseball, and catching fish with your bare hands. The childhoods of these seven Western writers were full of discovery. They witnessed first-hand the gold prospectors and the discovery of oil, the developing system of the railroad, and the novelty of the streetcar. They learned to use weapons as a means of survival, as well as for recreation.

Life could be hard in the Old West. A. B. Guthrie's brothers and sisters died at an early age; Wright Morris lost his mother when he was an infant; and David Lavender's parents obtained a divorce—he had to learn to live with a new stepfather. These are heartaches that still must be endured.

But the hardships were mixed with adventure. These men dealt with avalanches, mail robbery, and train wrecks. For an enticing look at the lives of "modern cowboys" turned authors, read *Growing Up Western.*

—*Mary Cosper*

Hare's Choice   **Grade 3-Adult**
By Dennis Hamley

A clear, starry night with a low moon. Hare, the fastest creature in the forest, was racing a strange but friendly red beast that seemed to roll on legs that were round. The beast began to fall behind; in ecstasy Hare began to tear around in great circles next to the road. "Look at me! Look at me!"

Suddenly she disappeared. There was a light but audible bump at the front of the car. The driver braked hard. She was stone dead. The only wounds were scratches on her flanks where the blood was sticky.

"I'm going to lay it out on the roadside grass properly," said the woman. "Perhaps someone will find it who has a little time to spare." She placed two buttercups and a sprig of cow parsley alongside the hare. The next day Harry and Sarah, ten-year old twins, found the hare and carefully carried her to the village school. "Poor Puss," said Sarah. "I want to write a story about her."

"So do I," said Harry, unexpectedly.

By the end of the day the whole class had worked together to create a wonderful story about the Queen of the Hares. A story of animal homes, a kindly witch, and a destructive society.

As for Hare, she became aware of a new reality, and the most important choice—the one she would make for all eternity. She, alone of all the Hares, could choose to spend eternity with the wild animals—or with the storybook creatures of fantasy. What would she do?

An extraordinary hare, and an extraordinary story.

—*Lesley S. J. Farmer*

The Harmony Illustrated   Grade 7–Adult
Encyclopedia of Rock, sixth edition
By Pete Frame and others, with Mike Clifford

From the group ABC to Frank Zappa, from the roots of rock to the late '80s, this encyclopedia is an essential reference guide to rock 'n' roll's past, present, and future, with over 700 entries and 500 photos and album covers.

Need to know which of your favorite albums are available on compact disc? Want to find out how high on the singles charts, in both the United States and Britain, a song climbed? Curious about the family trees of heavy metal or country rock, or the twenty-two years of Fleetwood Mac? Want to know who in the world Captain Beefheart, the Blockheads, Little Feat, Uriah Heep, or Bananarama are? Then this is the book for you.

—*Jeff Blair*

Harry Newberry   Grades 5-9
and the Raiders of the Red Drink
By Mel Gilden

Harry loves to read comic books, especially ones about superheroes. His favorite is *Tales of the Tuatara*, in which the Tuatara, with the help of her trusted assistant, Pennyperfect Lieberman, fights the sinister Bonnie Android. Unfortunately Harry's mom and dad and his revoltingly germ-conscious brother Theodore don't share Harry's fanatical devotion to the Tuatara.

One day Harry's mom sends him to the shopping center for some Norwegian Bachelor Farmers' Processed Cheese Food Product Substance. There something absolutely remarkable occurs—the Tuatara herself appears before his very eyes! What's more, she demonstrates her super-powers—she has to, to keep her spaceship, Mitzemacher 260, with Pennyperfect at the controls, from crashing into the crowded parking lot. Harry can hardly believe it—his superhero really exists!

Soon he is very much involved in helping foil an evil plot by Bonnie Android to wipe his home town off the map with the Slingshot of Doom. Harry's mom and brother are kidnapped and held by Bonnie Android, who demands the super-making Red Drink for ransom. Using clues found on a map on a day-old pizza from the Flat Earth Map and Pizza Company, Harry and Pennyperfect locate the Red Drink. But the more clues they unravel, the more it begins to look like Harry's *mom* may be the Tuatara; and his eccentric Aunt Agnes, Bonnie Android. Can this be possible?

If you have read and liked any of Daniel Pinkwater's off-the-wall science fiction, such as *Fat Men from Space*, *Lizard Music*, or *The Snarkout Boys and the Avocado of Death*, you'll love *Harry Newberry and the Raiders of the Red Drink*.

—Diane L. Deuel

The Haunting of Frances Rain   Grades 5-9
By Margaret Buffie

Lizzie is sick to death of her family. Her father walked out two years ago and rarely calls or writes. Her cold, unattentive mother has just gotten married again—to a man that Lizzie and her brother Evan don't like. And when Evan isn't tormenting their new dad, he's making Lizzie's life miserable. Even Erica, Lizzie's little sister, won't stop whining and crying. Lizzie can't stand it—the only sane one in the family is Gran, and even she doesn't seem like herself lately.

So Lizzie takes her canoe over to Rain Island to get away. While exploring there she discovers a pair of old-fashioned spectacles. When she puts them on, she can escape from the troubled present, but she finds herself in an equally troubled past. Can it be that somehow that past is connected to Lizzie's life in the present?

—*Kaite Mediatore*

Heartbeat   Grades 7–12
By Norma Fox Mazer and Harry Mazer

Tod has Amos to thank that his heart is beating at all. Years before, Amos had pulled a drowning Tod out of the lake. They'd been friends before, but that act had cemented the relationship. As he lay there on the bank, still spitting out water, Tod had said, "If you ever need me, if you ever want me, I'm your man."

Years passed before Amos asked Tod for anything. And when he did, it seemed so easy. All he wanted was for Tod to introduce him to Hillary, a girl who went to Tod's school. All Tod had to do was tell Hillary about Amos, what a great guy he was, and let her know how Amos felt about her.

Such a simple thing. Who would have thought the results would be so complicated? Who would have known Tod would fall for Hillary himself, and that Hillary would find herself in love with both Tod and Amos?

In the face of the ties that bind them to each other, the three of them struggle with their definitions of love and loyalty. Can a heart still beat when it's broken? How many hearts will be stilled before the situation is resolved?

—*Jeff Blair*

Heartbeats and Other Stories   Grades 7–12
By Peter D. Sieruta

A teenager's heart beats about seventy times a minute. There are people and events, though, which can set the heart to beating like a snare drum or make it boom like a kettle drum. This is a collection of stories about those times. For instance, "The Substitute."

All of us in the senior honors English class were still pretty shook up over Mrs. Morganstein's death on the day that *he* came in the room. The door slammed shut and everyone jumped, as if a bolt of electricity had passed through us all. He had a sort of sarcastic half-smirk on his face that got even broader as he picked up the copy of Dickinson lying on the desk and tossed it aside with a snort.

"My name is Eugene Trippman, and I will be your substitute for the remainder of the year. It is my understanding that honors classes in this school are designed with an open curriculum, so that you can waste both your time and that of the instructor by dabbling in poetry, plays, and basket-weaving.

"This will no longer be the case. I believe in hard work. I believe in the basics. I have a Masters degree in English literature and have taught college composition for almost ten years. Without even looking at your work, I can safely say that there is no one in this room who can come close to that level of performance."

He was just so patronizing, so superior, that I had to speak up. "Test us then."

He looked deep into me, almost staring through me, and I wished I could have taken the words back. He walked slowly toward me and said, "What is your name?"

"James O'Brien," I finally answered.

"Well, Mr. O'Brien, since you are so confident, we'll test you first. Tell me, what is a nonrestrictive appositive?" I had to admit he had me. Everyone in the class had heard me go on at one time or another about becoming a great poet or novelist someday. Did any of them know what it was? I sputtered out something about being sure that I would know one when I saw it in a sentence.

"Oh, so it's something you'd use in a sentence?"

"Well, yes," I said; then, "It is, isn't it?"

"Not so sure, are you? You strike me as a young man who thinks he knows quite a lot. You intend to go to college?"

"Notre Dame," I said. The last four generations of O'Briens had gone there. Of course I would too.

"Oh, I see," he said sarcastically. "And let me guess, honors student, star athlete, class officer. And a nice girlfriend and a nice new car, too, I suppose?"

I nodded numbly. He had me on all counts.

"All that, and Notre Dame, too. Very nice. And you're sure that you'll get into the school?"

Of course I was sure, but how would that sound? I sort of smiled and said, "Well, with any luck."

"In my class, Mr. O'Brien, we don't deal with luck. We deal with the basics like nonrestrictive appositives. Remember that."

I knew right then that I had an enemy. An enemy who stood between me and all of my dreams. An enemy who wielded all the power. An enemy who would change my life forever.

That's only one of the stories. There's also the brother who's dating the girl you love while you sit at home and write out a list of the twenty-five reasons you hate him, the girl who tries to smash into you with a driver's ed car, the runner who pushes a friend in a wheelchair through a race because some things are more important than winning, and many more.

These stories are full of the force of life, and those moments of truth when everything becomes clear in the space of a heartbeat.

—Jeff Blair

Herbie Jones and Hamburger Head   Grades 3-4
By Suzy Kline

He was the kind of dog only a kid could love: a mutt whose hairless head looked like raw hamburger. And it was love at first sight for Herbie Jones, especially after that dog helped Herbie foil a bank robbery.

Hamburger Head was just the kind of dog that Herbie had wanted all his life. The only problem was his dad, who hated dogs and had always refused to let Herbie have one.

Herbie and Hamburger Head won't give up easily, though. How can his dad *not* want a dog around that likes to watch the Yankees and loves to eat Spaghetti-O's—even if he does leave dog-doo in all the wrong places?

Will Herbie be able to keep Hamburger Head after all? You'll find out in *Herbie Jones and Hamburger Head.*

—Jeff Blair

Herds of Thunder, Manes of Gold: Grades 5-9
A Collection of Horse Stories and Poems
Edited by Bruce Coville

I came running down the mountain as fast as I could. As soon as I reached my mother's tent, I gasped, "I met a fanged cat!" even before I realized that The People's Aunt sat by my mother. Aunt knew the spirit world and had the gift of magic. She was very important to our people. She knew where I had gone and why, but for Mother's sake she asked what had happened. I told her I had gone up Magic Mountain on a dream quest. Only boys went on dream quests; being female, I knew I would never have a chance to go. But in spite of that, I climbed Magic Mountain last night. I don't know if what I saw was real or a dream, but I know I will never forget.

It was towards the dawn when I saw them in the valley below. The horses were pure white, like the windflowers. The stallion was grazing, and nearby in a crevasse a mare and her brand-new foal were resting. I have always had the gift of picture-making, but there was no stick to draw them with. I sat for awhile memorizing every detail so I could draw them later. I don't know what made me look up, but as I did I saw the fanged cat. He was crouching, ready to attack the mare and foal. Quickly I sprang to my feet and threw my knife. It clattered harmlessly against the rocks, but it was enough—the stallion moved to protect the mare and foal. I now stood facing the fanged cat. My eyes never left his. He did not know I was young, female, and now unarmed, but he knew I was human. The Uncles say that the cat, bear, and wolf all fear humans. I know this is true now, because as I stared into his eyes, the cat slowly drew back, and then he was gone. The horses galloped away, and I went running down the mountain to my mother's tent.

After I finished my story, the Aunt told me that I had the power of the spirit world and of magic-making. She took me back up Magic Mountain to the Magic Cave, and there with the painted bison, reindeer, and brown horses, I painted my white horses. I have seen many things in the years since that day, but that morning was the only time I saw my white horses.

This is a collection of horse stories, some old, some new—like the one I just told you. If you love to read about horses, this book is for you!

—*Linda Olson*

Hey World, Here I Am!   **Grades 5-9**
By Jean Little

If you had Kate Bloomfield in your class, you'd either love her or hate her, but you would certainly know she was there. She has very definite opinions about lots of things, including Dominic Tantardini, who looks like a Greek god to Kate (even though he's Italian); old people; her parents and her big sister, this year's English class; notebooks, journals, and mosquitoes.

In this book, Kate tells what she thinks about all these things and more. It's as though you'd been allowed to peek at her most private journal. She shows us her serious, thoughtful side, for instance, with the four-line poem titled "Surprise":

> I feel like the ground in winter,
> Hard, cold, dark, dead, unyielding . . .
> Then hope pokes through me
> Like a crocus.

And she shows us her funny side in the longer poem "Smart Remark," which she ends by comparing her sister to a caterpillar, her father to a spider, and her mother to a queen bee. She writes about her best friend Emily and about writing poems. She writes about the mean substitute teacher she had for one day, and about an old woman she has known all her life. Kate feels very deeply about all the things she experiences and writes these feelings for us to share.

If you've ever kept a private journal and then been required to write a daily journal for your teacher, you'll empathize with Kate when she tells about "My Journals." If you've ever had a friend with whom you've shared very special moments, you'll know what Kate means by "Not Enough Emilys." Sure, Kate is Canadian, Jewish, and a girl, but even if you aren't any of those things, you'll understand what Kate means in another poem, called "Yesterday":

> Yesterday I knew what was Right and what was Wrong.
> But today . . . everything's changing.
> Life is harder now . . . and yet easier . . .
> And more and more exciting!

Hey world, here's Kate!

—JoEllen Rice

High Wizardry   Grades 7–12
By Diane Duane

Dairine was smart—too smart to be Nita's little sister; too smart period. When she was three years old, she saw Nita come home crying from her first day of kindergarten because she hadn't known the answers to some of the questions that the teacher asked. Right then Dairine decided that *she* wasn't going to be like her sister. If she only knew enough, the world would lose its power to hurt her. So she began to learn everything there was to know, including the fact that her big sister was a wizard and she wasn't. That is, she wasn't until the day she found Nita's wizard's manual, opened it, looked through it, and then repeated the words of the Oath of Power. The silence that suddenly crashed down upon her for a moment didn't frighten Dairine—it exhilarated her: there was more to know, and she was going to be able to find it out!

But the next day she woke up in the same bed, in the same world she had gone to sleep in, and thought, "Nothing's happened—it's all still the same." But she was wrong, very wrong. Nothing would ever be the same again. That morning their new computer arrived, and while her parents were arguing over the manuals that came with it, Dairine plugged it in and turned it on. She knew that the first thing you do with a computer is to copy the systems disk onto the hard disk, so she used the copy command. And suddenly there on the desk beside the computer she was using was another computer, exactly like it. Dairine was horrified—her folks would kill her for messing with the new computer without permission. So she pulled up the directory again and found the Hide command. She punched the buttons on the keyboard frantically, and the copy-computer vanished, just as her father turned around to see her playing with the original. Within minutes, she was off to New York, with Nita and Kit, who was Nita's partner in wizardry, to see a new show at the Museum of Natural History.

But Dairine had no intention of staying with Nita and Kit, and she lost them as soon as she could. She went to a restroom, entered a stall, and locked the door behind her. Then she told the computer to reappear, having cued it to voice-only commands. And there it was.

A few minutes later, when Nita opened the restroom door looking for her sister, she stepped, not into the restroom, but onto the surface of Mars. Dairine was nowhere to be seen.

It wasn't just a computer. It was a wizard's manual on disk, with many of the safeguards removed and many of the commands simplified. Dairine had been heard by the Powers when she repeated the Oath, and her manual had found her the next morning. Now she was on her Ordeal, the test that all new wizards must undergo—a test far more difficult than those of any of the other wizards, for after all, Dairine was much smarter than most people, and she had the new computer and the software that could make her more powerful than any other wizard on Earth—or off it.

—*J. R. B.*

The Hitchhiking Vampire   Grades 5-9
By Stephen Mooser

My thirteenth birthday party was one I would never forget. Dad had
taken my sixteen-year-old brother Luke and me to one of the fanciest,
most expensive restaurants in San Diego. Unfortunately, Luke and I
both knew that Dad didn't have any money. I figured if we got out of
the Coronado with our skins that night, it would be a miracle.

Dad ordered lobster, caviar, the works—he was having a great time.
When he returned from a trip to the men's room, his fly was open, and
I had to remind him to zip it up. We were at one of the center tables,
so naturally after dinner he insisted that everyone in the restaurant join
in singing Happy Birthday to me. It was at this point that the manage-
ment presented the bill and asked us to leave—quietly. But of course
our Dad wouldn't leave without a fuss. Oh, no—he got really obnox-
ious and started bellowing. As he leapt to his feet the tablecloth he'd
accidentally zipped into his pants came with him, and with that tablecloth came all the glasses, dishes, and silverware, and a lot of food.

Luke and I made a run for it, but Dad got arrested. He was going to
be in jail for thirty days, so Luke and I packed up and headed for Utah.
It was on the road to Las Vegas that we picked up the hitchhiking vampire. My wild thirteenth birthday party was nothing compared to what
happened next.

—Marianne Tait Pridemore

Horror Movies   Grades 5-12
Movie Monsters
By Tom Powers

Horror. Fear. Menacing eyes that gleam as they focus on *you*, the
next victim. The smooth hands of the vampire as they reach hungrily
for the unwary. Or the ghastly realization that the disturbance beneath
the surface of the waves is not caused by happy swimmers but by a
monstrous shark, wheeling to attack its next victim.

Such is the stuff of horror movies, fantasy worlds so skillfully con-
trived that we find ourselves believing the unbelievable, even though
we know that the shark really is a robot and the werewolf a concoction
of synthetic fur, fake blood, and putty. Yet the stories behind some of
moviedom's most famous horror films are as fantastic as the creatures
themselves.

What actor would actually wear boots that weighed thirteen pounds *each* to play Frankenstein's monster? Boris Karloff, perhaps the most famous movie monster of them all. Bela Lugosi, the actor who played Count Dracula, was actually buried in the black cape he wore in the movie. Have you ever wondered how long it took to make some of the most famous horror scenes? The shower scene in *Psycho* runs forty-five seconds on the screen, but it took seven days to film.

Learn the secrets and discover what it takes to bring these blood-curdling stories to life, in *Horror Movies* and *Movie Monsters* by Tom Powers.

—Nancy L. Chu

House of Heroes   **Grade 10-Adult**
and Other Stories
By Mary La Chapelle

When you were a kid, did you ever make up silly superstitions? Step on a crack, break your mother's back! Getting out of bed wrong means the whole day will go wrong.

Ten-year-old Frances had lots of superstitions. After she got out of bed in the morning she had to walk through the hall with her eyes closed. When she found the attic door left open one summer morning, she was filled with dread—she knew that something terrible would happen that day.

It did. Her eight-year-old brother Jimmy wanted to play war. He was going to lead the troops (Frances) in taking control of an important bridge. Jimmy was hyperactive and epileptic. Frances would much rather have gone to the pool. She lagged too far behind and lost sight of her little brother as he ran toward the bluffs high above the Mississippi River. When Frances finally caught up with him, he was teetering semiconscious in midair on a narrow old iron beam.

Most of these stories leave the reader suspended, too. "House of Heroes" is narrated by the night counselor at a home for mentally ill and mentally retarded boys. Laura cares about the boys, hopes they'll make it eventually in the real world, but she gets discouraged sometimes and she's frightened by their violent reactions to their growing sexuality.

In "Faith," Tiffany is a troubled teen who crashes Catholic weddings. At one reception she forms a relationship with a psychologist who's as vulnerable as she is. "Anna in a Small Town" portrays the lifelong harassment of a nice but physically gigantic woman.

Misfits, struggling against the demands of society—can they ever succeed?

—Susan Rosenkoetter

How It Feels to Fight for Your Life   Grades 7-12
By Jill Krementz

If you were to meet Anton Broekman, Alisha Weissman, or Spencer Gray, you'd have no idea they were any different from you. And in most ways, they aren't. Ten-year-old Anton is a soccer whiz who is getting to be a pretty good defense man. Sixteen-year-old Alisha also loves sports and plays basketball, volleyball, and softball. Much of Spencer's time goes to Junior ROTC. That is, when he's not on dialysis, or receiving follow-up treatment for his kidney transplant.

Like Spencer, Alisha and Anton have had battles with serious illness. Anton has asthma; Alisha is an epileptic. They've all had to make their illnesses part of their lives—or die. They take the medications, visit the doctors, and sometimes can't do what other kids can. But they also go to school, have families, friends, favorite sports, hobbies—just like anyone else. Perhaps the way they are most different is in their conscious determination to keep on living. They have had to fight for their lives on a daily basis, and they all know that the one sure way to lose is to give up—so they don't. Meet these kids and discover how it feels to fight for your life.

—Nancy L. Chu and J. R. B.

How Many Spots Does a Leopard Have? Grades 3-6
By Julius Lester

"Long before this time we call today, and before that time called yesterday, and even before 'What time is it?' the world wasn't like it is now." No, it was a time of curiosity, of questions like, Why do dogs chase cats? Why do monkeys live in trees? and How many spots does a leopard have? People all over the world have puzzled over these mysteries and told stories to try to explain them.

In *How Many Spots Does a Leopard Have?* you'll find tales of crafty animals and cruel monsters, quick-witted, brave heroes and dastardly cowards, tales that give you the answers to all those questions about why animals are the way they are today.

—Pamela A. Todd

Hurray for Ali Baba Bernstein   Grades 3-4
By Johanna Hurwitz

When David Bernstein was 9 years, 4 months, and 12 days old, he told his parents, teacher, and classmates to call him Ali Baba. He liked his new name: it set him apart from all those other Davids in his class. There were a lot of Davids, but there was only one Ali Baba.

On the Friday morning in September that Ali Baba was 9 years, 4 months, and 17 days old, his fourth-grade class was scheduled to make a trip to the public library. But Ali Baba had forgotten to bring his library card to school that morning. No problem—while the class was walking to the library, he would dodge away, take a short cut back to his apartment building, pick up his card, and rejoin the group before the teacher missed him. There was just one small flaw in his plan: by the time he got to the library the whole class was inside, and the door was locked!

On the day that Ali Baba was 9 years, 4 months, and 29 days old, he had to find out just what, exactly, Mr. Salmon did for a living. Ali Baba's father had said Mr. Salmon was a CPA. What did that mean? Mr. Salmon acted so strange and sneaky, he had to be some kind of secret agent!

On the Tuesday in November that Ali Baba was 9 years, 5 months, and 28 days old, he and his mother went shopping. On that day he met the underwear king, the egg-roll king, and the donut king; went to the Sweater Palace and ate at the China Castle. Ali Baba hadn't known there was so much royalty in the world, let alone in New York City!

On the Sunday that Ali Baba was 9 years, 11 months, and 4 days old, his best friend Roger invited him to go to the circus. Great! But then Roger called back to say his mom couldn't find the tickets she had bought. Not so great. And the only way Ali Baba and Roger can solve the mystery of the missing circus tickets is by untangling the raincoat mystery.

But after all, Ali Baba has already faced a locked library door, a mysterious CPA, and His Majesty the underwear king. Surely he can make it to the circus! To see if he does, you'll just have to read *Hurray for Ali Baba Bernstein*.

—*Betty A. Holtzen*

Husband Is the Past Tense of Daddy,   Adult
and Other Dispatches from the Front Lines of Motherhood
By Teryl Zarnow

Consider this book a survival manual for adults living in the precarious AC (after children) time period, specifically the years between breast-feeding and first grade. After all, parents, especially those fighting in the infant and toddler trenches, need to hear the reassuring message that others have been through these skirmishes too, and most have even survived to tell about it. Or write about it, as Teryl Zarnow does.

Zarnow's book provides the perfect pep-talk for a battle-fatigued parent. As an experienced veteran of six years of parenthood herself, she can sympathize with all the feelings of her fellow combatants, including the occasional urge to desert the battle altogether. What beleagured parent wouldn't empathize with this description of combat fatigue: "When it comes to having more children, I think it's time for me to stop. The other morning I left them all peacefully upstairs while I went outside to get the newspaper. Moments later the crescendo of their screams, pouring out the open window, shattered the early morning peace. I had this tremendous urge to wrap my bathrobe tightly about me, muster my dignity while I still could, and just keep going."

She didn't, of course. And the reason is simple: these things too shall pass—and all too quickly. The Mommy Years are really very short in the total span of parenthood. As Zarnow puts it: "I will always be a mother . . . but I will not always be a mommy. A mommy can heal owies with a kiss; a mom calls the doctor. A mommy takes walks with her children; a mom chauffeurs them in the car. A mommy gets kisses for no apparent reason; a mom must ask for them when nobody is looking."

Mommies, like the one who wrote this book and the ones who will read it in between washing clothes, diapering infants, and chasing down escaping toddlers, will recognize themselves in these anecdotes. A few years later, now moms instead of mommies, they can read this again and enjoy the memories.

—Margie Reitsma

I Feel Like the Morning Star   Grades 7–12
By Gregory Maguire

Buried alive!

Are Ella, Mart, and Sorb truly buried alive? That's not the way the elders of the Pioneer Colony see it. They would rather think of the colony as a survival community, a refuge from nuclear war. The people of the Colony were driven underground in the middle years of the twenty-first century, and they've stayed there ever since.

But Sorb has strange dreams, dreams that keep coming back. Can it be that by not drinking the larmer drug he is seeing the Colony for what it really is? His two friends, Ella and Mart, don't have these dreams. They don't get a trapped feeling whenever they think of the ice-wall barrier, and what (*what*?) lies beyond it.

Now, it's a known fact that no one can question the judgment of the elders—Garner Jones' death two years ago proved that. But as the days pass, Sorb becomes more and more obsessed by his dreams. He cannot shake off the feeling that he must be the risk-taker, or else grow up to be a zombie like Mem Dora or the Elder St. Gabriel. So Sorb dares to raise the question to the council, and for that he receives the same electro-chemical therapy that Garner Jones received. But Sorb is a little luckier—he survives the cure.

Ella and Mart are torn between loyalty to the Colony and loyalty to Sorb. They would like to believe, as he does, that the tunnels to the surface are still passable, but the elders say those tunnels collapsed long ago.

Sometimes trust in a friend is hard to hold on to. Can they trust Sorb's dreams? Dreams that say, Your whole world is artificial, built on fear, maintained by lies? Join Ella and Mart as they test the strength of that trust, and the truth of Sorb's dreams.

—Pam Swafford and J. R. B.

I Hate Your Guts, Ben Brooster!   Grades 3–6
By Eth Clifford

Charlie Andrews, aged eleven, had been looking forward to summer vacation until his mother spoke those dreadful words at breakfast: "Your cousin Ben Brooster will be here tomorrow." And what was so dreadful about that? Oh, nothing—except that Ben was only nine, had spent most of his life in Japan, and would be sharing Charlie's roon for a whole year. Plus he was a genius, especially at getting into trouble.

Once Ben arrived, things went from bad to worse. To find out the connection between the mixed-up suitcases, the stuffed pillow embroidered with "Mothers come and mothers go, but I go on forever," and the last, final, and only will of Barney Bangam (complete with a riddle about hidden treasure), read *I Hate Your Guts, Ben Brooster!*

—*Mary K. Hobson*

If I Never Get Back   Grade 10–Adult
By Darryl Brock

One moment I was stretching my legs at the Amtrak station, somewhere in the middle of nowhere; the next, I was lying on the platform—and when I got up and looked for my train, the silver Amtrak cars were gone, and in their place was an old black steam locomotive pulling a string of wooden coaches. I couldn't figure it out—maybe someone was making a movie, maybe I'd been out longer than just a minute or two. Then I heard someone calling me: "Hey, come on! Get on, it's pulling out!" "You talking to me?" "Are you from Cleveland?" "Yeah." "Well, come on aboard, I've got your ticket right here—we've been waiting for you!"

And with that, Sam Fowler's adventure in the 1860s begins, a hundred years before he was born. He's gone from 1989 to 1869 in one small step. He's no longer a reporter for the *San Francisco Chronicle*, divorced, with two daughters that he hardly sees and a bottle that keeps that loss from hurting too much. He's a member of the first professional baseball team, the Cincinnati Reds, with no time or need for a bottle. In fact, since he's also become one of the Red Stockings' substitute players, the uppermost thing in his mind is learning the differences between the baseball he played growing up and the game as it's played now, in 1869—and there *are* a few differences: the bunt doesn't exist, no one uses a mitt to catch, and the scoreboard hasn't been invented yet.

And worst of all for Sam, no one sells food at the games—no popcorn, hot dogs, hamburgers, or fries—nothing, except beer. So Sam makes a deal with the manager to spend his spare time hustling money for the club, which is badly in debt. He invents hamburgers, hot dogs, french fries, ice cream sodas—and the money comes rolling in! Sam is a man who changes history, in more ways than you might expect. And on the way he has some almost unbelievable adventures, one of which begins when he meets the man he was named for, Samuel Langhorn Clemens—the author Mark Twain. Sam also takes on one of the most vicious hit men of all time and falls in love with a beautiful but quite unavailable lady.

But can he ever go back? Taste pizza again, take a hot shower, ride
in a plane or even in a car? How long can a twentieth-century urban
man survive in the world of 1869? How long can that world survive?
Read *If I Never Get Back* and find out.

—*J. R. B.*

Illuminations   Grades 3–9
By Jonathan Hunt

Illuminations—the delicate, colorful artwork used by medieval
scribes to make the books they copied by hand beautiful. In the margins
and around the capital letters, imps play and angels sing, knights stroll
with their ladies, and small animals peep out from behind the leaves
and flowers. Unicorns may appear; these mysterious, magical creatures
were much sought after, because their horns had the power to heal.

Discover unicorns and much, much more as you wander through
this illuminated medieval alphabet.

—*Carol Kappelmann and J. R. B.*

In Lane Three, Alex Archer   Grades 10–12
By Tessa Duder

Everyone envies Alex Archer. At fifteen, she has everything going for
her. She looks like a model—tall and sleek, with chiseled features that
would be called handsome or striking rather than baby-doll pretty. Her
grades are tops, partly because of intelligence but also because of
dogged hard work and a competitive bent that few adults possess, much
less teenagers. But those parts of Alex's life are not what make her the
focus of her country's attention.

Alex is a world-class swimmer and New Zealand's best hope to win
gold medals at the 1960 Olympic Games in Rome. Her need to be The
Best pushes her through predawn practice sessions, endurance training,
and time trials that would dull the edge of seasoned athletes. Until a
few months ago, no one could come close to Alex in talent and stami-
na—until Maggie Benton showed herself to be Alex's equal, and in
some cases her better.

On top of the threat of real competition, Alex must deal with difficult
new feelings. Maggie lives for swimming and nothing else, even training
with the world-famous Australian team. Alex has always craved the water like a dolphin and is sustained by competition the way other people

are sustained by food or oxygen. But other interest are pressing on her now—her studies, which could lead to a law career, her love of drama and music, her need for friends.

Can Alex Archer have all these thing and continue the heartbreaking pace that is required of Olympic-class swimmers? Can anyone?

—*Nancy L. Chu*

In the Forest   Grade 3–Adult
By Jim Arnosky

Have you ever looked into a painting—I mean really looked? And just for a moment felt the cool, crisp air of the morning, or that shaft of warm sunlight through the trees of the forest, or the give of the spongey earth beneath your feet? Or maybe just for a moment you could hear the deer rustle in the bushes.

In this book, Jim Arnosky takes you on an adventure of heightened awareness in the forest. You discover the ever-changing colors of the sunset, the fir stand, and the beaver pond. You sense the majesty of the great white pine and feel the stillness of the copse and the playfulness of the streams. You see the shy animals—the fox, the deer, and the lynx—which inhabit different parts of the forest. Look at the paintings, and let yourself walk in the forest.

—*Cara A. Waits*

It Was on Fire   Adult
When I Lay Down on It
By Robert Fulghum

Remember when you were a kid and had to take something to school for Show-and-Tell? Or the last time one of your own kids came home with tales of what someone else had brought?

Maybe you think you're too old for that now—but Robert Fulghum wouldn't agree. He thinks we're never too old for Show-and-Tell. In fact, that's how he describes his new book. He says that he's showing us a collection of the stuff that's filled his life—marriages and parenting; traveling and meditating; climbing trees and singing "Jingle Bells"; weeping and laughing (but especially laughing). And while he's showing us these things, he's also telling us why they're so special—special enough to share.

If someone tells you that this book is a collection of essays, don't believe them. "Essay" sounds much too finished and complete for what Fulghum has in mind. Instead, the stories and thoughts in this book reflect the ongoing, moving, doing and redoing aspects of the human condition, which won't be finished until life itself is finished.

Maybe that's why Fulghum says that we're never too old for Show-and-Tell. Because we're never too old to try something, fail, and try again. Or to learn from someone else. We're never too old to share.

So go ahead and relax for an evening. Enjoy Fulghum's newest Show-and-Tell. And then share it with a friend. That's what I did.

—*Margie Reitsma*

Jack   Grade 10–Adult
By A. M. Homes

Jack is the kind of guy who wants everyone to be happy, including himself. He's trying to maintain his sense of humor despite the fact that his life is totally typical: he's fifteen years old and can't work up the nerve to ask a girl out; his best friend is crazy, and his parents are divorced. Then one day Jack is thrown one of life's little curves. His father tells him he's in love again—with another man. Jack's father is gay. What now?

—*Kaite Mediatore*

Janie's Private Eyes   Grades 5–9
By Zilpha Keatley Snyder

Hi, I'm David Stanley. Maybe you remember me and my family from Zilpha Keatley Snyder's other books: *The Headless Cupid, The Famous Stanley Kidnapping Case*, and *Blair's Nightmare*. If not, it doesn't matter, because you'll get to know us very well in this story.

Some of the townspeople of Steven's Corners wished they hadn't gotten to know us at all after our New Year's Eve party. That's when my ten-year-old sister Janie tried to use a hidden tape recorder to obtain clues about a murder she thought had taken place in our town. She accidently played the tape back over the stereo system, so it was broadcast to the whole party. She hadn't recorded any murder clues, but all the guests did hear the bank president's wife making nasty comments about them. After that incident, even though she is so smart and loves making deductions and solving mysteries, Dad told Janie she absolutely could not do any more detective work. That only slowed her down.

You see, she's got my six-year-old twin brother and sister, Blair and Esther, helping her as private eyes. Now, as you'll soon learn, Blair can sometimes tell what's going to happen in the future. He doesn't say much about this talent, so we don't understand just how it works yet. And Esther has her own ideas about the way things should be.

That's how we all got mixed up in the real mystery in our town—who was stealing all the dogs? Esther has these friends, Thuy and Huy Tran. They're Vietnamese kids, and some of the people started thinking their family was kidnapping the dogs. Esther knew they weren't doing it, and she got us all involved in proving the Tran family's innocence. Even our stepsister Amanda helped with the investigations.

Would you believe that all five of us kids ended up being arrested and taken to jail? We were trying to trap the dognappers in the town park when a policeman stumbled upon us. Read *Janie's Private Eyes* to learn how we got out of that situation, and who had really been stealing the dogs.

—*Lenna Lea Wiebe*

Jason Cosmo   Grade 10–Adult
By Dan McGirt

Jason Cosmo woke up one morning and discovered that he had become famous overnight (or perhaps infamous would be the more appropriate term). Instead of the nondescript woodcutter from Little Hicknittle that he'd been when he'd gone to bed, Jason woke up as a dreaded and dangerous demon-warrior, with a ten-million-crown bounty on his head. And he couldn't undo the transformation because he had no idea what had caused it in the first place. Although he still felt exactly the same as he had when he was Jason Cosmo the woodcutter, everyone else now saw him as some kind of bloodthirsty criminal.

Everyone, that is, except Mercury Boltblaster, a renegade master magician whom Jason had met when he was fleeing the bounty hunters. Mercury was also a fugitive. The Dark Magic Society, a band of evil magicians who wanted to conquer the world, was after him, and so was the League of Benevolent Magic, a society of good magicians who were trying to save the world from their evil colleagues. So far, Mercury had managed to elude both groups. Being somewhat of a nonconformist, he really preferred to remain an independent free-lancer.

That's why he decided to take Jason under his protection. According to Mercury's wizardly reasoning, the wildfire rumors about the criminal Jason Cosmo and the ten-million-crown bounty had to be a cover-up for a much bigger plot. Jason must be the vital link in some scheme to conquer the entire Eleven Kingdoms! Why else would all these people be chasing him? Why else would two different magic societies be desperate for Mercury's help?

And then there was the little matter of Jason's aura. From an aura, which was invisible to everyone but a magician, you could tell a person's magical power level, emotional state, and general importance. As a magician, Mercury could usually read an aura quite easily. But Jason's was written in a language Mercury had never seen before—a language that looked like some sort of ancient, secret code. All the more reason to suspect that something major was afoot. Why would the gods have chosen to give an ancient, secret aura to a simple woodcutter, unless he had a very important mission?

But when Mercury explained all this to Jason, he could tell that his companion had no idea what he was talking about. If Jason *did* have a mission to save the world, he obviously knew nothing about it. And unless they could find out what was going on soon, Mercury suspected that they weren't even going to be able to save themselves.

—Margie Reitsma

Journey   Grade 7–Adult
By James A. Michener

Just how far will Lord Evelyn Luton go to pursue his adventurous goal, to reach the "tons of gold" in the Klondike? Luton selects his crew with skill. Harry, an old friend and seasoned adventurer, is a must. Philip, Luton's nephew, is more than game to accompany his uncle. Blythe, the aspiring poet, sees this as a romantic adventure. And Fogarty, Luton's "ghillie" or farmhand, is selected as the muscle to serve the crew.

Luton's route will be like no other, to avoid at all cost touching American soil. And there's the rub—the near-Arctic Canadian route means a perilous journey that perhaps none of these Englishmen will survive.

—Barbara Diment

Journey   Grades 5–9
By Joyce Carol Thomas

Meggie Alexander is sixteen, and something is happening to the teenagers in her town. They have been disappearing, but now one of her missing classmates has been found—dead. Teenagers are warned not to go out at night, especially not to Meggie's favorite park, the Eucalyptus Forest, where many of the teens have vanished. The police are mystified; they don't seem to have a clue, and Meggie, feeling caged in, wants to investigate on her own. However, her probing soon tumbles her into the lab of a mad doctor—as his latest victim! Will she ever return to live as Meggie Alexander, or will her body be used in one of his evil experiments?

—*Faye A. Powell*

The Journey: Grade 7–Adult
Japanese Americans, Racism, and Renewal
By Sheila Hamanaka

Auschwitz, Bergen-Belsen, Buchenwald. Concentration camps whose reputations for misery have lived well past the time of their evil purposes. Add to those names others perhaps less familiar: Manzanar, Topaz, Heart Mountain, Tule Lake. These were also concentration camps, hastily built during World War II to imprison persons considered dangerous to the government and the war effort. But these were not Nazi death camps where Jews were persecuted. These camps were located in the United States, and they were designed to imprison persons of Japanese ancestry.

Persons of all ages were herded into these camps—some who were as little as one-sixteenth Japanese. Men, women, small children, the elderly, even orphan infants were packed into waterless, tar-paper shacks. Many had been born in the United States. They owned businesses, farms, and were proudly raising their families in America. Now their possessions and land were gone, auctioned off for pennies while the former owners stood behind barbed-wire fences and faced the rifle barrels of the soldiers who guarded them and would shoot them if they carelessly ventured too close to the fence. After all, who knew what traitors lurked there?

A long battle for a safe and dignified life seemed doomed to end in humiliation, perhaps even death. But *The Journey* is not yet over—how will it end?

—*Nancy L. Chu*

Junglerama   Grades 3-9
By Vicki Grove

TJ thought that the old trailer would be a good place to hide out from all the shouting going on at home. Mike's new home was a lot more crowded than his old one, so the trailer would be like his own private place. Easy was pretty much on his own all the time, but the colorful pictures on the side of the trailer reminded him of the jungle and the voodoo his uncle talked about. The boys made great plans to turn this old trailer into a traveling wild animal show. They'd call it the Junglerama! They started working on their plan by catching snakes and lizards in the woods behind the trailer.

But their plans were interrupted. TJ's little sister disappeared. Was this old witch-lady that the children called "the toytaker" responsible? After all, they said she took toys to lure children into her house, where she'd change them into other things. There was a lot of weirdness going on, all over town. And it all started the summer the carnival left behind that old trailer—the *Junglerama*.

—Frances W. Levin

Just Friends   Grades 7-12
By Norma Klein

Senior year, and back with my friends. Andria was smug and settled with her lifetime boyfriend. Lois was her usual kind and wispy self. And Kelli was ready for the next "flavor-of-the-month."

"Who're you aiming for this year?" I asked her. "Stuart?"

"Should I? Is he my type?"

Stuart was one of the few presentable guys that she hadn't latched onto, perhaps because Stuart and I were friends. We always had been, from way back in preschool. His mom even moved to an apartment close to ours, and he was like my adopted brother.

"Do I have your permission then?" Kelli asked. "You know, Gregory Arrington would be a great match for you, Iz. So intelligent and literary."

Gregory was *not* my type, and Stuart and I were just friends—we'd never been what you'd call a "hot item." So why did I already regret cluing Kelli about Stuart?

*Isabel and I have always been friends. I can talk to her about any-
thing. And Mom's such a flake that it's great to go over to Isabel's place
and feel like a natural part of a normal family scene.*

*You may wonder why I, Stuart, a reasonably bright, OK-looking guy,
don't have a main squeeze. I'm not 100% pure, but I'm not head-over-
heels about anyone either. Iz? She's warm, open, fun—the best girl I
know. But we're just friends.*

Friends are special. They're *never* "just friends". . . .

—*Lesley S. J. Farmer*

Just Like a Friend   **Grades 5–8**
By Marilyn Sachs

Did you ever wish you got along better with your mother? Do you
look up to her, think that she's pretty, wish that you could be just like
her?

Patti and her mother Vi are just like sisters. They look alike and have
many of the same interests. They love to go shopping together, plan
parties, listen to music, dance, and flirt. But best of all, they can really
talk. Patti feels like she can tell Vi anything. Maybe it's because they're
so close in age—Vi got married and had Patti when she was only sixteen
years old.

But now everything's changed. Patti's father wasn't feeling well one
evening, and Patti suddenly awoke at 4:15 a.m. when she heard him in
the living room. He was pale and frightened, and he clutched his chest.

"'Call an ambulance, Patti,' he said. 'Right away'

"I wanted to scream for help when he said that. I wanted to run and
get—who? Somebody who would know what to do, because I was only
a kid and I was scared.

"'Heart attack,' Daddy was whispering. 'Hurry, Patti.'"

Patti knew there was nobody else to handle this. Vi would just get
hysterical and go to pieces, so it was better to let her stay asleep. Patti
gritted her teeth and made the call, but it was the longest twelve minutes of her life, waiting for the ambulance to come.

Now everything's changed. Patti can't stand to be compared to Vi—
beautiful, sweet, delicate Violet, who can't handle anything. Patti wants
to be respected for her strength and intelligence, not just liked because
she's pretty. How can she make her family and friends understand her
feelings?

—*Susan R. Farber*

Kareem   Grade 10–Adult
By Kareem Abdul-Jabbar and Mignon McCarthy

Take a look inside the world of professional basketball through the eyes of legendary center Kareem Abdul-Jabbar. Go along with him on his last run through the long NBA season, the 1988–89 campaign with the defending champion Los Angeles Lakers. Kareem takes you from fall training camp to the NBA finals in late spring. Get a rare look at the behind-the-scenes world of the Lakers, meet superstars such as Magic Johnson, James Worthy, and Jerry West. It was a year of sell-out crowds and the dramatic push for a third consecutive world championship; of highs and lows; of emotional farewells around the league, beginning in New York's Madison Square Garden and ending with a last good-bye in the L. A. Forum; of a consummate athlete facing the ultimate challenge of ending his career on par with his own reputation and standards of excellence. *Kareem* is a glimpse into the heart and soul of a champion—a basketball immortal's farewell to the game.

—Barbara Bahm

The Kid Who Ran for Principal   Grades 5–9
By Judy Morris

Bonnie was a good girl. She never did anything she shouldn't do, or anything that would make people angry. So how did she end up running for principal of her school? You can't stay squeaky-clean and run a political campaign. You can't keep all those campaign promises you made if you weren't thinking when you made them. And most of all, you can't please everybody if you decide to do what's right for you. Bonnie has never really had to stand up to peer pressure—she's always just gone along. Now she discovers what it means to do what *she* thinks is right, no matter what anyone says—her parents, her teachers or *even* her friends.

—J. R. B.

Knight in Shining Armor   Grade 10–Adult
By Jude Deveraux

It was more horrible, more unbelievable than Douglass' worst nightmares. She watched Robin and Gloria drive away, her purse dangling from Gloria's outstretched hand so Douglass couldn't miss seeing it. She turned, sobbing, and stumbled back into the small seventeenth-century church and collapsed on the floor, leaning against the tomb of a young knight. The effigy on the tomb showed a handsome face and a strong body clothed in armor.

Douglass cried and cried. She couldn't believe Robin had deserted her, had believed his fat, spoiled, spotty daughter instead of her. He loved her—or did he? She'd been sure that one day they would be married. And now he was gone, believing all Gloria's lies, taking her only suitcase and her purse with him. She was completely alone in the English countryside, with no passport, no identification, no money, no plane ticket home, nothing. She would have to call her family collect to rescue her—again! And that meant that they'd have one more story to add to all the others they had been telling for years about her faults, her failures, her endless problems, and all the times she'd had to be rescued from one mess after another.

Thinking of what she'd lost and what she would have to go through to get home again, Douglass' sobs redoubled, and far away, across hundreds of years, a dark-haired man looked up from the letter he was trying to write. Who was that woman crying? Why didn't someone comfort her, or at least make her be quiet? He covered an ear with his free hand and went back to his letter. But the crying continued, louder and louder—it was impossible to ignore.

And in the church, Douglass realized she was leaning against a knight's tomb. "That's what I really need," she thought bitterly. "A knight in shining armor—someone to take care of me, someone who will want to please me, instead of me trying to please him all the time."

Suddenly the very air in the church seemed to shimmer, and when she looked up, there he was. A knight, a real knight, drawn from the seventeenth century by her tears, come to rescue her. "What have you done to me, witch? How come I hence?" Even angry, which he undoubtedly was, the man was incredibly handsome—dark hair, blue eyes, his body clad in shining silver armor inlaid with gold.

Douglass had wished for a knight—a knight in shining armor—and now she had one. But what was she going to do with a seventeenth-century nobleman who firmly believed that she was a witch and who had *not* traveled all this way through time to comfort her and dry her tears?

It's a love story, about a love that overcomes the constraints of time and space, and makes you wonder if maybe love really can last forever!

—J. R. B.

Knights   Grade 5–Adult
By Julek Heller and Deirdre Headon

For those who liked to eat and eat well, the age of the knights was pure pleasure. A feast might begin at ten in the morning and go on until after dark, through as many as fifteen elaborate courses—a roast peacock, for instance, served with all its feathers in place so that it looked almost alive, whole suckling pigs, fine wines, and pies from which live birds emerged, only to be seized by the knights' falcons, which came to the feast with their masters. Tables were lavishly and precisely set, for guests gauged their status by the seating arrangements, and protocol determined the placement of everything from the salt cellars to the aquamaniles (these were vessels in the shape of a knight or a monster, containing perfumed water for hand-washing). Although knives and forks were available, most food was eaten with fingers. Plates were licked clean. The knights ate with enormous enthusiasm and with little regard for the mess that resulted, so the aquamaniles were essential! And there was plenty to enjoy besides the food—no feast would have been complete without entertainment by singers, jugglers, and acrobats.

Such revelry helped pass the dull winter days between campaigns and crusades, and was one of the greatest pleasures of the knight's life. What were some of the other pleasures? Knights lived as lavishly as they dined. Discover who they were and how they lived in *Knights*.
—*Carol Kappelmann*

Landing on Marvin Gardens   Grades 5–9
Rona S. Zable

Things could be worse, Katie thinks, but she's not sure how much worse, since things are pretty rotten now. Katie and her mother were forced to move out of their apartment when the building went condo and they couldn't afford to buy. They had to move in with Aunt Rose, Katie's mother's older sister—twenty-five years older. Aunt Rose is neat, nosy, and a nag. She's making Katie's new life miserable. Katie can't *wait* to move out of her aunt's house, but it doesn't look like that will happen anytime soon. So Katie keeps her body out of the house and her mind off Aunt Rose by focusing on her schoolwork, on the upcoming essay contest, and on catching the eye of that cute Chris McConnell. But Aunt Rose can ruin anything. She interrupts Katie when she's studying, she has *lots* of suggestions for essay topics, and she embarrasses Katie every time they run into Chris. It takes an old friend, another victim of the housing crunch, to show Katie that her life isn't quite as awful as she thinks.

—*Kaite Mediatore*

The Last Dinosaur   Grade 3–Adult
By Jim Murphy

Why did the dinosaurs disappear? Scientists speculate on the reasons. Some believe it was a deadly disease. Others think a giant comet crashed into the earth, making a huge cloud of dust that blocked the sun so that the temperature of the earth suddenly dropped. Whether it was a change in the climate, a shortage of food, or an epidemic of sickness, the dinosaurs disappeared, leaving only their fossils to tell their story. What would it have been like to be the last of a breed? To know that you were truly alone in the world? We can never really know how it was, but in this book you can discover how it might have been.

Three Triceratops wander through the forest in search of food. But suddenly they're stopped by the pungent smell of smoke. Knowing it means danger, they flee. When the smell is gone and she feels safe, the female searches for a nesting spot to deposit her eggs. She finds a warm, sandy area where she builds a nest and lays fifteen eggs. She stays close to protect her eggs from the clumsy males and other, egg-eating creatures.

But two days later, the smell of smoke returns and with it a hungry Tyrannosaurus Rex who challenges the three Triceratops. The two males die fighting (and mortally wounding) the enemy, but the fire is coming closer and the female must flee, leaving her eggs behind. She is alone now, separated from both her nest and her companions. Will she find other dinosaurs, or is she now the only one left—the very last of the dinosaurs?

—*Susan Wolfe*

Learning How to Fall   Grades 10–12
By Norma Klein

Knowing how to fall is the most important thing you can learn in life—knowing how to fall, and knowing that you can survive and go on. But before you discover how to survive, there's the fall, that time when you feel worse then wishing you were dead—you feel like you already *are* dead, and there's nothing and no one that can make you feel alive again.

That's where Dusty is right now. His father had him put in a mental institution because he didn't like what Dusty and his girlfriend Star were doing when he came home and found them in bed together. And as soon as Star heard about the institution, she dumped Dusty. She said he was too intense and they were bad for each other.

Dusty gradually begins to recover, and then in one crazy moment, betrays everything he has begun to believe in, including himself. He thought he knew how to fall. He thought he knew how to survive. But when you betray yourself and all that you are, it may be the final fall—the one without a parachute. The one you can't survive.

—J. R. B.

Leave the Cooking to Me   Grades 5-8
By Judie Angell

Fifteen-year-old Shirley has a problem—her mother. It's not that there's anything major wrong with Shirley's mom. Mrs. Merton's a successful lawyer, doesn't have a drinking or drug problem, doesn't beat her kids, and she's basically nice. It's just that she wants to be sure that Shirley and her younger sister keep their noses to the grindstone, learn to be responsible, and widen their horizons in the process. That would be simple, if only she didn't watch over them so closely and insist on approving everything they want to do—including Shirley's summer job. Shirley's a super cook, and she wants to run a catering business. So she invents "Vanessa." "Vanessa" is her alias, so she can run her catering business without her mother's knowledge. That way she can keep her mother from knowing everything she's doing during summer vacation. If Mrs. Merton should happen to answer the phone and someone asks for "Vanessa," she will think that it's a wrong number. But if Shirley answers the phone it won't be the wrong number, it *will* be "Vanessa."

Running a catering business isn't exactly easy, especially when you have to hide flour and sugar in with your clean underwear. And keeping Vanessa's Catering a secret from her mom is just part of Shirley's summer. She also has to convince Terry Peltz, the school's number-one jock and the answer to a schoolgirl's prayer, that waiting tables is not "woman's work." She needs his muscles and his car for deliveries. But it turns out to be easy to persuade him to work for Vanessa's the entire summer, after he discovers that older women will gawk and drool over him just like the high school girls. And there are other crises, too—one right after another. Like the time she's going to serve a mousse in the shape of a clown's head, and at the very last minute discovers that it's lost its shape because of the heat. But she takes a chance, renames it, serves it anyway, and gets rave reviews. Then there's the spoon wrapped with celery and caught in the garbage disposal; the host who doesn't have a table, chairs, or dishes; and the race to clean up the kitchen when Shirley's mom arrives home unexpectedly. And those are only a few of the things that happen to Shirley that summer, as she tries to fool her mother and run a business—at the same time!

—*Sandra Carpenter*

LeMond: **Grade 9–Adult**
The Incredible Comeback of an American Hero
By Samuel Abt

Imagine yourself riding at top speed on a racing bike. Your lungs are burning, your calf muscles are tied in knots. Your back aches from the way you lean over the handlebars. You want to sit up in the saddle, just to stretch, but you don't dare; you'd lose precious seconds. So you stay with the pack, riding elbow to elbow across flatlands, up long slow hills, careening around the curves of a mountain pass. This is the Tour de France—you've trained hard to be here, but now the strain is just too much. The beautiful countryside is just a blur. You wonder if you're going to "bonk"—slow down, drop back, drop out.

Then you look down and see your reason for being here. You're wearing the yellow jersey! Suddenly you're alert again—you earned the privilege of wearing the leader's yellow by winning the previous day's leg of the race. That jersey means instant recognition! Spectators along the way will be craning their necks to catch a glimpse of you and their other heroes as you go hurtling though the villages along the way. You breathe in your new-found strength and pump a little harder. Your competitors want that jersey too, and they are waiting for you to show the first sign of fatigue, looking for you to falter so they can challenge you for the lead. You concentrate. Will someone dynamite the race—that is, set an impossibly fast pace, daring you to keep up and risk burning out? Or will your teammates do their job and dog the competition to allow you to surge to a bigger lead by the end of the day's leg? That's how teams are designed—to help the strongest member—and that's how it has worked all season, in the sprints, in the time trials, and in the big races in Holland, Italy, and Spain.

The Tour has been going on for almost three weeks, and now you think ahead to the last day of the race—the long frantic stretch from Versailles to Paris, and the last mad dash through the streets to emerge on the Champs-Elysées, the sprint to the finish line as half a million people cheer.

This is the world of big-money, high-pressure European cycling that Greg Le Mond stepped into in 1978. An American, joining the strict, traditional fraternity of cyclists? Greg knew that he didn't exactly fit in. He knew the road would be rough. But he had broken molds before, and he was willing to try.

Why would this personable young man leave the warm, secure sunshine of California to greet the cold gray dawn in an unheated flat in Belgium? Even before his first argument with his new landlady, Greg hit the streets for his daily workout—a sixty-mile training ride!

His wife Kathy says Greg went to Europe because of his determination. Greg says he wanted to challenge his skills. Greg's Dutch masseur Jacome taps his chest and explains that the key to Greg's success is his extraordinary cardio-vascular system—a gift, Jacome calls it: a heart that beats forty-one times a minute at rest, and that pumps so efficiently under stress that fatigue and pain set in much later in Greg's body than in the normal competitive athlete's.

Whatever the reason, during the decade of the eighties, Greg Le-Mond captured the respect of the racing community and the admiration of the world. He won several big races, including the Tour de France.

Greg has had to face some hurdles, though. The business end of racing has never been easy—so often one feels like the pawn of corporate sponsors. Bruised feelings among teammates have been difficult to avoid, but that's the nature of an aggressive sport where people ride in teams but the glory of victory belongs to one individual. Most devastating, though, was a hunting accident which almost cost Greg his life. His recovery was so slow and painful that sometimes he thought he'd never make it. This is the story of twelve absolutely unbelievable years in the life of Greg LeMond, the Sun King, and *Sports Illustrated*'s 1989 Sportsman of the Year.

—*Mark Anderson*

Let Me Tell You Everything: Grades 7–12
Memoirs of a Lovesick Intellectual
By Barbara Bottner

How much of yourself should you change for the person you love? Especially when what *you are* doesn't seem to attract the slightest response!

Brogan tries to dazzle Rowland with her brilliant classroom discussion and her sharp awareness of feminist issues. But handsome Rowland only has eyes for gorgeous Rosanna. Brogan knows she should hold onto her beliefs no matter what, but Rowland makes her want to "slip into something comfortable" and forget the ERA. Is Rowland worth all this anguish? Why won't he notice her mind? After all, he *is* her social studies teacher!

—*Kaite Mediatore*

Life and Death: Grade 10–Adult
The Story of a Hospital
By Ina Yalof

Meet the Studs Terkel of Columbia Presbyterian Hospital of New York [show jacket photo]. Skillfully editing and sequencing interviews with seventy-four hospital employees, from a laundress to the medical school president, Ina Yalof provides a rare and human look behind the stone walls of medicine.

Columbia Presbyterian is one of the largest hospitals in the United States. There are 2,000 doctors there and 1,600 nurses. In 1987 alone, more than 133,000 people walked or were wheeled or were carried through the doors of the emergency room.

The hospital was founded in 1872 by James Lenox, a businessman and philanthropist. A doctor friend of his was helping a critically-ill black servant and couldn't find an adequate hospital that would admit her. Furious, he told Lenox that New York needed a hospital that was "broad enough to admit patients without regard to color or creed." And that was the beginning.

Ina Yalof describes a scene in the hospital's busy emergency room which captures the spirit of the staff—and the book. A heavy-set grandmother was rushed in to the doctors, leaving behind a slim little girl. Hands clasped and eyes anxious, she couldn't wait forever. She tentatively whispered to a guard, "Mister, my grandmother was supposed to buy me McDonald's. Could you go in there, please, and tell her to come out?" Realizing the situation, the guard knelt down to meet the little girl eye to eye. Pulling out some change and pointing to the hospital coffee shop, he said, "Your grandmother wants you to go down the hall and get some lunch. And then you come right back here and wait for her, okay?" That's when Ina Yalof knew she had found the right hospital.

Each person's story reveals the truth of one registrar's statement: "I'm a spoke in a wheel, and if my co-workers and I are strong together, the wheel spins quickly and the patient's life is saved."

—*Lesley S. J. Farmer*

Living with a Parent Who Takes Drugs   Grades 3-9
By Judith Seixas

Sometimes Jason was afraid to go home after school. He would check for telltale signs before he opened the door to go in . . . signs that his dad was inside, stoned. If he was, Jason would just turn around and walk back toward school, or stop at his aunt's house down the street. It was such a scary situation.

Jason couldn't really talk about it with his aunt, but he needed to talk to somebody. It was getting harder to concentrate at school. His headaches were getting worse. He needed to confide his fears to someone who would understand, but he didn't know which way to turn.

If you and Jason have any of these things in common, or if you know someone like Jason, this book can help you figure out what to do.

—*Carol Kappelmann*

Long Live the Queen   Grades 10-12
By Ellen Emerson White

Meg had had to adjust to living in the White House, with all the publicity and restrictions, the Secret Service protection, the lack of privacy and the danger that went along with having a mother who was President of the United States—a mother who had almost been assassinated just a short time ago.

Now Meg and her family were trying to get back to a White House-kind of "normal." Meg was at the end of her senior year, deciding what to wear to the prom, getting ready for college, playing great tennis, and keeping in shape for even greater skiing. But as she left school one afternoon with her Secret Service escort, explosions suddenly went off along the road ahead, and a car and a van came speeding out of nowhere through the smoke, veering right up over the sidewalk, right at her.

"Get her inside!" Chet, one of the Secret Service guards, yelled, his gun already out, shielding her. For a second Meg was too stunned to move as she saw masked figures leap out of the van and the car, firing as they came. Chet stumbled backward, blood spurting from his neck and chest. Horrified, she turned toward the other guard and saw him lying face down on the sidewalk. Behind her the school door was opening—Josh!—and she had just time enough to yell "Get down!" before she felt herself being lifted right off the ground and slammed into the van, the impact of the metal floor jarring up through her hands and knees. Men piled in after her, still shooting as the van skidded away.

When Meg came to, she didn't know where she was, but she did know it was dark. She was chained to a bed, and her entire body hurt, especially her mouth. There was a bloody gap where one of her teeth had been. With sinking certainty she knew that the men holding her captive would kill her—eventually. If she were to get out alive, Meg would have to use her brain and all her strength, and find the courage to do things she had never, ever imagined.

—*Sue Padilla*

Looking for Home   Grades 7–12
By Jean Ferris

Sometimes home isn't where you look for it, where you want it to be, but where you find it—and with whom you find it. For seventeen-year-old Daphne, home is not with the father who beats her or the mother who bears the bruises from his temper tantrums, nor is it with Scott, the father of the child she is carrying. Home is something that can't even happen until she has had the baby and given it up for adoption, and can get on with her life. Then maybe after college she will meet the kind of person who will care about her, and make the home she has never had.

But that isn't the way things work out. There is no way she can stay uninvolved in the lives of the people that she sees every day, that she learns to care about, and that learn to care about her. There's T. Peter, the owner of the cafe where she works, the Gourmaniac. In his previous life he had been a doctor until he decided that what he *really* wanted to be was a restauranteur, one who would serve only round food—no square meals at his place. Then there's Junior Lee, tall, skinny, and the color of bittersweet chocolate—the cook at Gourmaniac. He's only a part-time chef; he goes to college at night, and someday he's going to wear three-piece suits and work with other guys who wear them too.

Then there's Mattie, one of their steady customers. Wearing overalls, she arrives on her motorbike every day about eleven-thirty, and she always orders soup.

It doesn't happen overnight, but eventually they all become friends, as they realize that they are important to each other, as their lives progress, and as Daphne's pregnancy comes to term. Friends aren't always the people you pick out, the pretty ones or the rich ones, or the ones you think you *should* be friends with. They are the people that you care about and that care about you—the ones that make room in their lives for you and take up room in your own life. They're the people that you sometimes don't realize you miss until they aren't around any more, and suddenly you see the gaps they've left behind.

Daphne was looking for a new life and a new home. Sometimes you look so hard that you can't see what you've found. Discover what and who she found when she was *Looking for Home.*

—*J. R. B.*

Lost Boys Never Say Die   Grades 3-6
By Alan Brown

Eleven-year-old Lewis stutters, and that alone is tough enough to deal with; but Lewis also has to cope with a gang of bullies (male and female!). Facing them in school makes him stutter even worse.

This summer Lewis is supposed to go away to camp while his parents are exploring the Arctic. But Lewis jumps off the train and sneaks back to his home, and he stays there by himself the entire summer!

What fun! He hides from his nosy neighbor by day and explores the forest in his backyard after dark. On one day of his explorations he meets Max. Max is a most unusual boy and just a little older than Lewis. Max sort of lives with his father and sort of camps out in the woods. The two boys decide to camp in at Lewis' house for the rest of the summer.

Max is appearing in the summer production of *Peter Pan* at the local college theater, and he encourages Lewis to try out for a part too. Lewis gets it—and to his amazement, he hardly stutters at all when he is on stage performing.

Then a gang of bullies makes an appearance at rehearsal and nearly demolishes the stage set. It doesn't look as if *Peter Pan* will open at the end of the week, if ever! Lost Boys never say die, but can they work a miracle?

—*Betty A. Holtzen*

Ludie's Song   Grades 5-9
By Dirlie Herlihy

Sometimes you know something isn't right, even when everyone
around you pretends it is. And sometimes, even at twelve-going-on-
thirteen, you just have to do what your heart says, without thinking
about the consequences.

That's what Marty—Martha Chafin Armstrong—does during her
summer in backwoods Caldwell, Georgia. Prepared for a boring two
weeks with her Aunt Letta and Uncle Ray, Marty sets out to discover
excitement. She's certain that Ludie, the disfigured daughter of Sister,
the black washerwoman who does the Armstrongs' sheets, is really a
witch, and she's determined to catch Ludie in the act of making her potions. So she sneaks up on the little shack in the woods, only to be surprised by Chili, Ludie's brother, who brings Marty round to meet Ludie
and Sister. Instead of black magic, Marty finds magic of a different
kind—the magic of friendship with Ludie and her close-knit family.

Marty's white friends and relations tell her that "our kind don't hang
around with niggers," but she ignores the warning until it is too late.
Stung by her Uncle Ray's accusations that she's been carrying on with
"that colored boy Chili," Marty builds a wall of lies. Then, on her way
to visit Ludie one morning, Marty stumbles upon Jewel Turner and
some of his friends savagely beating Chili. The boys kidnap Marty and
Chili and concoct a scheme to make it look like Chili has abducted her.

It is only then that Marty begins to understand the extent of the prej-
udices she has ignored, and discovers the true cause of Ludie's disfig-
urement and its connection to her own family.

—*Kim Carter Sands*

Ma and Pa Dracula   Grades 3-4
By Ann M. Martin

This was the most daring thing that Jonathan had ever done—
volunteering his house for the class Halloween party. He thought the
idea was great, and he had the perfect house for it! It would be the best
party ever—or would it?

Jonathan could remember a time when he thought all families were
just like his: working at night, sleeping during the day, having sharp
white teeth and pointy fangs, and long, long fingernails. He had actually
believed his parents when they told him that things like TV and school
existed only in fairy tales—that is, until he met Tobi, who was his very

first best friend. He couldn't let Tobi and the class down—he just *had* to have that Halloween party! But would inviting twenty-three humans to his house be a trick on his parents or a treat? Like giving them a Halloween feast!

—Cara Waits

Magicians of Erianne   **Grades 5-9**
By James Berry

Hardly anyone has had the chance to study magic on the legendary island of Erianne. I did, and I only wish I could tell you why I, Ronan, was chosen to be the student of Yorba, the most learned dragon magician of them all.

I don't even know how I got to Erianne. One moment I was aware of swords clashing and bodies striking together in battle, and the next thing I knew I was in another land, befuddled, bruised, and in rags. The only possessions I seemed to have were a small wooden flute and a curious iron amulet around my neck.

I might have wandered about for a long time, confused and lost, except for an unusual occurrence. On the path ahead, I saw an old couple struggling to free a young dragon from a big rock slide. All at once, I knew how I could help—I could use the Spell of Rise, the incantation that lightens heavy things.

How did I know about the Spell of Rise? After all, I was an ordinary fourteen-year-old boy—or was I? The harder I tried to remember my past, the thicker the fog in my mind became.

Maybe it was because I didn't know who I was that Yorba the dragon became my tutor and set me on the greatest adventure of my life. Yorba explained to me that Excalibur, the magical sword of King Arthur and the symbol of all England, had been stolen. Without it, despair and evil would overwhelm both Arthur and his kingdom. So far, only a few people knew of Excalibur's disappearance: the thief, Arthur, and Merlin, the greatest human magician who ever lived. Merlin had created a duplicate Excalibur with a Spell of Illusion, but even mighty Merlin could not maintain an illusion forever. The real sword must be found, and I was the only one to do it.

Could I save Arthur and his sword? Could I defeat the evil Morgan le Fay? Puppets, a black knight, keystones, and the smell of lilacs— these were all part of my adventures as one of the *Magicians of Erianne.*

—Sue Young

Making Cents: Grades 3–9
Every Kid's Guide to Money
By Elizabeth Wilkinson

"Money doesn't grow on trees, you know!" You've probably heard that line a few million times—like every time you ask one of your parents for a little money to pay for the "necessities of life." And then they go right into telling you how rough they had it when they were your age, like you've never heard *that* story before either. If that's your situation, then *Making Cents* is the book you need to help your cash flow. *Making Cents* is "every kid's guide to money." It is filled with ideas and projects you can use to make money in your spare time—money-making projects that fit your interests and schedule. Working doesn't have to be a boring, gruelsome task; you can have a good time doing it while lining your pockets with the green stuff (and we're not talking grass clippings here!). If you need some cold cash or a jingle in your pocket, then you should try *Making Cents: Every Kid's Guide to Money.*

—*Sandra Carpenter*

Manifold Destiny: The One! The Only! Guide to Adult
Cooking on Your Car Engine
By Chris Maynard and Bill Scheller

It all started with a pastrami sandwich, a hot pastrami sandwich that wasn't—hot, that is. That's when the authors of this book remembered the stories they'd heard about truckers cooking hot dogs and beans on their engines. If hot dogs, why not pastrami? They wrapped the meat in foil, tucked it onto the engine of their VW Rabbit, and an hour later pulled off at a roadside park and had their hot pastrami, still steaming.

And if pastrami, why not chicken? Or fish? Or even a roast for a long trip? Manifold cooking may have its limitations, but for the real tailgate picnic enthusiast, it's the only way to travel! Indeed, as car engine cooking spreads, rest stops may take on their own homey flavor, as people ask each other what smells so good, and share recipes and oven mitts. There's no doubt, it's the cuisine of the future—and if you don't believe it, try some of the recipes you'll find here the next time you have to take a trip around mealtime. Feel like fish for dinner? Try Cutlass Cod Supreme or Hundai Halibut with Fennel, Cajun Shrimp, Blackened Roadfish, or, for a longer drive, a Whole Stuffed Snapper. More of a meat-and-potatoes person? How 'bout Enzo's Veal (named in honor of

Enzo Ferrari); Dwight David Eisenhower Pepper Steak; To Grand-mother's House Road Turkey; Out of the House, Onto the Engine Stew; or Cruise Control Pork Tenderloin. And depending on where you are, you can tailor your menu to your roadmap. For instance, in California you might want to try Melrose Avenue Chicken or Three Pepper Salm-on Steaks, or even Abalone Allanté.

You don't have to make everything from scratch, of course—you can heat up almost anything, assuming that your trip is long enough and that you have enough room inside your engine compartment. Just triple-wrap it in foil, make sure that it's firmly braced, and take off. Leave the cooking to your car—all you have to do is enjoy the results. This little book could not only change the way you cook, it could even change the way you commute! Consider coming home to a hot meal, ready when you get there, hot off the engine. Car engine cooking may not be for everyone, but don't laugh too hard till you've tried it—afterwards, you just might have the last laugh!

—*J. R. B.*

Masquerade   Adult
By William X. Kienzle

They had all expected a week full of mystery, a week full of murder, but they never thought that anyone would actually end up dead. The four of them—the nun, the Episcopal priest, the monk, the rabbi—had been invited to lead a writing seminar on the role of religion in the murder mystery. They were all successful mystery writers, but they had more in common than expertise in that rather specialized field. They were all united in their loathing for the fifth panelist at the conference, the televangelist and publisher Klaus Krieg. The books his firm put out were a mixture of religion and sleaze—and hugely popular.

But the four authors felt more than just contempt for Krieg. They felt another emotion—fear. Each of them was a religious person, but none was without sin. In fact, each was guarding a dark secret, and these secrets, if exposed, could ruin careers and shatter lives. Small wonder, then, that someone was driven to break the Sixth Commandment—"Thou shalt not kill."

—*Rosanne Tricoles*

McKenzie's Boots   Grade 10-Adult
By Michael Noonan

Rod McKenzie was only fifteen when he joined the Australian army to fight for his homeland against the Japanese. He was young, but he was tall and wore size-13 boots, boots that had to be custom-made—the army didn't issue boots large enough for him.

He became a jungle fighter in the forests of New Guinea. One day he was in the forest alone and came face to face with a Japanese soldier. They were armed only with butterfly nets, and suddenly the war and the fact that they were enemies mattered less than their mutual search for beauty.

Rod was only fifteen when he had to begin to answer hard questions, questions that men in war have always had to answer: What's important to *me*? How can someone tell me that someone else is my enemy just because of the country he lives in and the shape of his eyes? Can't eyes see beauty, no matter what their shape is? How can people call themselves civilized when they kill and torture and mutilate their enemies? But how can anyone be a savage who can create beauty from glowing fragments of butterfly wing?

When Rod first pulled on his huge boots, he hadn't even thought of the questions—or of the answers he would very shortly be forced to find.

—*J. R. B.*

Meet My Cats   Grade 3-Adult
By Lesley Anne Ivory

Everyone has a family, and some families include animals as well as humans. My family does—I live with Samantha, who's 19, Annie, who's 9, and Angie, who's 3. They're all Siamese cats, and are just as much a part of my family as the human members are. That's one reason I like this book so much—Lesley Anne Ivory also has family members who are cats, and she introduces you to twelve of them in *Meet My Cats*.

Gemma is the oldest—some of her children and grandchildren still live with her. She's a tabby with a passion for feathers, which she steals and hides behind a curtain in the sitting room.

Muppet is Gemma's daughter and very intelligent—she's even discovered how to open the refrigerator door to get at the chicken she loves so much!

Twiglet likes to sit at the kitchen counter watching the faucet drip, and he's the one who discovered the best way to get milk from out of a milk carton: the nearer the bottom he bites, the bigger the jet of milk!

Spiro is the ringleader in some very creative escapades—like the time he, Chesterton, and Twiglet discovered that together they could get the lid off the garbage can and rummage around for goodies inside.

And those are only a few of the mischievous, beautiful, affectionate, and demanding cats that make up part of the Ivory household. You can get to know them for yourselves, as Lesley Anne Ivory invites you to *Meet My Cats.*

—*J. R. B.*

Merlin Dreams
By Peter Dickinson
Grade 10–Adult

Have you ever wondered about your dreams? What are they, anyway, and what, if anything, do they mean? Usually dreams seem to be nothing more than a jumbled kaleidoscope of selected memories from the past, but then there is the rare dream that almost carries the aura of a vision or glimpse into the future. Why, some people even claim that certain types of dreams can actually shape or alter events in the waking world.

Let me tell you about some of Merlin's dreams. You remember Merlin, don't you? He was the legendary wizard who brought King Arthur to the throne and then finally met his own doom when he was trapped forever under an unmarked stone on the English moors. Under that rock, Merlin still dreams.

Some of his dreams, such as the tale of Sir Tremalin, appear to be nothing more than straightforward memories of past adventures. Sir Tremalin, a sorry excuse for a knight, who had never met a challenge or done a noble deed in his life, was suddenly forced to accept a perilous quest that not only involved fighting two hardy and undefeated warriors but a deadly invisible foe as well. To all outward appearances, Sir Tremalin was a disastrous choice for such a quest; in Merlin's dreams, however, appearances can be deceiving—things are never quite what they seem. This is what Prince Alexander also discovered, in another of Merlin's dreams. When Alexander decided to hunt down and destroy the evil dragon that was terrorizing his country, he discovered—just as Sir Tremalin had on his quest—that the enemy was not quite what he had expected.

But perhaps I shouldn't tell you any more of Merlin's dreams, especially not the strange tale of the beautiful enchantress who held an entire country under her spell. Listening to a wizard's dreams can be dangerous. Dreaming itself can be dangerous because, as Merlin once said, "Dreams are their own masters." So don't treat dreams lightly; if you do, you might just find yourself mastered by your own or someone else's dreams. After all, look at what happened to Merlin.

—*Margie Reitsma*

Millie Cooper, Take a Chance   Grades 3–4
By Charlotte Herman

Millie Cooper hated to take chances. But she wanted a new bicycle more than anything in the world. When winning one didn't work, Millie started selling subscriptions, but she couldn't quite face her customers. And her parents seemed oblivious to her hints.

Not getting a bike wasn't Millie's only problem, either. Shyness affected her life in other ways—at school, for example. Have you ever felt afraid to try something? Has it ever looked as though other kids could do things that you just couldn't even try? (And besides, what if you failed!) Well, Millie had discovered that if she never tried she couldn't fail, but she was missing out on a lot of fun and good feelings.

Find out what happens when Millie finally decides to go after what she wants—sometimes being "safe" is no fun!

—*Kelly Jewett*

Moondream   Grades 3–9
By Victor Osborne

Rupert watched in horror as the cloud thing that had been the Grabbly flew off into the night. Sticking out from the cloud, his cousin Katy's legs were kicking wildly.

Just a few moments before, the Grabbly had been standing by his bed, ready to grab Rupert. The thing was a terrible sight, like a moving bag of potatoes, with swamp steam rising from the cracks in its skin. It had no head, but a face had rippled across the body, scowling and snapping at Rupert, ready to grab him away.

That was when Katy had come to his rescue, kicking the creature and smacking at it with her slipper. The Grabbly suddenly sprouted four webbed arms, snatched Katy with two of them, and launched itself and Katy out the window.

Rupert jumped as a shadow flew across the moon. Was the Grabbly coming back for him? He snatched up the first thing he could find to defend himself—his tennis racket—and braced for the attack. Then he was staring out the window in astonishment. For this time it was no monster, but a flying clipper ship, manned by an all-animal crew.

The crew of the *Dainty Duck* were hot on the trail of the Grabbly themselves. Rupert joined them, vowing to rescue Katy and defeat the Grabbly and its wizard master before the evil could spread.

—Jeff Blair

Moonkid and Liberty　　　　　　　**Grades 7–12**
By Paul Kropp

You've heard about the typical American family—and how there's no such thing any more? Well, this book is a good example of that. Just look at the main characters. First, there's Moonkid (earth-name Ian) who says he's an alien (but that's really just a defensive, superior attitude). Then there's Liberty (or Libby), who wants desperately to be popular but falls in with a bunch of glamour kids who won't be around when things get bad. Libby and Ian live with their father, an aging hippie whose different lifestyle confuses and embarrasses them. It must have embarrassed their mom, too, because she decided to quit being a hippie some time ago and is now a successful businesswoman in California. She wants Ian and Libby to come live with her. The Moonkid's problems at school get heavier, Dad gets in trouble with the law, and Libby just wants to solve it all by moving to California. It's time to either pull together or bail out.

These people have drifted so far apart—will they ever be able to pull together into a family? Will Moonkid and Liberty realize that perhaps they need each other to survive?

—Mark Anderson

More to Life than Mr. Right:　　　**Grades 10–12**
Stories for Young Feminists
Compiled by Rosemary Stones

Three-thirty in the morning! Can you believe it?

Three-thirty! When she told me that she had a date after school, I never thought that she'd stay out this late! Oh yes, I know she's with Alex, and he's all right. At least he seems to be trustworthy—but can you really be sure? It's not as if life weren't complicated enough for a woman today. Work, school, trying to have some kind of a sane social life—and now this!

She's changed since the divorce. It didn't matter much to me—my life stayed pretty much the same. If anything, it got more peaceful and that wasn't bad at all. But her—it's as if she'd bloomed. First pierced ears, then the new job, and now Alex. She could have warned me, but no-o-o. No consideration for anyone.

What time is it now? Maybe I should call the police. Maybe there's been an accident and nobody knows who to call. Oh heck, I've got to cool down. She's old enough to take care of herself—she's my mother! But am I going to have a talk with her when she gets home! I wonder—can you ground your own mother? Find out, in "Twelve Hours—Narrative and Perspectives," by Adele Geras. It's only one of the stories in *More to Life Than Mr. Right*.

—*Nancy L. Chu*

The Mother's Almanac II: Adult
Your Child from Six to Twelve
By Marguerite Kelly

I don't believe in Super Moms. Fortunately, neither does Marguerite Kelly. That's why she's put together this almanac for mothers.

Like any self-respecting almanac, this one gives information and advice about all aspects of the subject. But instead of the best weather for planting potatoes, the topic here is how to create the best family climate for raising confident, happy kids between the ages of six and twelve. The problems are as familiar to mothers as weeds are to farmers: how to encourage your child to do homework well and on time; how to limit extra-curricular activities so that they don't take over the child's and the whole family's life; and how to help your child fit in with other children and still develop unique interests.

As Kelly warns, children from six to twelve years old present some of the greatest challenges—as well as the greatest rewards—of parenting. That's why all mothers with children in the age bracket will want to check out the information in this book. After all, prevention is still the best policy, in parenting as well as in farming.

Think about it this way: although we might not believe in Super Moms, we certainly want our children to!

—*Margie Reitsma*

Motherwit   Grade 10–Adult
By Onnie Lee Logan and Katherine Clark

Onnie Lee Logan wants to tell you a story—the story of her life. A life filled with love for the thousands of mothers and babies she has known, and for the God who has guided her. Onnie Lee Logan is a black "Granny" midwife who, in this era of massive medical intervention, still delivers babies at home—delivers them with a slow love and patience lost in the stark efficiency of a hospital. Born in rural Alabama, fourteenth of sixteen children, Onnie Lee learned the art of midwifery at her mother's knee. She learned to make do and to have faith. She found it was no use calling white doctors for help because the babies could be walking before they got there. She learned that old wives' tales and superstitious remedies sometimes worked miracles, because of faith and love maybe. She tells of the first delivery she attended, where a small black baby was laid aside as dead by the other midwife. Onnie picked it up and brought it to life with mouth-to-mouth resuscitation, which she had never even seen done before. "You know why I did that?" she says. "I asked God to help me bring that baby to life, if life was in it, and he gave me the power to do that. God gave me wisdom, motherwit, common sense." Filled with this faith and with experience and Motherwit, Onnie Lee Logan was determined to share her story with the world, determined to "scratch it out" if she had to. "I want to show that I knew what I knew," Onnie says. "I want to share what I know before it dies with me." Read *Motherwit* and share more than a story of midwifery. This is a story of the personal odyssey of a rural black woman determined to lead a life of meaning and fulfillment.

—*Jan L. McConnell*

The Mouse Rap   Grades 5–8
By Walter Dean Myers

With tenth grade behind him and summer vacation ahead, the Mouse (real name: Frederick Douglas) looked forward to long weeks of tubing and hooping, taking it easy and playing it cool. But that summer brought a whole lot more than just basketball and TV. To begin with, his father, better known as Mr. D., reappeared after an eight-year absence—just showed up at their Harlem apartment and began romancing Mouse's mother, obviously trying to get back together with his wife and son. Mouse tried to avoid him as much as possible and even allowed his friend Sheri to con him and his main man, Styx, into entering a dance contest. That's when things really got hot! First Beverly, a foxy new girl from California, claimed the Mouse as her own. Then Sheri's grandfather admitted that he used to know the mobster Tiger Moran, even did some moving for him. And he just might be able to lead Mouse and company on a search for the gangster's hidden loot! With all that action, vacation breezed by. But as for what happened between the Mouse and Beverly, and between Mr. D. and the Mouse's mom, and whether or not the hidden cash stayed hidden—tune in to *The Mouse Rap!*

—*Sister Mary Anna Falbo, CSSF*

The Mummy   Grade 9–Adult
By Anne Rice

It was his eyes she noticed first, his deep blue, magnetic, compelling eyes. As the mummy's ancient wrappings fell away, disintegrating in the bright sunlight, she found herself looking at a handsome blue-eyed man, who gazed back at her with intelligence and curiosity. Her father had been right—his translation of the papyrus scrolls found with the mummy had been correct. The sun had brought the mummy back to life, and now here he was, Ramses the Great, who called himself Ramses the Damned because he could neither die nor be killed. He'd had himself sealed up in the tomb after his beloved Cleopatra had committed suicide. Rather than continue to live alone forever, he'd had himself wrapped as a mummy, put into a sarcophagus, and sealed up where the sun could not reach him, with many warnings and curses on the door designed to discourage anyone who might be curious. It was as close to death as he could get, and it lasted for two thousand years, until Lawrence Stratford, archaeologist and Egyptologist, ignored the warnings, blasted the door, and let the sunlight spill into the tomb-like room that had been dark for so long.

He was only partly awake for many days, while his body was brought to London, and now that he was fully awake, he found himself faced with a woman almost as beautiful and vibrant as Cleopatra had been. Julie was Lawrence's daughter, and after his death, the famous mummy he had unearthed just before he was killed was taken to her house as part of a special display honoring her father's last find. Intelligent, spirited, independent, educated, *and* an Egyptologist, Julie was uniquely suited to help Ramses learn how to survive in the early twentieth century. In addition, since she had seen the sun restore him to robust health in a matter of minutes, she knew he was just exactly who he said he was, and she almost instantly fell under the spell of his magnetic personality. She knew Latin and Greek, so she could speak to him and help him learn English. She was an heiress, and so she had both time and money to show him the new world he had waked up in. Her quick thinking and her social position made it possible for her to convince everyone that he was Reginald Ramsey, an Egyptian colleague of her father's, who had recently arrived in London. And when Ramsey wanted to visit his homeland one last time, money was no problem—the trip was quickly arranged.

But the trip turned into a disaster as one person after another discovered the secret of Ramsey's elixir of immortality and wanted it for themselves, not realizing that eternal life can be just as much a curse as a blessing. And then Ramsey made a terrible, impulsive mistake that changed the lives of everyone in their party and almost separated him forever from Julie, whom he had come to love even more than Cleopatra. Can they survive these terrible consequences, or will Ramses the Damned be condemned once more to spend his immortal life alone?

—*J. R. B.*

My Brother Stealing Second   Grades 7-12
By Jim Naughton

Sometimes when I think that I'm really losing it, I talk to myself. I pretend I'm two people: one trying to make friends, one who doesn't want to because he thinks no one can understand him. The friendly guy never wins.

My brother Billy's dead.

I'm sorry.

You're sorry, but you don't understand.

I do *understand.*

Maybe you understand, but you can't know. You can't know what it feels like, for me or my parents. You can't know what it feels like to be responsible.

Responsible for what?

Responsible for his death. Responsible for the Durhams' deaths, too, and Richie Munley's mangled leg. Knowing he was drunk with his friends the night they rounded a 35-mile-an-hour curve at 65 and smashed into the Durhams' car. Knowing he's the one to blame. Knowing he crushed so many lives at one time. Knowing things will never be the same.

Sounds tough. Don't you have anyone to talk with?

My parents have their own problems and ways of dealing with it all. The school psychologist is worthless. There's just you, and you're pretty worthless too.

Well, how about Annie?

Annie? Annie Durham? Oh sure, she can't even look at me without seeing Billy and what he did to her parents. We try to go our own ways, but our lives are linked by death.

And then I usually can't think of anything else for the nice guy to say. Told you he never wins.

No one around me feels like much of a winner these days. Not like when Billy was alive. We've all got to find something else to believe in, something to live for. Something like baseball used to be for Billy and me.

—Jeff Blair

My Brother the Star   **Grades 3–4**
By Alison Jackson

Leslie's biggest problem, other than his girly name, is his little brother Cameron. Cameron is a TV-commercial star. He has one of those cute, pudgy, round faces strange women can't resist pinching, perfect blond curls, and aqua-blue eyes. Cam can get pretty stuck-up at times, and Les is getting awfully tired of being "brother of the star."

But now maybe it's Les's turn. He and his best friend Mike have been invited to try out for the annual summer basketball camp. Les is tall and thin and an excellent ball-player. He and Mike are some of the "exceptional" fifth-graders who have been invited to the elimination tournament.

Will Les make the cut at the tournament, playing against those middle-class kids who've all been to the basketball camp before? Will a speedy little munchkin named Bobby beat him out of the game? Does Les realize that the strawberry bubblegum–chewing Bobby is a *girl?* Will Mike still want to be friends if Les goes to camp and he doesn't?

Read *My Brother the Star* to find out if Les finally gets his chance to be the star of the family.

—Diantha G. McCauley

My Daniel Grades 5-9
By Pam Conrad

"I loved my brother with a white fire. And like a burnt-out buffalo chip will crumble into dust if you stomp your foot beside it—that's what I was like once Daniel was gone."

Twelve-year-old Julia Creath was having the summer of her life, no matter that it was very dry and hot on the family farm in Nebraska. She knew that her sixteen-year-old brother Daniel would take her along on his treasure hunts to the river. Once their chores were done, they could spend the summer days swimming in the river and turning over every stone, looking for the one special treasure that would help bring money to the family.

As the summer drifted by, Julia was certain that nothing bad could happen to her or her brother. Why should she worry herself about something that just wasn't going to happen? What she did concentrate on was the secret hidden in the earth—the secret that only Daniel, his best friend, and Julia could know. Or were they the only ones? What about that steely-eyed stranger who came riding onto Pa's land on that smelly camel? Was he there to find the same secrets and treasures that Daniel had found? Why was Daniel trying to keep his discovery to himself? Was the treasure so special that it was worth dying for?

—Pam Swafford

My Name Is Not Angelica Grades 3-6
By Scott O'Dell

Raisha was going to become an African princess, because she was going to marry her love, Prince Konji. But instead, both were captured, torn from their African homes, brought to the West Indies, and enslaved. They were renamed Angelica and Apollo by the man who bought them.

The royal Konji became a common field hand, while Raisha forced the smile she had learned on the slave ship and became a house servant.

However, it wasn't long before Konji escaped and became the leader of 300 runaways. He began to plan a great revolt against the few rich plantation owners, a revolt that would eventually make Raisha fear for her own life. Yet it would also make her brave and rebellious enough to declare to the world, "My name is *not* Angelica!"

—Faye A. Powell

My War with Goggle-Eyes   Grades 5-9
By Anne Fine

Why me, wonders Kitty Killin when she is sent by Mrs. Lupey after
a tearful Helen Johnston. Why did the teacher pick *me* out for this
mission? But as she follows her weepy classmate into the locker-room
and tries to get her calmed down, she starts to see why she, Kitty Killin,
the world's greatest expert on domestic strife, would be the chosen one.
Mrs. Lupey must have guessed that Helen would want to hear the tale
of Kitty's war with Goggle-Eyes.

When Gerald Faulkner changed her "normal, workaday mother"
into "a radiant, energetic fashion-plate," Kitty lost her cool as well as
her sense of humor, and she launched an all-out war of wits against Gerald Faulkner, aka Goggle-Eyes, that "horrible, slimy, creepy and revolt-
ing middle-aged silver-haired pest"!

"I hated the whole house whenever he was in it," she tells Helen. "I
can't describe exactly what it was, but it just didn't feel like home any
more if he was ambling from room to room in search of a pencil to do
the crossword, or slipping out of the downstairs bathroom, leaving the
tank hissing behind him, or lifting my schoolbag off the coffee table so
he could lean back on the sofa and watch the news on television."

It was war, and Goggle-Eyes knew it—and he was a serious fighter.
He never let up on Kitty, making sure that she always heard his soft,
polite (but very opinionated) remarks. He criticized her sloppy room,
he thought she shouldn't charge her mother for the potatoes from her
garden, and he announced to the world that she ought to help more with
the housework.

Who would win the war—Goggle-Eyes Faulkner or Kitty Killin?

—*Susan Wolfe*

Nadja: On My Way   Grades 7-12
By Nadja Salerno-Sonnenberg

Nadja says, "You have to work hardest for the thing you love most,
and when it's music that you love, you're in for the fight of your life!"
And she knows what she's talking about! Nadja Salerno-Sonnenberg
started playing the violin before she started school, and began giving
concerts and competing in international contests shortly afterwards.
But just in case you think she's stuffy or boring, I can assure you she's
not! From her antics in school to her flamboyant and unconventional
stage performances all over the world, Nadja does what she wants to

do—and what her music requires her to do. Follow her as she takes you inside her life, shows you what it's like to be a child prodigy, to play on the concert stage, and to struggle to be yourself in the conservative world of classical music.

—Barbara Bahm and J. R. B.

Never Too Young to Die: Grades 10-Adult
The Death of Len Bias
By Lewis Cole

To the people who knew him, Len Bias was childlike, shy, spontaneous, and pleasure-loving; but to everyone else he was a celebrity—a valuable commodity, somebody in the national spotlight, playing basketball for Maryland.

On June 17, 1986, Len Bias had it made. He had just been chosen in a first-round draft to begin a brilliant professional athletic career with the Boston Celtics. His agent had worked out an endorsement contract with Reebok that would pay one million dollars for five years, and would assure Len of lifelong financial security.

On June 19, 1986, Len Bias died of an overdose.

In *Never Too Young to Die*, you can search for the key to this tragedy. Go through Len's last night alive, the investigation into his death, and the trial of the accused drug-dealer, his best friend Brian Tribble. Decide for yourself if Len was the victim of a seductive dealer or of a too-fast rise from urban ghetto to millionaire superstardom. Or was he simply the victim of a dangerous illusion—a belief in his own invincibility?

—Barbara Bahm

The New Medically Based Grade 10-Adult
No-Nonsense Beauty Book
By Deborah Chase

I can hear some of you already: "Oh, no, not another beauty book!" To be perfectly honest, that's pretty much the way I reacted when I saw it too. But the most important words in this title are "medically based" and "no-nonsense," not "beauty."

So give it a chance. It might not be the kind of book you'd want to curl up with at home after a long day at work, but it could be just what you need to help you look your best back at work the next morning. Let me give you an example. If you're over twenty and don't like acne, you should avoid any cosmetics that contain mineral oil. Want to hear more? Well, those special soaps that contain Vitamin E or aloe may give you a psychological boost, but they won't help your skin, no matter what they cost. In fact, according to this no-nonsense evaluation, Vitamin E may even cause allergic reactions in some people.

But if you're interested in more of these helpful hints, you'll just have to check this book out yourself. You see, I've already read it . . . and I just got back from work and I have this great mystery novel I'm dying to finish. . . .

—Margie Reitsma

New Zealand by Motorhome   Adult
By David Shore and Patty Campbell

When you were a kid, did you ever want to dig a hole to China and find out for yourself how the people there managed to walk around on the bottom of the earth without falling off? How far did you get? Two feet? Three? So much for budding scientific curiosity! But even though I discovered I couldn't dig 'way to the other side of the world, I never stopped wondering about it—what was it like, that part of the world where people walked upside down without falling off?

It wasn't until I saw a globe that I discovered that those people didn't live in China—the people on the bottom of the earth lived further south than that. They were literally "down under"—they lived in Australia and New Zealand, two islands with so little contact with the other continents that not only were their cultures unique but even their wildlife. They had plants, animals, and birds that could be found nowhere else in the world. But no matter how much I wanted to see these things for myself, they stayed half a world away—that is, until now. This book, *New Zealand by Motorhome*, has convinced me that anyone who wants to explore this fascinating part of the world can do so.

David Shore and Patty Campbell, a husband-and-wife writing team, have traveled all over Europe seeing the world from the front seat of a VW van, and in this book, they explain how to do the same thing in New Zealand. Reading their books could convince anyone that this is the only way to travel, especially in a country like New Zealand, where there is so much to see in such a small space.

But how do you get started? Find a van? Figure out what to take with you, where to go, and what and where to eat? Fear not—David and Patty will get you there and back in style, whether you travel alone, with another person, or with your whole family. They'll tell you which van would be best for you. how to stock it, what to make sure you include, and what you can safely leave out. From getting along with other people in the close quarters of a van to discovering which roads are the best, you'll find all the details here.

Wondering how to feed yourself and your family without going out to eat every night? Patty has a group of tried-and-true recipes and a collection of hints about where to find their ingredients, which can range from the standard to the exotic. For example, try a Pavlova with Kiwis or a Tamarillo Cream for dessert, after a meal of wonderful New Zealand beef or grilled fish—gurnard, opacapaca, or hapuku, or maybe steamed sweet scallops or giant mussels, or—well, the list goes on and on. (Patty doesn't suggest taking a scale along, but I do!)

You'll have a chance to follow Patty and David all over New Zealand as they discover how to read the highway signs, where to camp, how to save money by feasting on lambchops ("Heck," says Patty, "they're so cheap, have a whole dozen!"), and where to find the most spectacular views. Imagine luxuriating in a spa pool and gazing up at floodlit falls, after a budget meal of spicy lambchops and silverbeet with bacon. Get up the next morning and feed the greedy ducks that cluster around your van door, and then take off for a day of exploring the Kauri forest, the only one left in the world, with trees so straight and tall that they were once used for the masts of ships. In Rotorua, you can discover the three M's—mineral baths, Maori culture, and mud pools. From the Mount Cook airport you can charter a plane to fly you to the Tasman Glacier, where you can step out onto the snow and dig down to the solid ice beneath, that may have been frozen for centuries.

And those are only a few of the attractions that Patty and David describe—you can discover the beaches, the shops, the tearooms, the incredible birds, and the Plunket rooms for yourselves. Whether you prefer to hit the open road or just vacation from your armchair, this book will introduce you to a country full of wonders.

—*J. R. B.*

Newfound   Grade 7-Adult
By Jim Wayne Miller

I've never been one to talk much about myself. I'm just plain Robert Wells, from Newfound Creek, Tennessee. But then, no one in my family is much on talking about themselves. Not that there's much to talk about. We've always lived here, not like some families that wind up spread all over the country. Since my mom and dad split up, we've lived with my mom's folks, Grandma and Grandpa Smith. We—that's Mom, me, my little brother Eugene, and my little sister Jeannette.

But since I've gotten old enough to notice, there *are* some things that seem different about my family. For one thing, my Grandma and Grandpa Smith are sharecroppers on my other grandparents' farm. When I was little, I figured everyone lived close like this. Then I began to see how my mother looked when Grandma Wells (that's Dad's mother) would talk about Dad losing "another job in some big-headed scheme." Grandma Wells always sounded like she thought it was my mother's fault that Dad had dropped out of college to get married.

Don't get me wrong—I love all my grandfolks, and I love Newfound Creek the way anyone loves the place where they were born. After all, you don't really think about it as being anyplace special. It just *is*. I used to feel that way about my family too. Families aren't something you have to choose or think about. They're just there. At least, I felt that way until my family began to change, and I began to ask questions.

Trouble is, every time one question gets answered, another one comes up.

—*Nancy L. Chu*

The News About Dinosaurs   Grades 3-6
By Patrick Lauber

Go on, pick up the book! Yes, I know, Tyrannosaurus Rex is charging across the cover, but he can't really bite you. However, I warn you, this book can bite in another way: if you don't already have it, when you put down *The News About Dinosaurs*, you'll have Dinosaur Fever—and there's no known cure!

The traditional view of dinosaurs was based on observation of modern reptiles: cold-blooded and often slow-moving animals that leave their eggs to hatch and their young to survive on their own. But new discoveries are showing that this may not be an accurate description of dinosaurs. Pictures here bring these creatures to life and illustrate nine new ideas about their behavior and their fate. The illustrations are so real they look like photographs—they catch your eye and make you curious about what the author has to say. And what the author has to say makes you want to look even more closely at the illustrations. What does this all add up to? Dinosaurs are Big News, and this book is a great place to start finding out about them!

—*Susan Perdaris*

Night Riding   Grades 7–12
By Katherine Martin

Dear Diary,
Things are still turned upside down because my daddy's sick and in the hospital. But we've got new neighbors. The B. Z. Hammonds. B. Z. Hammond. Why is it that every time his name is mentioned, people whisper it and look like they're being forced to swallow something that tastes awful? And what about his daughter, Mary Faith? She's sort of weird, with dyed hair and too much make-up. But she's nice enough. She spends time with me and tells me 'bout things Mama says I shouldn't be askin' about. My sister Jo Lynn says that Mary Faith isn't a nice girl 'cause she's expecting a baby that doesn't have a daddy. But Mary Faith says her husband is away and that she's gonna meet him soon as she can. There's nothing wrong with that, is there? Jo Lynn says I have a lot to learn.

I like Mary Faith. I want her to be my friend. She always seems so sad. But her daddy—he scares me. He's always looking at me and smiling, but he makes me feel bad. Mary Faith is afraid of him too. She always has these awful bruises, and the first time I met her she had a black eye. She said she fell, but I think her daddy did it. One time I saw him push Mary Faith down the porch steps.

I know I shouldn't eavesdrop, but nobody wants to talk in front of me. It's always "Prin, you go outside, now" or "Prin, get on up to bed." One night, though, I heard Aunt Map and Mama talking about Mary Faith's baby and about Mary Faith's daddy. He's scary—daddies aren't supposed to be like that. *My* daddy would never hurt me.

Wish I could go night riding. It's so cool outside, and I can hear the horses running in the new field. But what if that Mr. B. Z. Hammond is out in the field, waiting for me? Like the last time.

Wish I could talk to my daddy!

—Paula Paolucci

The Night the White Deer Died   Grades 7–12
By Gary Paulsen

Some people live in dreams. Janet Carson may not have believed in dreams, but her life would not be the same after her experience. Her dream left her frightened. It always ended the same way. Like a frame in a movie, the action froze. What did it all mean?

At fifteen, Janet had moved to a small town in New Mexico with her artist mother. While her mother spent a great deal of time working on her pictures and relaxing with her friends, Janet spent most of her time alone. One day, one of the town drunks, an old Indian, introduced himself to Janet. He said his name was Billy Honcho. She should have been repulsed by him. But there was something about him that made her stop and listen. Without knowing why or how, she had walked back to her house to get him the dollar he had asked for to buy wine.

How was this old warrior's life connected to hers? The answer became quite clear the night her dream had a different ending: *The Night the White Deer Died*. Read it, and experience a dream come true.

—*Kathleen Ellis*

Nightmare   Grades 7-12
By Willo Davis Roberts

It all started when the man crashed down on top of my car. I caught a glimpse of a terror-stricken face, and then the splintering glass blocked everything out and I ran into the concrete piling that supported the bridge the man had fallen from. There was no question of its being my fault—the skid marks where I'd tried to stop proved that, and the cigarette butts on the bridge above showed he'd been standing there a while before he jumped. If he jumped. The police thought it was suicide, but I was pretty sure he hadn't wanted to die—I'd seen his face.

But I had problems of my own. Lisa had just dropped me for some college man, my new stepfather was being a royal pain in the butt, and then, later on that same night, a burglar shot my dog. At least Steve—my stepfather—didn't believe that the burglar was searching my room for drugs, but no one could figure out what he *was* looking for. I decided to cut out, and talked my mother and Steve into letting me drive the motorhome to Texas over spring break to see my brother. Little did I know that my pesky neighbor Daisy would stow away and complicate matters—or that it was no accident that Paul Valerian fell onto my car. He *was* pushed—and the two guys that did it were behind us all the way. They hadn't found what they wanted when they broke into our house, but they were sure we still had it—whatever it was. Is there any way to hide a huge motorhome on a lonely stretch of highway? Can we escape from two crooks who are as determined to catch up with us as we are to get away from them? And can we figure out what they're after—and why—before they strike again?

—*J. R. B.*

Nightmare Mountain   Grades 3-6
By Peg Kehret

Dear Mom,
   Someone is trying to kill me. It's too complicated to explain in a letter, but will you cut your trip short so I can come home?
   Love, Molly
   P.S. This is no joke!

   Well, what would you think? She'd only been at her aunt and uncle's llama ranch a few days when strange things started to happen. First her aunt became seriously ill after taking one of Molly's vitamins. Had they been poisoned? That same night Molly was almost hit by a truck speeding down a path—without any lights. The next day a bale of hay toppled down from the barn loft and landed right on top of her!
   But Molly is only twelve years old. Who could hate her that much? Enough to want to kill her. Just one name keeps coming to mind— Glendon. He always acts so strange and unfriendly. Glendon knows Molly takes a vitamin pill every day. He knows how to drive a truck. And he had mysteriously disappeared the morning she had the accident in the barn. But Glendon's her cousin. He couldn't possibly hate her enough to want to kill her—they just met! But why is it that every time Molly catches Glendon looking at her, all she sees in his face is hate and resentment?
   Before Molly's nightmare is over, she is forced at gunpoint to help a thief steal from her uncle. Then she spends a cold and lonely night on a mountain after barely escaping an avalanche. Molly has never felt so alone or so scared.
   Who can she talk to? Her aunt is in a coma. Her uncle would never belived his son had anything to do with what's been happening. Molly's not quite sure she believes it herself! She needs to talk to her mother! So she begins her first letter:

Dear Mom,
   Someone is trying to kill me. . . .

                                            —*Paula Paolucci*

The Ninth Issue   Grades 7-12
By Dallin Malmgren

In Hale High School's newspaper, *The Town Crier*, there is a something to offend everybody. The principal hates the drugdog story. The assistant principal hates the bomb-scare photos. The coaches hate the football coverage, and the students hate the stolen-test exposé. As if that weren't enough, the yearbook advisor, Mrs. Woodley, hates Mr. Choate, the newspaper advisor. And while the staff members are discovering that they're not the best-liked kids in school, they're certainly the best-known—they're notorious! *The Town Crier* has never gotten this much attention before.

But maybe it's starting to get a little too much. Maybe staff members Blue, Austin, Rachelle, and Lori Jo will have to decide where they stand—with their school or with their newspaper.

—Kaite Mediatore

No Kidding   Grades 7-12
By Bruce Brooks

There is little to be cheerful about in fourteen-year-old Sam's life. Of course, that's true for just about everyone in twenty-first-century Washington, DC. By that time, alcoholism has spread to epidemic proportions in America, with the majority of citizens officially classified as alcoholics. Sam himself is classified as an AO—alcoholic offspring. Whole families (including Sam's) are paralyzed by this plague.

Sam's main concern is his ten-year-old brother Ollie. After he had their alcoholic mother committed to a rehabilitation institution, Sam placed Ollie in a foster home. Though Ollie lives with a kind family who want to adopt him, it is Sam who has the authority to control his life, and Sam is still worried about him. Where does Ollie go late at night, when he takes bus after bus deep into the city? The instrument case he carries says that he is going to music practice, an excuse that his foster parents accept. But Sam is afraid that Ollie is being drawn into one of the fanatical churches that are rising, quietly but ominously, on the ruins of the disintegrating society.

This fear threatens Sam's dream of rebuilding his family after his mother is released from the rehab center. A job, a new apartment, a re-union with her sons—isn't that all it will take for his mother to regain the strength she needs to hold the family together, and take over some of Sam's reponsibilities?

A tough situation? *No Kidding!*

—*Nancy L. Chu*

No Promises   Grades 7–12
By Pamela Curtis Swallow

Just when things are going so well, something happens to change everything. And there are no promises that the change will be for the better.

Dana's been happy with her life. She has a horse to ride, a funny best friend, and a blond, blue-eyed boyfriend who can play the trumpet like an angel. Then, in the middle of October, black-haired Jared appears in Dana's geometry class, capturing the heart of her best friend Lynn and astonishing everyone by speaking fluently in French.

But it isn't Lynn who gets Jared's attention—it's Dana. It's Dana to whom he offers a ride home after school in a classic little white MG. It's at Dana's house he shows up to go riding, Dana's little brother he talks to so easily, and Dana's snooty cat that befriends him immediately.

But Dana already has Paul! Besides, her best friend is crazy about this new transfer student. Actually, Jared never does or says anything to intentionally cause trouble for Dana, and when Paul starts getting jealous, Dana feels trapped, as if she has to choose between her friends. It isn't fair! She hasn't done anything wrong!

Yet she finds herself humming the songs Jared strums on his guitar. She can't say no to his spontaneous invitations. Then, at a picnic, Dana slips on a rock and starts to fall into the pond. As Jared reaches out to grab her, she imagines a scene in a movie where the guy grabs the girl just in time; they look into each other's eyes and embrace passionately. And she realizes Jared has become more to her than just a friend.

There are no promises in life. You make your choices and take your chances. Read *No Promises* by Pamela Curtis Swallow to see how many chances Dana is willing to take.

—*Tracie Pruitt*

No Way Out   Grades 5–12
By Ivy Ruckman

Clyde and Ben had just reached the small tree and were hanging on to it and each other like koala bears when the wall of water hit them.

It sounded like ten freight trains. Churning flash-flood water was smashing Clyde into the tree with the same powerful force it was using to wrest Ben away from the down-side of it. Sand was being sucked out from under the roots. The earth rocked with the explosion of water. Logs and rocks as big as Volkswagens surged past them, mud sprayed into their mouths and eyes. Everything shook. Their tree dipped and swayed with their weight.

What had started out as a perfect weekend hike had turned into a watery nightmare. Just minutes before, sixteen-year-old Clyde and eleven-year-old Ben had been sleeping in a small cave above the river in the beautiful Zion Narrows. Ben's older sister Amy and four other people had been sleeping down on the beach. Now there was no beach. Ben and Clyde couldn't help Amy and the others now. The boys and the tree were linked together, clinging for survival.

Six or maybe eight hours later, the two boys began to work their stiff, cold fingers and bodies loose from the tree. The water had gone down, but the current was still treacherous. Clyde didn't know if they could make it through another night with no fire or dry clothes. His leg was injured and numb from something that had struck it. Now they had to find their way out the canyon, hoping to locate Amy and the others. He prayed for no more rain.

—Ann Provost

Nobody's Fault   Grade 10–Adult
By Nancy Holmes

Nobody's Fault is a love story. The story of Amanda Gordon and Lord Charles Warrington: their meeting, courtship, and marriage. The story of their attraction, passion and love for one another.

Nobody's Fault is also a crime story. The story of a murder. The story of how—and why—Charles Warrington broke into his own home late at night under the cover of darkness, and brutally murdered a woman he mistook for his wife.

Nobody's Fault—the story of a love gone sour, a marriage gone bad. All too common these days. And as in real life, it's really nobody's fault . . . or everybody's.

It's a fine line between love and hate.

—Melinda Waugh

A Nugget of Gold
By Maureen Pople

Grades 7-12

The bottom of the large hole that Sally has fallen into is cold and damp and very, very hard. She is feeling shaky and sick, but she soon realizes she's not hurt, except for her bruised ego and her ruined jeans (which are now missing a button in front and a seam in back). Embarrassed though she is at having fallen down an old mine shaft on this Australian farm, Sally calls for help, and is soon rescued by her best friend Annie and Annie's two brothers. But before they haul her up from the pit, Sally sees something shiny in the soft soil near her right leg. She quickly digs out the object, which feels like a mud-coated pebble, and slips it into the front pocket of her jeans. Later, in secret, Sally cleans off the object and sees that it's a very old brooch, made from a nugget of solid gold and inscribed with these words: *Ann Bird Jem Ever*. Sally can't begin to figure out what that could mean, but as she spends more and more time on her friend's farm, she beings to decipher the mystery of the brooch, and a love story a hundred years old.

—Diane P. Tuccillo

On Fortune's Wheel
By Cynthia Voight

Grades 9-12

What a shock when she saw he was not bearded! When Birle defiantly climbed into her father's boat to prevent this man from stealing it, she had no idea that the thief was one of the Lords. And not just any Lord, but the heir to the Earl of Sutherland. Fearing for his life and the future of his lands, Orien has fled his home to seek his fate on Fortune's wheel. And now Fortune has put him and Birle in the same boat!

Little do the two know as they drift downriver that it will be months, years, before they see their homeland again. Shipwreck awaits them and war, slavery and escape. What can become of an Earl who was once a slave and does not wish to rule, or a girl who served as the Philosopher's scribe and does not wish to be a Lady? Can there be a place for them somewhere, together?

—Kathleen Beck

On the Devil's Court   Grades 7–12
By Carl Deuker

Had I really sold my soul to the Devil? I kept telling myself that was just my imagination, but still . . . what about the facts? Ever since I'd made that pledge in the shadows of a hollow, deserted gym—"Give me a full season, give me twenty-four games of this power, and my soul is yours!"—my game and my luck had been unstoppable.

Why would I even think of selling my soul? Because I wanted to play on a real basketball team, where the other guys were all jocks who lived for the game the way I did.

My name is Joe Faust, and my parents and I had just moved to Seattle from Boston. I was hoping to go to the local high school instead of another rich private school with a mediocre basketball team, but I blew my chance when I got drunk at a party, passed out cold on the front lawn, and was brought home in a police squad car. Now I'm going to Eastside Academy. Actually, they have a pretty good team, but right away the coach let me know that even though I was a senior, I was new, so I'd have to start out on the junior varsity. I had been cut, and I hadn't even tried out!

It was then that I felt the power of the Devil reach out to me. I *had* to play, so I made my deal. "Give me a full season, give me twenty-four games of this power, and my soul is yours." I made my deal and I made the team, but had I made a pact with the Devil, or just with myself? You decide.

—Marianne Tait Pridemore

One Day in the Tropical Rain Forest   Grades 3–6
By Jean Craighead George

Hi there! My name is Tepui, and I want to tell you about the day I raced against time. To most people, it probably seemed like any ordinary day, but I knew that it was Doomsday for my home, the Tropical Rain Forest of the Macaw. You see, on that day a caravan of bulldozers and trucks was scheduled to arrive from the city of Caracas to cut down the forest and prepare the land for crops. It would be a terrible disaster! The forest was alive with millions of species of wild plants and animals. And of course, all rain forests are vital to the health of our planet—they supply oxygen and remove polluting carbon dioxide from the atmosphere. My rain forest had to be saved, and there was only one way to do it! If the scientist who worked in the rain-forest laboratory could find a new, unnamed species of butterfly, a wealthy man had promised to buy and preserve the entire forest so that the butterfly could be named for his daughter. For many months the scientist and I had been searching for such a butterfly, but always without luck. Today was our very last chance! Join our race against the bulldozers, *One Day in the Tropical Rain Forest.*

—*Sister Mary Anna Falbo, CSSF*

One Green Leaf   Grade 7-Adult
By Jean Ure

I remember so many things. I remember meeting Abbey on the first day of a new school for the both of us. We were eleven. I also remember meeting Zoot and David that first day, but when you're eleven, boys are not a very high priority. By the end of the year, though, we were about as close as four friends can get. I remember our visiting each other's houses, and tea at Abbey's or horseback riding at David's. I remember that Zoot and David were always doing stupid things, like riding a bicycle downhill with no hands, just to impress us. I remember it was Zoot who paid dearly for those stunts, with chipped teeth and broken bones. David seemed to come through without a single scratch. I remember how Zoot got his nickname. It was David who named him. We were studying French that year, and Zoot was never any good at languages. Usually all he could think of to say was, "Zut alors!" He's been Zoot ever since.

I remember talking about death one day, and how we wanted our remains disposed of. Zoot wanted to be thrown into the sea with a note saying "Food for Sharks: Human Beings Keep Off!" I wanted a full-blown funeral service with lots of flowers and chanting priests. Abbey and David had simpler tastes. Abbey wanted a humanist ceremony; David, just a simple, honest farewell. Death seemed so far away then. The four of us were best friends, a unit, inseparable forever. But there are only three of us now, and I remember so many things.

—*Linda Olson*

One in a Million   Grade 10-Adult
By Harry A. Cole and Martha M. Jablow

Harry Cole rummaged in the refrigerator, searching absent-mindedly for something to spread on his morning toast. Grocery shopping had become the last thing on his mind after Jackie had been hospitalized. Now there was nothing but margarine on the shelves. Groping farther, Harry found an almost empty jar pushed to the back. The fancy label read "Color Me Raspberry" and was written in Jackie's prettiest script. The sight of his wife's handwriting and the memory of her making the jars of preserves last summer brought a fresh wave of pain.

Jackie had always lived life with the energy God would normally have given three people but instead had packed into one trim, vital personality. The divorced mother of four, she had raised her children alone until she met Harry Cole, a Presbyterian minister who fell in love with her *and* the children. Together they meshed into a family and made a home. That is, until Easter Saturday in 1986, when a terrific headache assaulted Jackie. This was no ordinary migraine. It was a stroke of the worst kind.

Jackie lay in a coma, and her family began the process of adjusting their lives to absorb their pain. The beloved mother and wife would probably die—maybe in days, maybe in weeks. Oh yes, some people come out of comas; the doctors wouldn't rule that out entirely. But they also advised caution, and their eyes were more honest: Don't get your hopes up. Be ready for the worst.

Harry struggled with his doubts, but one thought kept returning: Jackie wouldn't want to live this way, hooked to tubes that ate and breathed for her, her body a battleground for painful infections. The only answer was to seek court permission to unhook the tubes and end his wife's humiliation and suffering. And Harry was ready now to do just that.

But doctors can be wrong. Harry always said that Jackie was one in a million. Soon he was to discover how very true that phrase could be.
—*Nancy L. Chu*

**1001 Things Everyone   Grade 10–Adult
Should Know About American History
By John A. Garraty**

Do you remember your last American History course? More important, do you remember what you learned there? No? Have no fear, John A. Garraty's *1001 Things Everyone Should Know About American History* will put you at ease. Get ready for an entertaining and fact-filled trip through American history from the landing of Columbus to SALT II. Who were those men who signed the Declaration of

Independence? "Tippecanoe and Tyler Too"—I remember the slogan, but what did it mean? Who was known as "Old Fuss and Feathers"? Did LBJ really say that Gerald Ford was "a nice fellow who spent too much time playing football without a helmet"? With wit and wisdom, the author discusses America's bloodiest battles and noisiest elections, cites famous quotes (including some that the people in question never uttered), tells you the nicknames and slogans of the time, and describes some of the inventions that transformed daily life in the twentieth century.

If you are a trivia buff or need to put more punch into a term paper or sinply want to feel inspired about this colorful country of ours, then read *1001 Things Everyone Should Know About American History*. Definitely a history-lover's delight.

—Blair Reid

The Outside Child   Grades 3-6
By Nina Bawden

Have you ever felt that you were outside a group and just didn't fit in? What if that group was your own family? That's how Jane feels.

Jane's mother died when she was an infant, and since her father was a ship's captain and away from home most of the time, Jane was adopted and raised by two aunts. But she visits her dad on his ship whenever it gets into port. Imagine her surprise when one day she finds a picture of two other children in her father's cabin. He has remarried and he has two children and no one ever told her. Jane is very curious about her half-brother and sister, but it's hard to get any answers to her questions. Plato, her friend, tells her she'll have to become a spy if she wants to find out anything. But what Jane discovers most is how it feels to be *The Outside Child*.

—Frances W. Levin

Ozzy on the Outside   Grades 10-12
By R. E. Allen

More than anything else, Ozzy Mills wants to be a writer. Not something like a newspaper reporter, but a Writer with a capital W. He wants to create his own worlds where he'll have all the answers, put his creative talent into overdrive, and let his pencil do the talking.

But according to his Famous Authorship course, you have to live life to write about it. How can anyone really experience Life in Capitol, Colorado? He ought to be roaming the streets of Paris or somewhere, having exotic adventures to be insightful about.

Not that he hasn't tried to make his life in Capitol interesting. Didn't he attempt a unique sexual experience? Hasn't he done his best to make himself memorable to his classmates by always dressing in black, so they'll have something to talk about when his biographers come calling after he's famous? But it's just not the same.

When his mother suddenly dies and the rest of the family ignores her last wishes, Ozzy decides to head out into the world and start discovering Real Life. And on a bus bound for New Orleans, he encounters Life, all right, in the form of Maysie Fontaine. Maysie's a real woman, the kind Ozzy's only read about, and she teaches Ozzy that there's more to life and to literature than he ever dreamed.

—Jeff Blair

Paper Doll   Grades 9–12
By Elizabeth Feuer

Leslie is a senior in high school and she has never been in love. When the other girls meet in the cafeteria at lunch to talk about boys, Leslie hides in the basement practice rooms with her violin. For the last ten years, ever since she lost her legs in an automobile accident, Leslie's music has been the center of her life. After high school she hopes she'll be accepted at the Julliard School of Music. And it's not just her dream—it's her father's dream too, maybe even more than it's hers.

But then she meets Jeff. He's not much to look at, and he has cerebral palsy so he walks funny, but he's fun, and he thinks she is pretty and desirable. No other boy ever has. Suddenly Leslie realizes that there can be more to her life than music—there can be love. But her father, who has always loved and supported her, forbids her to see Jeff. Can Leslie find a way to have both Jeff and her music? Is she strong enough?

—Marianne Tait Pridemore

The Paper Knife   Grades 3–6
By Marc Talbert

Jeremy's the new kid at his school, and from the start, things don't work out too well. One day at recess he gets in trouble for pulling a knife on two other boys. It's just a small pocketknife, but still, it's sharp and dangerous. Some of the kids and most of the teachers and parents in town start to think of Jeremy as a real troublemaker.

But nobody knows Jeremy's real story, not even his own mother. Nobody knows about the things that George, his mother's former boyfriend, used to do to Jeremy. And Jeremy is so scared and ashamed about what George did that he can't tell anybody about it or ask for help.

The boys at school scare him a little, but his greatest fear is that George will come back. And now, with his pocketknife gone, Jeremy feels more helpless than ever. So he decides to make another weapon. Jeremy goes into his room, takes out a pen and paper, and writes down everything that happened to him when he and his mother were living with George. He keeps this paper in his pocket where his knife used to be, because he feels that somehow, when his secret becomes too much to bear, the truth may be the only thing that can save him.

What kind of courage does it take to tell the truth, when the truth may ruin the lives of people you love?

—*Steven Engelfried*

Paterno: By the Book Grade 10–Adult
By Joe Paterno and Bernard Asbell

When someone asks Joe Paterno to name an all-star squad from his twenty-plus years of coaching football at Penn State, he refers to a quote from another great coach, Knute Rockne of Notre Dame. The measure of greatness was the same for both coaches—not statistics, but rather the ways in which their players contributed to society after their playing days were over.

In this autobiography, Paterno tells us about football and about his complex strategies. But strengths and weaknesses of character, in himself or in others, matter more than on-field combat or final scores. And it is this expansive, probing aspect that makes this a book not only about a life but about a philosophy.

Paterno works hard to make his athletic program a success. He is active on NCAA committees and sponsors rule changes to benefit not only the colleges but also the lives of student athletes. He wants confident, serious players whose life experiences will help them function in the pressure-cooker of high-profile college sports. And Paterno is right there in the soup with them, helping them all the way. Which is one of the reasons why, after it's over, his players point to him with pride.

Paterno has his own inspirational characters, and he revels in them—people he knew in his years at Brown, or an old teacher. Or he will tell us about his favorite book, *The Aeneid*. Indeed, Paterno's analysis of the Virgilian hero as opposed to the Homeric is extraordinary, and complete with modern-day applications. Aeneas was a team player, you see, and, well—Virgil would have loved football!

—Mark Anderson

Phoenix Rising,   Grades 7–12
or How to Survive Your Life
By Cynthia D. Grant

"My sister Helen is dead. My older, beloved sister is dead. Helen is dead." Jessie could say the words, but she could not accept their meaning. All she could do was to try somehow to survive it all.

The whole family had known all along that Helen was sick, so it wasn't like it was a big shock when she never came home from her last trip to the hospital. The first tumor had appeared when Helen was fourteen. Cancer, for the past four years, had become a part of the family's life, but a part they treated like a big mistake that could get corrected any second. Helen had been such a great person—talented, funny, and wise. Not like me, Jessie thought, but the sort of person who ought to live.

Everyone who had known Helen had to come to terms with her death. To Jessie, Mom and Dad seemed calm and accepting, dealing with grief with mature intelligence. Lucas, Jessie's older brother, was full of anger, but he could find release in his music. Friends could remember Helen with fondness. Only Jessie was full of panic, horrible thoughts and nightmares, and terrible fears. The only one who could help Jessie was Helen herself.

When Jessie's very life hangs in the balance, it is Helen who does manage to reach Jessie through the diary she kept throughout her illness. Day by day, Jessie reads and absorbs. Slowly Jessie begins to understand life from Helen's point of view, and to gather the courage to go on.

—Sue Young

Phone Call from a Ghost   Grades 5-9
By Daniel Cohen

Ghosts don't have to live in spooky old houses or in graveyards, or even in haunted castles. The ghosts in this book live right here in America, and they are as likely to haunt an apartment house as a graveyard. You might even talk to one the next time you pick up the phone.

Don't believe me? Well, you're not alone—I'll bet that Patricia Adams never expected to get a phone call like that either. She was just a little girl at the time, and her mother had a very close friend whose daughter had been killed in a car accident several years earlier. The dead girl's name was Barbara, and she had been a college student. One Thanksgiving, Patricia and her family were visiting at this friend's house when the phone rang. Patricia picked it up. A long-distance operator said she had a collect call for her mother's friend from her daughter Barbara. Patricia didn't know quite what to do—she thought someone was playing a sick joke. But she went and got her mother's friend, and when the woman picked up the receiver she listened for a minute, then turned absolutely white and fainted.

Later she told what had happened: when she picked up the phone, she recognized not only her daughter's voice but the words she said as well—"Mommie, it's me. I need twenty dollars to get home." It was a phrase that she had often used before coming home—so often it had gotten to be a family joke. Her mother would always send the money. But this time the phone company had no record of where the call came from.

Then there's the story of Marie, who had a dream about her old friend Lana—a nightmare where she saw her sinking into a pool of blood. The next day she called her friend, and Lana said that she had been ill and in the hospital, and would be going back to the hospital the next day. Marie said she would like to come visit her there, but Lana said no, no visits, no phone calls. She would call Marie as soon as she was better. But she never did. Marie finally got in touch with her husband, who told her that Lana had died six months before, long before Marie had talked with her on the phone.

These are only two of the spooky stories in this book, stories that couldn't possibly have happened . . . and yet, somehow, they did.

—J. R. B.

Plague Year   Grades 7–12
By Stephanie S. Tolan

Molly called what happened that October a plague, but I'm not all that sure she was right. A plague comes from outside and infects people. What happened in our home town wasn't something from outside—it was something that was inside all the people that lived in that town, or almost all of them. It was surely inside Molly and inside me.

It all started the day Bran Slocum moved to town. From the very beginning he was different, with his long ponytail and his big gold earring, and he acted different too. He never reacted to the things that Nick and his gang said or did to him—Bran just shrugged it all off and went on, always quiet, always alone. That is, until the day the reporter came to town, with the story about the son of a serial killer who was going to our high school—the son whose description fit Bran like a glove. It was all over school that day and all over town the next—and the ugly side of the people that I'd known and trusted all my life came to the surface. It was as if they'd all changed personalities when I wasn't looking, just like the town I thought I knew so well. It was different—it was wrong. And they all said that Bran was the reason, he was the cause. They said he was a bad seed, and that he'd helped his father kill all those kids, and that he would start doing the same thing to the kids in our town. It was crazy from the beginning. I knew it wasn't true, he hadn't killed anyone—and when I saw him playing with his twin cousins, I didn't see how anyone could think that he had. His cousins were about four or five, and they'd been holy terrors before Bran moved here. Then they just latched on to him and wouldn't let go. The only time he got a break was when they were in daycare. But he loved it—you could tell as soon as you saw them together that he loved those kids.

Maybe if I had done something it would have made a difference, and it wouldn't have ended up the way it did. Or maybe Molly was right, and it was a plague that had infected everyone in town, and once they were contaminated, there was no cure. All I know now is that I don't like this town as much as I used to, and I'm not even sure I like *me* too much.

—*J. R. B.*

Poems of A. Nonny Mouse   Grades 3-6
By Jack Prelutsky, comp.

When we don't know the name of an author or poet, we say the poem or book was written by Anonymous. There are lots of poems signed Anonymous, and now someone has stepped forward to admit that she was their real author. Her name is Ms. A. Nonny Mouse, and she claims that because of an unfortunate misspelling of her name long ago, she never received the proper credit for all those poems. This book, *Poems of A. Nonny Mouse*, is the very first collection of her verses. And you can find Ms. Mouse herself, wearing a straw hat and carrying an umbrella, on every page.

Ms. Mouse has a very off-beat sense of humor. Consider this poem about a goat:

> There was a man—now please take note—
> There was a man who had a goat.
> He loved that goat—indeed he did—
> He loved that goat just like a kid.
>
> One day that goat felt frisk and fine,
> Ate three red shirts from off the line.
> The man, he grabbed him by the back
> And tied him to a railroad track.
>
> But when the train drove into sight,
> That goat grew pale and green with fright.
> He heaved a sigh as if in pain,
> Coughed up those shirts, and flagged the train.

Then there is her version of a familiar nursery rhyme:

> Mary had a little lamb,
> A lobster, and some prunes.
> A glass of milk, a piece of pie,
> And then some macaroons.
>
> It made the busy waiters grin
> To see her order so,
> And when they carried Mary out,
> Her face was white as snow.

A. Nonny Mouse's work includes limericks like those of the famous Edward Lear and tongue-twisters worse than the one about the woodchuck chucking wood. At last this hard-working author is getting the recognition she deserves!

—Diane L. Deuel

The Potato Kid   Grades 5-9
By Barbara Corcoran

You would not believe how the arrival of the Potato Kid affected my family during what I'd thought would be a dream summer. But the Potato Kid changed everything, in ways that we'd never expected.

Let me tell you about that incredible summer. To begin with, my mother dropped the bomb on us at the very end of the school year by announcing that she planned to take in a child for the summer, an underprivileged ten-year-old from a poor potato-farming family in Maine. This was one of Mrs. Hallowell's do-good projects—she had donated the money, and Mom had fallen for it hook, line, and sinker! And of course Mom was already committed to working at the church thrift shop three days a week. And of course Diantha, my older sister, was getting ready for college with lots of reading, and my brother Jay had a summer job at a nearby stable. My own summer was supposed to be glorious—I was going to spend a whole month at a Massachusetts stable that trained horses for world competition. I'd waited forever to do this, and now I could see it crumbling around me.

You see, I was the only one who would be free at the start of the summer to watch over this new arrival—Lilac, a.k.a. the Potato Kid. Grandma and Grandpa had been planning to keep her on the farm after I went away, but then Grandpa became very ill . . . That left me, Ellis, as the number-one Lilac-sitter all summer.

But I could never have imagined what a difference Lilac would make to us all—it turned out to be a really unforgettable vacation. Why? Well, I'll let you discover that for yourself in *The Potato Kid*, by Barbara Corcoran.

And if you then want to learn everything there is to know about the potatoes Lilac had to harvest every year, check out another title, called *The Great Potato Book* [Macmillan, 1986], Meredith Sayles Hughes.

—Sharon Thomas

The Princess in the Pigpen   Grades 3-9
By Jane Resh Thomas

Elizabeth lay in the feather bed under the fur covers. She was very, very ill. "It's the fever," she heard the servants whisper. Sukie, the nurse, bathed Elizabeth's face in cold water. Then she tucked Mariah the doll under Elizabeth's arm and turned the crank on the music box. As Sukie pulled the heavy bed-curtains closed, Elizabeth thought about her mother, also bedridden with the fever. Would she ever see her again? A shaft of sunlight shone through a crack in the curtains and struck Elizabeth in the face. It hurt her eyes and made her head pound.

An instant later Elizabeth heard a screeching noise like that of a rusty hinge. She looked around and couldn't believe her eyes! The bed and the curtains had vanished. She was standing in the middle of a pigpen. The screeching noise was the pigs squealing as they pushed past her to get to the food trough. Elizabeth turned and saw a man standing in a patch of sunlight that filtered into the dusty barn. He looked about as shocked as she felt. He was dressed like a peasant, but she was sure he was not one of her father's servants. She demanded to be taken to her father. At once!

Little did Elizabeth realize that going home would be so difficult. Especially since home was seventeenth-century England and she was now standing in a barn in twentieth-century Iowa. Can she be happy three hundred years in the future? Will she ever get back to her own home and her own time?   —*Linda Olson*

Probably Still Nick Swansen   Grades 7-12
By Virgina Euwer Wolff

To Nick Swansen, Room 19 is an endurance test. Other kids make fun of the kids in Room 19, because that's where the special classes for the learning-disabled are held. Nick has a hard time understanding things. But he already knows that Room 19 means an end-of-the-year project and not being able to drive, even though he is sixteen. He's hoping to have his own "Going Up" party. Once you have a "Going Up" party, you can stop being Special Ed and start being like everybody else the next day. The thing Nick really isn't sure about is the prom—does being in Room 19 mean you'd better not go? There's no rule that says you can't, so Nick decides to ask someone. But he knows that no matter how things turn out, he will probably still be Nick Swansen in the end.
                                                           —*Barbara Bahm*

Proud Knight, Fair Lady: Grade 10–Adult
The Twelve Lais of Marie de France
By Marie de France, translated by Naomi Lewis

There was a time (long, long ago) when knights roamed the land
seeking adventure, and fair ladies waited for true love. *Proud Knight,
Fair Lady* is a collection of stories written during that time. In these
stories, warriors rescue princesses, werewolves roam in the forest, love
and danger lie in wait, and magic makes life more interesting. In "Le
Fresne," twin girls are separated at birth, but fate contrives to reunite
them years later. "Launfal" tells of the exploits and trials of one of King
Arthur's greatest champions.

These are the stories that entertained proud knights and fair ladies
when the day's adventures were done—stories from another world.

—*Kimi Patton*

Radio Fifth Grade   Grades 3–6
By Gordon Korman

Benjy Driver and Mark Havermayer stare at their new teacher, Ms.
Panagopoulos, in steadily deepening horror. Hearing about what you're
going to learn is even worse than learning it, they think, as she drones
on, explaining that theirs will no longer be a "class" but a "seminar":
"a fifth-grade seminar—an adventure in learning"! Benjy and Mark roll
their eyes. Translated, all it really means is more homework—math
homework, science homework, social studies, and eight chapters of
reading a night, not to mention a research assignment for every
weekend—given out on Friday afternoon! How will they ever find time
for "Kidsview," the school radio program they write and produce?
Then Benjy has an inspired idea—they'll start a quiz show on
"Kidsview" using the research assignment for questions. They'll give
prizes for the right answers, and do the show and their homework at
the same time! Brilliant! They even talk their grouchy sponsor, Mr.
Whitehead, the pet store owner, into supplying both the prizes and the
mascot of the week—Winston Churchill, a large parrot. Now all they
have to do is keep Ms. Panagopoulos from listening to the program and
convince all the potential contestants that pooper-scoopers are great
prizes—even if you don't have a dog. When Winston Churchill gets

birdnapped and Ms. Panagopoulos shows up at the station, Benjy and Mark wish they'd never heard of "fifth grade seminars" or "Kidsview." Can Winston be found? Can Ms. Panagopoulos be fooled? Are Mark and Benjy fools? Read *Radio Fifth Grade* to find out.

—Jan McConnell

The Random House Book — Grades 3–6
of 1001 Questions and Answers
By Bridget Ardley and Neil Ardley

Did you know that the first matches appeared in 1827? A British chemist, John Walker, was trying to invent an explosive material for guns. He stirred the material with a stick and then scraped the stick on the floor to clean it off. It was like a giant match, and it burst into flame.

Did you know that the panda bear is not a bear at all, but a relative of the raccoon?

Did you know that there are little animals called bush babies with paws that look like human hands? Bush babies live in Africa and hide away during the day, but they come out at night to catch insects with their tiny hands.

Did you know that a chukka is a period of play in the gameof polo? It lasts seven minutes, and there are eight chukkas to a game.

Did you know that a hydrofoil is a boat with wings, but the wings are underwater? It can skim through the water at speeds of up to one hundred miles an hour.

Did you know that you can find all sorts of fascinating facts in *The Random House Book of 1001 Questions and Answers*? Facts that will amaze your friends, and astound your brothers and sisters!

—Eileen Gieswein

Raymond — Grades 5–9
By Mark Geller

Raymond's father beats him. He beats Raymond's mother too. She never fights back; she says he can't help it and really he loves Raymond. But if you really love your son, do you beat him till the gym teacher notices the bruises on his back? Raymond's father does just that—until the night Raymond can't take it any longer and fights back. He hits his father with a small statue and leaves him bleeding on the floor.

So, what do you do when you're thirteen years old, you know that if you go home again your father will kill you, and you don't have the money to go anyplace else? Raymond's sister lives in Milwaukee, a $24 bus ride away. How can he make 40¢ into $24 without attracting the attention of the police? How can he escape his father, and the beatings? And what about his mother—how can he leave her alone without any protection? He's desperate, and he's only got one chance—so he takes it.

—*J. R. B.*

Rebel Without a Clue   Grades 10-Adult
By Holly Uyemoto

You know Thomas Bainbridge—he's the eighteen-year-old who has it all. Born wealthy in Marin, he's the rich-boy-makes-good story of the year. You've seen his picture a hundred times in *Vogue, GQ,* and *People.* You've probably watched him on Oprah and Barbara Walters, and you must have seen his movies. Maybe you're even wearing a turban because he wore one in his last picture. Yes, Thomas has it all, all right—including AIDS.

Through the eyes of his friend Christian, we see Thomas at home, on the set, and at his exclusive parties. From the Bay Area to the California beach scene, we follow him as he languidly lounges toward death. Christian has a lot of time with Thomas that summer. A lot of time to think—and to remember. Even in Marin, growing up can be very, very hard, and that underlies all the lazy fun and games.

Finally when Christian has to confront the truth about himself and his feelings about Thomas, it is surprising, grotesque and pathetic all at once. But can Christian wake up and realize that he is a *Rebel Without a Clue?*

—*Douglas Rees*

Remembering and Other Poems   Grade 7-Adult
By Myra Cohn Livingston

Sometimes the smallest fragments of daily life are the most vividly remembered long after the moment has slipped away. And sometimes a familiar sight or smell, arriving at some unexpected time, can bring back wispy memories of days past. *Remembering and Other Poems* is a collection of childhood memories in verse which captures those

small, seemingly unimportant moments. Memories—of a day spent at
the beach collecting shells, of a picture of Lincoln hanging on the
classroom wall, of a Fourth of July decked in full-fire array—memories
that recall a time when life seemed so uncomplicated. Though many
things have changed, some things have hardly changed at all. If you
enjoy spending a quiet moment wondering what life is all about,
Remembering and Other Poems is for you.

—*Mary MacNeil*

Rewind to Yesterday   Grades 3-6
By Susan Beth Pfeffer

Chances are you don't remember your family's first TV—it's always
been around. But I remember the excitement at our house when our
first TV arrived and we finally got *The Flintstones* in our living room,
even if it was just on a black-and-white portable. This memory came
back to me when I read *Rewind to Yesterday*. The Forrest family are
just as excited when they get their first VCR. Everyone wants to learn
how to use it, so they all experiment with changing channels, recording,
rewinding, and setting the 24-hour timer/pre-set.

The next morning, eleven-year-old Kelly is up before the rest of the
family. She realizes that this is her chance to try out the VCR. She especially wants to outdo her twin brother Scott—he'll still be looking at
the instructions while she'll be using the VCR like a professional. But
things don't go quite the way Kelly plans. She accidentally pushes
"Rewind" when there is no tape in the machine and ends up back in
yesterday. This could be great! But is it? What happens when Kelly,
Scott, and their friend Miri use the VCR to travel in time?

—*Susan Perdaris*

Risky Times   Grades 7-12
By Jeanne Blake

At 23, Ali Gertz had everything: looks, lots of money, a good
education—and AIDS. The looks and money she inherited from her
folks; the AIDS came from sleeping with a guy—a nice guy—when she
was sixteen.

These are risky times. Certain behavior—unprotected sex, doing
drugs—could always get you in trouble. You could get pregnant—or get
herpes. You could overdose or get hepatitis. But AIDS is different. Peo-

plc go through pregnancies, they cope with herpes. They can survive
ODs, they recover from hepatitis. But AIDS will kill you—sooner or
later—every time. And living with AIDS is for always too: as long as
you have AIDS—two years, ten years, before you know you have it and
until you die—there is always some chance that having sex will kill the
person you love. There is also a chance that your friends, your neighbors, even your own family, will avoid you. And there is almost *no*
chance for kids: you don't dare have babies.

There are kids around—maybe you know them—who won't drink
from the school water fountain or swim in the town pool or hug their
uncle (because he's homosexual). And there are kids who think there's
something "dirty" about planning for sex; that AIDS only happens to
homosexuals, to grown-ups, or to scruffy people in big cities, so why
worry about it here? And so there are kids who are scared for the wrong
reasons or for no reason at all. And there are kids who are going to die.

Risky Times lets you meet people who have AIDS—and their best
friends and their boyfriends and their moms. It lets you meet kids who
don't have AIDS, and who don't ever want to get it! Above all, it gives
you the facts—the facts you need to make good choices, to stay well—
to stay alive.

—*Rene Mandel*

Rosy's Romance   Grades 5-9
By Sheila Greenwald

"My name is Rosy Cole. I go to Read, which is a small private school
on the Upper East Side of Manhattan. At Read our teacher, Mrs.
Oliphant, assigns us books that are very interesting. Some are about
adventure, some are about friendship, some are even about love. But
none of them ever is about romance. We have to find out about
romance on our own." [Use this paragraph alone for a short booktalk.]

With the help a friend—Hermione Wong—and the books in the two
romance series of Sugarwater High and Sakrinhill Quints, Rosy begins
Project Romance. The goal of the project get Rosy's two sisters ready
for the prom in less than three weeks.

It's a tough job, but Rosy and Hermione are confident they can do
it. All they have to do is make over Pippa and Anitra from head to toe,
from hair to nails to the proper romantic perfume. Then there's the
matter of the proper prom attire. And finally, once Rosy's sisters are
ready, all that's left to be done is to find them romantic dates. Everything will be just like the Sakrinhill Quints. Or will it? Read *Rosy's*

Romance to see if everything goes according to Project Romance.

—*Linda Olson*

The Runaways   Grades 5-6
By Ruth Thomas

What would you do if you found thousands of dollars hidden under the floorboards of an old abandoned house? Would you run away like Nathan and Julia did?

The old house was Nathan's secret place, and he had never told anyone about it. There really was no one to tell, since Nathan didn't have a single friend at school and none at home either. He was skipping school that rainy morning because he was in trouble for fighting (as usual). He had run into Julia hiding behind a tree. She had never skipped school before—she was too much of a wimp—but she was in trouble too. She was so stupid. She didn't know that after Assembly they came looking for you. If you didn't hide, you'd get caught. So Nathan invited Julia to the secret place, and she found the money—lots of it.

Nathan thought if he saved his half of the money, maybe he'd have enough to buy a house when he was older. But then Julia started spending her half on presents for the girls at school—trying to buy friends. It had worked for a day or two, so Nathan had tried it too, and then the teacher found out. Now their parents knew, and maybe the police. . . .

They couldn't give the money back. It was theirs. They had to run! *The Runaways*, by Ruth Thomas.

—*Marianne Tait Pridemore*

Running West   Grade 10-Adult
By James Houston

Snowblindness comes after days of walking in a brilliant white wilderness. That is, if you haven't already frozen, starved to death, or been killed by hostile natives or wild animals. In the year of our Lord 1721, all the land west of Fort York on the great Hudson Bay was marked as "Terra Incognita," and anyone who ventured into that frozen wasteland would probably encounter death before snowblindness.

In that year a young Scottish indentured clerk, William Stewart, and his Indian guide Thanadelthur begin a "walk-across" that will last nine months. The great white governor of Fort York needs more furs to send to England, and he needs new Indian tribes to trade with. Thanadelthur, a young woman of the Dene Nation whose family was massacred, has been adopted by the Cree but wishes to return to her own tribe in the Northwest. By following the great and steady wolf star and invoking the protection of "The Big Woman" spirit, she knows she can lead the white traders west. Her land runs wild with beaver, mink, otter, and lynx—pelts to trade for the magical gifts brought by the white man—beads, mirrors, and most impressive, the booming thunder-guns. But while Governor Knight knows that furs will make good trading, his eye has been caught by the soft yellow metal Thanadelthur's people casually form into beads, fur scrapers, and the occasional knife blade, though it is too soft to be really useful. She has told him and William Stewart that this metal lies in profusion in the rivers near her tribe. Driven by duty, greed, and love, Thanadelthur, William and an untrustworthy band of Cree begin "running west," through a land where death can seem a friend compared to the cruelty of life.

—*Jan L. McConnell*

The Sacred Circle of the Hula Hoop   Grades 6-9
By Kathy Kennedy Tapp

"I was eating a tuna-salad sandwich in the kitchen when the gun went off in the bedroom. From now on, whenever I look at tuna, or even smell it, my brain will think, bang! I'll remember . . . running down the hall to the bedroom . . . finding Jen . . . the red circle spreading over her pink blouse . . . the gun in her hand."

Thirteen-year-old Robin will never forget her sister Jen's suicide attempt. It was a serious attempt—her second—and it seems a miracle that Jen survived. Is it possible that the sacred Hula Hoop saved Jen's life?

Trying to understand, Robin thinks back to two years ago, when Jen began to change. At times she became a different person—she would put on some bizarre outfit, or talk in a strange, baby voice. Jen never remembered these spells afterwards. At about the same time, Robin's life changed too. She won the Hula Hoop contest, and she and her friends Lynn and Georgie all divided the winnings. They made a pact to stay friends forever, using the lucky Hula Hoop as a friendship ring around the three of them. One night when Robin was lying awake worrying about her sister, the miracle happened: the Hula Hoop formed a golden ring of light, and Robin, believing it was a vision, prayed, "Please—make Jen okay."

The first time Jen tried to kill herself, Robin turned to her parents for an explanation. What was wrong with Jen? Why had she done it? But her parents couldn't really explain anything. It was only when Robin happened to see *The Three Faces of Eve* at the drive-in that she learned the name of Jen's problem.

Now, two years later, with Jen in the hospital, Robin discovers the shocking reason for her sister's illness—a reason that has more to do with history—family history—than with magic.

—*Eldean Kechely*

Saturday Night   Grade 9–Adult
By Susan Orlean

Saturday night. The night when rules are made to be broken and life is meant to be lived. On Saturday nights people eat, drive, play, and love more than on any other night of the week. Money flows, whether it is spent in restaurants, theaters, music clubs, video-rental stores, bars, poker games, polka clubs, bowling alleys, or shooting galleries. Even popular music has had a love affair with Saturday night—after all, can anyone name a song written about Thursday night? Wednesday afternoon? No, Saturday night is special.

But not everyone relaxes on Saturday night. For every person who kicks back, there is someone else who has to work. Babysitters. Waiters and waitresses. Theater employees. Musicians. Doctors and nurses and police officers, for Saturday night is also the night when people are most likely to die from car accidents or drug overdoses or shootings and stabbings.

Just what goes on on Saturday night? How have changes in American society affected the way we spend this special night? And why is Saturday night still so important, no matter how you spend it? Follow Susan Orlean as she explores the romance and reality of *Saturday Night*.

—*Nancy L. Chu*

Secret City, U. S. A.   Grades 5–8
By Felice Holman

Benno has a dream—he would like to be a pioneer in a new land where there is space and light and fresh air. Benno lives in a crowded tenement in a crowded, noisy city, and he longs for something better.

One day while Benno is exploring, he and his friend Moon discover an area of the city that is no longer inhabited. The buildings there have collapsed or have been torn down, and the streets are filled with debris. Benno sees this wasteland as the open space he's dreamed of. He and Moon discover one house that is still in fairly good shape, and they claim it as their own. They have marvelous plans about how they will fix it up and share it with some homeless boys they know. They face many dangers in fulfilling their dream—wild dogs, the Poison gang, and a mysterious old man. But despite these obstacles, Benno and Moon are determined to establish Secret City. Can a group of kids reclaim a neighborhood? Find out in *Secret City, U. S. A.*

—*Terrie Ratcliffe*

The Secret of the Indian   Grades 3-6
By Lynne Reid Banks

It all started a year ago when Omri discovered the wonderful power of the battered old cupboard which his brother had given him for his birthday. Though it looked like an ordinary medicine cabinet, Omri was astonished to learn that the small cupboard had magical powers—plastic objects placed inside it would come to life! That's how Omri transformed Little Bear from a plastic model Indian into a living, breathing, flesh-and-blood Iroquois transported from eighteenth-century America to twentieth-century London. Stubborn and domineering, Little Bear was every inch a chief, and Omri learned that the incredible power of the cupboard brought with it terrible responsibilities.

Now Omri is faced with a new challenge—a tempting yet frightening one. The old wooden chest that he rescued from a junk shop possesses an odd magic of its own, which would enable normal-sized people like Omri and his friends Patrick and Emma to travel through time. Exciting as that might sound, Omri's experiences with Little Bear and Boone, the cowboy visitor from the Old West, have taught him that such adventures can involve dangerous risks. Little Bear and Boone are now real people who must be cared for and protected. They can be hurt, and unlike plastic toys, they cannot simply be put away on a shelf when Omri gets tired of playing with them. Then there are the prying eyes of all the people who do not know the secret of the cupboard and the chest—Omri's parents, teachers, and classmates. Worst of all is the task of convincing the people who *do* learn the secret to be careful—their new-found power is not a plaything. When Patrick decides to test the magic of the wooden chest and travels back to the Old West, Omri must find a way to explain his friend's mysterious disappearance—and bring him home again!

Playing with time travel may sound like fun, but it also means playing with people's lives and futures. There is always the possibility that someone won't make it back—someone like Patrick. On top of that, the threat of discovery is coming closer. Perhaps Omri can no longer control *The Secret of the Indian*.

—*Nancy L. Chu*

Self-Portrait with Wings   Grades 2–6
By Susan Green

Suppose I told you I had wings—would you believe me? Of course you wouldn't, especially since you couldn't see them. But—I do! It's a long story, one I really don't understand myself.

All I wanted was to be able to ice-skate as well as Penelope, to fly across the ice and make those wonderful pivots and jumps. One evening I got out Mom's anatomy and drawing books, studied where wings would have to be to give a person the correct balance, etc., and drew a picture of myself with wings. When I awoke the next morning, I had grown wings . . . wings that could only be seen when you looked in the mirror.

My best friend Angela said, "You'll be famous! Can't you just see yourself in the *Enquirer*? Right next to 'Woman Gives Birth to Two-Headed Snake,' there you'll be: 'Girl Sprouts Wings!'"

That was my first clue that having wings might not be as wonderful as I'd thought it would be. And let me tell you, not even the prospect of being an ice-skating star is worth what I went through!

—*Carol Kappelmann*

A Serpent's Tooth   Grades 7–9
By Robert Swindells

Moving to a new school is the pits at any age. At thirteen it's a disaster. For Lucy the first day was all she'd been dreading—and more. Not only did she have hostile teachers, she had ugly, overbearing classmates as well. Then to top it off her mother became involved in a protest against a nuclear waste dump right across the road at Pit Fields. Lucy could have died.

She had always hated the way her parents fought about her mother's causes, but this time her dad went too far. While her mother was camping on the road into Pit Fields, he locked her out . . . in the rain. Faced with a choice, Lucy joined her mother. It meant going to school the next morning in clothes still damp from being outside all night, and in weeks to come it meant sleeping in a car and studying in the home of the "crazy lady" who lived at Pit Fields. But it meant more than that to Lucy—at last she had a chance to learn what was really important.

So why did she accept Tim's invitation to a party at his house when his parents were away? She should have known there would be trouble, but she wasn't thinking, or perhaps wasn't honest with herself. . . .

—*Sarah M. Thrash*

Seventeen Against the Dealer   Grades 10-12
By Cynthia Voight

Dicey Tillerman is a boatbuilder. Correction—Dicey Tillerman *wants* to be a boatbuilder. At twenty-one, Dicey has dropped out of college to open her own business. Nights of working at McDonald's have given her the money she needs for a start; days working in Ken's boatyard have given her the experience she needs to make her plans work.

And the boats she plans to build! Not chintzy little plywood dinghies like those her landlord throws together to sell to summer people who don't know any better. No, Dicey plans to build sleek, solid-wood sailboats with curved planks that fit seamlessly. Boats from Tillerman's Boatyard will be special. Dicey's hard work will see to that.

Dicey's not afraid of hard work. If it takes fourteen-hour days to get her business running, she'll put them in. Her family says they understand her need to succeed. And Jeff, her boyfriend, is busy finishing his senior year at college and understands why marriage isn't high on her agenda right now. Yet when Gram's illness turns to pneumonia and Jeff doesn't return her phone calls, Dicey begins to realize that even understanding families and friends need attention.

On top of everything else, Dicey begins to wonder if sacrifice is really enough to make a business work. First her prized tools are stolen during a break-in at the shop. Then materials cost more than she had planned. Contracts, insurance, and all the other nit-picky details that seemed to have little to do with boat-building suddenly become very important. But Dicey doesn't know much about them. For all her planning, Dicey learns about running a business alone the hard way through mistakes. Big ones.

When a drifter named Cisco Kidd drops by her shop, picks up a paintbrush and begins working, Dicey finds the companionship she needs. But can she afford to trust Cisco? Can she afford not to?

—Nancy L. Chu

Shabanu: Daughter of the Wind Grade 5–Adult
By Suzanne Fisher Staples

Shabanu sits upon her father's shoulders and surveys the Sibi Fair. Here in Pakistan, it's the most thrilling event she can imagine, so different from the peaceful desert home she shares with her parents, her sister, and other family members. There herds of camels run free, and water is the most precious thing on earth.

Shabanu hears the music of the fair blending with the roar of motorcycles from the daredevil pit. Her father treats her to exotic foods she's never tasted before and takes her on a Ferris wheel ride. Later, back at their camp, it's down to business—the real reason for traveling to the fair. Shabanu's father plans to sell some of his camels at the fair so he will have enough money to pay for both his daughters' weddings. You see, here in Pakistan, even today, a good father chooses a husband for his daughter when she is very young, and then she marries at age thirteen. And a daughter must obey her father always, or she can be severely punished—even killed—no matter how much her father may love her.

Shabanu's sister Phulan is thirteen now, and her wedding day is approaching quickly. Shabanu is almost twelve, and she knows she will be next. She knows that the days of riding on her Dadi's shoulders, running free with her camels, and feeling the peace and joy of childhood are almost over. There won't be dates or parties or trips to the shopping mall when she becomes a teenager, because those things are unheard-of in her culture. And although most teenagers have a hard enough time coping with their changing bodies and changing relationships, Shabanu will also have to deal with becoming a married woman—with a husband, in-laws, a house to keep, and children of her own.

So she savors the ride on her Dadi's shoulders, knowing there will be no fair with him hext year. Next year, though he loves her dearly, her father will force her to prepare for marriage. It doesn't seem so bad at first. But when circumstances change and things happen that no one expects, trying to obey him becomes the hardest thing Shabanu has ever had to do.

—Diane P. Tuccillo

Shadow of the Wall   Grade 7-Adult
By Christa Laird

Misha feels much older than his thirteen years. Like most young people in Warsaw's Jewish ghetto, he has abandoned his youth in the struggle for daily survival. Since his father's death, his mother, ill and unable to take care of her three children, has entrusted Misha and his two sisters, Rachel and Elena, to the care of Doctor Korczak at the Orphans' Home. But Misha has to support his mother, and that means making frequent, dangerous trips out of the ghetto to trade his father's remaining possessions for food or money. The price for getting caught outside the ghetto is instant death at the hands of the Nazis. Inside the ghetto as well, there are daily demonstrations of Nazi brutality. Misha sees the baker and his son hauled into the street and shot to death, their bodies left to rot where they fell. People inside the ghetto are dying by inches of starvation, and typhus is epidemic. Rumors have begun to circulate, suggesting that the ghetto residents will soon be relocated to death camps. Luckily, the good doctor has been able to find a foster family on the outside for baby Elena.

As his fourteenth birthday approaches, the age at which children usually leave the orphanage, Misha must decide what to do. He knows that Doctor Korczak will not ask him to go, but he feels he must. There are so many other, younger children in greater need of the orphanage's care. Yet he hates to leave Rachel, and he has nowhere to go. Then his mother dies, and an acquaintance asks him to join the Dror, an underground resistance organization. Misha soon learns that it is one thing to fight for personal survival but a different matter altogether to fight for the survival of your people.

—*Kathy Ann Miller*

Shadow over Mousehaven Manor   Grades 3-4
By Mary DeBall Kwitz

Minabelle Mouse never dreamed that this Christmas would be quite different from any she'd ever experienced. It all started when she learned that her dear Aunt Pitty Pat and her new husband, Magnus, were not coming to share her cozy Christmas fire. In fact, Aunt Pitty Pat lay very ill, and Minabelle was instructed to bring her aunt's will to Mousehaven Manor immediately.

Minabelle set out on the dangerous journey from Rodentville to Mousehaven Manor. With her own eyes she saw the massacre of chickens by the Chicago Rats. She was warned on the way by Secret Agent Weasel that she would be wise to turn back and not press on to Mousehaven Manor, which was the center of danger. What was really happening at her aunt's home? Why did the name S U N G A M make her attackers on the road flee in terror?

You see, Minabelle had to find out, and the answer lay at Mousehaven Manor. Join Minabelle against the Chicago Rats as the mystery unfolds in *Shadow over Mousehaven Manor.*

—Sharon Thomas

Shark Beneath the Reef   Grades 7-9
By Jean Craighead George

Fourteen-year-old Tomas Torres is a dreamer. He dreams mainly of one thing—catching the huge whale shark by himself. Oh yes, with the money from the sale of the shark, he would certainly be the hero who could save the family fishing business for Grandfather and Uncle Miguel! How proud his mother would be when he paraded down the streets of Loreto carrying the shark overhead, glistening in the sun. His friend Griselda would smile and shout his name aloud so that everyone would know of his bravery. But Tomas has other dreams too . . . dreams of finding a legendary Spanish ship with golden shafts wrecked atop the Coronados volcano. He dreams of his future as a student at the high school and then at the university.

Yes, Tomas dreams and dreams . . . but as he dreams, he is unaware of the round black eye peering through the clear water at him. Tomas has too much on his mind to notice that the birds are acting strangely and that the smaller fish are looking for safe places to hide. Will his dreams prepare him for the moment when he finally comes face to face with the shadow hiding beneath the coral reef?

—Pam Swafford

The Shimmershine Queens   Grades 5-9
Camille Yarbrough

Angie is a dreamer. She wants her dad to come back home so her mother won't be so depressed. She wishes the kids at school would stop teasing her about her dark skin and kinky hair.

Cousin Seatta tries to help Angie by telling her how to shake off Mr. Fear and glory in knowledge. She encourages Angie to use her git-up-and-git, to do her best and shimmershine.

Angie shares Cousin Seatta's advice with her best friend Michelle. Both girls are determined to shine in knowledge, to be proud of their African heritage, and to do their best. But when Charlene and her gang continue to taunt Angie about her looks, she realizes she must do more.

With Michelle's help, Angie speaks up for herself, only to discover that Charlene and her gang won't quit. The insults continue until Michelle attacks Charlene. Mrs. Cooper sends Michelle to the principal's office after school, and Angie is left alone to face Charlene and another fight.

Will she ever be able to stand up to Charlene, to glow and feel good about herself? Can she and Michelle ever become *The Shimmershine Queens*?

—*Susan Wolfe*

Short Subject   Grades 5-9
By Binnie Kirshenbaum

For Audrey Feldman, life is not just boring, it's chaotic. It's nothing like a movie with a beginning, middle, and end—which is probably why Audrey spends all her afternoons at Mr. Eisenstein's Variety Theatre. Audrey doesn't want to go home so her mother can begin another fight. She can't stand to be in the same room with her creepy brother Alex, and she'll never hear the end of her "psychological adolescent problems" from her sister Ruth. So with a box of popcorn and a cherry Coke, Audrey escapes to the movies of the '30s and '40s. But you can't sit in a movie theatre forever. And, as Audrey soon discovers, you can't take life off the silver screen and try to live it, either.

—*Kaite Mediatore*

The Sierra Club   Grades 3-6/Adult
Summer Book
By Linda Allison

Booktalk for Children

I know you've all planted seeds in your garden at home or for a project in school or perhaps in Sunday School, but have you ever started a peanut farm? It really can be done—it takes time, but it's not difficult. You'll need a raw, unroasted peanut, the kind you can buy at a health-food store. Carefully remove the shell but leave the red skin on. After soaking the peanut in water overnight, place it on some yarn inside a jar. Each day add just enough water to keep the yarn damp. A root should begin to grow. When the root is about three inches long, plant it in an eight-inch flowerpot, with pebbles in the bottom and potting soil nearly up to the rim. Move the pot to a sunny place and water it regularly. Soon leaves will sprout, and in six or eight weeks, yellow flowers will appear. About a month after the flowers have fallen off, the green plant will turn brown. Then the peanuts can be harvested—just dump out the pot and there they'll be. And imagine what your friends will say when you offer them peanuts you grew yourself!

This is just one of the suggestions in the Garden chapter of *The Sierra Club Summer Book*. That chapter also tells you how to make raisins and sunjam, how to get a free Dennis the Menace comic, and how to recognize garden birds and garden bugs, good and bad.

In other words, if you want to try something new and different this summer, if you want to be creative and learn while having fun, take a look at *The Sierra Club Summer Book*, and enjoy!

Booktalk for Parents and Teachers

It's summer vacation. The kids are home. The neighbor kids are home. They've been home for a week now, and they're already complaining: it's boring, it's hot; they want to be entertained.

You could tell them that "humans can survive several hours at 200 degrees Fahrenheit with no serious effects" but I'm sure they won't be impressed. Then you can bring out the *Summer Book*, a collection of ideas for summer fun and learning put out by the Sierra Club. In the chapter on keeping cool, they can learn to make fans, the old-fashioned accordion-pleated kind or the leaf kind. The heat can be a lesson in looking at the animal kingdom to see how various animals keep cool— by finding shade, hiding under rocks or in the mud, becoming nocturnal, panting, or just staying still.

In addition to fans, kids can make sun hats or set up a water garden, a water whip, a water slide. A water war might be fun. If they like to send away for things, Captain Hydro will supply directions on making your own rain gauge, as well as experiments, puzzles, and problems dealing with water. The Soil Conservation Service has a free pamphlet on water conservation. And if you can stand some junior chefs in the kitchen, why not let them try Easy Vanilla Ice Cream, Frozen Bananas, Watermelon Ice, or any of the other summer treats offered in this chapter? Don't forget, this chapter is only one of many, all cram-packed with ideas and suggestions, facts and fancies, crafts, games, and trips that you and your family, scout troop, or class can enjoy this summer and throughout the year. Projects are illustrated and directions are easy to follow. Supplementary material is available free or for a very low price. Don't let summer get you down. It's too good to waste!

　　　　　　　　　　　　　　　　　　　　　　　　　—Carol Kappelmann

Silver　　　　　　　　Grades 10-12
By Norma Fox Mazer

Sarabeth wasn't rich, and she wasn't sophisticated. Grant Varrow and her friends were, and Sarabeth couldn't believe it when they asked her to join their crowd. *Her* mother cleaned houses for a living, and Sarabeth had never known what it was like to have enough money. 'Course, she never thought of the things she had that money couldn't buy—the friends she'd made in the trailer court where she and her mother lived, andthe trust her mother had in her, the love they shared. All she saw was the money they didn't have and the things they couldn't buy. Sarabeth was sure that having enough money would solve everything.

But that was before she met Grant and her friends, and before she found out about Patsy's secret. Money didn't buy Patsy anything except fear and mistrust and terror. Money couldn't buy her mother's trust or even her attention. It did buy Patsy her uncle's attention, and then his interest—and the horror that came with it. Sometimes there's a lot that money can't buy, problems that money can't solve.

　　　　　　　　　　　　　　　　　　　　　　　　　—J. R. B.

Silver Days　　　　　　　Grades 5-12
By Sonia Levitin

America. For Lisa Platt, her sisters, and their parents, America means life, first and foremost. By coming to America, they can live.

Lisa and her family are Jews, living in Germany, with the Nazis in full power. So they leave, they escape, to America. They have to leave everything behind: possessions, friends, relatives. But they have no choice if they are to survive.

So now they are in America. Though America means life for them, it also means great hardship. In Germany, the Platts were a very wealthy family. In America, they live in a filthy tenement in New York City. In Germany, Lisa's father was an important and successful businessman. In America, he is a peddler on the street. In Germany, Lisa's mother led a life of leisure. In America, she's a scrubwoman. In Germany, Lisa and her sisters had everything they could want. In America they have nothing. But they *are* alive, and if they had remained in Germany, in all likelihood they would not be.

Then Lisa's father moves them again—this time to California. He's sure that they can make it there. In America, anything is possible—even for poor immigrants who can barely speak the language.

But things are tough in California too. Lisa's parents work very hard and there is still not enough money. And once America enters the war, the Platts are looked upon with suspicion because they are German—no matter that they fled to America to escape the Nazis.

Lisa, however, still has her dreams. She wants to be a dancer. She wants to have friends, and boyfriends. She wants to be an American. She is so busy pursuing these dreams that she forgets how fragile her world really is—until it begins to crumble.

—*Melinda Waugh*

The Silver Kiss
By Annette Curtis Klause

Grade 7–Adult

It seemed as though everyone was leaving her—her mother slowly dying of cancer, her father, whose concern for his wife had made him all but forget he had a daughter, and now Lorraine, her best friend, moving to Oregon. "Soon," she thought, "I'll be all alone." But just then, gazing across the small park with the few lights making golden pools in the darkness, she saw a movement in the gazebo, and then, as he stepped into the light, she saw him—slight, pale, dressed in black; with dark eyes and silver hair. Suddenly she realized how beautiful he was, and as she began to cry he fled, disappearing as silently as he'd appeared, and Zoe sat alone, crying for all she had lost.

Simon thought of the girl, how beautiful she was, dark-haired like the night, and thin, so very thin, as if one of his brethren had already claimed her. But no, she didn't have that smell about her—she was untouched. She had surprised him. He didn't like surprises—he might let his guard slip down, and that could be dangerous. He was amazed that he kept thinking about her, that he wanted to talk to her. He didn't talk much with people—they were food. One didn't talk to food, or learn its speech patterns. But still he wanted to see this girl again, talk to her, maybe even kiss her—the silver kiss, that could make her his forever.

And so on Halloween night, after the trick-or-treaters had gone, Zoe opened her front door and invited the real monster inside.

—*J. R. B.*

Silver Pigs   **Grade 10–Adult**
By Lindsey Davis

The girl wasn't exactly what you would call streetwise. When I first saw her, she was dashing across the Forum with two evil-looking thugs in hot pursuit. Maybe she was planning on losing herself in the afternoon crowd, but the bad guys would have to have been blind to miss her. The expensive outfit and jewelry she was wearing made her an easy target to spot among the drab, work-a-day Romans in the Forum.

Since I like to think of myself as a good guy, I decided to help the poor girl. Actually, what really happened was that when she almost ran me down on the steps of the Temple of Saturn, I got a good look at her face and decided that she was far too beautiful to waste on those guys. Besides, why miss such a golden opportunity? Some very worried and very wealthy Roman father would probably offer a generous reward to the kind person who returned his wayward daughter.

Well, I was right on two counts, which gives you some hint about my abilities as an informer, or private detective as you moderns like to call us. Sosia *was* wealthy, and her father, Senator Decimus Camillus, was very glad to have her returned safely. But I missed out on the reward.

What I got instead was a job. It seemed that someone was stealing silver from the government-owned mines in Britain. The Senator was trying to investigate the crime because rumors had reached some very high-placed ears that this stolen silver was going to be used to finance a plot against the Emperor Vespasian. Needless to say, Sosia was also lending a hand with the case—hence the chase scene in the Forum. My job was simple enough: Discover who was stealing the silver and thus save the Empire. Piece of cake, right? The really big question, of course, is, do I get the girl?

—*Margie Reitsma*

Singin' Somebody Else's Song   Grades 7–12
By Mary Blount Christian

Nashville. Country music capital of the world. The city that spawned all the greats—Johnny Cash, Dolly Parton, Kenny Rogers. And now Gideon Bullock was there to make a name for himself.

For as long as Gideon could remember, he and his best friend Jeremy had planned on going to Nashville and making it big. At home in West Texas they played in a band, practiced their music, and wrote songs. Really good ones, too—as good as anything on the radio. As soon as they finished high school, they were going to Nashville, and the rest would be history.

But things didn't work out according to plan. Life became too much for Jere to deal with, and he committed suicide, leaving Gideon all alone—all alone to carry out their big plan.

Gideon feels that he let Jere down—that he didn't do the things a best friend should do. Maybe if he'd been a better friend, Jere would be here with him now, in Nashville. Both of them should be here, not just Gideon.

Trying to find a publisher for their music in a city where hundreds of others are trying to do the same thing is hard, discouraging, depressing work. Gideon can't help but feel that if Jere were here with him, everything would be going smoothly. Jere knew how to do things like this. He was the leader, Gideon was the follower.

Gideon is determined not to give up, though, no matter what the odds. Jere died because Gideon wasn't there for him, and Gideon isn't about to let that happen again. Jere will live on. He'll live on through his music.

But what about Gideon? What about his life?

Singin' Somebody Else's Song, by Mary Blount Christian.

—*Melinda Waugh*

Sleeping Arrangements   Grade 7–Adult
By Laura Cunningham

Before Lily was twelve years old her sleeping arrangements had change drastically three times. At four years old, Lily remembered vaguely, she had slept in odd places in relatives' homes, once even under a dining-room table. But at five she had moved with her mother to their very own apartment, a New York efficiency right beside Yankee Stadium.

During the days she was left on her own a lot, since her mother worked until six p.m. Lily's play consisted of shoplifting, exploring the dark, forbidden regions of the park, and making the neighbors talk. But when her mother came home in the evening, they were together, inseparable now in their new home. Lily knew she was deeply loved, and life was fairly uncomplicated. That is, until she was eight.

That year her mother died. Since Lily was not told why or even allowed to attend the funeral, her mother's death wasn't real to her. Confused and lost, she was clucked over by neighbors and sighed over by relatives. Lots of well-meant sympathy, no real mothering. In the end the only two people willing to step in and care for her were unlike and unlikely: Len and Gabe, her mother's grown brothers.

Len looked and acted like Abraham Lincoln, whom he idolized. Gabe, on the other hand, strictly adhered to his own, somewhat unconventional version of the Jewish faith, cleaned the house ferociously, and lived in a mystical dream world, composing Jewish gospel songs. They sent their clothes to a cleaners that returned them clean, all right, but with hundreds of creases everywhere. They couldn't cook, so popcorn became the breakfast favorite. And since Lily was officially in mourning and the only female in the house, the two uncles bowed to her decorating ideas for their new "family" apartment: a polka-dot sofa, pink striped walls, and boxes for chairs and tables.

In this three-bedroom apartment, the dog got a room of its own while one uncle's bed was squeezed in the front hall for all their visitors to bump into (not that they had very many). Gradually their apartment took the shape of a child's imagination, but still, it was home for them.

While Lily waits for her mother to return, her uncles provide a sense of security, love, and the magic of goodness. They provide a family, eccentric through it may be. But what will happen when Lily must face the outside world?

—Faye A. Powell

Small Victories: Grade 10–Adult
The Real World of a Teacher, Her Students,
and Their High School
By Samuel G. Freedman

Jessica Siegel is more than a teacher at Seward Park High School: she's a mother figure, mentor, journalist, supporter, nag, and inspiration.

Seward is an inner-city high school, situated on the Lower East Side of New York City, packed with Spanish and Asian immigrants, surrounded by crime and poverty, and submerged in city bureaucracy. Yet Jessica and other teachers there somehow pull the students through, with ninety percent going on to college. What's their secret? Knowledge and caring.

So many students, yet each so individual.

See Wai was born in China, his bare yard set off by bamboo stakes. When he was seven his family fled from the flood waters of Yong He Le River, beginning a journey that would take them halfway round the world.

Carlos came from the Dominican Republic. By age ten he was smoking pot and skipping school.

Lun had a troubled father, overbearing brothers, and a mother straining to hold her fissioning family together. Then he discovered his sole friend—on the streets. When his friend invited Lun to join the Chinatown gang Ghost Shadows, Lun remembered their warning: "Join another gang, and we'll kill you!"

Aracelis received her first proposal of marriage at age twelve, but her mother told her to finish her education. Now she's seventeen and in love with Miguel. Yet she also wants college and a career—how can she let down her seamstress mother, who sacrificed so much for her?

Jessica touched each of these students' lives, just as she will touch yours.

—Lesley S. J. Farmer

Sniper **Grades 7–12**
By Theodore Taylor

Rocky had been abandoned by his mother. She simply shut her ears to the high-pitched hunger screams, and it was a waste of words to tell her she was being a bad mother. Instead, Ben's dad said, "He's all yours. Good luck, boy. You'll need it."

So ten-year-old Ben became a surrogate mother, and formula time came every two hours, round the clock. Ben's own mother said, "You should have been a girl. I've never seen such a maternal instinct." So began the love affair between Benjamin Jepson and Rocky Lion. And the time-bomb at the heart of it began to tick away.

Ben's father was a researcher and writer. His mother was a famous nature photographer. Together they had created a game preserve in Orange County, California, in spite of the neighbors' opposition. Now

Ben, fifteen, had to take care of the place while his parents were off on an expedition in Africa. Alfredo was actually in charge, but he was out of commission, in the hospital. Some prowler had let the lions loose, and Ben had to retrieve them. Someone was killing the animals—shooting them.

But the worst was yet to happen. The worst was when Ben found his beloved Rocky—shot by the sniper who was killing off the game preserve's animals, one by one.

—Lesley S. J. Farmer

So Much to Tell You   Grades 10-12
By John Marsden

Marina won't talk, but she does write, and little by little she shows us her world.

February 6

This is my third day at boarding school. I don't know what everybody is expecting me to do here. Actually, I do know, but I can't do anything about that. Mr. Lindell, our English teacher, has given us journals to write in during Prep. It scares me. I thought I wouldn't write in it. But I'm already writing, sharing secrets I want to keep hidden.

February 13

Ann has noticed me looking at her quilt. It looks like a jigsaw of stars, and I lie in bed and try to fit the pieces together. Now I'm so embarrassed, I've turned my face to the wall, into my pillow. She seems kind, but I don't want to be noticed by anyone, for anything. And with my face, that's so hard.

February 20

Tonight Sophie pretended I was a ventriloquist's doll. She put her hand up my sweater and moved me around as if I were a puppet. The girls laughed at her as she talked for me in a squeaky voice. I think Sophie is angry because I won't talk. Even though she's noisy and I'm silent, I can still win "arguments" with her.

February 24, 4 p.m.

I watched the girls returning from Sunday afternoon outings with their families. Their laughter is natural and relaxed. They live in a strange world of love that I envy but cannot understand—and will never enter.

Fourteen-year-old Marina's journal presses her relentlessly to share her pain, wonder, anger, and yearning with us. There are so many things she wants to share, if only she can find the courage and the words. Will she opt for life, or shrink back into the terrible cloud from her past?

—*Tracie Pruitt*

Soda Jerk   Grade 5–Adult
By Cynthia Rylant

I work the counter at Maywell's Drugstore here in Cheston, Virginia. It's not much of a job, but it's mine. It's not much of a town either, like living in a dream that somone else is having and we're all freeze-dried into our own little poses and semblances of life. But it's my town.

Maywell's has that sort of sweet-sour smell to it that clings to you after you've left. Sometimes people leave tips behind, sometimes secrets they don't mean for a guy like me to have, but they always take away with them some of that special smell.

I see just about everyone in the whole town come through here at one time or another: the rich kids who look like they're in a Tide commercial, the poor ones who belong in one for Clearasil, the hippies who bring another smell or two in with them, the police, the old ladies, the jocks, their girls, the hunters. They all come through. It's the advantage of being the only drugstore in town. From my spot behind the counter, I see them and their dreams and secrets.

I've yet to see, though, anything that'll tell me why some people get what they want and some people don't. I've been at this job for almost a year now, amidst the smells of face-powder and frying cheeseburgers, but that secret still eludes me. Some day maybe I'll find that answer tucked away somewhere, like a tip stuck under a plate, and I'll know where to find my dreams as well. Until then, I'm just the jerk behind the counter at Maywell's. See you there.

—*Jeff Blair*

Somehow Tenderness Survives: Grades 5–12
Stories of Southern Africa
Edited by Hazel Rochman

You have heard about Apartheid in South Africa, but have you ever
really thought about how it would be for someone your age—black or
white—to live under such a restrictive system?

Could you take the bitter cold mornings, walking miles for your daily
meal of pork rinds, as the young African boy does in the story
"Crackling Day"? Or would you feel the respect "Old Chief Mislanga"
demanded and received from black and white people alike? Where
would you be on "A Day in the Country," when some high-spirited
white men have a little sport with a "young animal," chasing it and tap-
ping it playfully with their car, while its kin watch scared and helpless
because that "young animal" is a small black child? Even love could be
affected: Paulus (white) and Thebedi (black) meet secretly, because in-
terracial romance is forbidden in South Africa. When their baby is
born, Paulus is terrified: now he will be exposed as a lawbreaker and
scorned by his own people. To protect his secret, he becomes a real
criminal—a murderer—and he is caught.

There are six more stories here of sadness and heartache, and yet,
even under Apartheid, *Somehow Tenderness Survives*.

—*Faye A. Powell*

Somerset Homecoming: Grade 10–Adult
Recovering a Lost Heritage
By Dorothy Spruill Redford

The backwoods of Columbia, North Carolina, held a secret. A secret
no one wanted to talk about or admit to. Dorothy Redford had been
born in Columbia, North Carolina, but had spent nine years with her
aunt and uncle in New York City. They were proud of being "Northern
Blacks" and instructed Dorothy to tell people they originally came from
Jamaica—"The Islands." But Dorothy knew she wasn't from any
island.

Where did her family come from? Years later, still haunted by that
question, she asked her mother. Could she tell her, could she take her
back—back to North Carolina and Virginia, back to her family, back
to a hazy town of dirt streets and distant cousins, to hogs in a pen and
prayers in the living room, back to the edge of the woods where the
vaguest family memories and whispered stories stopped. And beyond
that . . . back to the legacy of slavery that every black American must

face, and either deny or be proud of. Distant relatives were found in leather-bound volumes of the 1870 census: Fred Littlejohn, born 1816—a slave; Alfred Littlejohn, born 1847—slave. Information Dorothy had been denied as a child and had refused to think about as a woman was now staring her in the face. Of course it was no surprise, where else could she have come from? This information hit Dorothy Redford in the heart, and she chose to be proud of it. Proud enough to begin a ten-year journey through volumes of census statistics, property deeds, and bills of sale. Lists of slaves were intertwined with names belonging to their masters, and now to Dorothy's family. She followed dirt roads and dead-end streets till they began to point, inexorably, to one southern plantation—Somerset—in North Carolina. She branched out from there to all the slaves and their families who had lived and loved, worked and borne children, grown old and died on Somerset, their names and faces falling into ashes as so much property. By the end of 1984 Dorothy had begun to "see" a homecoming, a gathering of her "family" at the Somerset Plantation, a way to give her people an Ellis Island, a Plymouth Rock, a way to know where they started and a way to stop keeping secrets and telling lies, a way to start being proud. This book is the story of her journey, her people's proud roots, and a joyous homecoming!

—*Jan L. McConnell*

A Song for Uncle Harry   Grades 3-6
By David Kherdian

Uncle Harry is very special to me. In fact, he's my best friend. He knows how to have fun—real fun—without worrying about what anybody thinks. He has a Model-A Ford, and he lets me sit in it and pretend I'm driving. He takes me fishing, which is neat because we get to ride in the car all the way to Thompsondale, a place without a single house, just a wonderful river with big trees growing almost right out of it. I have my own favorite tree which has a branch right over the river where I sit and fish. Uncle Harry and I collect things together: I collect box tops for prizes, coupons, and bottles for deposit, and Uncle Harry collects all sorts of things to look at and to eat. He is a sight sometimes, carrying branches and stuff in his arms, with his pockets bulging with other things he's found. And he's interested in everything I do, like my drawing. He just gave me a new drawing tablet that I'm using to make pictures of trees and plants that can be eaten. I'm going to call it "Edible Trees and Plants I Have Observed." Only thing is, the last couple of times I went to Uncle Harry's house to show him my drawings, his house was shut up tight. So I finally asked my mother about it, and she said he's been in Chicago. When I asked what for, she said he's engaged to a young lady from there. I can't believe it! What's going to happen if Uncle Harry gets married? Will I still see him? Will he still have time for me? I just know everything's going to be different now.

—*Kim Carter Sands*

Soup's Hoop
Grades 3–6
By Robert Newton Peck

Ever hear of a place called Pretzelsteiner? Know what a spintzentootle is? Ever play hooperdunken? And just what is the correlation between sheepdogs, wool, and scoring baskets? If you don't know the answers to these questions, then you definitely should read *Soup's Hoop*, the latest adventure of Luther Wesley Vinson (better known as Soup) and his best buddy Bob Peck.

The two boys are determined to save their hometown basketball team from another shut-out season. Their plan involves Piffle Shootensinker, a seven-foot-tall giant from a tiny country situated somewhere near the Bavarian Alps; a very shaggy and befuddled sheepdog (or should I say, sheependag?); and the not-so-willing assistance of their arch-enemy, Janice Riker.

To find out what all this has to do with a losing team's basketball game, read *Soup's Hoop*, by Robert Newton Peck.

—*Rebecca E. Jenkins*

Soweto, My Love:
Grades 7–Adult
A Testimony to Black Life in South Africa
By Molapatene Collins Ramusi

Molapatene Collins Ramusi, or Ram, grew up in Molemole, South Africa. When he was twelve years old he went through his tribe's traditional ritual for boys, called Bodika. Ram thought he would die of the pain, but he and all the boys were also proud: they knew that in the end they would be strong tribal men. Men who could sit with the elders and listen to heroic tales of bravery and manhood.

Ram knew that in Molemole he was loved, cherished, and respected as a human being. But by the time he was nineteen, he had found out that being black in South Africa was dehumanizing—and expensive.

For instance, while the government paid for white children's education, black children were not thought to be educable. This meant that by the time Ram was nineteen his family was just barely able to pay his way through the eighth grade! Later, after he almost died of cold and starvation in the rich city of Johannesburg, he received a scholarship to attend a boarding school. Once a month, so that he would have something to eat, his sister would walk twenty miles to bring him a supply of food. Once his mother even sent him money, and since Ram know she must have sold everything she owned to raise such a large sum, he put it in a bank account—it was all of twenty-five cents.

After being forced to work for fifty cents a month, called a Kaffir (a nigger), jailed for walking in the white man's cities, made to sleep in a three-by-four box (he was six feet tall), Ram became ashamed of his blackness. Then one day a teacher told him that life began in Africa—that the word *primitive* did not mean "backward," it meant "first"! From that day on, Molapatene walked proud and began to help his people. He realized that his and his people's sufferings had made them strong, beautiful, and sensitive. When he became a lawyer, he returned to Soweto, his home, to fight for his people's rights, even though he knew he could be imprisoned for the speeches he made all over the world, and for telling the truth in this book . . . *Soweto, My Love*.

—Faye A. Powell

Squeeze Play   Grades 3–4
By Mel Glenn

Mr. Shore made sixth grade feel almost like boot camp. He was all Jeremy had feared—and worse! It was bad enough when they were in school, but they had to put up with Mr. Shore after school too. His main interest was baseball, and he "convinced" his whole class to challenge the elite Penwell Prep School to a match. But the more Mr. Shore ranted and raved and bullied his team into doing what he wanted, the less spirit and enthusiasm they had. And when Jeremy tried to stick up for one of his teammates, Mr. Shore banished him to the left outfield, off by himself.

Have you ever felt alone and powerless against a teacher or some other grown-up? If you have, you'll know just how Jeremy felt, and why he did what he did.

—Kelly Jewett and J. R. B

Star Baby   Grades 7–12
By Jean Lowery Nixon

Cookie Baynes, age seven, was a star—everyone's favorite child. With her adorable, dimpled little-girl smile, she had people lined up at the box office for all her films. But now, at age seventeen, Cookie's a has-been.

Cookie knows she's a has-been; her friends know it; the public knows it. But Cookie's mother, who manages her career, doesn't know it. She can't accept the fact that Cookie isn't going to make a comeback as a child star.

How can Cookie convince herself, her mother, and the public that she is an adult? How can she make people see her as Abby and not as Cookie? How can she make everyone see her, not as a has-been child actor, but as an up-and-coming young comedienne?

Join Cookie in her quest for self in Joan Lowery Nixon's *Star Baby*.

—*Olivia D. Jacobs*

The Starstone   Grades 5–12
By Grace Chetwin

Everyone yearns for a little bit of adventure, and when Gom apprenticed himself to the wizard Folgon, he was expecting great adventures. But Folgon treated him like a scullery-boy. He had to clean the house, tend the animals, and cook all the meals for his master. Slowly, as Gom learned his lessons in patience, Folgon began to show him how to make simple potions and cast simple spells. He also taught him to control his own mind.

But Gom disobeyed Folgon and was sent away in disgrace. Back in his mother's house, he found her old books of magic, and using these and the techniques he had learned from Folgon, Gom proceeded to teach himself to be a wizard.

As he was studying, unrest and evil came upon his world. Soon it became obvious that only Gom and his wizardry could save Ulm from the evil Katak and protect the precious crystal stair, the doorway to the stars.

Is Gom enough of a wizard to defeat the powerful Katak? Can he conquer his own fear? And who is the mysterious warrior who comes from the stars to help him?

—*Patsy Launspach*

Stories I Ain't Told Nobody Yet: Grade 7–Adult
Selections from The People Pieces
By Jo Carson

Jo Carson is a poet, a short-story writer, a radio performer, and an eavesdropper. She has collected stories from East Tennessee and other regions of Appalachia, eavesdropping in grocery-store lines, beauty parlors, drug stores, and emergency rooms; and reconstructing what she heard into poems that capture the rhythms of the speakers' lives, the pattern of life in Appalachia.

> I spent the first years of my life
> sittin' on what we called splinter benches
> 'cause we were too poor for store-bought furniture.
> You scooted, you got splinters.
> My mama used to cry
> 'cause she wanted a bed with a real mattress
> for Grandma Lynn to die on.
> Turned out Grandma Lynn didn't need it.
> She died mid-sentence at the women's circle.
> But the first money I ever earned
> I got mama a store-bought mattress.
> Daddy bought her two straight-back chairs
> so she and him could sit proper at the table.
> It was her birthday.
> I never seen anybody since
> made so happy by a gift.
> When Daddy finally found regular work
> first thing they did was ride down to McEnniss's
> and choose a houseful of fancy stuffed furniture.
> Bought it on time, had it delivered, and paid for years.
> The day it came, Mama and I stood out back
> bustin' the old stuff with an ax.
> Mama said if they couldn't pay for their bed
> she'd rather sleep on the floor than have that one back.
> We burnt furniture for kindling all that winter.
> Mama'd say, "Here goes the table, Charlie!"
> and she and Daddy'd laugh and raise their coffee cups
> to toast their new prosperity.
> Turns out we burnt what could have been
> my fortune in antiques. My wife collects 'em.
> She likes what she calls primitive;

it's the very stuff my mama didn't like,
and now I'm supposed to fix it so it don't ruin clothes
instead of bust it up.
I don't mind, might as well be this as something else,
but if I do get to heaven, if I do get to meet my mama again,
I don't know how in this world or that one
I'm gonna explain why I still got splinters in my seat.

                                                    —*Kristina Peters*

Storm Rising   Grades 7-12
By Marilyn Singer

I never meant to fall in love with her, but I did. I can still remember the day I met her. She stood there at the door, a short dumpy woman in baggy pants and workshirt and dark glasses. I just looked at her and when she didn't say anything, asked rudely, "Who are you?" "I'm here to fix the switch," she said in a beautiful low voice that didn't seem to fit with the rest of her. Her name was Joycelyn, and somehow it did fit, but I didn't find that out till later, after I started working for her, helping her fix up her house. At first I didn't really want to work for her—in fact, I told my best friend Gary that he could have the job. But when he showed up to work that Sunday morning, she just looked at him and said, "Tell Storm the job is his and not to send anyone else for it." I didn't know what to do—there was something strange about her, and I didn't understand what she wanted from me. But when I went to talk to her about it, I suddenly found myself saying that I'd work with her. She was like no one else I'd ever known—different, special. I started to see just how special and how different the day she held a cardinal with a broken wing, and he flew out of her hands, healed. What did it all mean? Who was she? Why did she haunt me so?

                                                    —*J. R. B.*

Stray   Grade 5-Adult
By A. N. Wilson

Stray is the autobiography of a cat. He is not a pampered house-pet but a cat who has been buffeted by life—and come through. He tells his story to his grandkitten Kitchener, as they sit in the sun upon the garden wall.

"I have known love and unspeakable cruelty, tenderness and great tragedy at the hands of the two-footed things—humans. So I have become a 'gentleman of the road,' proud and independent, owned by no one, not even accepting the name, Pufftail, by which I am known in the neighborhood. I enjoyed peaceful early years after my brother and I were sold to Old Granny Harris. We rewarded her for her kindness with an offering of freshly killed thrush. But our life of freedom and comfort and regular meals ended when Granny died—and her scatterbrained daughter took us home and sometimes remembered to feed us and sometimes not. If only we had run away from her, our lives might have taken a far different course! But our choice set up a chain of events which tore my poor brother violently from me and set me against human beings forever. Oh, some have been kind, like the nun, Sister Caroline Mary, who cared for me when I was injured. But I could not stay; the call of the road was too strong. And some of the two-footed ones have been so inhumane that I can hardly bear to recount the horrors I have seen and endured. When I came at last to love a beautiful tabby, your grandmother, she was snatched from me by an engine of murder, a car.

"So remember, my little one, never trust a two-footed thing. Remember. . . . "

Stray is not a comfortable story; we humans do not come off well, but the indomitable spirit of this irascible tomcat shines through.

—*Diane L. Deuel*

Struggle
By Sara Zyskind

Grade 7–Adult

Struggle is a true story.

It is the story of Luzer, a teenager, a lot like many of you. He had a family—grandparents, aunts, uncles, cousins, parents, a sister—and spent his time going to school and hanging around with his friends, just like you all do. But that's where the similarity ends. For one day (September 1, 1939, to be exact) Luzer's life became unlike anything that any of us have ever experienced.

You see, Luzer and his family were Jewish, living in Poland when Germany invaded. While life became tougher for all Poles, for Jews it became hell.

First came all the rules and regulations about what Jews were and were not allowed to do. Then came the yellow star that they all had to wear, to let everyone know they were Jewish. Finally one small area of their town was fenced off, and all the Jews were forced to live in this ghetto, entire families in one room.

But it didn't stop there. Sick people, old people, small children, were "relocated"—and never seen again. The remaining Jews were moved again, crammed into another ghetto in another town. Luzer had lost many friends and relatives by this point, but he still felt fortunate, for he, his sister, and his parents were still together.

Time passed, and conditions got much worse for Luzer and the other Jews of Poland. At last the day came that Luzer had feared most of all— the day that he and his family were separated, and he was alone.

Alone . . . in Auschwitz.

Alone to die . . . or to survive.

Struggle, by Sara Zyskind.

—*Melinda Waugh*

A Summer Like Turnips Grades 3-6
By Louann Gaeddert

Do you like turnips? Well, Bruce doesn't like them either. He thought he would have a "milkshake summer"—just him and Gramps playing golf with the old duffers, swimming, and batting tennis balls around—while his parents took a vacation in Europe. He knew things would be different with his grandmother gone, but he wasn't prepared for the strange, moody old man who picked him up at the airport. A milkshake summer? It sure looks as though it's going to be *A Summer Like Turnips* instead.

—*Frances W. Levin*

Supersense: Grades 7-Adult
Perception in the Animal World
By John Downer

Anyone who's ever owned a pet knows that animals are very complicated creatures. In many ways animals are more difficult to understand than people. With people, we often have the advantage of experience; we can sympathize with their feelings because we've probably felt that same way ourselves. But how can we, as humans, ever really know what animals feel or how they experience events? Well, for a start, try reading this book: John Downer's *Supersense: Perception in the Animal World*.

This book will tell you how animals experience the world around them, including you. And it's full of surprises. Take this example: You've probably always assumed that your cat rubbed its face against your leg because it liked you and your smell. Actually, what your cat is trying to do is make you smell better—in cat terms. A cat recognizes familiar objects through smell; therefore, this rubbing ritual is your cat's way of claiming you as its property. And cats aren't the only animals that use smell to guide them. Pigeons also depend on their sense of smell to bring them home on their travels.

What about sight? Next time you use your remote control to change the television channel, sneak a look at your goldfish. He or she can actually see the infra-red beams that travel from the remote control to the television set. And you thought you had good eyesight!

The surprises in this book are endless. For instance, do you know why air-rescue helicopters may endanger the same animals they're being used to save? Or why moving from one state to another can spell disaster for the love-life of a frog? Well, I'm not going to tell you why, but Downer's book will. So use your sense—even if it's only human!
                                                                            —*Margie Reitsma*

Sweetgrass   **Grades 5-9**
By Jan Hudson

Sweetgrass, a girl of the Blackfoot Indian tribe of the western plains, is fifteen years old—and still not married. Even her best friend, thirteen-year-old Pretty-Girl, has been given away in marriage by her parents. Sweetgrass dreams of the handsome young warrior Eagle-Sun and fervently hopes he will capture enough horses to offer her father a bride-price. But her father, Shabby-Bull, does not wish his oldest daughter to leave his tipi yet—he finds first one excuse, then another, while Sweetgrass tries to control her impatience and wishes for the power to control her own life.

Life among the Blackfoot is hard, an endless round of foodgathering to prepare for the long, cold months of winter. Berries are picked and dried, and buffalo butchered. The only bright spot for Sweetgrass is the annual Sun Dance, a time for visiting and ceremonies for all the bands of the tribe. Will Sweetgrass's father announce her marriage at this great gathering? Oh, how she hopes—but it is not to be. Instead, her father decrees that she must prepare twenty-eight buffalo hides, alone, before spring. Then, and only then, will he consider arranging a marriage.

Each family spends the winter months in isolation, so Sweetgrass is stuck with her bratty twelve-year-old brother Otter, the two babies, her demanding stepmother, and the twenty-eight hides. Food is running low and game is scarce, so Shabby-Bull goes on a hunting trip, out into the endless snow. He has no sooner left than the babies fall ill—it is the dreaded smallpox! Despite Sweetgrass's efforts, the babies die. Then Otter and Bent-Over-Woman fall ill too, and only Sweetgrass is left to care for them. She must break one of the tribe's most sacred taboos if she hopes to save what is left of her family.

—Diane L Deuel

Sydney, Herself   Grades 5–9
By Colby Rodowsky

My junior year in high school was the year I decided that the father I never knew was a member of the famous Australian rock group, the Boomerangs. My mother had always said that my father was a student at the University of Sydney when she met and married him. He had been killed, she said, in a car accident a month before I was born. But why did she have only one small, dog-eared snapshot of my supposed father, Arthur Downie? I just *knew* that my father was a Boomerang— after all, my name was the same as the title of one of their albums, *Sydney Downie Down Down.*

Only a few of my best friends would have known of my Boomerang blood if we hadn't had this class assignment to write a letter to the editor of the local paper, the *Sun.* In my letter I told how my mother had met and married one of the famous Boomerangs. I wanted to be an author, so it was really exciting to see my letter in print with every word just the way I'd written it.

Unfortunately, my mother wasn't as excited as I was. She was so upset she wouldn't even let the reporter from the *Sun* interview me. And that was only the beginning!

I kept a record of that year in my diary, and you can read the whole story for yourself.

—Marianne Tait Pridemore

Tehanu: The Last Book of Earthsea   Grades 7–12
By Ursula Le Guin

Tenar, a young woman, was summoned to the house of Ogion, the wizard of Re-Albi. She made the long journey as quickly as she could, for the summons had been an urgent one, and with her she brought Therru, her gypsy foster child. When they reached Ogion's house, Tenar could see why the summons had been so urgent: the old wizard was dying. He could hardly speak, but Tenar knew he had summoned her for a reason. There was something she must stay and wait for, something she must do. She didn't know what; she wasn't sure. . . .

When she looked out to sea again she saw, blue in the blue haze where sea met sky, the line of an island—Oreanea, easternmost of the Inner Isles. She gazed at that faint dream-shape, dreaming, until a bird flying from the west over the sea drew her gaze. It was not a gull, for it flew steadily, and too high to be a pelican. Was it a wild goose, or an albatross, the great rare voyager of the open sea, come among the islands? She watched the slow beat of the wings, far out and high in the dazzling air. She got to her feet, retreating a little from the cliff's edge, and stood motionless, her heart going hard and her breath caught in her throat, watching the sinuous, iron-dark body borne by long, webbed winds as red as fire, the out-reaching claws, the coils of smoke fading behind it in the air. . . . She saw the glitter of rust-black scales and the gleam of the long eye. She saw the red tongue that was a tongue of flame. The stink of burning filled the wind, as with a hissing roar the dragon, turning to land on the shelf of rock, breathed out a sigh of fire.

—Cara W. Waits

[The second paragraph is drawn from p.37 of the hardcover edition.]

Tell Me How the Wind Sounds   Grades 7–12
By Leslie D. Guccione

This isn't your average love story, no more than Jake and Amanda are your average teenagers. Jake is deaf, and Amanda is determined to talk to him, to really *communicate* with him—and that makes her very different from all the other people he has ever met. She struggles to talk to him, to understand what he says in his seldom-used, muffled voice, and what he says in the signs he uses to substitute for sounds. He watches her, paying close attention to everything she says, trying to read her lips and her face, trying to communicate with her as intensely as she is trying to communicate with him. That intensity, that caring, makes him very different from the other boys she's known, even different from the boy whose class ring she wears.

Amanda and her family have come to spend the summer on a small island off the New England coast, the island that is both Jake's home and his family's livelihood. His father is a lobsterman, and Jake works with him and also runs his own lobster pots. He has no friends to speak of, because few people want to take the extra time that a conversation with Jake requires. No one, that is, till Amanda arrives on the island. At first she is frightened by the intense way he looks at her, and by his silence. But when he finally tells her that he's deaf, instead of withdrawing, like other people always have, Amanda apologizes for not understanding him and wants to learn how to sign. She even fights with him, something no one outside his family has ever done—it's just too hard to communicate abstract feelings (not like talking about concrete objects). Slowly, little by little, Jake and Amanda begin to share their feelings and their lives. But just about the time they begin to think that perhaps their love can work out, the real world steps in—Amanda's boyfriend arrives on the island for a visit, and suddenly everything is very, very different. Can Amanda and Jake learn to share their worlds, or will they stay apart, separated by the silence and the distance that they have so recently begun to fill with their love?

—*J. R. B.*

Tell Us Your Secret   Grades 7–12
By Barbara Cohen

Crunch's broken arm ruined his plans for a lifeguard job while his parents were in Italy, so his mother signed him up for the Hudson Manor Writers' Conference instead (she'd do anything to keep him from staying home by himself). So you can imagine how he felt about the conference from the start. But things began to look up when he figured out the ratio of boys to girls: 4 to 8. And at the first meeting, he realized there were no set rules; everybody had a different idea about what to expect from the conference.

Crunch decided to write a ghost story for his final paper and arranged for a ghost-story hour in the basement of an old building on campus. But during the hour, more than ghost stories came to light. The aspiring writers not only learned about each other but began to reveal their secret selves. That is, all but Eve. She was holding back a secret that had Crunch on edge, and he kept pushing her about it. After a harmless prank unlocked the fury behind Eve's secret, Crunch won-

dered if he had gone too far. Find out, in *Tell Us Your Secret.*
                                                                      —*Barbara Bahm*

Thanksgiving: An AIDS Journal   Adult
By Elizabeth Cox

By 1986 Elizabeth and Keith had settled into about as much comfort
and routine as they would ever have. After all, musicians generally
don't have nine-to-five jobs with regular paychecks. But Keith
Avedon's reputation was finally established, and projects were coming
in. Elizabeth's career as a classical flutist was on hold for a while
because of the birth of their son, but she still found time to practice her
music and teach. They were happy and content.

Keith's trip to Europe to record a commercial for Chanel was a symbol of his success. Though he had felt vaguely ill before leaving New
York, the trip was too important to cancel. Then, in the middle of the
night, Elizabeth received a telephone call from London: Keith had collapsed and been hospitalized. Her frantic pleas for information were
met only with a cryptic "Your husband is a very sick man." For days
no one would say just how sick.

When the final diagnosis was made, Elizabeth knew that their nightmare was just beginning. Keith had AIDS. Even with treatment, death
was a certainty. Elizabeth was faced with the responsibility of helping
him live his final days with as much peace and dignity as possible. Her
journal became a record of their last few months together. It also became a voice for the love she felt for her baby boy and the gentle, handsome man who was his father. A love story about real
people—*Thanksgiving.*
                                                                      —*Nancy L. Chu*

These Good Men: Grade 10–Adult
Friendships Forged from War
By Michael Norman

Can you smell it? The dust, the exhaust from the convoy trucks that
wind along the Quang Tri River on their way from Khe Sanh? The
smell of fear that the soldiers recognize as they approach Bridge 28?
Once so real . . . and now a part of the past.

For many people Vietnam will never be past. The ambush at Bridge
28 ensured that the war would always be with them. There is Craig

Belknap, the handsome Texan whose hip was torn open at Bridge 28 and who will limp for the rest of his life. Squeaky Williamson, so skinny he looks like a coathanger, whose wounds brought him to the brink of blindness. Bob Hagen, the dedicated soldier who even as a child wanted to be a Marine. His parents still cling to the slim hope that one day their MIA son will miraculously walk through the door of their genteel Savannah home. For these people and their families, the ambush at Bridge 28 was the event that changed their lives forever.

To help himself deal with these changes, Michael Norman, a *New York Times* columnist, sought out the survivors of the ambush at Bridge 28. In a journey that took him halfway around the world, he reforged the ties with his old comrades from Charlie Squad. He also discovered much about himself as he learned the fate of *These Good Men*.

—*Nancy L. Chu*

Things That Go Bump in the Night   Grades 5–12
Jane Yolen and Martin Greenberg

Have you ever peered out from under the blankets, eyes wide open to the blackness of your bedroom, while you listened to *noises*—rustles and creaks and thumps—that could be made by almost anything? Has your mind been invaded by horrible pictures of who or what might be moving around out there? Were you almost disappointed to discover that it was just the cat or the dog, or someone getting up late at night for a glass of water? If you enjoy the sensation of being scared, the suspense of not knowing quite what waits behind the almost-closed door, of being not quite sure that it isn't the boogeyman, then this is the book for you. It will give you a chance to shudder and look over your shoulder while the light is still on, and make the darkness after it's turned off even more menacing. After all, we all create our own worst nightmares. The things we are most afraid of come from within . . . and these stories can help us get started! Maybe we need the things that go bump in the night to remind us of the daylight, of honor and courage, of hope and faith—and of laughter, at ourselves, at our fears, and perhaps even at life itself.

So these stories take place at night, when shadows seem to be everywhere, when daylight is too far away, when the sounds we hear are magnified and changed into horrible, fearful images drawn from our darkest dreams. But don't try to read the whole book in one night, because even though not all the stories will make you stop and look up and wonder what made that noise, there are enough to make you bunch up the covers in an attempt to hide from that *thing* with long bristly legs that is marching down the long dark hall straight for your bed.

Nightlights were made for people who read books like this—be sure that yours is working before you open this one! And . . . have fun!

—*J. R. B.*

Those Other People   Grades 10-12
By Alice Childress

Seventeen-year-old Jonathan Barnett had some things in his life that he needed to sort out. The major one was that he had known for some time that he was gay, but he hadn't been able to get up the courage to tell either his parents or Fern, the girl who cared too much for him.

He *had* told his parents that he wasn't ready for college, that he needed time to think, to be alone. That seemed to worry them, so he ran away to New York City where he met Harper Mead. They became roommates, and then they became lovers.

For a time Jonathan was happier than perhaps he'd ever been. But Harper was always after Jon to come out of the closet—to admit that he was gay. One day Jon entered the apartment just in time to overhear Harper on the phone saying, "Jonathan Barnett is gay. He's too chicken to emerge from his dark, secret closet, so I'm giving him this coming-out announcement. I'm his lover."

Jon grabbed the phone out of Harper's hand and found himself talking to his own father, saying it was all just a bad joke. He had walked out on Harper then and gone back home, but still hadn't been able to tell his parents or Fern. He tried, but no one wanted to hear what he was trying to say.

So he had run away again, but this time he found himself in even more trouble: he was a witness to an attempted assault on a fifteen-year-old girl. The girl had a bad reputation and the man was her PE teacher. Jonathan knew he had to speak up, but at what cost? For he too had a secret to keep hidden.

—*Marianne Tait Pridemore*

Too Young to Die
By Lurlene McDaniel

Grades 7-12

Prequel to *Goodbye Doesn't Mean Forever*

Melissa Austin meets the world head on. She wants things from life: to make the school's Brain Bowl team, to be named a National Merit Scholar, to win the unobtainable senior Brad Kessing. For Melissa, life is more than an endless round of parties and days spent at the country club, as it is for her best friend Jory. Melissa is determined that *her* junior year of high school will be something special.

But if she is going to give the SAT, the Brain Bowl, and Brad her best shot, she will have to get better. She's been tired too often lately; dark circles have formed beneath her eyes, and ugly purple bruises have appeared on her arms and legs. Melissa's doctor checks her into the hospital, where she is poked and prodded, bled and tapped. She is impatient to go home and resume her regular schedule, but until the test results come back, there is nothing to do but wait.

Then one morning, while she's studying her history book, Dr. Pace and Dr. Rowan walk into her room, and behind them she can see her mother and her older brother Michael. Her mother's face is pasty white. Melissa's surprise turns immediately to fear.

"Why so many of you? Will it take all of you to hold me down for today's tests?"

Dr. Rowan sighs, "No more tests, Melissa."

"Mom? Why aren't you at work?"

"I wanted to be here when they talked to you, so I took the day off."

Melissa tries to catch Michael's attention, but he won't meet her eyes.

"Okay. So it's more than anemia."

"Melissa, it isn't anemia. Or mono." Dr. Rowan is grasping her small hands, and she can feel the strength of his.

"Or rheumatic fever," she finishes his sentence. She's staring at Dr. Rowan's white lab coat with the faint brown stain on the pocket, unable to look anywhere else. "All right. I give up," she says, determinedly cheerful, "What do I have?"

Dr. Rowan's voice forces her to look at him. "The diagnosis is lymphocytic leukemia, Melissa." He sounds clinical, and very far away. "It's a form of cancer."

What? Cancer? Why is this happening to her? Yesterday she'd been a normal sixteen-year-old girl on the verge of everything wonderful. Today she has cancer. Sixteen is too young for cancer. Sixteen is *Too*

Young to Die.

—*Judy Druse*

Tough Girls Don't Knit,   **Grade 10-Adult**
and Other Tales of Stylish Subversion
By Freda Garmaise

Feeling crowded by the Mass-Media World? by Social Expectations? Take heart! There's Freda Garmaise! She's the Erma Bombeck of shop till you drop, of wrapped nails, of killer sunrays. Just listen to this:

"The other day I picked up a bran cracker sample from Sweden in a health food store and it exploded in my mouth like so much Scandinavian sawdust. Usually, though, samples taste good. Even if they don't, I always eat them as if they do—licking my fingers, smacking my lips—in case a TV crew is lurking nearby, looking for someone to deliver the glowing endorsement that will allow her to buy a yacht on the residuals.

"On a couple of occasions, I have bought a slab of cheese based on my enthusiasm for the store sample, only to get it home and find it tastes like soap. Do manufacturers do something to these samples to make them taste better? It is too unsettling to think marketers are that perfidious. I prefer to believe that it is a question of size: however tasteless the fish cake is in the larger quantity, in the nibble, it is tolerable.

"And then, of course the sample is free. Everything tastes better free. Yet I've joined the millions of others who prove that getting a taste of the product is not the same as getting a taste for it."

Or the horror of trying on clothes:

"I have a fitting-room phobia. And is it any wonder? I enter with a simple desire to find out if the maillot swimsuit is for me and I exit not only knowing it is not, but with a lot of other information I can live without.

"Perhaps I could send someone else into the fitting room for me. A stand-in. It wouldn't have to be human. It could be one of those rubber dolls lonely guys have found to be such a comfort. Deflated, it could go with me everywhere, to be brought out and blown up (rate of inflation pegged to figure fluctuation) when needed for try-ons. With such a surrogate, I wouldn't be dashed by disappointments and, if there were triumphs, I'd savor them to the full later."

Get the last laugh on life's little surprises with Freda.

—*Leslie S. J. Farmer*

The Toynbee Convector   Grades 10–Adult
By Ray Bradbury

That was the autumn they found the genuine Egyptian mummy out past Loon Lake.

Certainly, nothing was happening the day before, nothing for a thirteen-year-old boy. No murders. No maniac lawnmowers. No dirigibles falling on the Masonic Temple, squashing 6,000 Masons at a time. Green Town was a boring, boring place. Why, if Julius Caesar had been born in Green Town, he would have knifed himself at age ten, he would have been so bored. Boredom by the funeral mile. What's a guy to do?

Well, the colonel took pity on me—or maybe rose to the challenge. "Charles, I'll bet you six Baby Ruth candy bars against your mowing my lawn that Green Town, upper Illinois, population 5,062 people, 1,000 dogs, will be changed forever, changed for the better, by God, some time in the next miraculous twenty-four hours. That sound good? A bet?"

"Gosh! A bet! Colonel Stonesteel, I knew you could do it!" The old man grabbed a lizard tail, patches from a 1922 Kissel Kar inner tube, nicotine bandages, and half-forgotten memories, and wove them together.

"Voila! Boredom's savior: Amon Bubastis Rameses Ra the Third, just arrived on the four o'clock limited!"

"Now what are you going to do with him, Colonel?"

"Boy, what we've got here is a giant seed. And seed's no good unless you plant it. Then watch it grow. Then—harvest time! Come on, boy, and bring your Egyptian friend!"

And sure enough, the phones rang all across town and lunches burned on stoves the next day.

Your life will never be the same either, once you read Ray Bradbury's stories in *The Toynbee Convector*.

—*Lesley S. J. Farmer*

Traitors from Within   Grades 7–12
By R. A. Montgomery

When our government ran out of money we were no longer the United States. The country had broken apart into independent geographical sections, at war with each other. Dorado, which used to be Texas, New Mexico, and Arizona, is now run by a brilliant but warped man, Arthur Gladstone. It is a dangerous, aggressive nation, and our enemy.

My name is Matt and I live in Turtalia, which covers what used to be Colorado, Montana, Wyoming, and Utah. I'm part of a group that helps defend Turtalia.

However, there's a story going round that someone is involved in a game of corruption, and it's not just a casual rumor. Headquarters believes that at least one member of our group is corrupt. Which one?

And to make matters even more interesting, a ghost from my past seems to have turned up alive and thriving—in Dorado. Could my brother Steve really be a turncoat?

To discover the verdict and share our adventure, read *Traitors from Within*, by R. A. Montgomery.

—*Suzi Smith*

Travel Tips from Harry: Grades 3–4
A Guide to Family Vacations in the Sun.
By Amy Hest

How are you? We are having a major snowstorm here in New York, the Big Apple. It is so major there's no school today. Because I have this whole long day with nothing better to do, I, your cousin Harry, am going to do you a big favor. I am going to prepare a kind of survival kit, so that your Easter holiday at Gram and Grampa's new condo in Florida will be every bit as good as mine was last Christmas. In other words, I'm handing out free advice.

You'll need to know how to get your bike to Florida—or risk having to rent one that's rusted and has no handbrakes.

You'll have to be prepared for the first fight—which may happen as early as fifteen minutes after settling in at the condo. Vacation or no vacation, you probably won't get through the week without getting punished at least once. Listen to me and you'll get Gram and Grampa to defend you against your parents to the bitter end.

See what I'm driving at? A person's first vacation in Florida ought to be perfect, but that takes planning. No problem. My experiences are written down in Amy Hest's book, *Travel Tips from Harry: A Guide to Family Vacations in the Sun.* Sue Truesdell drew some wacky pictures to go with them, and I came out looking pretty good. Let me know how you make out.

—*Anna Biagioni Hart*

Trevor's Place   Grade 10–Adult
By Frank and Janet Ferrell, with Edward Wakin

Eleven-year-old Trevor Ferrell could not believe what he had seen
on his television set. There were homeless people in America, even in
his own home town, the city of brotherly love, Philadelphia. After
discussing the story with his parents and finding out that it was true,
he convinced them to take him to the area of town where the homeless
were, so that he could help them. That night, when Trevor offered first
a yellow blanket and then his special pillow to a man of the streets, was
the quiet beginning of a thunderous change in the Ferrells' lives. Follow
Trevor as he leads people from the socialite suburbs to the dank, dirty
alleys of Philadelphia, where no one knows who benefits more, the
giver or the receiver. Discover how one person *can* make a difference
in a world too busy to respond to the broken lives that lie forgotten in
the shadows of dark streets.

—Barbara Bahm

The Trolley to Yesterday   Grades 5–10
By John Bellairs

Johnny and his friend Fergie were not too sure what was going on
with their friend the professor. He was acting weird. He'd always been
kind of strange, but now he really had the boys worried. He hadn't
invited them over for a visit or a chess game for ages. He kept the house
closed up and the shades drawn. Sometimes he seemed to be talking
to himself. Johnny thought that maybe he was suffering from some
mental illness, or else getting senile. Fergie suggested that he might be
drunk.

The boys finally decided to sneak into the professor's house (Johnny
had a key) and try to discover what was going on. They found the professor talking with a statue—the statue of a falcon, *and* it talked back!
The professor had traveled back in time to 14 BC, where he had found
the falcon in the temple of Abu Simbel in Egypt, and he'd brought it
home with him. Johnny and Fergie knew they had stumbled onto
something exciting and possibly dangerous. Now the question was,
would the professor let them go along on his next journey back in time?

—Carol Kappelmann

Truckers
By Terry Patchett

Grade 7-Adult

This is the story of the Going Home. This is the story of the Critical Path. This is the story of the huge truck roaring through the sleeping city and out toward the country lanes, smashing through streetlamps and swinging from side to side and shattering shop windows and rolling to a halt when the police chased it. And when they looked inside and discovered that there was no one driving it, then it became the story of the truck that started up again, rolled away from the astonished policemen, and vanished into the night. And the story didn't end there—but it didn't start there either.

This is the story of the nomes, creatures that look just like humans, except they are about four inches high. It is also the story of one particular nome, named Masklin. When we first meet Masklin, he is wet and cold and frustrated. He has decided that it is time for his group to leave their burrow behind the roadside diner and find a new place to live, a better shelter than the burrow, with more to eat than diner scraps and the occasional rat. So he persuades the other members of his group, even the old ones, to climb up a rope into the back of a truck stopped at the diner. He has been watching this truck and knows they haven't much time. But they all make it, even Masklin himself, who has to go back down the rope at the last minute to get The Thing, the black box the nomes have carried with them longer than anyone can remember.

When the truck stops, it is inside the garage of a large department store in the middle of a busy city, although the nomes don't know that. They have always lived outdoors in the country, and they believe that the eight of them are all the nomes that are left in the world. Masklin goes out to explore and finds not only an apple core but also a huge rat wearing a red leather collar, and a nome holding the other end of the leash. At least, Masklin though he was a nome (he was certainly the right size), but the way he was dressed—in such bright colors, when everyone knew that colors like that would attract the attention of other creatures, and make it much more likely that you'd end up as someone else's dinner. It was better, and safer, to wear dull browns and greens, and blend in with your surroundings.

"Where did you come from?" the strange nome demanded.

"From the truck," Masklin replied.

"And what were you doing in there? Answer me!"

"We were traveling—going from one place to another."

The brightly dressed nome looked stunned. "But that's impossible! There's nothing Outside!"

"Oh, really," said Masklin, "well, we all seem to have come from it anyway. It is all right if the rest of us come down? It's been a long journey."

Well, Masklin may think they have come a long way, but it is nothing compared to what they find when they get inside The Store. The thousands of nomes who live there don't believe that there *is* any other place—Outside doesn't exist, and neither does Sun or Rain or Day or Night. Nothing that Masklin and his group can say will convince them otherwise—even when the big Closing! Going Out of Business! signs appear on every floor, and all the merchandise begins to disappear off the shelves. Can Masklin do anything to change their minds, or will the end of their store be the end of the nomes?

—J. R. B.

True Detectives: Grade 10-Adult
The Real World of Today's Private Investigators
By William Parkhurst

Have you ever wanted to locate a missing person? What about tracking down con artists or recovering stolen art? You can do these things and lots more by coming on a journey into a bizarre world few outsiders are allowed to see. This book will take you inside today's multi-billion-dollar investigative and security industry. You will be able to follow the daily dramas of private investigators—a colorful cast including Vinny Parco, whose staff can find almost anybody; Joel Howard, a former hero cop; Barry Silvers, who tracks world-class sleaze; Ray Melucci, the debugger; and Peter Castillo, a soft-spoken bounty hunter. Discover what goes on in the real world of *True Detectives*.

—Barbara Bahm

Tucker   Grades 3-6
By Tom Birdseye

Life was OK until *she* came along: a nine-year-old sister Tucker hasn't seen in seven years; a nine-year-old who can out-burp Tucker's best friend, Joe Allen; a nine-year-old who laughs and smiles all the time and ingratiates herself with Tucker's dad, Duane; a nine-year-old who has taken over eleven-year-old Tucker's room and life. For unexplained reasons, when Tucker and Livi's mom and dad divorced seven years ago, Tucker and Duane moved to Idaho. Livi and Cathy, their mom, stayed in Kentucky.

Tucker likes his life with Duane in the Idaho woods. It is simple and uncomplicated. Tucker is preparing himself to become a true warrior of the "Tribe" like the Indians who used to live in the area. Tucker and Joe Allen have a secret spot in the woods. They have built a tipi, made their own bows and arrows, and declared themselves blood brothers as they prepare for their first kill of deer season. They are totally immersed in their game of becoming true warriors of the Tribe which they have created.

Then *she* arrives. She's Olivia, or Livi, the sister Tucker not only doesn't know but doesn't want to know. She's the sister who writes to their mother every day and even gets letters back (Tucker hasn't heard from his mom in seven years). She's the sister who says, "We *can* be a family again. I just know Mom wants it to happen." So does Tucker, and gradually he begins to believe her.

Then Tucker intercepts one of the many letters that Livi receives. Tucker, the warrior of the Tribe, painfully discovers that life is not what Livi says it will be. Tucker, the warrior, discovers the difference between fantasy and reality. Which will he choose?

—*Marvia Boettcher*

Turning Thirteen   Grades 5-9
By Susan Beth Pfeffer

Dina and I have been best friends since before we were born. Our moms attended Lamaze classes together. But lately Dina doesn't have much time for me. Amy's her new superfriend. I'm old hat! But now I've come up with a foolproof plan to get Dina back.

The plan involves a rabbi, a very special party, the truth, and turning thirteen. To discover if friendships really last forever (and if I can survive all of the above), read *Turning Thirteen*, by Susan Beth Pfeffer.

—*Suzi Smith*

21st Century Fox   Grades 7-12
By Scott Eller

The other guys said Pioneer High was tough, and were they right! It was a fierce game—and dirty too. Brad had been cleated, given kidney punches, and gouged through his face mask. In the fourth quarter,

Pioneer ran the sweep. Brad, who played left corner, and his older brother Dean, who played strong safety, were in on the Maples defense.

Everybody was doing what they were supposed to. Brad saw that the Pioneer halfback, Weeks, had the ball and went after him. He came in low, trying to split the blockers. They took him down. He saw Dean steamrolling toward Weeks. It was the hardest hit Brad had ever seen. The ball popped free and Maples recovered. Brad watched Dean shrug his shoulders, get up, and walk off the field. Weeks stayed on the ground. Brad didn't move either. He wondered why his face hurt so much, and what that salty, sticky stuff in his mouth was. His trainer and manager came on to the field and helped him off. Doc Carter said his nose was broken.

As Brad waited to be taken to the hospital, a couple of cheerleaders came over to see how he was doing. Denise, of course, and Paula Mason. And then the Fox, Christiana Fox Renard, movie star dressed as cheerleader, came over. She leaned over Brad, asked him his name, told him he was going to be ok, kissed him on the cheek, and walked away.

So what everybody had been talking about all week was true. If the Fox was here, acting like a cheerleader, Leonard Rampis must have brought the entire film company here, to Adrian, Michigan, to make a movie. What would life be like for Brad now?

—Barbara Hawkins

The Twenty-Four-Hour Lipstick Mystery Grades 3-6
By Bonnie Pryor

There was a rumble, and the entrance to the tunnel filled with dirt, rocks, and rotten timbers. Cassie waited for the room to come crashing in on them, but—amazingly—the ceiling remained steady. Then it was deathly quiet—they were trapped in an underground room in absolute darkness. They were going to die, locked in this black prison until they ran out of air or starved.

Cassie, her brother Danny, and their friend Jason had discovered where the burglary loot was hidden—and the thieves had left them in the tunnel and started a cave-in. Was there a way out? Could anyone help them escape? *Would* anyone?

—Eileen Gieswein

Two-Part Invention: **Adult**
The Story of a Marriage
By Madeleine L'Engle

If you like to read kiss-and-tell books, you should try this one. Or then again, maybe you shouldn't. Because unlike most of the books which fall under this category, Madeleine L'Engle's book wasn't written as an expose of her or her husband's secret love affairs or illicit activities. It couldn't have been; neither one of them ever had any. Instead this book was written as a celebration of her forty-plus years of marriage with Hugh Franklin and of the people and events that helped shape those years.

Today the challenges and strains of a two-career marriage are familiar topics. In 1946, however, when Madeleine L'Engle and Hugh Franklin married, both the problems and the rewards were still relatively unexplored. When they married, L'Engle had already had one novel published and a second one accepted for publication; Franklin was a well-established actor who had appeared in a number of leading roles. Both of them had made New York the center of their lives, professionally and socially.

But with the birth of their first child, all their relatively clear-cut plans hit a major obstacle. How could they build the kind of stable family life they both wanted and yet continue to develop in their chosen careers? Anyone who has ever faced this problem or ever expects to will find L'Engle's reflections about her and her husband's solutions interesting. But remember—don't read this book if you're looking for titillating details or headline scandals. Do read it if you're interested in love—the long-lasting, lifetime variety, which includes friends, children, work, and intimacy of all kinds.

Hugh Franklin proposed to Madeleine L'Engle with the words from a poem by Conrad Aiken: "Music I heard with you was more than music, And bread I broke with you was more than bread." No wonder L'Engle wrote about her marriage. The memories she shares are more than memories; they reveal the stuff of which true love is made.

—Margie Reitsma

The Unfrightened Dark   **Grades 5-12**
By Isabelle Holland

Five years ago, when Jocelyn was twelve, her world was darkened by an automobile accident. She lost her sight and both her parents in that crash. Ever since then she has lived with her aunt Marion, cool and distant, and her loyal seeing-eye dog, Brace.

Jocelyn is a good student, working toward being a professional pianist. She has many friends and does volunteer work, helping serve food to the homeless. But several people Jocelyn knows have mysteriously lost their pets, and Jocelyn begins to be tormented by voices she has never heard before. The voices accuse her of using Brace as a slave animal—and the voices promise to set Brace free. Then Brace vanishes, and now Jocelyn's world is not only dark, but totally black and empty.

—*Cathy Crowell*

Unlived Affections   Grades 7–12
By George Shannon

For as far back as Willie can remember, he can't remember anything about his parents. His mother died when he was two, and his father had left before Willie was even born. Willie's grandmother will tell him stories about his mother when she was a little girl, but nothing about what she was like as a young woman. About Willie's dad, all she'll say is, "Better off dead. Unfit to be a father!"

But now Willie's grandmother is dead, and while cleaning out the old room, Willie finds a box of letters from his father to his mother. In these letters Willie not only discovers what his parents were really like but also sees a side of his grandmother he never knew existed. How *could* the people who loved him best have lied to him for so long?

—*Kaite Mediatore*

Up Country   Grades 7–12
By Alden R. Carter

The police. Again. When sixteen-year-old Carl sees the police at the door, he wonders what his mother's done this time. Did she get drunk and hurt somebody? Did she get drunk and ram her car into a tree? Or maybe for once it's *not* his mother. Maybe the police are coming for *him*. What if they finally caught on that Carl is the brains behind the local car-stereo theft ring, and he has a basement full of stolen radios and tape decks?

But Carl hasn't been caught. Not yet. He can still make all the money he needs to carry out his big plans and get away from his awful homelife forever. It *is* his mother the police are after, and they arrest her for a hit-

and-run accident. Of course she had been drinking (as usual!). Carl isn't surprised at that. He *is* surprised when he discovers that this time he can't get her out of jail. This time, the court decides to remand his mother to an alcohol-abuse facility for several months.

Carl, of course, won't be allowed to stay by himself at home. The social worker informs him he'll have to move in with relatives he hasn't seen in eight years—an aunt, uncle, and cousin who live far away from his home in Milwaukee on a farm up country in Blind River. Great. Just what he needs. A bunch of hicks he barely remembers running his life and sending him off to Hillbilly High School. But before he knows it, Carl is on bus heading north for Blind River. He doesn't even have tim to get rid of the stolen stereos before he goes. Well, how could the cops ever find out, anyway?

When Carl goes up country, he is convinced that life in Blind River will be just as boring and backward as he can imagine. He's in for a few surprises, though, when friendship and romance sneak up on him—things he never had back in Milwaukee. But can Carl really feel secure in his new life, when the police may still discover his secret? He begins to think so—to hope so, but there are *more* surprises in store, possibilities he's never even dreamed of!

—Diane P. Tuccillo

The Ups and Downs of Carl Davis III   Grades 5-9
By Rosa Guy

The Ups and Downs of Carl Davis III is a collection of letters from Carl Davis to his parents. The easiest way to describe Carl is by reading an excerpt from his first letter:

Dear Mother,

In our family, it has always been generally accepted that I am quite an intelligent boy. That's because in our family we have always regarded truth and openness as our greatest virtue. As you know, there are few things that happen in this world of which I am unaware, or on which I do not hold an opinion. . . . Therefore, I regret to admit (while conceding my distaste for such an admission) being thoroughly confused. Ma, why did you and Dad send me to stay with Grandma?!

Carl is a young black New Yorker, an only child, an extremely self-aware loner given to making rather pompous speeches (although he'd never admit it). He has been used to living with his doctor father and his nurse mother, two intellectuals with whom he can converse freely. But now he's stuck with Grandma, who seems a trifle dull. What can one expect from a person living in this slow, Southern, country town? According to Carl, "Grandma's greatest occupation, outside the church, is the thought-consuming programs on that stultifying tube which takes up half her living room."

When school opens, Carl finds an enemy right off the bat in his homeroom/social studies teacher. She firmly believes that Jefferson Davis was a hero and Abraham Lincoln was not. She will not discuss black history beyond enslavement. And she refers to Carl Davis III as an "arrogant, fat little beast"! To top it off, Carl's grandmother's response to all this is, "Junior, you go to that school to learn, not to make a nuisance of yourself."

Carl's stuck. For all his brilliance, he can't for the life of him figure out why his parents abandoned him in this sinkhole. So he writes home, telling of his life, telling of his one friend, of his grandmother, and asking for answers. It's these letters that let us peer over Carl's shoulder as he learns that the answers he wants are not in a book, not to be taken from his parents or grandmother, but are to be found in the heart and mind of Carl Davis III.

—Dominique Hutches

Valentine and Orson   Grades 5-Adult
By Nancy Ekholm Burkert

At first glance, you might think this was a children's book, but it isn't. It's a classic tale from the year 1555, and includes romance, adventure, deception, evil, revenge, kidnapping and mystery!

It all begins in the days when Pepin was King of France. His sister, Bellisant, was a beautiful, wonderful lady. When Alexander, the Emperor of Greece, heard about her, he fell instantly in love and traveled to France to ask Pepin for his sister's hand in marriage, a request Pepin readily granted. The royal couple sailed back to Greece, where the people came to love them both and where they lived in harmony.

But evil forces were at work in the kingdom. Alexander put his trust in the Archbishop, who appeared to be a holy man on the outside but who was really evil on the inside. The Archbishop decided he wanted Bellisant for himself. When she refused his advances, he became very angry and lied to Emperor Alexander, telling him his wife loved another man.

Bellisant tried and tried to defend herself, but it was no use. In great anger, Alexander banished her from their country, even though she was expecting their child.

Bellisant left the palace with her loyal squire, Blandyman, as a guide. They traveled through the woods seeking refuge, and one day Bellisant realized that her baby was about to be born. Blandyman left her in the woods and went in search of some help. While he was gone, Bellisant gave birth by herself. To her great joy, she found she had delivered not one but two babies—twin boys! Her joy was suddenly changed to fear, though, when a huge brown bear loomed up and took one child into its great jaws, then plunged into the wood with him. Bellisant followed in pain on her knees, but she couldn't retrieve her son. While she was gone, she left her other son lying safely near the base of a tree. And who happened to be traveling by and find the seemingly abandoned baby in the woods? Why, King Pepin, Bellisant's brother, who had heard the news of his sister's unfaithfulness and had sided against her with the Emperor. He took the child he found, not knowing it was his nephew, back to France with him to raise as his son. When Bellisant returned to the tree, she found her other son missing as well. She was all alone. Little did she know that the bear would raise one son with its cubs, and her own brother would raise her other son in his royal court. The story of how the wild brother and the royal brother finally meet one day and what happens when they do is just the beginning of the amazing ordeals to come!

—Diane Tuccillo

Veronica Meets Her Match   Grades 3–6
By Nancy K. Robinson

The weekend's events had been planned right down to the last minute. First thing Saturday morning, the welcome ceremony— complete with strawberry tarts and hot cocoa. In the afternoon, the introduction of pets, a discussion of favorite subjects, and a tour of the neighborhood. All topped off with pizza in the evening. The next day there was to be a luncheon of striped soup and groundhog salad, then a walk in the park. All systems were go.

When Veronica discovers that a new girl her age is moving into the apartment next door, she plans a grand welcome weekend. It will be the perfect opportunity for them to get to know each other. And when Crystal skates off the elevator, Veronica can't believe her eyes. They could be twins. The likeness goes beyond looks; they soon discover that they have many of the same interests, right down to the same career choice—librarian. But some things about Crystal puzzle Veronica. Things like, why does she avoid talking about her past? Why isn't she allowed to have visitors in her apartment? And why does she have to move after the TV interview at the Save the Library Rally?

Find out, in *Veronica Meets Her Match.*

—Linda Olson

Veteran's Day   **Grade 10-Adult**
By Rod Kane

My worst day in Viet Nam was when I realized I'd never get out alive. I spent the rest of my tour just missing an ambush or a booby trap, just missing getting hit. I became a survivor by accident—surviving in jungles and bomb craters, rice paddies and hell. Awakened every night at 3:00 a.m. for radio watch, I would think and dream and want. . . . Is this way of life forever? Are there still families? Will anyone be waiting when I get back? No one is. I'm home—I have survived, only to relive the war, relive death and almost-death a thousand times. I can't sleep in the house. I lie awake in the tiny room until all is dark and I can escape to the backyard to doze and dream until three a.m., when I wake for radio watch—only there is no radio watch. I'm home—but I'm not; I've survived, but I haven't. I can't celebrate Christmas—dates are anniversaries to me, and Christmas is still the nightmare of malaria and ice baths. Valentine's Day will always be losing my heart in Bong Song, struggling to save the life of a man I really cared about. And Veteran's Day—Veteran's Day is the carnage of Ia Drang Valley, charred bodies hanging from trees defoliated of autumn leaves.

Forget it! Forget it! "You have to forget it, son," my Dad says to me. Forget it? Is that what he said? Dad in World War II, Uncle Paul in Korea, did they forget it? Is that why we're in Viet Nam now, because the horror and the terror of war were forgotten? I can't forget, and it's wrecking my life. It's as if I'm still waiting—waiting in the bottom of a VC foxhole, waiting to die. It's real easy to go off to war. It's just so damn hard to come back.

—Jan L. McConnell

The Village by the Sea
By Paula Fox

Grades 3-4

It was so beautiful, so special . . . this village so intricately constructed in the sand. To build it, Emma and Bertie used only the things they could salvage from the beach or dig up out of the sand—shells, bits of seaweed, driftwood, pieces of colored glass. Each building had a special meaning and a unique design, and each was built of special and different things. And as each was completed, Emma moved one day closer to the time when she could leave Uncle Crispin and Aunt Bea's strange and uncomfortable home—the time when her dad's open-heart surgery would be over, and their life could return to normal.

It was a visit Emma fervently hoped would never be repeated, but it was also one she'd never forget.

—*Carol Kappelmam*

Viola, Furgy, Bobbi, and Me
By Kenneth Ethridge

Grades 5-12

Money, that was my problem, or actually, the lack of money. My sister's birthday was coming up, and I had already spent my allowance. Now in the past, I wouldn't have worried about not having money for my sister's birthday. You see, I can't stand my sister. But this year I had the perfect gift in mind, and I was $8.00 short. My mother quickly put an end to any thoughts of a loan, but she did have a suggestion. I could raise the money by doing yardwork for the old lady down the street. That's how I met Viola Spencer, probably the neatest old lady I've ever known. To be truthful, at first I was not too keen on the idea of working for an old lady. I figured she would always be talking at you about her aches and pains, and about neighbors who had moved away or died a hundred years ago. Not exactly what I'd call the thrill of a lifetime. Boy, was I surprised when I met Viola. First of all, she had a dog, so I figured she couldn't be all bad. Then when I saw she was wearing a Detroit Tigers baseball cap, I knew Viola and I would be great friends. You see, I love the Tigers more than anything, except maybe my parents, Viola, Bobbi, and Furgy. Bobbi is my girlfriend; we've been going together since last Christmas. Furgy has been my friend for ages. He is kind of, well, eccentric, which, considering his home life, isn't surprising.

The four of us—Viola, Furgy, Bobbi and me—had some great times together, doing yardwork and watching Tiger games on TV. But then Viola's mean, selfish daughters showed up, and everything changed—

and not for the better!

—Linda Olson

Vision Quest   **Grades 5–12**
By Pamela F. Service

It was just a stone, a smooth black stone, tapered at both ends and carved with a single line spiraling down its length. Kate ran her fingers up and down the groove, thinking of the person who'd made it so many years ago, and suddenly she seemed to see him before her, looking at her, holding the same stone in his own hand, reaching across the centuries to her. . . . And then it was gone, and she looked up to see instead the man who'd tried to sell her mother some Indian artifacts earlier that day. Her mother had realized that this man was one of the pothunters who looted archeological sites, and had refused to buy anything. He'd left the black stone behind by accident, and now Kate's mother had asked her to return it—she wouldn't have a stolen object around.

But it was such a wonderful stone, a connection to the past and to the long-ago person who'd carved it. Slipping it into her pocket, Kate realized how right it felt there. The last thing she wanted to do was give it back. But it was stolen, and much as she hated to, Kate knew she had to do just that. Then, as the pothunter snatched the stone from her hand, a bright flash dazzled her eyes, and she saw a swirling spiral of light that blinded her for a moment. Through the afterimage of light, Kate watched the pothunter's van drive away, and a sense of loss swept through her so deep and strong that she almost cried.

Kate didn't know it then, but the stone she had just given up was a charm stone. It had belonged to a shaman in one of the tribes that had lived in the region hundreds of years before. She *did* know that she kept seeing the strange spiral of light, and that she often felt the stone in her hand or her pocket, just as if it were really there. But it was not until she found a second charm stone—smooth, red, and carved with three curving lines—that she discovered the power these two stones had—they could make time disappear and perhaps even let her travel in time, back to when they were shaped, to see the man who made them and who carried the black stone in his medicine pouch, and his young companion, the boy who carried the red stone and was to be the next shaman.

They wanted her to do something for them, and it was up to her to discover what that was and how she might accomplish it. If she failed, their lives—and hers—could be changed forever.

—J. R. B.

The Voice from the   Grades 5–9
Mendelsohns' Maple
By Mary C. Ryan

Thirteen-year-old Penny Eagan has not been looking forward to this summer. Her best friend Cherie is away visiting her aunt in Virginia, and babysitting the out-of-control Lawler twins is about the only thing there is to do. Until the day the tree talks. Now Penny doesn't usually go around talking to trees, but as she cuts across her neighbors' lawn she distinctly hears the tree talking to her. She figures the only polite thing to do is answer back, especially when what she hears coming from the upper branches is the word "Help!" Pretty soon Penny discovers a nearly naked old lady in the branches of the tree, and it's all she can do to get her something to wear and get her down without the whole world knowing.

And Penny soon discovers something else. This is only the beginning of the strange behavior of the old folks at nearby Beacon Manor, and it's not because they are senile. Penny decides, like her favorite mystery character, Agatha Potts, to figure out what's going on. When other strange things begin to happen and Penny starts to piece together her clues, what she uncovers is an unexpected surprise! Read *The Voice from the Mendelsohns' Maple* to find out how Penny finally unravels this off-beat mystery.

—Diane P. Tuccillo

Voices from the Civil War: Grade 7–Adult
A Documentary History of the Great American Conflict
Edited by Milton Meltzer

Short booktalk

Another boring history report to write? Want to know how to impress your teacher? While everyone else writes a bunch of facts and figures, strategies and statistics (bor-ing), you can dazzle Mr. Marvel with personal letters and diaries from everyday people who lived through the Civil War. And where do you find these great letters? In this book, *Voices from the Civil War*, by Milton Meltzer. These men and women were there—Gettysburg, Andersonville, Richmond; listen to them. These are the *Voices from the Civil War.*

I don't read war books.

A bunch of names, dates, and places. Who cares?

I don't read war books, but I read this one. *Voices from the Civil War* isn't a textbook crammed with facts and figures, statistics and strategies. It doesn't talk about battles and troop maneuvers as if they were moves on a chessboard. Sacrificing some to save others. Acceptable losses. Cold. Emotionless.

Voices from the Civil War is a collection of the letters and diaries of soldiers and prisoners and nurses and civilians. They were not observers; they were participants. They don't try to present the "big picture"; they didn't see it. What they saw and lived was war on a personal level.

Any book about the Civil War tells of Sherman's march through Georgia. The number of men. The number of miles. The number of bridges blown up. The number of houses burned. But have you ever wondered about the humanity behind the statistics? Samuel T. Foster marched through Georgia. His voice rises from the page to describe the hell that was the battlefield: "Dead men meet the eye in every direction. . . . It seems like they have nearly all been shot in the head, and a great number of them have their skulls bursted open and their brains running out. . . . "

Andersonville. Quantrill's Raiders. Draft riots. History books tell us the facts, but *Voices from the Civil War* tells us more. It tells us the hopes and fears, triumphs and tragedies of the men and women who lived one day at a time through each of the one thousand, four hundred, and sixty days that were the Civil War. Let them speak to you. Hear them. Theirs are *Voices from the Civil War.*

—Tracy Chesonis Revel

The Voyage of The Frog   Grades 5-12
By Gary Paulsen

Maybe I was dead, and maybe it wasn't so bad. There was silence, wonderful quiet . . . But then I moved, and the most unbelievably intense pain jolted me into reality. I wasn't dead!

I opened my eyes slowly and gradually focused on the cabin of the boat. Contents of the drawers had been thrown all around the cabin, cans of food were rolling in eight inches of water on the floor, packets of tea floated in the crumpled mainsail that hung through the top hatch, and bits of Styrofoam cups and garbage were strewn everywhere.

Suddenly I remembered the deafening noise of the wind, the swells rolling higher and closer, and then the fifty-pound spruce boom swinging across the deck towards me. From the disarray, it was apparent that *The Frog* must have gone almost upside down, with me rolling around inside.

Now my whole life depended on *The Frog*, a small sailboat drifting about three hundred miles southwest of the California coast. A voice inside me said, "You're alone at least three hundred miles out at sea in a small boat. You deserve to panic. Go ahead and panic." *Wrong thinking*. Pain still sizzled in my head.

I had accomplished my mission. My uncle's ashes were somewhere out there, in that vast, never-ending ocean. But so was I. Now I had to think. I had to start somewhere.

Stay with David as he sits becalmed for days, without enough wind to even ruffle the sails. Stretch that jug of fresh water and those few cans of food, and force down the mounting fear as the shark attacks the underside of *The Frog*. And look for land, for other ships, for anyone or anything.

The Voyage of The Frog is one you'll never forget.

—*Sharon Thomas*

We Didn't Have Much,   **Grade 10–Adult**
But We Sure Had Plenty:
Rural Women in Their Own Words
Edited by Sherry Thomas

Inspired by Dorothea Lange's moving photographs of American country women in the 1930s, Sherry Thomas left her sheep farm on the California coast and traveled thousands of miles to see if women like those Lange discovered still exist today. Crisscrossing back roads from New Mexico to Georgia with stops at tiny communities that only appear on large-scale US census maps, Thomas discovered dozens of women who spoke honestly about a way of life that is rapidly disappearing.

Meet seventy-year-old Lillian Fox, whose gray stone cottage in North Carolina is surrounded by a rainbow of color—huge gardens that she still tends, despite her age.

Hear the voice of Irene Nixon, daughter of a slave, who spent her entire life working in the fields only to be forced off the land by a corporate buy-out.

Listen to Juanita Sutemeier tell of traveling west in a covered wagon with her mother and her horse-trader father. One night the wagon caught fire, and they lost everything except the feather-tick mattress they'd rolled Juanita in to toss her through the flames.

Bessie Jones, who homesteaded a spread of 1,920 acres in New Mexico during the Great Depression, lived and worked on her hard-won land for thirty years without even electricity. She sums up a lifetime and a generation when she says, "Well, we didn't have as much as some people, but we made the best of what we had. And when you do that, it doesn't make any difference if you have a lot or if you have a little."

—Kristina Peters

We Have AIDS   Grades 7-12
By Elaine Landau

You probably don't know anyone your age who's died of AIDS—and you probably never will. AIDS takes years to develop in your body. Babies born with it die before they are teenagers, and teenagers with AIDS are usually in their twenties when they die. But teenagers can have AIDS.

We Have AIDS is about Karen, whose family was always moving from place to place. She was always the new kid, always lonely, and just before her last move, she slept with a really popular guy at her school. Now a friend writes to tell her that Ken has AIDS.

We Have AIDS is about Jason. His family doesn't reject him, exactly. But this year the family reunion is held at his aunt's house, not his. A picnic, outdoors, off paper plates. And Jason knows why.

We Have AIDS is about Paul, who is a hemophiliac. Where Paul lives, a guy was run out of town because he was divorced, because he didn't date, because he had a male roommate—and because rumors started flying. When Paul and his brother Danny actually do get AIDS from blood transfusions, who'll help them and their family cope with the pain and sorrow? Whom will they dare to tell?

We Have AIDS. Because AIDS isn't really a mass epidemic. It's people living with—and dying of—AIDS. One by one.

—Rene Mandel

We Remember the Holocaust   Grades 5-12
By David A. Adler

On January 28, 1933, Adolf Hitler became chancellor of Germany. From that day on, life for anyone who was Jewish and living in Germany would never be the same again. Why? Because Adolf Hitler had decided that the Jews were an inferior race and should not be allowed to live.

From January 1933 until World War II ended in 1945, Hitler and his Nazi party set about destroying the Jews. Their goal? To rid Germany, and eventually all of Europe, of these people.

Oh, it didn't happen all at once—it was done a step at a time. Jews were banned from stores, theaters, and libraries. They were not allowed to go to school. They could not own or run a business. They couldn't walk on the sidewalks or own a radio. They had to wear yellow stars so everyone would know they were Jews. They lost all their rights—not only their rights as citizens, but their rights as human beings.

And this still wasn't enough. As the Nazis conquered one country after another, and all these same laws were put into effect in each place they took over, they found that there were still too many Jews. They forced them out of their homes and out of the small towns, and made them live all packed together in crowded areas of the big cities. These areas were called ghettos, and Jews died by the thousands of disease and starvation, not to mention being put to death for any small offense—real or imagined. Anyone could kill or do harm to a Jew; it was okay.

But still there were too many, so concentration camps were set up all over Europe, where Jews could be imprisoned—and killed. They were shipped to these places in freight cars. Some of the prisoners were worked and starved to death; some were used for "scientific" experiments; many were simply herded into gas chambers as soon as they arrived at the camps.

The result? By the end of the war, six million Jews were dead. Besides these six million, there were also several million dead prisoners of war, Communists, Gypsies, homosexuals, cripples, mentally-ill people, beggars, Jehovah's Witnesses—the list goes on and on—all dead at the hands of the Nazis.

We Remember the Holocaust is the story of those dark years, told in the words of the few who survived. People who were your age when it happened—when it happened to them, to their friends and their families.

Why tell it? Because hatred, bigotry, and fanaticism still exist today, and something like the Holocaust must never happen again. Only you can make sure that it never will.

—*Melinda Waugh*

Weetzie Bat   Grades 10-12
By Francesca Lia Block

Weetzie Bat, Dirk, Duck, Slickster Dog, My Secret Agent Lover Man, Cherokee, Witch Baby . . . they all come together here in the glitz, glitter, and dream-like glow of Hollywood.

Weetzie Bat had a bleach-blonde flat-top, wore pink harlequin glasses, strawberry lipstick, sugar-frosted eyeshadow, and lots of fringe, feathers, and glitter. She was unhappy because the rest of the world—the other kids at school—just didn't understand. They were blink to all the wonderful things out there in the world to be seen, done, and enjoyed.

Weetzie was alone, with no one to experience the world and all it held with—until Dirk came along. Dirk, with his shoepolish-black Mohawk and his red '55 Pontiac. All the girls wanted Dirk, but he chose Weetzie, and they developed the friendship of a lifetime.

But they needed more. They needed true love for their lives to be complete. A Duck for Dirk, My Secret Agent Lover Man for Weetzie, and a wonderful little house where they could all live together, happily ever after.

It seemed as if this dream of happiness would never be. It seemed as if no true loves were out there for Weetzie and Dirk, until. . . . Until the day when Grandma Fifi gave Weetzie a beautiful golden lamp, and Weetzie took it home and polished it. *Weetzie Bat*—a beautiful dream come true—brought to you by Francesca Lia Block.

—*Melinda Waugh*

A Well-Timed Enchantment   Grades 5-8
By Vivian Vande Velde

Deanna was having the most awful, rotten, lonely summer of her life. Her happy family had been torn apart by her parents' divorce, and then she had been dragged away from her best friend to go half-way around the world to France with her mother. "It's a great opportunity," they said; "travel broadens," said they.

Alas, all France is not the Riviera, and the area Deanna was in was farm country, about as romantic as Iowa. Deanna didn't speak French, not that there were any other people anywhere near her age to talk to anyway. Her only friend was Oliver, a cat she'd saved from the neighbors' dog.

Sitting on the edge of an unimaginably old well, thinking about the fun pool parties and dances she was missing back home in Colorado, Deanna noticed that the well looked remarkably like the wishing wells in cartoons. She threw in a coin, and suddenly Oliver started acting very strangely. Her digital Mickey Mouse watch accidently fell into the well, and then the water started rising, rising up to the top of the old stones. A hand reached out of the well and grabbed Deanna and pulled her in.

To find out what happens to Deanna and Oliver when elves wrench them out of this world, turn Oliver into a teenager, and send the two of them back to medieval times on an impossible quest, read *A Well-Timed Enchantment*.

—*Di Herald*

What Are the Chances? Grade 10-Adult
Risks, Odds, and Likelihood in Everyday Life
By Bernard Siskin, Jerome Staller, and David Rorvik

In what regions of the country are couples most/least likely to divorce? Are women who read a lot of romance novels likely to be lousy lovers? In which city are you most likely to be the victim of theft?

This is a book of interesting, bizarre, and sometimes frightening probabilities. Which spaces will you most likely land on in a Monopoly game? Illinois Avenue and the B&O Railroad. What are the chances you'll get correct change at your local fast-food outlet? Slim; fewer than half of the 21-to 25-year-olds working there can make proper change for a two-item meal. The odds are 1 to 600,000 against your being struck by lightning, but what are your chances of appearing on *The Tonight Show*? 1 in 490,000, better than your chances of being struck by lightning. Whether you're an armchair gambler or a trivia nut, chances are you'll enjoy this book.

—*Kaite Mediatore*

When Morning Comes   Grades 10–12
By Patricia Calvert

Call me Cat! That's who I've been for almost a year. Someone named
Cathleen Kincaid is dead and gone, not that anyone has really missed
her, not even her mother. Duke named me Cat. Duke said that I'm like
one of them big black cats in the jungle, all cool and calculating. Duke
is from Harley Street. That's where I crashed with Floss, Angie, Josie,
and Davey, never staying at the same place for too long. That is, until
the Social Services caught me shoplifting nine months ago. Since then
I've been shuffled in and out of foster homes. Now I'm on my way to
live on a farm with an old lady, Annie Bowen. Of all the kinds of
farmers I could be staying with, I get a *bee* farmer. My social worker,
Mrs. Allen, says if this placement doesn't work out, my next stop will
be the girls' home at Ellensburg. I tell her that I'll stay for now, but to
myself I say, when morning comes, I'll make plans. I'm outta here.

—Cathy Crowell

Where Have All the   Grade 10–Adult
Tigers Gone?
By Lynn Hall

Booktalk for Young Adults

Have you ever wondered what you'll be like years from now, who
you'll be? How will your friends turn out? And what about the others
in your class—the nerds, the ones that aren't part of your group,
because they're either too smart or not smart enough, too pretty or too
ugly, or maybe just because they don't fit in anywhere, with anyone. It's
been said that people who weren't popular in high school spend their
lives trying to show the kids who didn't like them that they are worth
something, even if those kids never know. If you think that you might
be that kind of person someday, then this book is for you. Read it now
and discover the secret: no one sees you exactly the way you see
yourself. You may be closer to being the person you want to be than
you think.

Jo Herne has become a successful writer by the time she goes back
to her high school reunion. She and her fellow classmates are fifty years
old. A lot of things have changed since their senior prom, but some
things haven't changed at all. Because of that, Jo and her friends have
some surprises in store. For each of them had a mask, but the face they

thought they were showing to everyone else was not exactly the one that others saw. It makes for an interesting reunion.

This isn't a book for everyone, but for the special few with the courage to look into the future and maybe see themselves, and get a glimpse of what their reunions may be like. If you're one of those people, this book is for you.

Booktalk for Adults

Remember how you felt in high school, when everyone was prettier and more confident and smoother? It was a time when you wished that you had just a little of whatever it was that the popular ones had, the ones at the top, the ones who had it all. Remember wishing that you could show them all—make them believe for just one night that you were as good-looking, smart, and smooth as they were? Well, this book is for you. Don't pay attention to the fact that it's called a young adult book—the narrator is fifty years old, and she speaks with the voice of a member of the class of '55, which is what she is. Jo Herne didn't set out to prove anything to the classmates who ignored her—she just decided to live the life that she was most comfortable with, and in the process she became a celebrity, a famous author. But she became someone else as well—she became herself, as much herself as she could be, as much as anyone could be.

Who are you? Who were you? Who were they, your classmates? What did they really think of themselves? Of you? You won't find the answers here, but you may find a different way of looking at the questions.

—*J. R. B.*

Where in the World Is the Perfect Family?
By Amy Hest

Grades 3-6

Eleven-year-old Cornie is one of those children who spend their time shuttling back and forth between mom's house and dad's house. Life sure is complicated, and it's getting more so every minute. Her dad's new wife is pregnant, and Cornie doesn't want her dad to love this new baby more than her. And her mother! She's in business for herself, and she made this trip to California. Now it looks like she wants to open a business out there. Cornie sure doesn't want to move to California. And, as if she didn't have enough trouble already, she has to come up with a super photography project for a school assignment.

How can anyone handle all that? Oh, *Where in the World Is the Perfect Family?*

—*Frances W. Levin*

Where's My Other Sock?   Grades 5–12
How to Get Organized and Drive Your
Parents and Teachers Crazy
By Claudine G. Wirths and Mary Bowman-Kruhm

Are you the kind of person who's always late for something? Or who can't get things finished on time? Or can't ever find what you're looking for because whatever you're looking in (the room, closet, locker, car) is so messy? If any of this sounds familiar, then maybe this book can help you out! It has lots of ideas about organizing things—not only to find missing socks but to gain study space, keep up with assignments, manage a social life, and just about anything else.

It shows you how you can make things easier for yourself by getting organized—and doing it in the way that's best for *you*. Everyone hates to be nagged for being messy or careless or late, and here you'll find lots of tricks to organize yourself, your stuff, and your time. People who are organized have personal power, a good feeling about how their lives are going. *They* are making their lives go, not Mom or Dad or a teacher. This book offers three suggestions: Break big problems down into smaller ones (after all, small problems are easier to fix). Be in charge of what you do and take responsibility for yourself. Finally, look for a way of organizing that works for you, even if it doesn't work for everybody else, and be creative about what you organize and how organized you get. *Where's My Other Sock?* contains information that can help you make schoolwork and studying easier. It can help you find more time for the interesting things you want to do, and it even gives you a hint or two about organizing your room. If this still isn't enough incentive to read it, imagine a new, calm, organized, efficient you. Wouldn't that drive your parents and teachers crazy? What better reason could you have?

—*Anna Biagioni Hart*

Whispers from the Dead   Grades 7-12
By Joan Lowery Nixon

Some say that after nearly dying, people become more sensitive to what you might call otherworldly beings. At least that's how Sarah's doctor tried to explain the shadowy stranger who followed Sarah around for months after she had nearly drowned. The shadowy stranger began to fade out and disappear as she came to terms with her trauma. But now the family had moved, and Sarah felt uneasy about her new home. When first stepping into the doorway, Sarah couldn't move; she felt as if she were being sucked into a cold, smothering mist that surged against her forehead like the tide, and she heard the echo of a scream beating against her. This was different—not like the other time. It was as if something horrible in the house were reaching out and touching her. She wanted to scream "Don't do this to me! I don't want to be a link to some other world! Leave me alone!" But the house seemed filled with whispers, frantic Spanish whispers that Sarah just had to understand, no matter how difficult or how dangerous.

—Barbara Bahm

White Rabbit   Grade 10-Adult
By Dr. Martha A. Morrison

Martha wasn't an easy baby. As an infant she had colic frequently and had to be held, petted, and walked endless nighttime hours.

Martha wasn't an easy youngster. Her family kidded her that her mom would have to put a baby bottle into Martha's lunch box. Martha couldn't have cared less what they said. She simply drank from her bottle after school.

Martha wasn't an easy adolescent. When she was twelve, she threw up rum and cherry Kool-Ade in bed, not even knowing it till she woke up to the mess in the morning. She embraced the drug culture with open arms by the time it reached her in Fayetteville, Arkansas. Forsaking her Baptist upbringing, she smoked, shot up, and drank her way right into a psychiatric ward.

Martha Morrison was a difficult child, but she was not stupid. She maintained straight A's and swore that someday she'd be a better doctor than those who treated her.

And she was. She went back to school, was admitted a year early to medical school, and won honors during her two years of residency.

Martha always did do things all the way. And she'd do them longer, harder, and better than anyone else. Martha was an excellent doctor. She was also a perfect addict.

For seventeen years, Martha Morrison denied her addiction. Her doctor in recovery told her she'd taken more drugs than anyone he'd ever seen and still lived. Not surprisingly, Martha wasn't an easy patient. But she clung to sobriety as stubbornly as she had once clung to addiction.

White Rabbit by Martha Morrison, MD, is a story of addiction and recovery. Martha says it wasn't an easy book to write. But then, Martha never did go easy on anything.

—*Tracie Pruitt*

Who Invited the Undertaker?   Grades 5-9
By Ivy Ruckman

How do you find a date for your mother? Since Dale's father died his mom doesn't sing anymore, and Dale's getting tired of being the man around the house. There are too many bills and broken-down cars, and even though his English teacher points out that one out of four families is headed by a single parent, he still feels "abnormal."

An ad in the newspaper! That's the perfect idea—it should read something like: "Loves cooking, country music, and commitment . . . ," signed "C." Then surely the right man will call—someone named "Blake"—and Dale's problems will be over. But they're just beginning! When he runs the ad in the paper without saying whether "C" is male or female, women call for dates instead of men, and his mother, who's furious, makes *him* answer the phone and explain. In this hilarious book, Dale learns that his mom is stronger than he realized, that an undertaker can be a friend, and that even when things change, a family is still a family.

—*Jan L. McConnell*

Why I Left Harry's All-Night   Grade 7-Adult
Hamburgers and Other Stories from Isaac Asimov's
Science Fiction Magazine
Edited by Sheila Williams and Charles Ardai

Did you know that aliens meet nightly at Harry's All-Night Hamburgers out near a little wide place in the road called Sutton, West Virginia, just off I-79? How do *I* know? I used to work there years ago, just before I got out of high school, and I saw them—heck, I even talked to lots of them. They weren't really aliens from other worlds, but folks that came from other, parallel universes.

What's a parallel universe? Well, think of all the things that have happened since the earth began, all the big and little decisions that were made, the battles that were fought, the things that were invented, and the hundreds of people, important or not, who made a difference in the way history happened. Every one of those decisions or battles could have gone the other way, or never been fought, or been won by a different side. Each of those inventions could have been invented at a different time, or never invented at all. And the people responsible for big and small turning-points in our history could have missed their appointments with destiny, or made history turn the other way. Now imagine that at every moment of decision, a new world was created, where things went the other way. We've been around for thousands of years now, and millions and millions of things that could have gone differently have happened. That means that there are millions, even zillions, of other, parallel universes out there, where life is either a little different or maybe a *lot* different from ours. And somebody out there in one of those universes figured out how to travel between them—go visiting around the neighborhood, so to speak—and spread the word on just how to do it. And Harry's was one of the places they ended up at. You see, it seems that there's a place like Harry's in just about all those universes. It's in more universes than Washington, D.C., one guy said. No one knows why; one of the travelers tried to explain it to me one night, but I didn't catch much of it—something about the earth's magnetic fields or something. Put that with the fact that this part of West Virginia is pretty much deserted in most of the worlds, whether they've been through nuclear wars (and apparently there have been a *lot* of those) or whether the Americas were settled by the Europeans or the Chinese—no matter; no one seems to think much of this part of the world. It's not a site for weapons or populated densely enough to be hit by them, and the mountains and forests make it a good place to hide. Not that everyone hides—every so often, one of our customers would just park a flying saucer right out in the parking lot. If any state cops cruised by and saw it, they never dared write it up—they could have, I guess, but no one would've believed them. But all the Harrys have a reputation for being quiet places, where you can meet other travelers, get a good burger, and pay with gold or silver if you don't have any of the local currency.

The one I knew was no exception. Every night we'd get some truckers coming through, and then, after they trickled off, the travelers would start to come in. Sometimes we even saw the same person from two or three different universes come in, looking like a flock of identical twins.

And every one of them had a story to tell about going from one world to another, and most of them were looking for the world they came from. You see, with all those millions and zillions of universes out there, there's no way you can get back to your own. The guys that invented the way to go from one world to another forgot to figure out a way to get home before they left, and now no one can get back. That's why we rarely saw any of the travelers more than once—they moved on to some other Harry's in some other universe. That's why all their stories were different, even though they were all exciting, and full of adventures and things and places I'd never seen or even thought of before. After a while I began to wonder why I stayed there in Harry's night after night. By that time I was out of high school, and since I didn't have either the money or grades for college, I thought, perhaps I could just hitch a ride with someone and see what other worlds I can find.

There was one guy, though, who came in over and over again. He'd decided to stay in this world and came back every so often so see if the steering device that would let him get home had been invented yet. And he was the one who gave me the ride out of town the night one of the travelers offered me a ride in his ship. Why didn't I leave this world when I had the chance? And go discover all those places I'd been hearing about for the past two years? Well, it was because of what the guy who'd decided to stay here said—if you don't know what's in your own world, why leave it to go somewhere else, when you know you can never get back?

Well, that's my story—that's how I got started traveling. So, what brings *you* to India?

—*J. R. B.*

Wiggie Wins the West   Grades 3-6
By Elisabet McHugh

Wiggie is a cat of substantial proportions, who looks a bit like a skunk. The Carter family is moving west. Our hero, having a vivid imagination, finds it easy to convince the other pets in the household that he is a descendant of the brave pioneers of olden days. Naturally, because of his heritage, Wiggie is chosen unofficial guide on their perilous journey. What should be a simple car trip turns into a series of hilarious adventures with Wiggie in the lead. Read *Wiggie Wins the West*, by Elisabet McHugh, and discover how Wiggie actually *does* become a hero.

—*Kelly Jewett*

The Wild Inside: Grades 3–6; Adult
Sierra Club's Guide to the Great Indoors
By Linda Allison

Your home is your protection. It's like a second skin, a controlled environment, a safe, private place that helps keep you and your family alive. But did you ever take a scientific look at the inside of your house? Your home contains the bones of mountains: rocks and minerals can be found in every room. For instance, you can find volcanic pumice stone in the bathroom, graphite in the pencil-drawer, clay in the china cupboard; sand, chalk, slate, limestone, and marble if you know where to look. Your mom's diamond ring, your baby brother's talcum powder, and that dangerous asbestos are all forms of rock.

Using various kinds of rock, you can make a plaster mold of your foot, or you can perform a simple experiment to discover if a rock is a carbonate (that's a substance found in fossilized shells). You can even order a Magic Crystal for free.

All this in just one of the chapters of *The Wild Inside*. Read on—you'll discover that there's a lot more to that building you call home than you thought!

—*Carol Kappelmann*

The Winter Room   Grades 5–12
By Gary Paulsen

Life on a farm in Minnesota revolves with the seasons. Spring is soft and sticky and stinky. Summer means long days of hard work. Fall is the killing time. But Winter stands alone. Winter is totally different from the other seasons. In winter no work can be done outside, so Eldon spends his evenings in the winter room, sitting around the wood stove with Mother and Father and his older brother Wayne. Two old men are there also, Nels and Uncle David. Every night in the winter room while Father whittles and Mother knits, Uncle David tells stories from the old country—Norway. His first story is always about his long-dead wife, Alida. Then he tells stories about Viking conquerors and heroes like Crazy Alen. He tells stories that, as Mother says, "are not so much for believing as for believing in." Then one night Uncle David tells the story about the Woodcutter. This story is different. This story makes things happen.

—*Sue Padilla*

Wishes   Grade 10–Adult
By Jude Deveraux

Berni looked as good in death as she had in life—maybe even better!
But no one was mourning at her funeral; the people who gathered
around her coffin cared about as much for her as she had for them—
which was not at all!

Suddenly Berni woke up. She had on her new designer pantsuit and
was standing in a sea of fog. The only landmark she could see was a pale
golden light in the distance. She walked toward it, and when she drew
near, saw a handsome gray-haired man sitting behind a golden desk.
She noticed at once that it was solid 24 carat; if there was one thing that
Berni had trained herself to do, it was to tell the difference between 12,
14, and 24 carat gold, and this desk was the real thing! When she demanded to know what was going on, the man said, "You're dead. You
died last night in your sleep. Heart attack." At first Bernie didn't believe
him, but when he summoned Pauline to show Berni her own death, funeral, and even her embalming, Berni had to believe.

"So where am I?" she demanded. "This doesn't look like heaven to
me!" "It isn't," Pauline responded. "This is The Kitchen." "You mean
I'm going to have to spend eternity scrubbing floors and making
dinners?" Berni was horrified. Then Pauline told her why this place was
called The Kitchen. It was where women who were too bad to go to
Heaven but too good to go to Hell ended up after they died. "But why
call it The Kitchen?" Berni asked. "Because," said Pauline, "When you
get married, you think that it will be heavenly, and you end up in the
kitchen. When you die, you think you must be going to Heaven, and
you end up here—The Kitchen."

In order to get to Heaven, Berni must do what she never did in her
life—help someone else, think of them first instead of herself. "You
mean I'm a fairy godmother? Can I give someone three wishes?" "You
can give them as many wishes as you like," Pauline responded. "Just
as long as you accomplish your task." It sounded like great fun—until
Berni discovered two important things: one is that you can't always
judge a book by its cover, and the other is that magic is very literal and,
hastily applied, may backfire with disastrous results for everyone,
including the careless fairy godmother!

All Berni has to do is get Jace and Nellie together to live happily ever
after. But when Nellie is an insecure, fat old maid with a spoiled younger sister (who's got her avaricious eye on Jace) and a skinflint old father (who enjoys having an unpaid servant and doesn't want Nellie to

ever get married), it's harder than Berni ever imagined. As she herself says desperately at one point, "The course of true love never did run smooth—but this is ridiculous!"

It's a love story with a sense of humor, that proves you shouldn't wish for something—you just might get it!

—J. R. B.

With a Name Like Lulu, Who Needs More Trouble?
By Tricia Springstubb

Grades 5–12

Hi, my name is Lulu Leone Duckworth-Greene. Some name, huh? Personally, I hate it, but what can you do?

There are some things you should know about me (I mean, besides the fact that I have a weird name). One is that I hate trying new foods. My mother is forever experimenting with things like bean curd and tofu. Yuck! Just give me plain everyday food and I'm happy. In fact, I go to Grammie's to eat as often as I can—at least she cooks normal.

Another thing you should know about me is that I absolutely *love* baseball, though maybe "love" isn't a strong-enough word. My favorite team is the Cleveland Indians. Grammie and I try to catch every game they play. I play baseball, too, on a Little League team. My dream is to play for the Indians someday. Oh, I know, there is the small matter of my being a girl, but I am only ten-and-a-half—that gives me ten years to practice, and the major leagues ten years to change their policies.

There is one other thing I suppose you ought to know, and that's that some people think I'm a hero. I guess I am, too—after all, I *did* catch the baby. You see, I was on my way to practice when I noticed this baby pushing the screen out of a window three stories up. I tried to get her to go back, but she kept pushing on the screen. Finally she tumbled out of the window—and I caught her! There's more to this story, but I haven't time to tell you all the rest. (I've got practice, you know.) You can get the whole scoop by reading *With a Name Like Lulu, Who Needs More Trouble?* by Tricia Springstubb.

—Linda Olson

Wonderful Me   Grades 7–12
By Barbara Wersba

Someone is sending 16-year-old Heidi passionate, poetic, anonymous love letters. The handwriting looks familiar, but she can't figure out whose it is. So in between fighting with her father, trying to be nice to her mother's foot-doctor boyfriend, and walking eight dogs in Central Park, Heidi puzzles over her secret admirer. Until the light dawns—it's her 23-year-old English teacher. What should she do *now?*

—Kaite Mediatore

A World of Ideas   Grade 10–Adult
By Bill Moyers

Have you ever dreamed of meeting a famous thinker and having a long conversation about life today and the ideas shaping our future? If you missed Bill Moyers' series *A World of Ideas*, or would like to preserve some of those talks, then this book will delight you. It contains forty-one windows into the American mind: serious, open-ended interviews with people like Asimov, Commager, Tuchman, Fuentes, Gregorian, Wilson—the insights of philosophers, writers, professors, historians, scientists, anthropologists, ethicists. Bill Moyers, one of the most thoughtful of television interviewers, considers this series a "continuing course in adult education." The reader will consider it enjoyable headwork. Here are a few tidbits to pique your curiosity:

"We have a much greater opportunity to cleanse and improve this country than we do to cleanse and improve the Soviet Union. But so long as we focus wholly on the other as enemy, whether it be our neighbors in this country or our neighbors around the world, and don't attend to our own ills and evils, then we're going to be deluding ourselves, and we will be quite dangerous, both to ourselves and others." (F. Forrester Church)

"Most people think of progress as man's increasing mastery of things. But we have arrived at the point at which man himself becomes a thing. What this world needs is not growth as much as stability. We have to conserve much of the world. We have to conserve much of the past." (John Lucas)

"The stories that we sometimes tell ourselves, that the free will is free no matter what conditions people are living in, and that these people in misery are really okay because they have free will—those are evasive and pernicious stories, because they prevent us from looking with the best kind of compassion at the lives of other people." (Martha Nussbaum).

—*Lesley S. J. Farmer*

Worlds Apart   Grades 3–6
By Jill Murphy

Imagine what your life would be like if you didn't know anything about your father. This year Father's Day really bothers Susan, so her mother finally tells her why she left Susan's father when Susan was just an infant. But she won't tell Susan anything else. Susan decides to find out about her dad on her own. She wants to meet him and see if he will answer her questions. She may be only eleven years old, but she's determined. Will she succeed?

—*Frances W. Levin*

The Wrong Way Home   Grades 7–12
By Liza Fosburgh

It was a beautiful apartment. The silk drapes, the fine antique furniture, the valuable paintings . . . Bent took another drag on the joint and sighed. Yes, the apartment was still lovely. Her mother had made it that way. But her mother was no longer lovely. Huntington's Chorea had taken everything from her and left her a feeble, mute bag of bones. But Bent still loved her mother with a fierce, protective love. She vowed that she would care for her mother to the end. Just she and Ani. In this apartment. Alone.

Bent inhaled again on the joint and thought angrily of her father. Deserter! Two-timer! She would never give her mother up to a home and go live with him! She had money. She could take care of her self after her mother . . . that was another thing. Huntington's Chorea is known to be hereditary. Every day Bent thought about that, and it scared her. Bad.

Bent took another drag and relaxed. The marijuana was her only escape. But reality was closing in. And there was no escaping reality.

—*Julie Bray*

Your Move, J. P.!   Grades 5–8
By Lois Lowry

It all started when Angela Patricia Galsworthy transferred into his seventh-grade class at the Burke-Thaxter School. She had long blonde hair, like spun gold. Straight white teeth, like pearls. Large, deep blue-green eyes, like pools. Skin like porcelain. And a voice like a rippling brook. Suddenly J. P. Tate was a wreck. He had an overpowering urge to use deodorant (he broke out in a sweat whenever he thought of her). He had trouble walking. He ran into things. He didn't pay attention in class. He couldn't even concentrate on chess.

Desperate to impress her, J. P. told Angela that he suffered from a hereditary disease called "triple framosis," and that the late Raymond Myerson, whose wealthy parents had donated the school science lab, was his cousin and had died of the disease. One lie led to another, and another. Angela's revelation that her father was a doctor specializing in hereditary ailments put J. P. into a panic. Learning that the Myersons were to attend the school's Spring Fling didn't help. Neither did knowing that J. P. would have to defend his title as the school's chess champion against hearing-impaired Kevin Kerrigan, whose pals had been enlisted to make noise to break his concentration. Things were turning into a real mess. How was J. P. going to hold onto his chess championship, keep from losing Angela, and get out from under all the lies he had told?

—Patricia Willingham

Yours Till Forever   Grades 7–12
By David Gifaldi

"All of life's a circle, sunrise to sundown. . . . " Is that true? Were all the things that happened to me *real*, or were they just some kind of crazy coincidence? I think sometimes that even I am beginning to doubt what happened to me, to cover it up, to forget it, because it's more comfortable that way. That's why I decided to write it all down, just as it happened, no matter how crazy it sounds, so I can remember and so I won't ever be able to forget.

Reincarnation? Living more than once? Is it possible? Does it happen? Pete and Samantha were new in town, and seemed to fall for each other the first time they met. They started dating just as naturally as they became my best friends. But when I saw the pendant that Pete gave Samantha, I began to wonder. It was a gold heart inscribed "Yours Till

Forever," just like the one that I'd found in the box of my parents' things—all I had left of them, since both my parents had been killed the night I was born. Pete and Sam had the same birthday I did—was that a coincidence, or could my parents' love have been so strong that they couldn't die until they had lived out their lives together? And if Pete and Sam are the souls of my parents reborn, then is there any way I can prevent their deaths—prevent the pattern from repeating itself once again?

—J. R. B.

BIBLIOGRAPHY BY AUTHOR

Aaseng, Nathan. *Better Mousetraps: Product Improvements That Led to Success.* Lerner 1990. (Grades 5-12; 3P, 4Q)
____. *The Fortunate Fortunes.* Lerner 1989. (Grades 5-12; 3P, 4Q)
____. *The Problem Solvers.* Lerner 1989. (Grades 5-12; 3P, 4Q)
____. *The Rejects.* Lerner 1989. (Grades 5-12; 3P, 4Q)
____. *The Unsung Heroes.* Lerner 1989. (Grades 5-12; 3P, 4Q)
Abdul-Jabbar, Kareem and McCarthy, Mignon. *Kareem.* Random 1990. (Grade 10-Adult; 1P, 3Q)
Abt, Samuel. *LeMond: The Incredible Comeback of an American Hero.* Random 1990. (Grade 9-Adult; 2P, 3Q)
Adler, David A. *We Remember the Holocaust.* Holt 1989. (Grades 5-12; 2P, 4Q)
Allen, R. E. *Ozzy on the Outside.* Delacorte 1989. (Grades 10-12; 2P, 3Q)
Allison, Linda. *The Sierra Club Summer Book.* Little 1989. (Grades 3-6, Adult; 3P, 3Q)
____. *The Wild Inside: Sierra Club's Guide to the Great Indoors.* Little 1988. (Grades 3-6, Adult; 2P, 4Q)
Anderson, Kevin J. *Gameplay.* Signet 1989. (Grade 10-Adult; 1P, 3Q)
Angell, Judie. *Leave the Cooking to Me.* Bantam 1990. (Grades 5-8; 3P, 3Q)
Anthony, Carolyn, ed. *Family Portraits: Remembrances.* Doubleday 1989. (Adult; 3P, 4Q)
Ardley, Bridgette and Ardley, Neil. *The Random House Book of 1001 Questions and Answers.* Random 1989. (Grades 3-6; 2P, 4Q)
Arias, Ron. *Five Against the Sea.* NAL 1989. (Grade 10-Adult; 3P, 4Q)
Arnold, Caroline. *Dinosaur Mountain: Graveyard of the Past.* Clarion 1989. (Grades 5-12; 2P, 4Q)
Arnosky, Jim. *In the Forest.* Lothrop 1989. (Grade 3-Adult; 1P, 4Q)
Auch, Mary Jane. *Glass Slippers Give You Blisters.* Holiday 1989. (Grades 5-9; 2P, 3Q)
Backes, Clarus and Brown, Dee, eds. *Growing Up Western.* Knopf 1989. (Grade 5-Adult; 3P, 3Q)
Banks, Lynne Reid. *The Secret of the Indian.* Doubleday 1989. (Grades 3-6; 4P, 3Q)
Bauer, Caroline Feller, comp. *Halloween: Stories and Poems.* Lippincott 1989. (Grades 3-4; 4P, 3Q)
Bawden, Nina. *The Outside Child.* Lothrop 1989. (Grades 3-6; 3P, 3Q)
Bellairs, John. *The Chessmen of Doom.* Dial 1989. (Grades 5-9; 2P, 4Q)
____. *The Trolley to Yesterday.* Dial 1989. (Grades 5-10; 2P, 4Q)
Berry, James. *Magicians of Erianne.* Harper 1988. (Grades 5-9; 3P, 3Q)
Birdseye, Tom. *Tucker.* Holiday 1990. (Grades 3-6; 2P, 3Q)
Blackwood, Gary. *The Dying Sun.* Atheneum 1989. (Grades 7-12; 3P, 4Q)
Blake, Jeanne. *Risky Times.* Workman 1990. (Grades 7-12; 3P, 4Q)
Block, Francesca Lia. *Weetzie Bat.* Harper 1989. (Grades 10-12; 3P, 3Q)
Bograd, Larry. *The Fourth-Grade Dinosaur Club.* Delacorte 1989. (Grades 3-6; 2P, 3Q)

Bottner, Barbara. *Let Me Tell You Everything: Memoirs of a Lovesick Intellectual.* Harper 1989. (Grades 7-12; 2P, 3Q)

Bradbury, Ray. *The Toynbee Convector.* Knopf 1988. (Grades 10-Adult; 2P, 3Q)

Brizzolara, John. *Empire's Horizon.* DAW 1989. (Grade 10-Adult; 1P, 3Q)

Brock, Darryl. *If I Never Get Back.* Crown 1990. (Grade 10-Adult; 2P, 3Q)

Brooks, Bruce. *No Kidding.* Harper 1989. (Grades 7-12; 2P, 3Q)

Brown, Alan. *Lost Boys Never Say Die.* Delacorte 1989. (Grades 3-6; 2P, 4Q)

Buffie, Margaret. *The Haunting of Frances Rain.* Scholastic 1989. (Grades 5-9; 2P, 3Q)

Burkert, Nancy Ekholm. *Valentine and Orson.* Farrar 1989. (Grades 5-Adult; 1P, 4Q)

Byars, Betsy. *Bingo Brown and the Language of Love.* Viking 1989. (Grades 4-6; 3P, 4Q)

Bylinsky, Tatyana. *Before the Wildflowers Bloom.* Crown 1989. (Grades 3-6; 2P, 4Q)

Calvert, Patricia. *When Morning Comes.* Scribners 1989. (Grades 10-12; 4P, 4Q)

Carson, Jo. *Stories I Ain't Told Nobody Yet: Selections from the People Pieces.* Orchard 1989. (Grades 7-Adult; 1P, 3Q)

Carter, Alden R. *Up Country.* Putnam 1989. (Grades 7-12; 3P, 4Q)

Catalano, Grace. *Alyssa Milano: She's the Boss.* Bantam 1989. (Grades 5-9; 2P, 4Q)

Chase, Deborah. *The New Medically Based No-Nonsense Beauty Book.* Holt 1989. (Grade 10-Adult; 1P, 3Q)

Chetwin, Grace. *The Starstone.* Bradbury 1989. (Grades 5-12; 2P, 4Q)

Childress, Alice. *Those Other People.* Putnam 1989. (Grades 10-12; 1P, 3Q)

Christian, Mary Blount. *Singin' Somebody Else's Song.* Macmillan 1988. (Grades 7-12; 2P, 3Q)

Clifford, Eth. *I Hate Your Guts, Ben Brooster!* Houghton 1989. (Grades 3-6; 2P, 4Q)

Cohen, Barbara. *Tell Us Your Secret.* Bantam 1989. (Grades 7-12; 3P, 4Q)

Cohen, Daniel. *Phone Call from a Ghost.* Dodd 1988. (Grades 5-9; 4P, 3Q)

Cole, Brock. *Celine.* Farrar 1989. (Grades 10-12; 2P, 4Q)

Cole, Harry A. and Jablow, Martha M. *One in a Million.* Little 1990. (Grade 10-Adult; 3P, 3Q)

Cole, Lewis. *Never Too Young to Die: The Death of Len Bias.* Pantheon 1989. (Grades 10-Adult; 3P, 3Q)

Colman, Hila. *Forgotten Girl.* Crown 1990. (Grades 5-8; 2P, 3Q)

Conford, Ellen. *Genie with the Light Blue Hair.* Bantam 1989. (Grades 5-9; 3P, 3Q)

Conrad, Pam. *My Daniel.* Harper 1989. (Grades 5-9; 2P, 4Q)

Cooney, Caroline B. *Family Reunion.* Bantam 1989. (Grades 5-9; 3P, 4Q)

———. *The Face on the Milk Carton.* Bantam 1990. (Grades 7-12; 3P, 2Q)

Cooper, Ilene. *Choosing Sides.* Morrow 1990. (Grades 5-6; 3P, 4Q)

Corcoran, Barbara. *The Potato Kid.* Atheneum 1989. (Grades 5-9; 3P, 4Q)

Coville, Bruce, ed. *Herds of Thunder, Manes of Gold: A Collection of Horse Stories and Poems.* Doubleday 1989. (Grades 5-9; 1P, 3Q)

Cox, Elizabeth. *Thanksgiving: An AIDS Journal.* Harper 1990. (Adult; 3P, 3Q)

Crew, Linda. *Children of the River.* Delacorte 1989. (Grades 7-12 3P, 4Q)

Cross, Charles and the editors of *Backstreets* magazine. *Backstreets: Springsteen—The Man and His Music.* Harmony 1989. (Grade 7-Adult; 1P, 4Q)

Crutcher, Chris. *Chinese Handcuffs.* Greenwillow 1989. (Grades 10-12; 4P, 4Q)

Cunningham, Laura. *Sleeping Arrangements.* Random 1989. (Grade 7-Adult; 3P, 4Q)

Dallas, Sandra. *Buster Midnight's Cafe.* Random 1990. (Grade 10-Adult; 3P, 4Q)

Daneman, Meredith. *Francie and the Boys.* Delacorte 1989. (Grades 7-12; 2P, 3Q)

Daniel, Mark, comp. *A Child's Treasury of Animal Verse.* Dial 1989. (Grades 3-9; 2P, 4Q)

Danziger, Paula. *Everyone Else's Parents Said Yes.* Delacorte 1989. (Grades 3-6; 4P, 4Q)

Davis, Lindsey. *Silver Pigs.* Crown 1989. (Grades 10-Adult; 3P, 4Q)

Day, Alexandra. *Frank and Ernest.* Scholastic 1988. (Grades 3-9, Adult; 3P, 4Q)

DeClements, Barthe. *Five Finger Discount*. Delacorte 1989. (Grades 5-9; 3P, 3Q)

De Treviño, Elizabeth Borton. *El Guëro: A True Adventure Story*. Farrar 1989. (Grades 3-6; 2P, 4Q)

Deuker, Carl. *On the Devil's Court*. Little 1989. (Grades 7-12; 2P, 4Q)

Deveraux, Jude. *Knight in Shining Armor*. Pocket 1989. (Grade 10-Adult; 3P, 4Q)

_____. *Wishes*. Pocket 1989. (Grade 10-Adult; 3P, 3Q)

Dickinson, Peter. *Eva*. Delacorte 1989. (Grades 7-Adult; 4P, 4Q)

_____. *Merlin Dreams*. Delacorte 1988. (Grade 10-Adult; 1P, 4Q)

Dines, Carol. *Best Friends Tell the Best Lies*. Delacorte 1989. (Grades 7-12; 2P, 4Q)

Downer, John. *Supersense: Perception in the Animal World*. Holt 1989. (Grade 7-Adult; 2P, 4Q)

Duane, Diane. *High Wizardry*. Delacorte 1990. (Grades 7-12; 3P, 4Q)

Duder, Tessa. *In Lane Three, Alex Archer*. Houghton 1989. (Grades 10-12; 3P, 4Q)

Duffy, James. *Cleaver of the Good Luck Diner*. Scribners 1989. (Grades 3-6; 2P, 3Q)

Duncan, Lois. *Don't Look Behind You*. Delacorte 1989. (Grades 7-12; 4P, 4Q)

Dygard, Thomas J. *Forward Pass*. Morrow 1989. (Grades 7-12; 3P, 4Q)

Elkington, John and others. *Going Green: A Kid's Handbook to Saving the Planet*. Viking 1990. (Grades 3-12; 4P, 4Q)

Eller, Scott. *21st Century Fox*. Scholastic 1989. (Grades 7-12; 2P, 3Q)

Ethridge, Kenneth. *Viola, Furgy, Bobbi, and Me*. Holiday 1989. (Grades 5-12; 4P, 4Q)

Ferrell, Frank and Ferrell, Janet, with Edward Wakin. *Trevor's Place*. Harper 1990. (Grade 10-Adult; 2P, 3Q)

Ferris, Jean. *Looking for Home*. Farrar 1989. (Grades 7-12; 3P, 4Q)

Feuer, Elizabeth. *Paper Doll*. Farrar 1990. (Grades 9-12; 2P, 3Q)

Fine, Anne. *My War with Goggle-Eyes*. Little 1989. (Grades 5-9; 3P, 3Q)

Forman, James D. *The Big Bang*. Scribners 1989. (Grades 7-12; 3P, 3Q)

Fosburgh, Liza. *The Wrong Way Home*. Bantam 1990. (Grades 7-12; 2P, 3Q)

Fox, Paula. *The Village by the Sea*. Orchard 1988. (Grades 3-4; 3P, 4Q)

Frame, Pete and others, with Mike Clifford, consultant. *The Harmony Illustrated Encyclopedia of Rock*, sixth edition. Harmony 1988. (Grade 7-Adult; 3P, 4Q)

Fraser, Craig and Sullivan, Deirdre. *Burnt: A Teenage Addict's Road to Recovery*. NAL 1989. (Grade 10-Adult; 3P, 4Q)

Freedman, Samuel G. *Small Victories: The Real World of a Teacher, Her Students, and Their High School*. Harper 1990. (Grade 10-Adult; 3P, 3Q)

Fulghum, Robert. *It Was on Fire When I Lay Down on It*. Random 1989. (Adult; 4P, 4Q)

Gaeddert, Louann. *A Summer Like Turnips*. Holt 1989. (Grades 3-6; 3P, 3Q)

Gallo, Donald R., ed. *Connections: Short Stories by Outstanding Writers for Young Adults*. Delacorte 1989. (Grades 7-12; 3P, 4Q)

Garfield, Leon. *The Empty Sleeve*. Delacorte 1988. (Grades 5-12; 3P, 4Q)

Garmaise, Freda. *Tough Girls Don't Knit, and Other Tales of Stylish Subversion*. Little 1990. (Grade 10-Adult; 3P, 3Q)

Garraty, John A. *1001 Things Everyone Should Know About American History*. Doubleday 1989. (Grade 10-Adult; 1P, 4Q)

Geller, Mark. *Raymond*. Harper 1988. (Grades 5-9; 2P, 3Q)

George, Jean Craighead. *One Day in the Tropical Rain Forest*. Harper 1990. (Grades 3-6; 2P, 4Q)

_____. *Shark Beneath the Reef*. Harper 1989. (Grades 7-9; 2P, 4Q)

Gifaldi, David. *Yours Till Forever*. Lippincott 1989. (Grades 7-12; 2P, 2Q)

Gilbert, Sara. *Get Help: Solving the Problems in Your Life*. Morrow 1989. (Grades 5-9; 3P, 4Q)

Gilden, Mel. *Harry Newberry and the Raiders of the Red Drink*. Holt 1989. (Grades 5-9; 2P, 3Q)

Gilmore, Kate. *Enter Three Witches.* Houghton 1990. (Grades 7-12; 2P, 2Q)
Glenn, Mel. *Squeeze Play.* Houghton 1989. (Grades 3-4; 4P, 3Q)
Grafton, Sue. *F is for Fugitive.* Holt 1989. (Adult; 3P, 4Q)
_____. *G is for Gumshoe.* Holt 1990. (Grade 9-Adult; 4P, 4Q)
Grant, Cynthia D. *Phoenix Rising, or How to Survive Your Life.* Atheneum 1989. (Grades 7-12; 3P, 4Q)
Green, Susan. *Self-Portrait with Wings.* Little 1989. (Grades 2-6; 3P, 3Q)
Greenwald, Sheila. *Rosy's Romance.* Joy Street 1989. (Grades 5-9; 3P, 4Q)
Grove, Vicki. *Junglerama.* Putnam 1989. (Grades 3-9; 3P, 3Q)
Guccione, Leslie D. *Tell Me How the Wind Sounds.* Scholastic 1989. (Grades 7-12; 4P, 4Q)
Guy, Rosa. *The Ups and Downs of Carl Davis III.* Delacorte 1989. (Grades 5-9; 3P, 3Q)
Hall, Lynn. *Dagmar Schultz and the Angel Edna.* Scribners 1989. (Grades 3-9; 3P, 4Q)
_____. *Dagmar Schultz and the Powers of Darkness.* Scribners 1989. (Grades 3-9; 3P, 3Q)
_____. *Where Have All the Tigers Gone?* Scribners 1989. (Grade 10-Adult; 2P, 4Q)
Hamanaka, Sheila. *The Journey: Japanese Americans, Racism, and Renewal.* Orchard 1990. (Grade 7-Adult; 1P, 3Q)
Hamilton, Morse. *Effie's House.* Greenwillow 1990. (Grades 7-12; 3P, 2Q)
Hamley, Dennis. *Hare's Choice.* Delacorte 1990. (Grade 3-Adult; 3P, 3Q)
Harris, Mark Jonathan. *Come the Morning.* Bradbury 1989. (Grades 7-12; 3P, 4Q)
Heller, Julek and Headon, Deirdre. *Knights.* Random 1989. (Grade 5-Adult; 1P, 4Q)
Herlihy, Dirlie. *Ludie's Song.* Dial 1988. (Grades 5-9; 1P, 3Q)
Herman, Charlotte. *Millie Cooper, Take a Chance.* Dutton 1988. (Grades 3-4; 4P, 4Q)
Hest, Amy. *Where in the World Is the Perfect Family?* Clarion 1989. (Grades 3-6; 4P, 4Q)
_____. *Travel Tips from Harry: A Guide to Family Vacations in the Sun.* Morrow 1989. (Grades 3-4; 1P, 3Q)
Hobbs, Will. *Changes in Latitudes.* Atheneum 1988. (Grades 7-12; 2P, 3Q)
Holland, Isabelle. *The Unfrightened Dark.* Little 1990. (Grades 5-12; 3P, 3Q)
Holman, Felice. *Secret City, U.S.A..* Scribners 1990. (Grades 5-8; 3P, 4Q)
Holmes, Barbara Ware. *Charlotte Shakespeare and Annie the Great.* Harper 1989. (Grades 5-6; 2P, 3Q)
Holmes, Nancy. *Nobody's Fault.* Bantam 1990. (Grade 10-Adult; 4P, 3Q)
Homes, A. M. *Jack.* Macmillan 1989. (Grade 10-Adult; 3P, 3Q)
Hoover, H. M. *Away Is a Strange Place To Be.* Dutton 1990. (Grades 6-8; 2P, 3Q)
Houston, James. *Running West.* Crown 1989. (Grade 10-Adult; 2P, 4Q)
Howe, Norma. *The Game of Life.* Crown 1989. (Grades 7-9; 2P, 3Q)
Hudson, Jan. *Sweetgrass.* Philomel 1989. (Grades 5-9; 2P, 4Q)
Hughes, Dean. *Family Pose.* Atheneum 1989. (Grades 5-6; 2P, 3Q)
Hunt, Jonathan. *Illuminations.* Bradbury 1989. (Grades 3-9; 1P, 4Q)
Hurwitz, Johanna. *Hurray for Ali Baba Bernstein.* Morrow 1989. (Grades 3-4; 3P, 4Q)
Irwin, Hadley. *Can't Hear You Listening.* McElderry 1990. (Grades 7-12; 3P, 4Q)
Ivory, Lesley Anne. *Meet My Cats.* Dial 1989. (Grade 3-Adult; 2P, 4Q)
Jackson, Alison. *My Brother the Star.* Dutton 1990. (Grades 3-4; 2P, 3Q)
Jackson, Bo and Schaap, Dick. *Bo Knows Bo.* Doubleday 1990. (Grades 7-Adult; 4P, 2Q)
Jenness, Aylette. *Families: A Celebration of Diversity, Commitment and Love.* Houghton 1990. (Grades 3-6, Adult; 3P, 4Q)
Johnston, Norma. *The Delphic Choice.* Four Winds 1989. (Grades 7-10; 2P, 3Q)
Jones, Rebecca C. *The Believers.* Arcade 1989. (Grades 3-6; 1P, 3Q)
Jong, Erica. *Any Woman's Blues.* Harper 1990. (Adult; 1P, 3Q)
Kane, Rod. *Veteran's Day.* Orion 1990. (Grade 10-Adult; 3P, 4Q)
Kaplow, Robert. *Alessandra in Love.* Lippincott 1989. (Grades 7-9; 3P, 4Q)

Kehret, Peg. *Nightmare Mountain*. Dutton 1989. (Grades 3-6; 3P, 3Q)

Kelleher, Victor. *Baily's Bones*. Dial 1989. (Grades 3-9; 2P, 4Q)

Keller, Beverly. *Fowl Play, Desdemona!* Lothrop 1989. (Grades 3-9; 3P, 4Q)

Kelly, Marguerite. *The Mother's Almanac II: Your Child from Six to Twelve*. Doubleday 1989. (Adult; 2P, 4Q)

Kennedy, X. J. *Ghastlies, Goops & Pincushions: Nonsense Verse*. McElderry 1989. (Grades 3-4; 3P, 4Q)

Kherdian, David. *A Song for Uncle Harry*. Philomel 1989. (Grades 3-6; 1P, 4Q)

Kienzle, William X. *Masquerade*. Andrews & McMeel 1990. (Adult; 3P, 2Q)

King, Stephen. *Four Past Midnight*. Viking 1990. (Grade 9-Adult; 4P, 4Q)

Kirshenbaum, Binnie. *Short Subject*. Orchard 1989. (Grades 5-9; 3P, 3Q)

Klause, Annette Curtis. *The Silver Kiss*. Delacorte 1990. (Grade 7-Adult; 4P, 4Q)

Klein, Norma. *Just Friends*. Knopf 1990. (Grades 7-12; 3P, 3Q)

_____. *Learning How to Fall*. Bantam 1989. (Grades 10-12; 4P, 4Q)

Kleinbaum, N.H. from the filmscript by Tom Schulman. *Dead Poets Society*. Bantam 1989. (Grade 7-Adult; 3P, 2Q)

Kline, Suzy. *Herbie Jones and Hamburger Head*. Putnam 1989. (Grades 3-4; 3P, 3Q)

Korman, Gordon. *Radio Fifth Grade*. Scholastic 1989. (Grades 3-6; 3P, 4Q)

Krementz, Jill. *How It Feels to Fight for Your Life*. Little 1989. (Grades 7-12; 2P, 4Q)

Kropp, Paul. *Moonkid and Liberty*. Little 1990. (Grades 7-12; 2P, 3Q)

Kuklin, Susan. *Fighting Back: What Some People Are Doing About AIDS*. Putnam 1989. (Grades 7-Adult; 1P, 3Q)

Kwitz, Mary DeBall. *Shadow over Mousehaven Manor*. Scholastic 1989. (Grades 3-4; 3P, 4Q)

La Chapelle, Mary. *House of Heroes and Other Stories*. Crown 1988. (Grade 10-Adult; 1P, 3Q)

Laird, Christa. *Shadow of the Wall*. Greenwillow 1990. (Grade 7-Adult; 2P, 4Q)

L'Amour, Louis. *Education of a Wandering Man*. Bantam 1989. (Adult; 2P, 4Q)

Landau, Elaine. *We Have AIDS*. Watts 1990. (Grades 7-12; 2P, 3Q)

Landis, James David. *The Band Never Dances*. Harper 1989. (Grades 7-12; 2P, 2Q)

Lauber, Patrick. *The News About Dinosaurs*. Bradbury 1989. (Grades 3-6; 4P, 4Q)

Le Guin, Ursula. *Tehanu: The Last Book of Earthsea*. Atheneum 1990. (Grades 7-12; 2P, 3Q)

L'Engle, Madeleine. *An Acceptable Time*. Farrar 1989. (Grades 7-12; 4P, 4Q)

_____. *Two-Part Invention: The Story of a Marriage*. Farrar 1988. (Adult; 2P, 4Q)

Lessac, Frané, comp. *Caribbean Canvas*. Lippincott 1989. (Grade 10-Adult; 1P, 2Q)

Lester, Julius. *How Many Spots Does a Leopard Have?* Scholastic 1989. (Grades 3-6; 3P, 3Q)

Levitin, Sonia. *Silver Days*. Atheneum 1989. (Grades 5-12; 3P, 4Q)

Lisle, Janet. *Afternoon of the Elves*. Orchard 1989. (Grades 4-6; 2P, 3Q)

Little, Jean. *Hey World, Here I Am!* Harper 1989. (Grades 5-9; 3P, 3Q)

Livingston, Myra Cohn. *Birthday Poems*. Holiday 1989. (Grades 3-4; 2P, 3Q)

_____. *Remembering and Other Poems*. McElderry 1989. (Grade 7-Adult; 1P, 3Q)

_____, comp. *Halloween Poems*. Holiday 1989. (Grades 3-4; 4P, 4Q)

Logan, Onnie Lee and Clark, Katherine. *Motherwit*. Dutton 1989. (Grade 10-Adult; 3P, 4Q)

Lowry, Lois. *Your Move, J. P.!* Houghton 1990. (Grades 5-8; 3P, 4Q)

MacLachlan, Patricia. *The Facts and Fictions of Minna Pratt*. Harper 1988. (Grades 3-6; 3P, 3Q)

Maguire, Gregory. *I Feel Like the Morning Star*. Harper 1989. (Grades 7-12; 3P, 4Q)

Mahy, Margaret. *The Blood-and-Thunder Adventure on Hurricane Peak*. McElderry 1989. (Grades 3-9; 3P, 3Q)

Malmgren, Dallin. *The Ninth Issue*. Delacorte 1989. (Grades 7-12; 3P, 3Q)

Manes, Stephen. *Chocolate-Covered Ants.* Scholastic 1990. (Grades 3-6; 3P, 2Q)
Marie De France (translated by Naomi Lewis). *Proud Knight, Fair Lady: The Twelve Lais of Marie de France.* Viking 1989. (Grade 10-Adult; 1P, 3Q)
Marino, Jan. *Eighty-Eight Steps to September.* Little 1989. (Grades 3-6; 4P, 3Q)
Marsden, John. *So Much to Tell You.* Little 1989. (Grades 10-12; 2P, 4Q)
Martin, Ann M. *Ma and Pa Dracula.* Holiday 1989. (Grades 3-4; 2P, 3Q)
Martin, Katherine. *Night Riding.* Knopf 1989. (Grades 7-12; 2P, 3Q)
Maynard, Chris and Scheller, Bill. *Manifold Destiny: The One! The Only! Guide to Cooking on Your Car Engine.* Villard 1989. (Adult; 1P, 4Q)
Mazer, Norma Fox. *C, My Name Is Cal.* Scholastic 1990. (Grades 7-8; 2P, 2Q)
_____. *Silver.* Morrow 1988. (Grades 10-12; 4P, 4Q)
Mazer, Norma Fox and Mazer, Harry. *Heartbeat.* Bantam 1989. (Grades 7-12; 4P, 4Q)
McDaniel, Lurlene. *Goodbye Doesn't Mean Forever.* Bantam 1989. (Grades 7-12; 4P, 4Q)
_____. *Too Young to Die.* Bantam 1989. (Grades 7-12; 4P, 4Q)
McGirt, Dan. *Jason Cosmo.* NAL 1989. (Grade 10-Adult; 2P, 3Q)
McHugh, Elisabet. *Wiggie Wins the West.* Atheneum 1989. (Grades 3-6; 4P, 4Q)
McKenna, Colleen O'Shaughnessy. *Fifth Grade: Here Comes Trouble.* Scholastic 1989. (Grades 5-9; 3P, 3Q)
Meltzer, Milton, ed. *Voices from the Civil War: A Documentary History of the Great American Conflict.* Crowell 1989. (Grade 7-Adult; 1P, 4Q)
Michener, James A. *Journey.* Random 1989. (Grade 7-Adult; 2P, 4Q)
Miklowitz, Gloria. *Anything to Win.* Delacorte 1989. (Grades 7-12; 3P, 2Q)
Miller, Jim Wayne. *Newfound.* Orchard 1989. (Grade 7-Adult; 2P, 4Q)
Miller, Sue. *Family Pictures.* Harper 1990. (Adult; 4P, 4Q)
Montgomery, R. A. *Traitors from Within.* Bantam 1990. (Grades 7-12; 3P, 3Q)
Mooser, Stephen. *The Hitchhiking Vampire.* Delacorte 1989. (Grades 5-9; 3P, 3Q)
Morris, Judy. *The Kid Who Ran for Principal.* Lippincott 1989. (Grades 5-9; 3P, 3Q)
Morrison, Martha A., M.D. *White Rabbit.* Crown 1988. (Grade 10-Adult; 3P, 4Q)
Morse, Jeff. *The Butterfly Jar.* Bantam 1989. (Grades 3-9; 3P, 4Q)
Moyers, Bill. *A World of Ideas.* Doubleday 1989. (Grades 10-Adult; 2P, 3Q)
Murphy, Jill. *Worlds Apart.* Putnam 1989. (Grades 3-6; 3P, 4Q)
Murphy, Jim. *The Call of the Wolves.* Scholastic 1989. (Grade 3-Adult; 4P, 4Q)
_____. *The Last Dinosaur.* Scholastic 1988. (Grade 3-Adult; 4P, 4Q)
Murrow, Liza Ketchum. *Fire in the Heart.* Holiday 1989. (Grades 5-9; 2P, 3Q)
Myers, Walter Dean. *Fallen Angels.* Scholastic 1988. (Grades 10-Adult; 4P, 4Q)
_____. *The Mouse Rap.* Harper 1990. (Grades 5-8; 4P, 4Q)
Naughton, Jim. *My Brother Stealing Second.* Harper 1989. (Grades 7-12; 2P, 4Q)
Newman, Barbara and Rogan, Barbara. *The Covenant: Love and Death in Beruit.* Crown 1989. (Grade 10-Adult; 1P, 3Q)
Nixon, Jean Lowery. *Star Baby.* Bantam 1989. (Grades 7-12; 3P, 4Q)
_____. *Whispers from the Dead.* Delacorte 1989. (Grades 7-12; 3P, 4Q)
Noonan, Michael. *McKenzie's Boots.* Orchard 1988. (Grade 10-Adult; 3P, 4Q)
Norman, Michael. *These Good Men: Friendships Forged from War.* Crown 1989. (Grade 10-Adult; 1P, 4Q)
O'Dell, Scott. *My Name Is Not Angelica.* Houghton 1989. (Grades 3-6; 1P, 3Q)
Orlean, Susan. *Saturday Night.* Knopf 1990. (Grade 9-Adult; 3P, 4Q)
Osborne, Victor. *Moondream.* Lothrop 1989. (Grades 3-9; 2P, 4Q)
Parkhurst, William. *True Detectives: The Real World of Today's Private Investigators.* Crown 1989. (Grade 10-Adult; 4P, 4Q)
Patchett, Terry. *Truckers.* Delacorte 1989. (Grade 7-Adult; 3P, 4Q)
Paterno, Joe and Asbell, Bernard. *Paterno: By the Book.* Random 1989. (Grade 10-Adult; 1P, 3Q)

Patterson, Nancy Ruth. *The Christmas Cup*. Orchard 1989. (Grades 3-4; 3P, 3Q)
Paulsen, Gary. *The Boy Who Owned the School*. Orchard 1990. (Grades 5-8; 3P, 4Q)
——. *The Night the White Deer Died*. Delacorte 1990. (Grades 7-12; 1P, 3Q)
——. *The Voyage of the Frog*. Orchard 1989. (Grades 5-12; 2P, 4Q)
——. *The Winter Room*. Orchard 1989. (Grades 5-12; 2P, 4Q)
Peck, Robert Newton. *Soup's Hoop*. Delacorte 1990. (Grades 3-6; 2P, 3Q)
Pendergraft, Patricia. *Brushy Mountain*. Philomel 1989. (Grades 5-9; 3P, 4Q)
Penn [Penn Jillette] and Teller. *Cruel Tricks for Dear Friends*. Villard 1989. (Grade 10-Adult; 3P, 4Q)
Peters, David. *A Gallery of Dinosaurs and Other Early Reptiles*. Knopf 1989. (Grade 3-Adult; 1P, 4Q)
Pfeffer, Susan Beth. *Rewind to Yesterday*. Delacorte 1988. (Grades 3-6; 2P, 3Q)
——. *Turning Thirteen*. Scholastic 1988. (Grades 5-9; 2P, 3Q)
Pinkwater, Daniel. *Borgel*. Macmillan 1990. (Grade 7-Adult; 2P, 4Q)
Pinkwater, Jill. *Buffalo Brenda*. Macmillan 1989. (Grades 5-9; 3P, 4Q)
Pople, Maureen. *A Nugget of Gold*. Holt 1989. (Grades 7-12; 1P, 3Q)
Powers, Tom. *Horror Movies*. Lerner 1989. (Grades 5-12; 2P, 3Q)
——. *Movie Monsters*. Lerner 1989. (Grades 5-12; 2P, 3Q)
Prelutsky, Jack, comp. *Poems of A. Nonny Mouse*. Random 1989. (Grades 3-6; 4P, 4Q)
Pryor, Bonnie. *The Twenty-Four-Hour Lipstick Mystery*. Morrow 1989. (Grades 3-6; 4P, 4Q)
Rabinowitz, Ann. *Bethie*. Macmillan 1989. (Grades 7-12; 2P, 4Q)
Radford, Ken. *The Cellar*. Holiday 1989. (Grades 5-12; 2P, 3Q)
Ramusi, Molapatene Collins. *Soweto, My Love: A Testimony to Black Life in South Africa*. Holt 1989. (Grades 7-Adult; 2P, 4Q)
Redford, Dorothy Spruill. *Somerset Homecoming: Recovering a Lost Heritage*. Doubleday 1988. (Grade 10-Adult; 3P, 4Q)
Reed, Don C. *The Dolphins and Me*. Little 1989. (Grades 3-6; 3P, 4Q)
Rice, Anne. *The Mummy*. Ballantine 1989. (Grade 9-Adult; 3P, 4Q)
Ritchie, Alan. *Erin McEwan, Your Days Are Numbered*. Knopf 1990. (Grades 5-8; 2P, 4Q)
Roberts, Willo Davis. *Nightmare*. Atheneum 1989. (Grades 7-12; 3P, 4Q)
Robinson, Mary. *Give It Up, Mom*. Houghton 1989. (Grades 5-9; 2P, 3Q)
Robinson, Nancy K. *Angela, Private Citizen*. Scholastic 1989. (Grades 3-9; 3P, 4Q)
——. *Veronica Meets Her Match*. Scholastic 1990. (Grades 3-6; 3P, 3Q)
Rochman, Hazel, ed. *Somehow Tenderness Survives: Stories of Southern Africa*. Harper 1988. (Grades 5-12; 3P, 4Q)
Rodowsky, Colby. *Sydney, Herself*. Farrar 1989. (Grades 5-9; 1P, 3Q)
Roe, Elaine Corbeil. *Circle of Light*. Harper 1989. (Grades 5-9; 2P, 4Q)
Rosenberg, Maxine B. *Growing Up Adopted*. Bradbury 1989. (Grades 5-12; 1P, 3Q)
Ruckman, Ivy. *No Way Out*. Crowell 1988. (Grades 5-12; 3P, 4Q)
——. *Who Invited the Undertaker?* Harper 1989. (Grades 5-9; 4P, 4Q)
Ryan, Mary C. *The Voice from the Mendelsohns' Maple*. Little 1990. (Grades 5-9; 2P, 3Q)
Rylant, Cynthia. *Soda Jerk*. Orchard 1990. (Grade 5-Adult; 3P, 4Q)
Sachar, Louis. *The Boy Who Lost His Face*. Knopf 1989. (Grades 5-9; 4P, 4Q)
Sachs, Marilyn. *Just Like a Friend*. Dutton 1989. (Grades 5-8; 3P, 3Q)
Sacks, Margaret. *Beyond Safe Boundaries*. Lodestar 1989. (Grades 5-9; 1P, 3Q)
Salerno-Sonnenberg, Nadja. *Nadja: On My Way*. Crown 1989. (Grades 7-12; 1P, 3Q)
Sanders, Scott Russell. *The Engineer of Beasts*. Orchard 1988. (Grades 7-Adult; 2P, 3Q)
Sanfield, Steve. *The Adventures of High John the Conqueror*. Orchard 1989. (Grades 5-9; 2P, 3Q)

Schultz, Ted. *The Fringes of Reason: A Whole Earth Catalog.* Harmony 1989. (Grade 7-Adult; 2P, 4Q)

Scott, Elaine. *Choices.* Morrow 1989. (Grades 7-12; 2P, 3Q)

Seixas, Judith. *Living with a Parent Who Takes Drugs.* Greenwillow 1989. (Grades 3-9; 3P, 4Q)

Service, Pamela F. *Vision Quest.* Fawcett 1990. (Grades 5-12; 3P, 4Q)

Shannon, George. *Unlived Affections.* Harper 1989. (Grades 7-12; 1P, 3Q)

Shore, David and Campbell, Patty. *New Zealand by Motorhome.* Pelican 1989. (Adult; 1P, 4Q)

Shusterman, Neal. *Dissidents.* Little 1989. (Grades 7-9; 2P, 3Q)

Sieruta, Peter D. *Heartbeats and Other Stories.* Harper 1989. (Grades 7-12; 3P, 4Q)

Singer, Marilyn. *Storm Rising.* Scholastic 1989. (Grades 7-12; 4P, 4Q)

Siskin, Bernard, Staller, Jerome and Rorvik, David. *What Are the Chances? Risks, Odds, and Likelihood in Everyday Life.* Crown 1989. (Grade 10-Adult; 2P, 1Q)

Skurzynski, Gloria. *Dangerous Ground.* Bradbury 1989. (Grades 5-6; 2P, 3Q)

Smith, Marya. *Across the Creek.* Arcade 1989. (Grades 5-9; 2P, 4Q)

Snyder, Zilpha Keatley. *Janie's Private Eyes.* Delacorte 1989. (Grades 5-9; 3P, 4Q)

Springstubb, Tricia. *With a Name Like Lulu, Who Needs More Trouble?* Delacorte 1989. (Grades 5-12; 2P, 4Q)

Staples, Suzanne Fisher. *Shabanu: Daughter of the Wind.* Knopf 1989. (Grade 5-Adult; 1P, 4Q)

Stolp, Hans. *The Golden Bird.* Dial 1990. (Grade 5-Adult; 3P, 4Q)

Stone, Bruce. *Been Clever Forever.* Harper 1988. (Grades 7-12; 2P, 3Q)

Stones, Rosemary, comp. *More to Life than Mr. Right: Stories for Young Feminists.* Holt 1989. (Grades 10-12; 2P, 3Q)

Strasser, Todd. *Beyond the Reef.* Delacorte 1989. (Grades 7-12; 3P, 4Q)

Swallow, Pamela Curtis. *No Promises.* Putnam 1989. (Grades 7-12; 3P, 4Q)

Sweeney, Joyce. *The Dream Collector.* Delacorte 1989. (Grades 7-12; 4P, 3Q)

Swindells, Robert. *A Serpent's Tooth.* Holiday 1988 (U.S. edition 1989). (Grades 7-9; 2P, 3Q)

Talbert, Marc. *The Paper Knife.* Dial 1988. (Grades 3-6; 2P, 3Q)

Tapp, Kathy Kennedy. *The Sacred Circle of the Hula Hoop.* Macmillan 1989. (Grades 6-9; 3P, 3Q)

Taylor, Theodore. *Sniper.* Harcourt 1989. (Grades 7-12; 3P, 4Q)

Tepper, Sheri S. *Grass.* Doubleday 1989. (Grade 10-Adult; 3P, 4Q)

Thomas, Jane Resh. *The Princess in the Pigpen.* Clarion 1989. (Grades 3-9; 4P, 3Q)

Thomas, Joyce Carol. *Journey.* Scholastic 1988. (Grades 5-9; 2P, 3Q)

Thomas, Ruth. *The Runaways.* Lippincott 1989. (Grades 5-6; 3P, 3Q)

Thomas, Sherry, ed. *We Didn't Have Much, but We Sure Had Plenty: Rural Women in Their Own Words.* Anchor 1989. (Grades 10-Adult; 1P, 4Q)

Tolan, Stephanie S. *Plague Year.* Morrow 1990. (Grades 7-12; 3P, 4Q)

Tsuchiya, Yukio, translated by Tomoko Tsuchiya Dykes. *Faithful Elephants: A True Story of Animals, People and War.* Houghton 1988. (Grade 3-Adult; 3P, 4Q)

Ure, Jean. *One Green Leaf.* Delacorte 1989. (Grade 7-Adult; 2P, 4Q)

Uyemoto, Holly. *Rebel Without a Clue.* Crown 1989. (Grades 10-Adult; 1P, 2Q)

Vande Velde, Vivian. *A Well-Timed Enchantment.* Crown 1990. (Grades 5-8; 2P, 3Q)

Van Leeuwen, Jean. *Dear Mom, You're Ruining My Life.* Dial 1989. (Grades 5-6; 2P, 4Q)

Van Raven, Pieter. *The Great Man's Secret.* Scribners 1989. (Grades 7-12; 3P, 4Q)

Voight, Cynthia. *On Fortune's Wheel.* Atheneum 1990. (Grades 9-12; 3P, 4Q)

———. *Seventeen Against the Dealer.* Atheneum 1989. (Grades 10-12; 3P, 3Q)

Ward, Kaari, ed. *Great Disasters: Dramatic True Stories.* Reader's Digest 1989. (Grade 3-Adult; 3P, 4Q)

Wersba, Barbara. *The Best Place to Live Is the Ceiling.* Harper 1990. (Grades 7-12; 3P, 3Q)
_____. *Wonderful Me.* Harper 1990. (Grades 7-12; 3P, 2Q)
Westall, Robert. *Blitzcat.* Scholastic 1989. (Grades 10-Adult; 3P, 4Q)
_____. *Ghost Abbey.* Scholastic 1989. (Grades 5-9; 2P, 3Q)
Wharton, William. *Franky Furbo.* Holt 1989. (Grade 10-Adult; 2P, 4Q)
White, Ellen Emerson. *Long Live the Queen.* Scholastic 1989. (Grades 10-12; 4P, 2Q)
Wilkinson, Elizabeth. *Making Cents: Every Kid's Guide to Money.* Little 1989. (Grades 3-9; 1P, 4Q)
Williams, Heathcote. *Falling for a Dolphin.* Harmony 1989. (Grades 10-Adult; 1P, 4Q)
Williams, Sheila and Ardai, Charles, eds. *Why I Left Harry's All-Night Hamburgers, and Other Stories from Isaac Asimov's Science Fiction Magazine.* Delacorte 1990. (Grade 7-Adult; 3P, 4Q)
Wilson, A. N. *Stray.* Orchard 1989. (Grade 5-Adult; 2P, 3Q)
Wirths, Claudine G. and Bowman-Kruhm, Mary. *Where's My Other Sock? How to Get Organized and Drive Your Parents and Teachers Crazy.* Crowell 1989. (Grades 5-12; 2P, 3Q)
Wolff, Virginia Euwer. *Probably Still Nick Swansen.* Holt 1988. (Grades 7-12; 1P, 4Q)
Wrightson, Patricia. *Balyet.* McElderry 1989. (Grades 7-9; 1P, 3Q)
Yalof, Ina. *Life and Death: The Story of a Hospital.* Random 1989. (Grade 10-Adult; 2P, 3Q)
Yarbrough, Camille. *The Shimmershine Queens.* Putnam 1989. (Grades 5-9; 2P, 3Q)
Yolen, Jane. *Best Witches: Poems for Halloween.* Putnam 1989. (Grades 3-4; 4P, 4Q)
_____. *The Devil's Arithmetic.* Viking 1988. (Grades 7-12; 3P, 4Q)
_____. *The Faery Flag: Stories and Poems of Fantasy and the Supernatural.* Orchard 1989. (Grades 7-12; 4P, 4Q)
Yolen, Jane and Greenberg, Martin. *Things That Go Bump in the Night.* Harper 1989. (Grades 5-12; 4P, 4Q)
Zable, Rona S. *An Almost Perfect Summer.* Bantam 1989. (Grades 7-12; 2P, 3Q)
_____. *Landing on Marvin Gardens.* Bantam 1989. (Grades 5-9; 3P, 4Q)
Zalben, Jane Breskin. *Earth to Andrew G. Blechman.* Farrar 1989. (Grades 3-4; 2P, 2Q)
Zarnow, Teryl. *Husband Is the Past Tense of Daddy: And Other Dispatches from the Front Lines of Motherhood.* Addison-Wesley 1990. (Adult; 3P, 3Q)
Zindel, Paul. *A Begonia for Miss Applebaum.* Harper 1989. (Grades 7-12; 4P, 4Q)
Zyskind, Sara. *Struggle.* Lerner 1989. (Grade 7-Adult; 2P, 4Q)

P's and Q's: Points to Remember

P (Popularity Level)

4P—This is one of the books everyone wants to read.

3P—Most people will want to read this just as soon as they hear about it.

2P—Booktalking can sell this, but it may need pushing.

1P—For the special reader, or for those into the subject.

Q (Quality Level)

4Q—Couldn't be better.

3Q—Some flaws, but nothing to hinder the story.

2Q—Major flaws; worth pushing only because of its high P rating.

All titles are recommended for use with the designated age groups. The rating scale is adapted from that used in *Voice of Youth Advocates.*

BIBLIOGRAPHY BY AGE LEVEL

Elementary (Grades 3-4)

Afternoon of the Elves (Lisle)
Angela, Private Citizen (Robinson)
Baily's Bones (Kelleher)
Before the Wildflowers Bloom (Bylinsky)
The Believers (Jones)
Best Witches: Poems for Halloween (Yolen)
Bingo Brown and the Language of Love (Byars)
Birthday Poems (Livingston)
The Blood-and-Thunder Adventure on Hurricane Peak (Mahy)
The Butterfly Jar (Morse)
The Call of the Wolves (Murphy)
A Child's Treasury of Animal Verse (Daniel)
Chocolate-Covered Ants (Manes)
The Christmas Cup (Patterson)
Cleaver of the Good Luck Diner (Duffy)
Dagmar Schultz and the Angel Edna (Hall)
Dagmar Schultz and the Powers of Darkness (Hall)
The Dolphins and Me (Reed)
Earth to Andrew G. Blechman (Zalben)
Eighty-Eight Steps to September (Marino)
El Güero: A True Adventure Story (De Trevino)
Everyone Else's Parents Said Yes (Danziger)
The Facts and Fictions of Minna Pratt (MacLachlan)
Faithful Elephants: A True Story of Animals, People and War (Tsuchiya)
Families: A Celebration of Diversity, Commitment and Love (Jenness)
The Fourth-Grade Dinosaur Club (Bograd)
Fowl Play, Desdemona! (Keller)
Frank and Ernest (Day)
A Gallery of Dinosaurs and Other Early Reptiles (Peters)
Ghastlies, Goops & Pincushions: Nonsense Verse (Kennedy)
Going Green: A Kid's Handbook to Saving the Planet (Elkington)
Great Disasters: Dramatic True Stories ((Ward)
Halloween: Stories and Poems (Bauer)
Halloween Poems (Livingston)
Hare's Choice (Hamley)
Herbie Jones and Hamburger Head (Kline)
How Many Spots Does a Leopard Have? (Lester)
Hurray for Ali Baba Bernstein (Hurwitz)
I Hate Your Guts, Ben Brooster! (Clifford)
Illuminations (Hunt)
In the Forest (Arnosky)
Junglerama (Grove)
The Last Dinosaur (Murphy)
Living with a Parent Who Takes Drugs (Seixas)
Lost Boys Never Say Die (Brown)
Ma and Pa Dracula (Martin)
Making Cents: Every Kid's Guide to Money (Wilkinson)
Meet My Cats (Ivory)
Moondream (Osborne)
My Brother the Star (Jackson)
My Name Is Not Angelica (O'Dell)
The News About Dinosaurs (Lauber)
Nightmare Mountain (Kehret)
One Day in the Tropical Rain Forest (George)
The Outside Child (Bawden)
The Paper Knife (Talbert)
Poems of A. Nonny Mouse (Prelutsky)
The Princess in the Pigpen (Thomas)
Radio Fifth Grade (Korman)
The Random House Book of 1001 Questions and Answers (Ardley)
Rewind to Yesterday (Pfeffer)
The Secret of the Indian (Banks)
Self-Portrait with Wings (Green)
Shadow over Mousehaven Manor (Kwitz)
The Sierra Club Summer Book (Allison)
A Song for Uncle Harry (Kherdian)
Squeeze Play (Glenn)
A Summer Like Turnips (Gaeddert)
(Grades 3-6) *Travel Tips from Harry: A Guide to Family Vacations in the Sun* (Hest)

Elementary (cont.)
The Twenty-Four-Hour Lipstick Mystery (Pryor)
Tucker (Birdseye)
Veronica Meets Her Match (Robinson)
Where in the World Is the Perfect Family? (Hest)
Wiggie Wins the West (McHugh)
The Wild Inside: Sierra Club's Guide to the Great Indoors (Allison)
Worlds Apart (Murphy)
The Village by the Sea (Fox)

Middle School (Grades 5-6)

Across the Creek (Smith)
The Adventures of High John the Conqueror (Sanfield)
Afternoon of the Elves (Lisle)
Alyssa Milano: She's the Boss (Catalano)
Angela, Private Citizen (Robinson)
Away Is a Strange Place To Be (Hoover)
Baily's Bones (Kelleher)
Before the Wildflowers Bloom (Bylinsky)
The Believers (Jones)
Better Mousetraps: Product Improvements That Led to Success (Aaseng)
Beyond Safe Boundaries (Sacks)
Bingo Brown and the Language of Love (Byars)
The Blood-and-Thunder Adventure on Hurricane Peak (Mahy)
The Boy Who Lost His Face (Sachar)
The Boy Who Owned the School (Paulsen)
Brushy Mountain (Pendergraft)
Buffalo Brenda (Pinkwater)
The Butterfly Jar (Morse)
The Call of the Wolves (Murphy)
The Cellar (Radford)
Charlotte Shakespeare and Annie the Great (Holmes)
The Chessmen of Doom (Bellairs)
A Child's Treasury of Animal Verse (Daniel)
Chocolate-Covered Ants (Manes)
Choosing Sides (Cooper)
Circle of Light (Roe)
Cleaver of the Good Luck Diner (Duffy)
Dagmar Schultz and the Angel Edna (Hall)
Dagmar Schultz and the Powers of Darkness (Hall)
Dangerous Ground (Skuzynski)
Dear Mom, You're Ruining My Life (Van Leeuwen)

The Dolphins and Me (Reed)
Eighty-Eight Steps to September (Marino)
El Guëro: A True Adventure Story (De Trevino)
The Empty Sleeve (Garfield)
Erin McEwan, Your Days Are Numbered (Ritchie)
Everyone Else's Parents Said Yes (Danziger)
The Facts and Fictions of Minna Pratt (MacLachlan)
Faithful Elephants: A True Story of Animals, People and War (Tsuchiya)
Families: A Celebration of Diversity, Commitment and Love (Jenness)
Family Reunion (Cooney)
Fire in the Heart (Murrow)
Fifth Grade: Here Comes Trouble (McKenna)
Five Finger Discount (DeClements)
Forgotten Girl (Colman)
The Fortunate Fortunes (Aaseng)
The Fourth-Grade Dinosaur Club (Bograd)
Fowl Play, Desdemona! (Keller)
Frank and Ernest (Day)
A Gallery of Dinosaurs and Other Early Reptiles (Peters)
Genie with the Light Blue Hair (Conford)
Get Help: Solving the Problems in Your Life (Gilbert)
Ghost Abbey (Westall)
Give It Up, Mom (Robinson)
Glass Slippers Give You Blisters (Auch)
Going Green: A Kid's Handbook to Saving the Planet (Elkington)
The Golden Bird (Stolp)
Great Disasters: Dramatic True Stories ((Ward)
Growing Up Adopted (Rosenberg)
Growing Up Western (Backes and Brown)
Hare's Choice (Hamley)
Harry Newberry and the Raiders of the Red Drink (Gilden)
The Haunting of Frances Rain (Buffie)
Herds of Thunder, Manes of Gold: A Collection of Horse Stories and Poems (Coville)
Hey World, Here I Am! (Little)
The Hitchhiking Vampire (Mooser)
Horror Movies (Powers)
How Many Spots Does a Leopard Have? (Lester)
I Hate Your Guts, Ben Brooster! (Clifford)
Illuminations (Hunt)

In the Forest (Arnosky)
Janie's Private Eyes (Snyder)
Journey (Thomas)
Junglerama (Grove)
Just Like a Friend (Sachs)
The Kid Who Ran for Principal (Morris)
Knights (Heller and Headon)
Landing on Marvin Gardens (Zable)
The Last Dinosaur (Murphy)
Leave the Cooking to Me (Angell)
Living with a Parent Who Takes Drugs (Seixas)
Lost Boys Never Say Die (Brown)
Ludie's Song (Herlihy)
Magicians of Erianne (Berry)
Making Cents: Every Kid's Guide to Money (Wilkinson)
Meet My Cats (Ivory)
Moondream (Osborne)
The Mouse Rap (Myers)
Movie Monsters (Powers)
My Daniel (Conrad)
My Name Is Not Angelica (O'Dell)
My War with Goggle-Eyes (Fine)
The News About Dinosaurs (Lauber)
Nightmare Mountain (Kehret)
No Way Out (Ruckman)
One Day in the Tropical Rain Forest (George)
The Outside Child (Bawden)
The Paper Knife (Talbert)
Phone Call from a Ghost (Cohen)
Poems of A. Nonny Mouse (Prelutsky)
The Potato Kid (Corcoran)
The Princess in the Pigpen (Thomas)
The Problem Solvers (Aaseng)
Radio Fifth Grade (Korman)
The Random House Book of 1001 Questions and Answers (Ardley)
Raymond (Geller)
The Rejects (Aaseng)
Rewind to Yesterday (Pfeffer)
Rosy's Romance (Greenwald)
The Runaways (Thomas)
Sacred Circle of the Hula Hoop (Tapp)
Secret City, U. S. A. (Holman)
The Secret of the Indian (Banks)
Self-Portrait with Wings (Green)
Shabanu: Daughter of the Wind (Staples)
The Shimmershine Queens (Yarbrough)
Short Subject (Kirshenbaum)
The Sierra Club Summer Book (Allison)
Silver Days (Levitin)
Soda Jerk (Rylant)
Somehow Tenderness Survives: Stories of Southern Africa (Rochman)

A Song for Uncle Harry (Kherdian)
The Starstone (Chetwin)
Stray (Wilson)
A Summer Like Turnips (Gaeddert)
Sweetgrass (Hudson)
Sydney, Herself (Rodowsky)
Things That Go Bump in the Night (Yolen and Greenberg)
The Trolley to Yesterday (Bellairs)
Turning Thirteen (Pfeffer)
The Twenty-Four-Hour Lipstick Mystery (Pryor)
Tucker (Birdseye)
The Unfrightened Dark (Holland)
The Unsung Heroes (Aaseng)
The Ups and Downs of Carl Davis III (Guy)
Valentine and Orson (Burkert)
Veronica Meets Her Match (Robinson)
The Voice from the Mendelsohns' Maple (Ryan)
Viola, Furgy, Bobbi, and Me (Ethridge)
Vision Quest (Service)
A Well-Timed Enchantment (Vande Velde)
We Remember the Holocaust (Adler)
Where in the World Is the Perfect Family? (Hest)
Where's My Other Sock? How to Get Organized and Drive Your Parents and Teachers Crazy (Wirths and Bowman-Kruhm)
Who Invited the Undertaker? (Ruckman)
Wiggie Wins the West (McHugh)
The Wild Inside: Sierra Club's Guide to the Great Indoors (Allison)
The Winter Room (Paulsen)
With a Name Like Lulu, Who Needs More Trouble? (Springstubb)
Worlds Apart (Murphy)
Your Move, J. P.! (Lowry)

Junior High (Grades 7–8)

An Acceptable Time (L'Engle)
Across the Creek (Smith)
The Adventures of High John the Conqueror (Sanfield)
Alessandra in Love (Kaplow)
An Almost Perfect Summer (Zable)
Alyssa Milano: She's the Boss (Catalano)
Angela, Private Citizen (Robinson)
Anything to Win (Miklowitz)
Away Is a Strange Place To Be (Hoover)
Backstreets: Springsteen-The Man and His Music (Cross)

Junior High (cont.)
Baily's Bones (Kelleher)
Balyet (Wrightson)
The Band Never Dances (Landis)
Been Clever Forever (Stone)
A Begonia for Miss Applebaum (Zindel)
Best Friends Tell the Best Lies (Dines)
The Best Place to Live Is the Ceiling (Wersba)
Bethie (Rabinowitz)
Better Mousetraps: Product Improvements That Led to Success (Aaseng)
Beyond Safe Boundaries (Sacks)
Beyond the Reef (Strasser)
The Big Bang (Forman)
The Blood-and-Thunder Adventure on Hurricane Peak (Mahy)
Bo Knows Bo (Jackson and Schaap)
Borgel (Pinkwater)
The Boy Who Lost His Face (Sachar)
The Boy Who Owned the School (Paulsen)
Brushy Mountain (Pendergraft)
Buffalo Brenda (Pinkwater)
The Butterfly Jar (Morse)
C, My Name Is Cal (Mazer)
The Call of the Wolves (Murphy)
Can't Hear You Listening (Irwin)
The Cellar (Radford)
Changes in Latitudes (Hobbs)
The Chessmen of Doom (Bellairs)
Children of the River (Crew)
A Child's Treasury of Animal Verse (Daniel)
Choices (Scott)
Circle of Light (Roe)
Come the Morning (Harris)
Connections: Short Stories by Outstanding Writers for Young Adults (Gallo)
Dagmar Schultz and the Angel Edna (Hall)
Dagmar Schultz and the Powers of Darkness (Hall)
Dead Poets Society (Kleinbaum)
The Delphic Choice (Johnston)
The Devil's Arithmetic (Yolen)
Dissidents (Shusterman)
Don't Look Behind You (Duncan)
The Dream Collector (Sweeney)
The Dying Sun (Blackwood)
Effie's House (Hamilton)
The Empty Sleeve (Garfield)
The Engineer of Beasts (Sanders)
Enter Three Witches (Gilmore)
Erin McEwan, Your Days Are Numbered (Ritchie)

Eva (Dickinson)
The Face on the Milk Carton (Cooney)
The Faery Flag: Stories and Poems of Fantasy and the Supernatural (Yolen)
Faithful Elephants: A True Story of Animals, People and War (Tsuchiya)
Family Reunion (Cooney)
Fifth Grade: Here Comes Trouble (McKenna)
Fighting Back: What Some People Are Doing About AIDS (Kuklin)
Fire in the Heart (Murrow)
Five Finger Discount (DeClements)
Forgotten Girl (Colman)
The Fortunate Fortunes (Aaseng)
Forward Pass (Dygard)
Four Past Midnight (King)
Fowl Play, Desdemona! (Keller)
Francie and the Boys (Daneman)
Frank and Ernest (Day)
The Fringes of Reason: A Whole Earth Catalog (Schultz)
A Gallery of Dinosaurs and Other Early Reptiles (Peters)
The Game of Life (Howe)
Genie with the Light Blue Hair (Conford)
Get Help: Solving the Problems in Your Life (Gilbert)
Ghost Abbey (Westall)
Give It Up, Mom (Robinson)
Glass Slippers Give You Blisters (Auch)
Going Green: A Kid's Handbook to Saving the Planet (Elkington)
The Golden Bird (Stolp)
Goodbye Doesn't Mean Forever (McDaniel)
Great Disasters: Dramatic True Stories (Ward)
The Great Man's Secret (Van Raven)
Growing Up Adopted (Rosenberg)
Growing Up Western (Backes and Brown)
Hare's Choice (Hamley)
The Harmony Illustrated Encyclopedia of Rock, sixth edition (Frame, Clifford)
Harry Newberry and the Raiders of the Red Drink (Gilden)
The Haunting of Frances Rain (Buffie)
Heartbeat (Mazer and Mazer)
Heartbeats and Other Stories (Sieruta)
Herds of Thunder, Manes of Gold: A Collection of Horse Stories and Poems (Coville)
Hey World, Here I Am! (Little)
High Wizardry (Duane)
The Hitchhiking Vampire (Mooser)
Horror Movies (Powers)

How It Feels to Fight for Your Life (Krementz)
I Feel Like the Morning Star (Maguire)
Illuminations (Hunt)
In the Forest (Arnosky)
Janie's Private Eyes (Snyder)
Journey (Michener)
Journey (Thomas)
The Journey: Japanese Americans, Racism, and Renewal (Hamanaka)
Just Friends (Klein)
Just Like a Friend (Sachs)
The Kid Who Ran for Principal (Morris)
Knights (Heller and Headon)
Landing on Marvin Gardens (Zable)
The Last Dinosaur (Murphy)
Leave the Cooking to Me (Angell)
LeMond: The Incredible Comeback of an American Hero (Abt)
Let Me Tell You Everything: Memoirs of a Lovesick Intellectual (Bottner)
Living with a Parent Who Takes Drugs (Seixas)
Looking for Home (Ferris)
Ludie's Song (Herlihy)
Magicians of Erianne (Berry)
Making Cents: Every Kid's Guide to Money (Wilkinson)
Meet My Cats (Ivory)
Moondream (Osborne)
Moonkid and Liberty (Kropp)
The Mouse Rap (Myers)
Movie Monsters (Powers)
My Brother Stealing Second (Naughton)
My Daniel (Conrad)
My War with Goggle-Eyes (Fine)
Nadja: On My Way (Salerno-Sonnenberg)
Newfound (Miller)
Night Riding (Martin)
The Night the White Deer Died (Paulsen)
Nightmare (Roberts)
The Ninth Issue (Malmgren)
No Kidding (Brooks)
No Promises (Swallow)
No Way Out (Ruckman)
A Nugget of Gold (Pople)
On the Devil's Court (Deuke)
One Green Leaf (Ure)
Phoenix Rising, or How to Survive Your Life (Grant)
Phone Call from a Ghost (Cohen)
Plague Year (Tolan)
The Potato Kid (Corcoran)
The Princess in the Pigpen (Thomas)
Probably Still Nick Swansen (Wolff)

The Problem Solvers (Aaseng)
Raymond (Geller)
The Rejects (Aaseng)
Remembering and Other Poems (Livingston)
Risky Times (Blake)
Rosy's Romance (Greenwald)
Sacred Circle of the Hula Hoop (Tapp)
Secret City, U. S. A. (Holman)
A Serpent's Tooth (Swindells)
Shabanu: Daughter of the Wind (Staples)
Shadow of the Wall (Laird)
Shark Beneath the Reef (George)
The Shimmershine Queens (Yarbrough)
Short Subject (Kirshenbaum)
Silver Days (Levitin)
The Silver Kiss (Klause)
Singin' Somebody Else's Song (Christian)
Sleeping Arrangements (Cunningham)
Sniper (Taylor)
Soda Jerk (Rylant)
Somehow Tenderness Survives: Stories of Southern Africa (Rochman)
Soweto, My Love: A Testimony to Black Life in South Africa (Ramusi)
Star Baby (Nixon)
The Starstone (Chetwin)
Stories I Ain't Told Nobody Yet: Selections from the People Pieces (Carson)
Storm Rising (Singer)
Stray (Wilson)
Struggle (Zyskind)
Supersense: Perception in the Animal World (Downer)
Sweetgrass (Hudson)
Sydney, Herself (Rodowsky)
Tehanu: The Last Book of Earthsea (Le Guin)
Tell Me How the Wind Sounds (Guccione)
Tell Us Your Secret (Cohen)
Things That Go Bump in the Night (Yolen and Greenberg)
Too Young to Die (McDaniel)
Traitors from Within (Montgomery)
The Trolley to Yesterday (Bellairs)
Truckers (Patchett)
Turning Thirteen (Pfeffer)
21st Century Fox (Eller)
The Unfrightened Dark (Holland)
Unlived Affections (Shannon)
The Unsung Heroes (Aaseng)
Up Country (Carter)
The Ups and Downs of Carl Davis III (Guy)
Valentine and Orson (Burkert)

Junior High (cont.)

Viola, Furgy, Bobbi, and Me (Ethridge)
Vision Quest (Service)
The Voice from the Mendelsohns' Maple (Ryan)
Voices from the Civil War (Meltzer)
We Have AIDS (Landau)
A Well-Timed Enchantment (Vande Velde)
We Remember the Holocaust (Adler)
Where's My Other Sock? How to Get Organized and Drive Your Parents and Teachers Crazy (Wirths and Bowman-Kruhm)
Whispers from the Dead (Nixon)
Who Invited the Undertaker? (Ruckman)
Why I Left Harry's All-Night Hamburgers, and Other Stories from Isaac Asimov's Science Fiction Magazine (Williams and Ardai)
The Winter Room (Paulsen)
With a Name Like Lulu, Who Needs More Trouble? (Springstubb)
Wonderful Me (Wersba)
The Wrong Way Home (Fosburgh)
Your Move, J. P.! (Lowry)
Yours Till Forever (Gifaldi)

High School (Grades 9–12)

An Acceptable Time (L'Engle)
An Almost Perfect Summer (Zable)
Anything to Win (Miklowitz)
Backstreets: Springsteen-The Man and His Music (Cross)
The Band Never Dances (Landis)
Been Clever Forever (Stone)
A Begonia for Miss Applebaum (Zindel)
Best Friends Tell the Best Lies (Dines)
The Best Place to Live Is the Ceiling (Wersba)
Bethie (Rabinowitz)
Better Mousetraps: Product Improvements That Led to Success (Aaseng)
Beyond the Reef (Strasser)
The Big Bang (Forman)
Blitzcat (Westall)
Bo Knows Bo (Jackson and Schaap)
Borgel (Pinkwater)
Burnt: A Teenage Addict's Road to Recovery (Fraser and Sullivan)
Buster Midnight's Cafe (Dallas)
The Call of the Wolves (Murphy)
Can't Hear You Listening (Irwin)
Caribbean Canvas (Lessac)
Celine (Cole)

The Cellar (Radford)
Changes in Latitudes (Hobbs)
Children of the River (Crew)
Chinese Handcuffs (Crutcher)
Choices (Scott)
Come the Morning (Harris)
Connections: Short Stories by Outstanding Writers for Young Adults (Gallo)
The Covenant: Love and Death in Beruit (Newman and Rogan)
Cruel Tricks for Dear Friends (Penn and Teller)
Dead Poets Society (Kleinbaum)
The Delphic Choice (Johnston)
The Devil's Arithmetic (Yolen)
Don't Look Behind You (Duncan)
The Dream Collector (Sweeney)
The Dying Sun (Blackwood)
Effie's House (Hamilton)
Empire's Horizon (Brizzolara)
The Empty Sleeve (Garfield)
The Engineer of Beasts (Sanders)
Enter Three Witches (Gilmore)
Eva (Dickinson)
The Face on the Milk Carton (Cooney)
The Faery Flag: Stories and Poems of Fantasy and the Supernatural (Yolen)
Faithful Elephants: A True Story of Animals, People and War (Tsuchiya)
Fallen Angels (Myers)
Falling for a Dolphin (Williams)
Fighting Back: What Some People Are Doing About AIDS (Kuklin)
Five Against the Sea (Arias)
The Fortunate Fortunes (Aaseng)
Forward Pass (Dygard)
Four Past Midnight (King)
Francie and the Boys (Daneman)
Franky Furbo (Wharton)
The Fringes of Reason: A Whole Earth Catalog (Schultz)
G Is for Gumshoe (Grafton)
A Gallery of Dinosaurs and Other Early Reptiles (Peters)
Gameplay (Anderson)
Going Green: A Kid's Handbook to Saving the Planet (Elkington)
The Golden Bird (Stolp)
Goodbye Doesn't Mean Forever (McDaniel)
Grass (Tepper)
Great Disasters: Dramatic True Stories (Ward)
The Great Man's Secret (Van Raven)
Growing Up Adopted (Rosenberg)
Growing Up Western (Backes and Brown)

High School (cont.)
Supersense: Perception in the Animal World (Downer)
Tehanu: The Last Book of Earthsea (Le Guin)
Tell Me How the Wind Sounds (Guccione)
Tell Us Your Secret (Cohen)
These Good Men: Friendships Forged from War (Norman)
Things That Go Bump in the Night (Yolen and Greenberg)
Those Other People (Childress)
Too Young to Die (McDaniel)
Tough Girls Don't Knit, and Other Tales of Stylish Subversion (Garmaise)
The Toynbee Convector (Bradbury)
Traitors from Within (Montgomery)
Trevor's Place (Ferrell and Ferrell)
Truckers (Patchett)
True Detectives: The Real World of Today's Private Investigators (Parkhurst)
21st Century Fox (Eller)
The Unfrightened Dark (Holland)
Unlived Affections (Shannon)
The Unsung Heroes (Aaseng)
Up Country (Carter)
Valentine and Orson (Burkert)
Veteran's Day (Kane)
Viola, Furgy, Bobbi, and Me (Ethridge)
Vision Quest (Service)
Voices from the Civil War: A Documentary History of the Great American Conflict (Meltzer)
We Didn't Have Much, but We Sure Had Plenty: Rural Women in Their Own Words (Thomas)
We Have AIDS (Landau)
We Remember the Holocaust (Adler)
Weetzie Bat (Block)
What Are the Chances? Risks, Odds, and Likelihood in Everyday Life (Siskin, Staller, and Rorvik)
When Morning Comes (Calvert)
Where Have All the Tigers Gone? (Hall)
Where's My Other Sock? How to Get Organized and Drive Your Parents and Teachers Crazy (Wirths and Bowman-Kruhm)
Whispers from the Dead (Nixon)
White Rabbit (Morrison)
Why I Left Harry's All-Night Hamburgers, and Other Stories from Isaac Asimov's Science Fiction Magazine (Williams and Ardai)
The Winter Room (Paulsen)

Wishes (Deveraux)
With a Name Like Lulu, Who Needs More Trouble? (Springstubb)
Wonderful Me (Wersba)
A World of Ideas (Moyers)
The Wrong Way Home (Fosburgh)
Yours Till Forever (Gifaldi)

Adult

Any Woman's Blues (Jong)
Backstreets: Springsteen-The Man and His Music (Cross)
Blitzcat (Westall)
Bo Knows Bo (Jackson and Schaap)
Borgel (Pinkwater)
Burnt: A Teenage Addict's Road to Recovery (Fraser and Sullivan)
Buster Midnight's Cafe (Dallas)
The Call of the Wolves (Murphy)
Caribbean Canvas (Lessac)
The Covenant: Love and Death in Beruit (Newman and Rogan)
Cruel Tricks for Dear Friends (Penn and Teller)
Dead Poets Society (Kleinbaum)
Education of a Wandering Man (L'Amour)
Empire's Horizon (Brizzolara)
The Engineer of Beasts (Sanders)
Eva (Dickinson)
F Is for Fugitive (Grafton)
Faithful Elephants: A True Story of Animals, People and War (Tsuchiya)
Fallen Angels (Myers)
Falling for a Dolphin (Williams)
Families: A Celebration of Diversity, Commitment and Love (Jenness)
Family Pictures (Miller)
Family Portraits: Remembrances (Anthony)
Fighting Back: What Some People Are Doing About AIDS (Kuklin)
Five Against the Sea (Arias)
Four Past Midnight (King)
Frank and Ernest (Day)
Franky Furbo (Wharton)
The Fringes of Reason: A Whole Earth Catalog (Schultz)
G Is for Gumshoe (Grafton)
A Gallery of Dinosaurs and Other Early Reptiles (Peters)
Gameplay (Anderson)
The Golden Bird (Stolp)
Grass (Tepper)
Great Disasters: (Ward)

Growing Up Western (Backes and Brown)
Hare's Choice (Hamley)
The Harmony Illustrated Encyclopedia of Rock, sixth edition (Frame, Clifford)
House of Heroes and Other Stories (La Chapelle)
Husband Is the Past Tense of Daddy: And Other Dispatches from the Front Lines of Motherhood (Zarnow)
If I Never Get Back (Brock)
It Was on Fire When I Lay Down on It (Fulghum)
Jack (Homes)
Jason Cosmo (McGirt)
Journey (Michener)
The Journey: Japanese Americans, Racism, and Renewal (Hamanaka)
Kareem (Abdul-Jabbar and McCarthy)
Knight in Shining Armor (Deveraux)
Knights (Heller and Headon)
The Last Dinosaur (Murphy)
LeMond: The Incredible Comeback of an American Hero (Abt)
Life and Death: The Story of a Hospital (Yalof)
Manifold Destiny: The One! The Only! Guide to Cooking on Your Car Engine (Maynard and Scheller)
Masquerade (Kienzle)
McKenzie's Boots (Noonan)
Meet My Cats (Ivory)
Merlin Dreams (Dickinson)
The Mother's Almanac II: Your Child from Six to Twelve (Kelly)
Motherwit (Logan and Clark)
The Mummy (Rice)
Never Too Young to Die: The Death of Len Bias (Cole)
The New Medically Based No-Nonsense Beauty Book (Chase)
New Zealand by Motorhome (Shore and Campbell)
Newfound (Miller)
Nobody's Fault (Holmes)
One Green Leaf (Ure)
One in a Million (Cole and Jablow)
1001 Things Everyone Should Know About American History (Garraty)
Paterno: By the Book (Paterno and Asbell)
Proud Knight, Fair Lady (Marie de France)
Rebel Without a Clue (Uyemoto)
Remembering and Other Poems (Livingston)

Running West (Houston)
Saturday Night (Orlean)
Shabanu: Daughter of the Wind (Staples)
Shadow of the Wall (Laird)
The Sierra Club Summer Book (Allison)
Silver Pigs (Davis)
The Silver Kiss (Klause)
Sleeping Arrangements (Cunningham)
Small Victories: The Real World of a Teacher, Her Students, and Their High School (Freedman)
Soda Jerk (Rylant)
Somerset Homecoming: Recovering a Lost Heritage (Redford)
Soweto, My Love: A Testimony to Black Life in South Africa (Ramusi)
Stories I Ain't Told Nobody Yet: Selections from the People Pieces (Carson)
Stray (Wilson)
Struggle (Zyskind)
Supersense: Perception in the Animal World (Downer)
Thanksgiving: An AIDS Journal (Cox)
These Good Men: Friendships Forged from War (Norman)
Tough Girls Don't Knit, and Other Tales of Stylish Subversion (Garmaise)
The Toynbee Convector (Bradbury)
Trevor's Place (Ferrell and Ferrell)
Truckers (Patchett)
True Detectives: The Real World of Today's Private Investigators (Parkhurst)
Two-Part Invention: The Story of a Marriage (L'Engle)
Valentine and Orson (Burkert)
Veteran's Day (Kane)
Voices from the Civil War (Meltzer)
We Didn't Have Much, but We Sure Had Plenty: Rural Women in Their Own Words (Thomas)
What Are the Chances? Risks, Odds, and Likelihood in Everyday Life (Siskin, Staller, and Rorvik)
Where Have All the Tigers Gone? (Hall)
White Rabbit (Morrison)
Why I Left Harry's All-Night Hamburgers, and Other Stories from Isaac Asimov's Science Fiction Magazine (Williams and Ardai)
The Wild Inside: Sierra Club's Guide to the Great Indoors (Allison)
Wishes (Deveraux)
A World of Ideas (Moyers)

SELECTIVE BIBLIOGRAPHY
BY THEME AND GENRE

Adventure

Away Is a Strange Place To Be (MS-JH)
Balyet (JH)
The Best Place to Live Is the Ceiling (JH-HS)
Beyond the Reef (JH-HS)
The Blood and Thunder Adventure on Hurricane Peak (EL-JH)
Buffalo Brenda (MS-JH)
The Call of the Wolves (MS-A)
The Cellar (MS-HS)
The Chessmen of Doom (MS-JH)
Dangerous Ground (MS)
The Delphic Choice (JH-HS)
The Dolphins and Me (EL-MS)
Education of a Wandering Man (A)
El Guero (EL-MS)
The Engineer of Beasts (JH-A)
Family Pose (MS)
Five Against the Sea (HS-A)
Gameplay (HS-A)
Grass (HS-A)
Great Disasters (HS-A)
High Wizardry (JH-HS)
I Feel Like the Morning Star (JH-HS)
If I Never Get Back (HS-A)
Jason Cosmo (HS-A)
Journey (Michener) (HS-A)
The Last Dinosaur (MS-A)
Long Live the Queen (HS)
Magicians of Erianne (MS-JH)
Merlin Dreams (HS-A)
Moondream (EL-JH)
The Mouse Rap (MS-JH)
My Daniel (MS-JH)
My Name Is Not Angelica (EL-MS)
Nightmare Mountain (EL-MS)
No Way Out (MS-HS)
On Fortune's Wheel (HS)
Proud Knight, Fair Lady (HS-A)
Running West (HS-A)
Secret City, U.S.A. (MS-JH)
Shadow of the Wall (JH-A)
Shadow Over Mousehaven Manor (EL)
Shark Beneath the Reef (JH)

Silver Pigs (HS-A)
Starstone (MS-HS)
Tell Us Your Secret (JH-HS)
Traitors from Within (JH-HS)
Trolley to Yesterday (MS-JH)
Truckers (JH-A)
The Twenty-Four-Hour Lipstick Mystery (EL-MS)
Valentine and Orson (MS-A)
The Voyage of the Frog (MS-HS)
Whispers from the Dead (JH-HS)
Wiggie Wins the West (EL-MS)

Aging

A Begonia for Miss Applebaum (JH-HS)
Brushy Mountain (MS-JH)
The Christmas Cup (EL)
Dangerous Ground (MS)
Earth to Andrew G. Blechman (EL)
G Is for Gumshoe (HS-A)
The Great Man's Secret (JH-HS)
A Summer Like Turnips (EL-MS)
Viola, Furgy, Bobbie and Me (MS-HS)
The Voice from the Mendelsohns' Maple (MS-JH)
We Didn't Have Much, But We Sure Had Plenty (HS-A)
Where Have All the Tigers Gone? (HS-A)

AIDS

Fighting Back (JH-A)
Rebel Without a Clue (HS-A)
Risky Times (JH-HS)
Thanksgiving (A)
We Have AIDS (JH-HS)

Animals (See also Dinosaurs)

Blitzcat (HS-A)
The Call of the Wolves (EL-A)
Changes in Latitudes (JH-HS)
A Child's Treasury of Animal Verse (EL-JH)

Animals (cont.)
Cleaver of the Good Luck Diner (EL-MS)
The Dolphins and Me (EL-MS)
The Engineer of Beasts (JH-A)
Eva (JH-A)
Faithful Elephants (MS-A)
Falling for a Dolphin (HS-A)
Fowl Play, Desdemona! (EL-JH)
Franky Furbo (HS-A)
A Gallery of Dinosaurs (EL-A)
Hare's Choice (MS-A)
Herds of Thunder, Manes of Gold (MS-HS)
Herbie Jones and Hamburger Head (EL)
How Many Spots Does a Leopard Have? (EL-JH)
Meet My Cats (EL-A)
One Day in the Tropical Rain Forest (EL-MS)
The Potato Kid (MS-JH)
Shark Beneath the Reef (JH)
The Sierra Club Summer Book (EL, A)
Sniper (JH-HS)
Stray (MS-A)
Supersense (JH-A)
The Unfrightened Dark (MS-HS)
Wiggie Wins the West (EL-MS)

Art

Celine (HS)
Illuminations (EL-JH)
Knights (MS-A)

Biography (See also Interviews)

Alyssa Milano: She's the Boss (MS-JH)
Backstreets: Springsteen (JH-A)
Better Mousetraps (MS-HS)
Bo Knows Bo (JH-A)
Burnt (HS-A)
Covenant (HS-A)
Education of a Wandering Man (A)
Family Portraits (A)
The Fortunate Fortunes (MS-HS)
Kareem (HS-A)
LeMond (HS-A)
Motherwit (HS-A)
Nadja: On My Way (JH-HS)
Never Too Young to Die (HS-A)
One in a Million (HS-A)
Paterno (HS-A)
The Problem Solvers (MS-HS)
Rejects (MS-HS)
Small Victories (HS-A)

Somerset Homecoming (HS-A)
Soweto, My Love (JH-A)
Struggle (JH-A)
Two-Part Invention (A)
Unsung Heroes (MS-HS)
Veteran's Day (HS-A)
White Rabbit (HS-A)

Child Abuse / Sexual Abuse

Chinese Handcuffs (HS)
Night Riding (JH-HS)
Paper Knife (EL-MS)
Raymond (MS-JH)
Sacred Circle of the Hula Hoop (MS-JH)
Silver (HS)
So Much to Tell You (HS)
Tehanu (JH-HS)
Those Other People (HS-A)

Cooking

Leave the Cooking to Me (MS-JH)
Manifold Destiny (A)
The Sierra Club Summer Book (EL, A)

Crafts

The Sierra Club Summer Book (EL, A)
The Wild Inside (EL, A)

Crime and Delinquency

The Boy Who Lost His Face (MS-JH)
Burnt (HS-A)
Buster Midnight's Cafe (HS-A)
Choices (JH-HS)
Fifth Grade: Here Comes Trouble (MS-JH)
Five Finger Discount (MS-JH)
The Forgotten Girl (MS-JH)
Moonkid and Liberty (JH-HS)
Nobody's Fault (HS-A)
Plague Year (JH-HS)
Runaways (MS)
Small Victories (HS-A)
True Detectives (HS-A)
Up Country (JH-HS)
When Morning Comes (HS)
White Rabbit (HS-A)
The Wrong Way Home (JH-HS)

Death and Mourning

Across the Creek (MS-JH)
The Band Never Dances (JH-HS)
A Begonia for Miss Applebaum (JH-HS)
Bethie (JH-HS)
The Big Bang (JH-HS)
Brushy Mountain (MS-JH)
Changes in Latitudes (JH-HS)
Children of the River (JH-HS)
Chinese Handcuffs (HS)
Covenant (HS-A)
The Devil's Arithmetic (JH-HS)
Dissidents (JH-HS)
Effie's House (JH-HS)
Eighty-Eight Steps to September (EL-MS)
Fallen Angels (HS-A)
*Fighting Back: What Some People Are
    Doing About AIDS* (JH-A)
Fire in the Heart (MS-JH)
*Get Help: Solving the Problems in Your
    Life* (MS-JH)
The Golden Bird (MS-A)
Goodbye Doesn't Mean Forever (JH-HS)
Hare's Choice (MS-A)
Life and Death: The Story of a Hospital
    (HS-A)
Long Live the Queen (HS)
My Brother Stealing Second (JH-HS)
My Daniel (MS-JH)
Nightmare (JH-HS)
No Promises (JH-HS)
One Green Leaf (JH-A)
One in a Million (HS-A)
Ozzy on the Outside (HS)
Phoenix Rising (JH-HS)
Plague Year (JH-HS)
Rebel Without a Clue (HS-A)
Sacred Circle of the Hula Hoop (MS-JH)
Secret City, U.S.A. (MS-JH)
Shadow over Mousehaven Manor (EL)
The Silver Kiss (JH-A)
Singin' Somebody Else's Song (JH-HS)
Sleeping Arrangements (HS-A)
A Summer Like Turnips (EL-MS)
Sweetgrass (MS-JH)
Thanksgiving (A)
These Good Men (JH-A)
Too Young to Die (JH-HS)
Two-Part Invention (A)
Unlived Affections (JH-HS)
The Village by the Sea (EL)
The Voyage of the Frog (MS-HS)
Weetzie Bat (HS)
The Wrong Way Home (JH-HS)

Dinosaurs

Dinosaur Mountain (MS-JH)
The Fourth-Grade Dinosaur Club (EL-
    MS)
The Last Dinosaur (MS-A)
A Gallery of Dinosaurs (EL-A)
News About Dinosaurs (EL-MS)

Environmental Issues

Changes in Latitudes (JH-HS)
Dangerous Ground (MS)
Falling for a Dolphin (HS-A)
Going Green (EL-HS)
One Day in the Tropical Rain Forest
    (EL-MS)
Someday I'll Laugh About This (MS-JH)

Facts and Statistics

*The Harmony Illustrated Encyclopedia of
    Rock* (JH-A)
*1001 Things Everyone Should Know
    About American History* (HS-A)
*The Random House Book of 1001 Ques-
    tions and Answers* (EL-MS)
*What Are the Chances? Risks, Odds and
    Likelihood in Everyday Life* (HS-A)

Family Relationships

Across the Creek (Ms-JH)
Angela, Private Citizen (EL-JH)
Baily's Bones (EL-MS)
Before the Wildflowers Bloom (EL-MS)
Believers (EL-MS)
Best Friends Tell the Best Lies (JH-HS)
The Best Place to Live Is the Ceiling (JH-
    HS)
Bethie (JH-HS)
Beyond Safe Boundaries (MS-JH)
The Big Bang (JH-HS)
Bingo Brown and the Language of Love
    (EL-MS)
Borgel (JH-A)
Brushy Mountain (MS-JH)
C, My Name Is Cal (JH)
Can't Hear You Listening (JH-HS)
Celine (HS)
Changes in Latitudes (JH-HS)
Children of the River (JH-HS)
Chocolate-Covered Ants (EL-MS)
Choosing Sides (MS)
The Christmas Cup (EL)
Cleaver of the Good Luck Diner (EL-MS)

Family Relationships (cont.)
Come the Morning (JH-HS)
Dangerous Ground (MS)
Dear Mom, You're Ruining My Life (MS)
The Dream Collector (JH-HS)
Earth to Andrew G. Blechman (EL)
Effie's House (JH-HS)
Eighty-Eight Steps to September (EL-MS)
The Empty Sleeve (MS-HS)
Enter Three Witches (JH-HS)
Erin McEwan, Your Days Are Numbered (MS-JH)
Eva (JH-A)
Everyone Else's Parents Said Yes (EL-MS)
The Face on the Milk Carton (JH-HS)
The Facts and Fictions of Minna Pratt (EL-MS)
Families (EL-MS)
Family Pictures (A)
Family Portraits (A)
Family Pose (MS)
Family Reunion (JH-HS)
Fire in the Heart (MS-JH)
Five Finger Discount (MS-JH)
The Forgotten Girl (MS-JH)
Fowl Play, Desdemona! (EL-JH)
Francie and the Boys (JH-HS)
The Game of Life (JH)
Get Help: Solving the Problems in Your Life (MS-JH)
Ghost Abbey (MS-JH)
Give It Up, Mom (MS-JH)
Glass Slippers Give You Blisters (MS-JH)
The Golden Bird (MS-A)
Growing Up Adopted (MS-HS)
Harry Newberry & the Raiders of the Red Drink (MS-JH)
The Haunting of Frances Rain (MS-JH)
Heartbeats (JH-HS)
Herbie Jones and Hamburger Head (EL)
Hey World, Here I Am (MS-JH)
High Wizardry (JH-HS)
The Hitchhiking Vampire (MS-JH)
House of Heroes (HS-A)
Husband Is the Past Tense of Daddy (A)
I Hate Your Guts, Ben Brooster! (EL-MS)
Jack (HS-A)
Janie's Private Eyes (MS-JH)
Just Like a Friend (MS-JH)
The Kid Who Ran for Principal (MS-JH)
Landing on Marvin Gardens (MS-JH)
Learning How to Fall (HS)
Leave the Cooking to Me (MS-JH)
Living with a Parent Who Takes Drugs (EL-JH)
Moonkid and Liberty (JH-HS)
More to Life Than Mr. Right (HS)
The Mother's Almanac II (A)
The Mouse Rap (MS-JH)
My Brother Stealing Second (JH-HS)
My Brother the Star (EL-MS)
My Daniel (MS-JH)
My War with Goggle-Eyes (MS-JH)
Newfound (JH-A)
Night Riding (JH-HS)
Nightmare (JH-HS)
Nightmare Mountain (EL-MS)
No Kidding (JH-HS)
No Way Out (MS-HS)
On the Devil's Court (JH-HS)
One in a Million (MS-A)
Outside Child (EL-MS)
Ozzy on the Outside (HS)
Paper Doll (HS)
Paper Knife (EL-MS)
Phoenix Rising (JH-HS)
Plague Year (JH-HS)
The Potato Kid (MS-JH)
Raymond (MS-JH)
Rewind to Yesterday (EL-MS)
Rosy's Romance (MS-JH)
Sacred Circle of the Hula Hoop (MS-JH)
Serpent's Tooth (MS-JH)
Seventeen Against the Dealer (HS)
Shark Beneath the Reef (JH)
Shimmershine Queens (MS-JH)
Short Subject (MS-JH)
Silver (HS)
Sleeping Arrangements (MS-A)
Sniper (JH-HS)
Somerset Homecoming (HS-A)
A Song for Uncle Harry (EL-MS)
Star Baby (JH-HS)
Stories I Ain't Told Nobody Yet (JH-A)
Struggle (JH-A)
A Summer Like Turnips (EL-MS)
Sydney, Herself (MS-JH)
Tell Me How the Wind Sounds (JH-HS)
Thanksgiving (A)
Too Young to Die (JH-HS)
Travel Tips from Harry (EL)
Twenty-First Century Fox (JH-HS)
Two-Part Invention (A)
Tucker (EL-MS)
Unlived Affections (JH-HS)
Up Country (JH-HS)
The Ups and Downs of Carl Davis III (MS-JH)
The Village by the Sea (EL)
We Have AIDS (JH-HS)

Weetzie Bat (HS)
When Morning Comes (HS)
Where in the World Is the Perfect Family? (EL-MS)
Who Invited the Undertaker? (MS-JH)
Winter Room (MS-HS)
With a Name Like Lulu, Who Needs More Trouble? (MS-HS)
Wonderful Me (JH-HS)
Worlds Apart (EL-MS)
The Wrong Way Home (JH-HS)
Yours Till Forever (JH-HS)

Fantasy (See also Science Fiction; Time Travel)

The Blood and Thunder Adventure on Hurricane Peak (EL-JH)
The Faery Flag (JH-HS)
Franky Furbo (HS-A)
Gameplay (HS-A)
Hare's Choice (EL-A)
Harry Newberry and the Raiders of the Red Drink (MS-JH)
High Wizardry (JH-HS)
Jason Cosmo (HS-A)
Genie with the Light Blue Hair (MS-JH)
Knight in Shining Armor (HS-A)
Magicians of Erianne (MS-JH)
Merlin Dreams (HS-A)
Moondream (EL-JH)
On Fortune's Wheel (HS)
Proud Knight, Fair Lady (HS-A)
Starstone (MS-HS)
Tehanu (JH-HS)
Truckers (JH-A)
A Well-Timed Enchantment (MS-JH)

Folklore

The Adventures of High John the Conqueror (MS-JH)
The Faery Flag (JH-HS)
How Many Spots Does a Leopard Have? (EL-JH)
Proud Knight, Fair Lady (HS-A)

Friendship

Across the Creek (MS-JH)
Afternoon of the Elves (EL-MS)
Away Is a Strange Place To Be (MS-JH)
Been Clever Forever (JH-HS)
A Begonia for Miss Applebaum (JH-HS)
Best Friends Tell the Best Lies (JH-HS)

Bethie (JH-HS)
The Blood and Thunder Adventure on Hurricane Peak (EL-JH)
Buffalo Brenda (MS-JH)
Buster Midnight's Cafe (HS-A)
C, My Name Is Cal (JH)
Can't Hear You Listening (JH-HS)
Celine (HS)
Charlotte Shakespeare and Annie the Great (MS)
The Chessmen of Doom (MS-JH)
Choices (JH-HS)
Connections (JH-HS)
Dead Poets Society (JH-A)
The Devil's Arithmetic (JH-HS)
The Dream Collector (JH-HS)
Eighty-Eight Steps to September (EL-MS)
The Empty Sleeve (MS-HS)
The Facts and Fictions of Minna Pratt (EL-MS)
Fallen Angels (HS-A)
Family Pose (MS)
Fifth Grade, Here Comes Trouble (MS-JH)
Fighting Back: What Some People Are Doing About AIDS (JH-A)
Five Finger Discount (MS-JH)
The Fourth-Grade Dinosaur Club (EL-MS)
Fowl Play, Desdemona (EL-JH)
Gameplay (HS-A)
Genie with the Light Blue Hair (MS-JH)
Ghost Abbey (MS-JH)
Glass Slippers Give You Blisters (MS-JH)
Goodbye Doesn't Mean Forever (JH-HS)
The Great Man's Secret (JH-HS)
Heartbeat (JH-HS)
Heartbeats (JH-HS)
Hey World, Here I Am (JH-HS)
House of Heroes (HS-A)
Hurray for Ali Baba Bernstein (EL)
I Feel Like the Morning Star (JH-HS)
Journey (Thomas) (MS-JH)
Junglerama (EL-JH)
Just Friends (JH-HS)
Just Like a Friend (MS-JH)
The Kid Who Ran for Principal (MS-JH)
Learning How to Fall (HS)
Leave the Cooking to Me (MS-JH)
Long Live the Queen (HS)
Looking for Home (JH-HS)
Lost Boys Never Say Die (EL-MS)
Ludie's Song (MS-JH)
Ma and Pa Dracula (EL)
McKenzie's Boots (HS-A)
Millie Cooper, Take a Chance (EL)

Friendship (cont.)
Moonkid and Liberty (JH-HS)
The Mouse Rap (MS-JH)
My War with Goggle Eyes (MS-JH)
Night Riding (JH-HS)
Nightmare (JH-HS)
The Ninth Issue (JH-HS)
No Promises (JH-HS)
Nugget of Gold (JH-HS)
One Green Leaf (JH-A)
Plague Year (JH-HS)
The Potato Kid (MS-JH)
Probably Still Nick Swansen (JH-HS)
Radio Fifth Grade (EL-MS)
Rebel Without a Clue (HS-A)
Rewind to Yesterday (EL-MS)
Runaways (MS)
The Sacred Circle of the Hula Hoop (JH)
Secret City, U.S.A. (MS-JH)
Self-Portrait with Wings (EL-MS)
The Shimmershine Queens (MS-JH)
Silver (HS)
Singin' Somebody Else's Song (JH-HS)
Sleeping Arrangements (HS-A)
Sniper (JH-HS)
So Much to Tell You (HS)
Soup's Hoop (EL-MS)
Squeeze Play (EL)
Stories I Ain't Told Nobody Yet (JH-A)
Storm Rising (JH-HS)
Tell Me How the Wind Sounds (JH-HS)
Tell Us Your Secret (JH-HS)
These Good Men (JH-A)
Too Young to Die (JH-HS)
Traitors from Within (JH-HS)
Trolley to Yesterday (MS-JH)
Turning Thirteen (MS-JH)
Twenty-Four-Hour Lipstick Mystery (EL-MS)
The Ups and Down of Carl Davis III (MS-JH)
Veronica Meets Her Match (EL-MS)
The Village by the Sea (EL)
Viola, Furgie, Bobbie and Me (MS-HS)
Weetzie Bat (HS)
A Well-Timed Enchantment (MS-JH)
Where Have All the Tigers Gone? (HS-A)
Yours Till Forever (JH-HS)

Handicaps

Across the Creek (MS-JH)
Baily's Bones (EL-MS)
Family Pictures (A)
The Great Man's Secret (JH-HS)
Heartbeats (JH-HS)

House of Heroes (HS-A)
How It Feels to Fight for Your Life (JH-HS)
Lost Boys Never Say Die (EL-MS)
Ludie's Song (MS-JH)
Paper Doll (HS)
Probably Still Nick Swansen (JH-HS)
So Much to Tell You (HS)
Tell Me How the Wind Sounds (JH-HS)
The Unfrightened Dark (MS-HS)
Your Move, J.P.! (MS-JH)

Health and Illness (mental and physical)

Afternoon of the Elves (EL-MS)
Burnt: A Teenage Addict's Road to Recovery ((HS-A)
Eighty-Eight Steps to September (EL-MS)
Family Pictures (A)
Fighting Back: What Some People Are Doing About AIDS (JH-A)
Get Help: Solving the Problems in Your Life (MS-JH)
Give It Up, Mom (MS-JH)
How It Feels to Fight for Your Life (JH-HS)
Learning How to Fall (HS)
Life and Death: The Story of a Hospital (HS-A)
Living with a Parent Who Takes Drugs (EL-JH)
The New, Medically Based No-Nonsense Beauty Book (HS-A)
One in a Million (HS-A)
Risky Times (JH-HS)
Thanksgiving: An AIDS Journal (A)
Too Young to Die (JH-HS)
Two-Part Invention (HS-A)
Tucker (EL-MS)
Veteran's Day (HS-A)
We Have AIDS (JH-HS)
Where's My Other Sock? How to Get Organized . . . (MS-HS)
White Rabbit (HS-A)
The Wrong Way Home (JH-HS)

Historical Fiction (See also Time Travel)

Before the Wildflowers Bloom (EL-MS)
Blitzcat (HS-A)
Buster Midnight's Cafe (HS-A)
Cellar (MS-HS)
El Guero (EL-MS)

The Empty Sleeve (MS-HS)
Faithful Elephants (MS-A)
If I Never Get Back (HS-A)
In Lane Three, Alex Archer (HS)
Journey (Michener) (JH-A)
Ludie's Song (MS-JH)
McKenzie's Boots (HS-A)
My Name Is Not Angelica (EL-MS)
Nugget of Gold (JH-HS)
Running West (HS-A)
Shadow of the Wall (JH-A)
Silver Days (MS-HS)
Silver Pigs (HS-A)
Sleeping Arrangements (HS-A)
Struggle (JH-A)
Sweetgrass (MS-JH)
Wishes (HS-A)

History

Better Mousetraps (MS-HS)
The Fortunate Fortunes (MS-HS)
Growing Up Western (MS-A)
Illuminations (EL-MS)
The Journey (Hamanaka) (JH-A)
Knights (MS-A)
1001 Things Everyone Should Know about American History (HS-A)
The Problem Solvers (MS-HS)
The Random House Book of 1001 Questions and Answers (EL-MS)
The Rejects (MS-HS)
Somerset Homecoming (HS-A)
Soweto, My Love (JH-A)
These Good Men (HS-A)
Unsung Heroes (MS-HS)
Voices from the Civil War (JH-A)
We Didn't Have Much, But We Sure Had Plenty (HS-A)
We Remember the Holocaust (MS-HS)

Homosexuality

Connections (JH-HS)
Fighting Back: What Some People Are Doing About AIDS (JH-A)
Jack (HS-A)
Rebel Without a Clue (HS-A)
Those Other People (HS-A)

The Homeless

Come the Morning (JH-HS)
Trevor's Place (HS-A)
The Unfrightened Dark (MS-HS)

Horror

Baily's Bones (MS-JH)
Best Witches (EL)
Four Past Midnight (HS-A)
Halloween: Stories and Poems (EL)
Halloween Poems (EL)
Horror Movies (MS-JH)
Ma and Pa Dracula (EL)
The Mummy (JH-A)
The Silver Kiss (JH-A)
Things That Go Bump in the Night (MS-HS)

Humor

The Adventures of High John the Conqueror (MS-JH)
Alessandra in Love (JH)
Angela, Private Citizen (JH)
A Begonia for Miss Applebaum (JH-HS)
Bingo Brown and the Language of Love (EL-MS)
The Blood and Thunder Adventure on Hurricane Peak (EL-JH)
Borgel (JH-A)
The Boy Who Owned the School (MS-JH)
Buffalo Brenda (MS-JH)
Buster Midnight's Cafe (HS-A)
Charlotte Shakespeare and Annie the Great (MS)
Chocolate-Covered Ants (EL-MS)
Cleaver of the Good Luck Diner (EL-MS)
Connections (JH-HS)
Cruel Tricks for Dear Friends (HS-A)
Dagmar Schultz and the Angel Edna (EL-JH)
Dagmar Schultz and the Powers of Darkness (EL-JH)
Enter Three Witches (JH-HS)
Erin McEwan, Your Days Are Numbered (JM-JH)
Everyone Else's Parents Said Yes (EL-MS)
Fifth Grade, Here Comes Trouble (MS)
Fowl Play, Desdemona (EL-JH)
Frank and Earnest (EL-JH, A)
The Game of Life (JH)
Genie with the Light Blue Hair (MS-JH)
Ghastlies, Goops and Pincushions (EL)
Give It Up, Mom (MS-JH)
Glass Slippers Give You Blisters (MS-JH)
Harry Newberry & the Raiders of the Red Drink (MS-JH)
Herbie Jones and Hamburger Head (EL)
Hey World, Here I Am (MS-JH)

Humor (cont.)
The Hitchhiking Vampire (MS-JH)
Hurray for Ali Baba Bernstein (EL)
Husband Is the Past Tense of Daddy (A)
It Was on Fire When I Lay Down on It
  (A)
Janie's Private Eyes (MS-JH)
Jason Cosmo (HS-A)
The Kid Who Ran for Principal (MS-JH)
Landing on Marvin Gardens (MS-JH)
Let Me Tell You Everything (JH-HS)
Ma and Pa Dracula (EL)
Manifold Destiny (A)
Poems of A. Nonny Mouse (EL-MS)
The Potato Kid (MS-JH)
The Princess in the Pigpen (EL-JH)
Radio Fifth Grade (EL-MS)
Rosy's Romance (MS-JH)
Soup's Hoop (EL-MS)
Stories I Ain't Told Nobody Yet (JH-A)
Sydney, Herself (MS-JH)
Tough Girls Don't Knit (HS-A)
Travel Tips from Harry (EL)
Viola, Furgy, Bobbie and Me (MS-HS)
Who Invited the Undertaker? (MS-JH)
With a Name Like Lulu, Who Needs
  More Trouble? (MS-HS)
Wonderful Me (JH-HS)
Your Move, J.P.! (MS-JH)

Immigrants

Children of the River (JH-HS)
Families (EL-MS, A)
The Fourth-Grade Dinosaur Club (EL-
  MS)
Janie's Private Eyes (MS-JH)
Silver Days (MS-HS)
Small Victories (HS-A)

Interviews

Families (EL-MS, A)
Growing Up Adopted (MS-HS)
Growing Up Western (MS-A)
How It Feels to Fight for Your Life (JH-
  HS)
Life and Death: The Story of a Hospital
  (HS-A)
Saturday Night (HS-A)
These Good Men (HS-A)
We Didn't Have Much, But We Sure
  Had Plenty (HS-A)
We Have AIDS (JH-HS)
We Remember the Holocaust (MS-HS)
World of Ideas (HS-A)

Minorities

Families (EL-MS, A)

Asian

Children of the River (JH-HS)
Janie's Private Eyes (MS-JH)
The Journey (Hamanaka) (JH-A)
Small Victories (HS-A)

Black

The Adventures of High John the
  Conqueror (MS-JH)
Beyond Safe Boundaries (MS-JH)
Caribbean Canvas (HS-A)
Junglerama (EL-JH)
Kareem (HS-A)
Ludie's Song (MS-JH)
Motherwit (HS-A)
The Mouse Rap (MS-JH)
My Name Is Not Angelica (EL-MS)
Runaways (MS)
Secret City, U.S.A. (MS-JH)
The Shimmershine Queens (MS-JH)
Small Victories (HS-A)
Somehow Tenderness Survives (MS-HS)
Somerset Homecoming (HS-A)
Soweto, My Love (JH-A)
The Ups and Downs of Carl Davis III
  (MS-JH)

Hispanic

El Guero (EL-MS)
The Fourth-Grade Dinosaur Club (EL-
  MS)
Shark Beneath the Reef (JH)
Small Victories (HS-A)

Jewish

The Devil's Arithmetic (JH-HS)
Earth to Andrew G. Blechman (EL)
Shadow of the Wall (JH-A)
Silver Days (MS-HS)
Struggle (JH-A)
Turning Thirteen (MS-JH)
We Remember the Holocaust (MS-HS)

Native American

Herds of Thunder, Manes of Gold (MS-HS)
The Night the White Deer Died (JH-HS)
One Day in the Tropical Rain Forest (MS-A)
Running West (HS-A)
Sweetgrass (MS-JH)
Vision Quest (MS-HS)

Music

Backstreets: Springsteen (JH-A)
The Band Never Dances (JH-HS)
The Harmony Illustrated Encyclopedia of Rock (JH-A)
Nadja: On My Way (JH-HS)
Paper Doll (HS)
Singin' Somebody Else's Song (JH-HS)

Mystery and Suspense

Balyet (JH)
The Best Place to Live Is the Ceiling (JH-HS)
Buster Midnight's Cafe (HS-A)
C, My Name Is Cal (JH)
The Cellar (MS-HS)
The Chessmen of Doom (MS-JH)
The Delphic Choice (JH-HS)
Don't Look Behind You (JH-HS)
F Is for Fugitive (A)
Family Reunion (JH-HS)
Fire in the Heart (MS-JH)
G Is for Gumshoe (HS-A)
Hurray for Ali Baba Bernstein (EL)
I Hate Your Guts, Ben Brooster (EL-MS)
Janie's Private Eyes (MS-JH)
Journey (Thomas) (MS-JH)
Masquerade (A)
Nightmare (JH-HS)
Nightmare Mountain (EL-MS)
Nobody's Fault (HS-A)
A Nugget of Gold (JH-HS)
Shadow over Mousehaven Manor (EL)
Silver Pigs (HS-A)
Sniper (JH-HS)
Traitors from Within (JH-HS)
The Twenty-Four-Hour Lipstick Mystery (EL-MS)
The Unfrightened Dark (MS-HS)
Veronica Meets Her Match (EL-MS)
The Voice from the Mendelsohns' Maple (MS-JH)
Whispers from the Dead (JH-HS)

Nature

The Call of the Wolves (EL-A)
Dinosaur Mountain (MS-JH)
Falling for a Dolphin (HS-A)
Five Against the Sea (HS-A)
Going Green (EL-HS)
Great Disasters (EL-A)
In the Forest (EL-A)
News about Dinosaurs (EL-MS)
One Day in the Tropical Rain Forest (EL-MS)
The Random House Book of 1001 Questions and Answers (EL-MS)
The Sierra Club Summer Book (EL, A)
Supersense (JH-A)
The Wild Inside (EL, A)

Nonfiction (See also Biography; Interviews; Poetry)

Cruel Tricks for Dear Friends (HS-A)
Dinosaur Mountain (MS-JH)
The Dolphins and Me (EL-MS)
Fighting Back: What Some People Are Doing About AIDS (JH-A)
Five Against the Sea (HS-A)
The Fringes of Reason (JH-A)
A Gallery of Dinosaurs (EL-A)
Get Help: Solving the Problems in Your Life (MS-JH)
Great Disasters (EL-A)
The Harmony Illustrated Encyclopedia of Rock (JH-A)
Horror Movies (MS-HS)
Husband Is the Past Tense of Daddy (A)
It Was on Fire When I Lay Down on It (A)
The Journey (Hamanaka) (JH-A)
Living with a Parent Who Takes Drugs (EL-JH)
Making Cents (EL-JH)
Manifold Destiny (A)
The Mother's Almanac II (A)
Movie Monsters (MS-HS)
The New Medically Based No-Nonsense Beauty Book (HS-A)
New Zealand by Motorhome (A)
News About Dinosaurs (EL-MS)
1001 Things Everyone Should Know About American History (HS-A)
The Random House Book of 1001 Questions and Answers (EL-MS)
Risky Times (JH-HS)
The Sierra Club Summer Book (EL, A)
Supersense: Perception in the Animal World (JH-A)

Nonfiction (cont.)

Thanksgiving (A)
Tough Girls Don't Knit (HS-A)
Trevor's Place (HS-A)
True Detectives (HS-A)
Voices from the Civil War (JH-A)
What What Are the Chances? (HS-A)
Where's My Other Sock? (MS-HS)
The Wild Inside (EL, A)

Occult and Supernatural

Afternoon of the Elves (EL-MS)
Baily's Bones (EL-MS)
Balyet (JH)
Best Witches (EL)
The Blood and Thunder Adventure on Hurricane Peak (EL-JH)
The Boy Who Lost His Face (MS-JH)
The Cellar (MS-HS)
The Chessmen of Doom (MS-JH)
Dagmar Schultz and the Angel Edna (EL-JH)
Dagmar Schultz and the Powers of Darkness (EL-JH)
The Empty Sleeve (MS-HS)
Enter Three Witches (JH-HS)
The Faery Flag (JH-HS)
Four Past Midnight (HS-A)
Franky Furbo (HS-A)
The Fringes of Reason (JH-A)
Genie with the Light Blue Hair (MS-JH)
Ghost Abbey (MS-JH)
Halloween: Stories and Poems (EL)
Halloween Poems (EL)
High Wizardry (JH-HS)
Journey (Thomas) (MS-JH)
Ma and Pa Dracula (EL)
The Mummy (HS-A)
Night the White Deer Died (JH-HS)
Phone Call from a Ghost (MS-JH)
Self-Portrait with Wings (EL-MS)
The Silver Kiss (JH-A)
Storm Rising (JH-HS)
Things That Go Bump in the Night (MS-JH)
Trolley to Yesterday (MS-JH)
Vision Quest (MS-HS)
Weetzie Bat (HS)
Whispers from the Dead (JH-HS)
Yours Till Forever (JH-HS)

Other Countries / Other Cultures

Baily's Bones (EL-MS)
Balyet (JH)
The Best Place to Live Is the Ceiling (JH-HS)
Beyond Safe Boundaries (MS-JH)
Caribbean Canvas (HS-A)
Cellar (MS-HS)
Children of the River (JH-HS)
Covenant (HS-A)
The Delphic Choice (JH-HS)
Dissidents (JH-HS)
Faithful Elephants (MS-A)
Fallen Angels (HS-A)
Ghost Abbey (MS-JH)
Hey World, Here I Am (MS-JH)
In Lane Three, Alex Archer (HS)
Janie's Private Eyes (MS-JH)
LeMond (HS-A)
McKenzie's Boots (HS-A)
The Mummy (HS-A)
New Zealand by Motorhome (A)
Nobody's Fault (HS-A)
A Nugget of Gold (JH-HS)
One Day in the Tropical Rain Forest (MS-A)
Shabanu: Daughter of the Wind (MS-A)
Shadow of the Wall (JH-A)
Silver Days (MS-JH)
Silver Pigs (HS-A)
Somehow Tenderness Survives (MS-HS)
Soweto, My Love (JH-A)
Struggle (JH-A)
Sydney, Herself (MS-JH)

Peer Pressure

Anything to Win (JH-HS)
Been Clever Forever (JH-HS)
Boy Who Lost His Face (MS-JH)
Chocolate-Covered Ants (EL-MS)
Choices (JH-HS)
Fifth Grade: Here Comes Trouble (MS)
Glass Slippers Give You Blisters (MS-JH)
Heartbeats (JH-HS)
The Kid Who Ran for Principal (MS-JH)
Moonkid and Liberty (JH-HS)
Ninth Issue (JH-HS)
On the Devil's Court (JH-HS)
Plague Year (JH-HS)
Probably Still Nick Swansen (JH-HS)
Tell Us Your Secret (JH-HS)

Poetry

Best Witches (EL)
Birthday Poems (EL)
The Butterfly Jar (EL-JH)
Caribbean Canvas (HS-A)
A Child's Treasury of Animal Verse (EL-JH)
Faery Flag (JH-HS)
Ghastlies, Goops and Pincushions (EL)
Halloween: Stories and Poems (EL)
Halloween Poems (EL)
Herds of Thunder, Manes of Gold (MS-HS)
Hey World, Here I Am (MS-JH)
Poems of A. Nonny Mouse (EL-MS)
Remembering and Other Poems (JH-A)
Soda Jerk (MS-A)
Stories I Ain't Told Nobody Yet (JH-A)

Religion

Believers (EL-MS)
Grass (HS-A)
Masquerade (A)
Struggle (JH-A)
Turning Thirteen (MS-JH)
Two-Part Invention (HS-A)

Romance

Alessandra in Love (JH)
An Almost Perfect Summer (JH-HS)
Any Woman's Blues (A)
The Best Place to Live Is the Ceiling (JH-HS)
Bingo Brown and the Language of Love (EL-MS)
Boy Who Owned the School (MS-JH)
Changes in Latitudes (JH-HS)
Connections (JH-HS)
Covenant (HS-A)
Dagmar Schultz and the Angel Edna (EL-JH)
Dagmar Schultz and the Powers of Darkness (EL-JH)
Delphic Choice (JH-HS)
Dream Collector (JH-HS)
Enter Three Witches (JH-HS)
Francie and the Boys (JH-HS)
Goodbye Doesn't Mean Forever (JH-HS)
Heartbeat (JH-HS)
Just Friends (JH-HS)
Knight in Shining Armor (HS-A)
Landing on Marvin Gardens (MS-JH)
Learning How to Fall (HS)
Let Me Tell You Everything (JH-HS)

Long Live the Queen (HS)
More to Life Than Mr. Right (HS)
The Mouse Rap (MS-JH)
The Mummy (HS-A)
My Name Is Not Angelica (EL-MS)
No Promises (JH-HS)
Nobody's Fault (HS-A)
Nugget of Gold (JH-HS)
On Fortune's Wheel (HS)
Ozzy on the Outside (HS)
Paper Doll (HS)
Proud Knight, Fair Lady (HS-A)
Rosy's Romance (MS-JH)
Seventeen Against the Dealer (HS)
The Silver Kiss (JH-A)
Silver Pigs (HS-A)
Storm Rising (JH-HS)
Tell Me How the Wind Sounds (JH-HS)
Too Young to Die (JH-HS)
Twenty-First Century Fox (JH-HS)
Two-Part Invention (HS-A)
Valentine and Orson (MS-A)
Weetzie Bat (HS)
Who Invited the Undertaker? (MS-JH)
Wishes (HS-A)
Wonderful Me (JH-HS)
Your Move, J.P.! (MS-JH)
Yours Till Forever (JH-HS)

Runaways

Effie's House (JH-HS)
Family Pose (MS)
Looking for Home (JH-HS)
Lost Boys Never Say Die (EL-JH)
Ozzy on the Outside (HS)
Raymond (MS-JH)
Runaways (MS)
When Morning Comes (HS)
Worlds Apart (EL-MS)

School

Alessandra in Love (JH)
Anything to Win (JH-HS)
Been Clever Forever (JH-HS)
Begonia for Miss Applebaum (JH-HS)
Blood and Thunder Adventure on Hurricane Peak (EL-JH)
The Boy Who Owned the School (MS-JH)
Buffalo Brenda (MS-JH)
Charlotte Shakespeare and Annie the Great (MS)
Choices (JH-HS)

School (cont.)

Circle of Light (MS-JH)
Dead Poets Society (JH-A)
Erin McEwan, Your Days Are Numbered (MS-JH)
Face on the Milk Carton (JH-HS)
Fifth Grade: Here Comes Trouble (MS)
Five Finger Discount (MS-JH)
Forward Pass (JH-HS)
Fourth-Grade Dinosaur Club (EL-MS)
Fowl Play, Desdemona (EL-JH)
Francie and the Boys (JH-HS)
Give It Up, Mom (MS-JH)
Glass Slippers Give You Blisters (MS-JH)
Goodbye Doesn't Mean Forever (JH-HS)
Hare's Choice (MS-A)
Kid Who Ran for Principal (MS-JH)
Landing on Marvin Gardens (MS-JH)
Let Me Tell You Everything (JH-HS)
Ma and Pa Dracula (EL)
Millie Cooper, Take a Chance (EL)
Moonkid and Liberty (JH-HS)
My War with Goggle Eyes (MS-JH)
Ninth Issue (JH-HS)
No Promises (JH-HS)
On the Devil's Court (JH-HS)
One Green Leaf (JH-A)
Paper Knife (EL-MS)
Plague Year (JH-HS)
Probably Still Nick Swansen (JH-HS)
Radio Fifth Grade (EL-MS)
Raymond (MS-JH)
Rosy's Romance (MS-JH)
Serpent's Tooth (JH)
Shimmershine Queens (MS-JH)
Small Victories (HS-A)
So Much to Tell You (HS)
Squeeze Play (EL)
Those Other People (HS-A)
Twenty-First Century Fox (JH-HS)
Ups and Downs of Carl Davis III (MS-JH)
Where Have All the Tigers Gone? (HS-A)
Wonderful Me (JH-HS)

Science

Dinosaur Mountain (MS-JH)
Going Green (EL-HS)
The Last Dinosaur (EL-A)
News About Dinosaurs (EL-MS)
One Day in the Tropical Rain Forest (EL-MS)
Sierra Club Summer Book (EL, A)
Wild Inside (EL, A)
World of Ideas (HS-A)

Science Fiction

Borgel (JH-A)
Dying Sun (JH-HS)
Empire's Horizon (HS-A)
Engineer of Beasts (JH-A)
Eva (JH-A)
Gameplay (HS-A)
Grass (HS-A)
High Wizardry (JH-HS)
I Feel Like the Morning Star (JH-HS)
Rewind to Yesterday (EL-MS)
Secret of the Indian (EL-MS)
Tehanu (JH-HS)
Toynbee Convector (HS-A)
Traitors from Within (JH-HS)
Why I Left Harry's All-Night Hamburgers (JH-A)

Self Help

Fighting Back: What Some People Are Doing About AIDS (JH-A)
Get Help: Solving the Problems in Your Life (MS-JH)
Going Green: A Kid's Handbook to Saving the Planet (EL-HS)
Living with a Parent Who Takes Drugs (EL-JH)
Making Cents: Every Kid's Guide to Money (EL-JH)
The Mother's Almanac II: Your Child from Six to Twelve (A)
The New Medically Based No-Nonsense Beauty Book (HS-A)
Risky Times (JH-HS)
Where's My Other Sock? How to Get Organized (MS-HS)

Self Knowledge

Afternoon of the Elves (EL-MS)
An Almost Perfect Summer (JH-HS)
Any Woman's Blues (A)
Anything to Win (JH-HS)
The Band Never Dances (JH-HS)
Been Clever Forever (JH-HS)
Beyond the Reef (JH-HS)
Big Bang (JH-HS)
The Boy Who Owned the School (MS-JH)
Brushy Mountain (MS-JH)
Changes in Latitudes (JH-HS)
Chinese Handcuffs (HS)
Choices (JH-HS)
Choosing Sides (MS)
Circle of Light (MS-JH)

Connections (JH-HS)
Dead Poets Society (JH-A)
Devil's Arithmetic (JH-)
Dissidents (JH-HS)
Dream Collector (JH-HS)
Dying Sun (JH-HS)
Eva (JH-A)
Face on the Milk Carton (JH-HS)
Facts and Fictions of Minna Pratt (EL-MS)
Fallen Angels (HS-A)
Family Pictures (A)
Fire in the Heart (MS-JH)
Five Finger Discount (MS-JH)
Forward Pass (JH-HS)
Grass (HS-A)
Growing Up Adopted (MS-HS)
Haunting of Frances Rain (MS-JH)
Heartbeat (JH-HS)
Heartbeats (JH-HS)
Hey World, Here I Am (MS-JH)
Husband Is the Past Tense of Daddy (A)
In Lane Three, Alex Archer (HS)
Jack (HS-A)
Junglerama (EL-JH)
Just Like a Friend (MS-JH)
Landing on Marvin Gardens (MS-JH)
Learning How to Fall (HS)
Long Live the Queen (HS)
Looking for Home (JH-HS)
Lost Boys Never Say Die (EL-MS)
McKenzie's Boots (HS-A)
Millie Cooper, Take a Chance (EL)
More to Life Than Mr. Right (HS)
Newfound (JH-A)
Ninth Issue (JH-HS)
No Promises (JH-HS)
Ozzy on the Outside (HS)
Paper Doll (HS)
Phoenix Rising (JH-HS)
Probably Still Nick Swansen (JH-HS)
Rebel Without a Clue (HS-A)
Sacred Circle of the Hula Hoop (JH)
Self-Portrait with Wings (EL-MS)
Serpent's Tooth (JH)
Seventeen Against the Dealer (HS)
Shark Beneath the Reef (JH)
Short Subject (MS-JH)
Silver (HS)
Silver Days (MS-HS)
The Silver Kiss (JH-A)
Singin' Somebody Else's Song (JH-HS)
Sniper (JH-HS)
So Much to Tell You (HS)
Soda Jerk (MS-A)
Somerset Homecoming (HS-A)

Soweto, My Love (JH-A)
Squeeze Play (EL)
Star Baby (JH-HS)
Starstone (MS-HS)
Storm Rising (JH-HS)
Sweetgrass (MS-JH)
Sydney, Herself (MS-JH)
Tell Us Your Secret (JH-HS)
These Good Men (HS-A)
Those Other People (HS-A)
Turning Thirteen (MS-JH)
Unlived Affections (JH-HS)
Up Country (JH-HS)
Ups and Downs of Carl Davis III (MS-JH)
Veteran's Day (HS-A)
Voyage of the Frog (MS-HS)
When Morning Comes (HS)
Where Have All the Tigers Gone? (HS-A)
White Rabbit (HS-A)
Why I Left Harry's All-Night Hamburgers (JH-A)
Winter Room (MS-HS)
With a Name Like Lulu, Who Needs More Trouble? (MS-HS)
Worlds Apart (EL-MS)
The Wrong Way Home (JH-HS)

Sex and Sexuality

Any Woman's Blues (A)
Chinese Handcuffs (HS)
Connections (JH-HS)
Learning How to Fall (HS)
Night Riding (JH-HS)
Paper Doll (HS)
Rebel Without a Clue (HS-A)
Risky Times (JH-HS)
We Have AIDS (JH-HS)

Short Stories

Adventures of High John the Conqueror (MS-JH)
Connections (JH-HS)
Faery Flag (JH-HS)
Four Past Midnight (HS-A)
Halloween: Stories and Poems (EL)
Heartbeats (JH-HS)
Herds of Thunder, Manes of Gold (MS-HS)
House of Heroes (HS-A)
How Many Spots Does a Leopard Have? (EL-MS)
More to Life Than Mr. Right (HS)

Short Stories (cont.)

Phone Call from a Ghost (MS-JH)
Proud Knight, Fair Lady (HS-A)
Somehow Tenderness Survives (MS-)
Things That Go Bump in the Night (MS-HS)
Toynbee Convector (HS-A)
Why I Left Harry's All-Night Hamburgers (JH-A)

Sports

Anything to Win (JH-HS)
Bo Knows Bo (JH-A)
Choosing Sides (MS)
Forward Pass (JH-HS)
If I Never Get Back (HS-A)
In Lane Three, Alex Archer (HS)
Kareem (HS-A)
LeMond (HS-A)
My Brother Stealing Second (JH-HS)
My Brother the Star (EL-MS)
Never Too Young to Die (HS-A)
On the Devil's Court (JH-HS)
Paterno (HS-A)
Random House Book of 1001 Questions and Answers (EL-MS)
Soup's Hoop (EL-MS)
Squeeze Play (EL)
Twenty-First Century Fox (JH-HS)
Viola, Furgy, Bobbie and Me (MS-HS)
With a Name Like Lulu, Who Needs More Trouble? (MS-HS)
Your Move, J.P.! (MS-JH)

Substance Abuse

Any Woman's Blues (A)
The Big Bang (JH-HS)
Burnt: A Teenager Addict's Road to Recovery (HS-A)
Can't Hear You Listening (JH-HS)
Get Help (MS-JH)
Give It Up, Mom (MS-JH)
Living with a Parent Who Takes Drugs (EL-JH)
My Brother Stealing Second (JH-HS)
Never Too Young to Die (HS-A)
No Kidding (JH-HS)
Up Country (JH-HS)
White Rabbit (HS-A)
The Wrong Way Home (JH-HS)

Survival

Balyet (JH)
The Call of the Wolves (MS-A)
Dangerous Ground (MS)
Five Against the Sea (HS-A)
Gameplay (HS-A)
Grass (HS-A)
Great Disasters (EL-A)
High Wizardry (JH-HS)
How It Feels to Fight for Your Life (JH-HS)
I Feel Like the Morning Star (JH-HS)
Journey (Michener) (HS-A)
Long Live the Queen (HS)
My Name Is Not Angelica (EL-MS)
No Way Out (MS-HS)
On Fortune's Wheel (HS)
One in a Million (HS-A)
Running West (HS-A)
Secret City, U.S.A. (MS-JH)
Shadow of the Wall (JH-A)
Struggle (JH-A)
Voyage of the Frog (MS-HS)

Theater

The Boy Who Owned the School (MS-JH)
Charlotte Shakespeare and Annie the Great (MS)
Enter Three Witches (JH-MS)
Francie and the Boys (JH-HS)
Glass Slippers Give You Blisters (MS-JH)
Lost Boys Never Say Die (EL-MS)
Star Baby (JH-HS)

Time Travel

An Acceptable Time (JH-HS)
Borgel (JH-A)
The Cellar (MS-HS)
The Devil's Arithmetic (JH-HS)
The Haunting of Frances Rain (MS-JH)
If I Never Get Back (HS-A)
Knight in Shining Armor (JH-A)
The Mummy (HS-A)
Princess in the Pigpen (EL-JH)
Rewind to Yesterday (EL-MS)
Secret of the Indian (EL-MS)
Trolley to Yesterday (MS-JH)
Vision Quest (MS-HS)
A Well-Timed Enchantment (MS-JH)
Wishes (HS-A)

Travel

Education of a Wandering Man (A)
Manifold Destiny (A)
New Zealand by Motorhome (A)
Travel Tips from Harry (EL)
Wiggie Wins the West (EL-MS)

War

Blitzcat (HS-A)
Children of the River (JH-HS)
Devil's Arithmetic (JH-HS)
Faithful Elephants (MS-A)
Fallen Angels (HS-A)
Franky Furbo (HS-A)
The Journey (Hamanaka) (JH-A)
McKenzie's Boots (HS-A)
Shadow of the Wall (JH-A)
Silver Days (MS-HS)
Struggle (JH-A)
These Good Men (JH-A)
Veteran's Day (HS-A)
Voices from the Civil War (JH-A)
We Remember the Holocaust (HS-A)

Women's Roles

Any Woman's Blues (A)
Erin McEwan, Your Days Are Numbered (MS-JH)
Forward Pass (JH-HS)
Glass Slippers Give You Blisters (MS-JH)
Hey World, Here I Am (MS-JH)
In Lane Three, Alex Archer (HS)
Let Me Tell You Everything (JH-HS)
More to Life than Mr. Right (HS)
The Mother's Almanac II (A)
Motherwit (HS-A)
Seventeen Against the Dealer (HS)
Shabanu: Daughter of the Wind (MS-A)
Tehanu (JH-HS)
Two-Part Invention (A)
We Didn't Have Much, But We Sure Had Plenty (HS-A)
With a Name Like Lulu, Who Needs More Trouble? (MS-HS)

Working

An Almost Perfect Summer (JH-HS)
Better Mousetraps (MS-HS)
Dead Poets Society (JH-A)
The Dolphins and Me (EL-MS)
Erin McEwan, Your Days Are Numbered (MS-JH)
Fortunate Fortunes (MS-HS)
Frank and Earnest (EL-JH, A)
Leave the Cooking to Me (MS-JH)
Life and Death: The Story of a Hospital (HS-A)
Looking for Home (JH-HS)
Making Cents (EL-JH)
Motherwit (HS-A)
Nadja: On My Way (JH-HS)
Problem Solvers (MS-HS)
Rejects (MS-HS)
Saturday Night (HS-A)
Seventeen Against the Dealer (HS)
Small Victories (HS-A)
Soda Jerk (MS-A)
Star Baby (JH-HS)
Those Other People (HS-A)
Two-Part Invention (A)
Unsung Heroes (MS-HS)
We Didn't Have Much, But We Sure Had Plenty (HS-A)
Where Have All the Tigers Gone? (HS-A)

LIST OF PUBLISHERS

Addison-Wesley. Addison-Wesley Publishing Co. Inc., Route 128,
Anchor. Anchor Books, Doubleday, 666 Fifth Avenue, New York, NY Reading, MA 01867
Andrews & McMeel. Andrews & McMeel, 4900 Main Street, Kansas City, MO 64112
Arcade. Arcade Publishing Inc., 141 Fifth Avenue, New York, NY 10010
Atheneum. Atheneum Publishers, 866 Third Avenue, New York, NY 10022
Ballantine. Ballantine Books, 201 East 50th Street, New York, NY 10022
Bantam. Bantam Books, 666 Fifth Avenue, New York, NY 10103
Bradbury. Bradbury Press, 866 Third Avenue, New York, NY 10022
Clarion. Clarion Books, 215 Park Avenue South, New York, NY 10003
Crowell. Thomas Y. Crowell Co. c/o HarperCollins, 10 East 53rd Street, New York, NY 10022
Crown. Crown Publishing Group, 201 East 50th Street, New York, NY 10022
DAW. DAW Books Inc., 375 Hudson Street, New York, NY 10014
Delacorte. Delacorte Press, 666 Fifth Avenue, New York, NY 10103
Dial. Dial Books for Young Readers, 375 Hudson Street, New York, NY 10014
Dodd. Dodd, Mead & Co. Inc., 6 Ram Ridge Road, Spring Valley, NY 10977
Doubleday. Doubleday, 666 Fifth Avenue, New York, NY 10103
Dutton. E. P. Dutton, 375 Hudson Street, New York, NY 10014
Farrar. Farrar, Straus & Giroux Inc., 19 Union Square West, New York, NY 10003
Fawcett. Fawcett Books, 201 East 50th Street, New York, NY 10022
Four Winds. Four Winds Press, 866 Third Avenue, New York, NY 10022
Greenwillow. Greenwillow Books, 1350 Avenue of the Americas, New York, NY 10019
Harmony. Harmony Books, 201 East 50th Street, New York, NY 10022
Harper. HarperCollins Publishers, 10 East 53rd Street, New York, NY 10022
Holiday. Holiday House Inc., 425 Madison Avenue, New York, NY 10017
Holt. Henry Holt and Co. Inc., 115 West 18th Street, New York, NY 10011
Houghton. Houghton Mifflin Co., One Beacon Street, Boston, MA 02108
Joy St. Joy Street Books, 34 Beacon Street, Boston, MA 02108
Knopf. Alfred A. Knopf Inc., 201 East 50th Street, New York, NY 10022
Lerner. Lerner Publications Co., 241 First Avenue North, Minneapolis, MN 55401
Lippincott. J. B. Lippincott Co., 227 East Washington Square, Philadelphia, PA 19106
Little. Little, Brown & Co. Inc., 34 Beacon Street, Boston, MA 02108
Lodestar. Lodestar Books, 375 Hudson Street, New York, NY 10014
Lothrop. Lothrop, Lee & Shepard Books, 1350 Avenue of the Americas, New York, NY 10019
Macmillan. Macmillan Publishing Co., 866 Third Avenue, New York, NY 10022
McElderry. Margaret K. McElderry Books, 866 Third Avenue, New York, NY 10022
Morrow. William Morrow & Co. Inc., 1350 Avenue of the Americas, New York, NY 10019
NAL. New American Library, 375 Hudson Street, New York, NY 10014
Orchard. Orchard Books, 387 Park Avenue South, New York, NY 10016

Orion. Orion Books, 201 East 50th Street, New York, NY 10022
Pantheon. Pantheon Books, 201 East 50th Street, New York, NY 10022
Pelican. Pelican Publishing Co. Inc., Box 189, 1101 Monroe Street, Gretna, LA 70053
Philomel. Philomel Books, 200 Madison Avenue, New York, NY 10016
Pocket. Pocket Books, 1230 Avenue of the Americas, New York, NY 10020
Putnam. G. P. Putnam's Sons, 200 Madison Avenue, New York, NY 10016
Random. Random House Inc., 201 East 50th Street, New York, NY 10022
Reader's Digest. Reader's Digest General Books, 260 Madison Avenue, New York, NY 10016
Scholastic. Scholastic Inc., 730 Broadway, New York, NY 10003
Scribners. Charles Scribner's Sons, 866 Third Avenue, New York, NY 10022
Signet. Signet Books, 375 Hudson Street, New York, NY 10014
Viking. Viking Penguin, 375 Hudson Street, New York, NY 10014
Villard. Villard Books, 201 East 50th Street, New York, NY 10022
Watts. Franklin Watts Inc., 387 Park Avenue South, New York, NY 10016
Workman. Workman Publishing Co., 708 Broadway, New York, NY 10003

INDEX